History of the Great War.

MILITARY OPERATIONS.

[*Crown Copyright Reserved*]

HISTORY OF THE GREAT WAR
BASED ON OFFICIAL DOCUMENTS
BY DIRECTION OF THE HISTORICAL SECTION OF THE
COMMITTEE OF IMPERIAL DEFENCE

MILITARY OPERATIONS EGYPT & PALESTINE
FROM JUNE 1917 TO THE END OF THE WAR
Part II

COMPILED BY
Captain CYRIL FALLS
LATE R. INNIS. FUS. AND GENERAL STAFF

MAPS COMPILED BY
Major A. F. BECKE
R.A. (RETIRED), HON. M.A. (OXON.)

The Naval & Military Press Ltd

Published by
The Naval & Military Press Ltd
5 Riverside, Brambleside, Bellbrook
Industrial Estate, Uckfield, East Sussex,
TN22 1QQ England
Tel: +44 (0) 1825 749494
Fax: +44 (0) 1825 765701
www.naval-military-press.com
www.military-genealogy.com
www.militarymaproom.com

In reprinting in facsimile from the original, any imperfections are inevitably reproduced and the quality may fall short of modern type and cartographic standards.

CHAPTER XVIII.

THE ARAB CAMPAIGN.
(Map 23 ; Sketch 27.)

THE LAST HALF OF 1917.

IN the first volume of this history the record of the Arab **Map 23.** campaign against the Turks was sketched from the outbreak of revolt at Mecca and Medina in June 1916 to the capture of 'Aqaba on the 6th July 1917. It will be recalled that by the latter date the Turks were confined to the Hejaz Railway itself, which they held by means of a series of blockhouses at the stations, and to its terminus, the town of Medina, where they had a considerable garrison. The capture of 'Aqaba was the first important news which greeted Sir Edmund Allenby on his arrival in Egypt, and he at once realized that it would alter the conditions of the desert war. The Arabs now had a base over two hundred miles north of Wejh, the northernmost Arabian port hitherto in their possession. Their raiding of the railway could therefore be extended, and in the event of a general British offensive it would be possible to enlist the tribes of eastern Syria for operations against the Turkish railway communications with Palestine. They might be able to capture—or at least interrupt traffic at—vital points on the railway such as Der'a, which were beyond the reach of the British. From the time of the capture of 'Aqaba and the almost simultaneous arrival of Sir Edmund Allenby there was at G.H.Q. a greater interest in the Arab operations, which resulted in fuller sympathy and support and in a more lavish provision of munitions and supplies. The assistance given by the Navy was as valuable as ever, Captain W. H. D. Boyle, Senior Officer Red Sea Patrol, being as enthusiastic and resourceful as Admiral Wemyss had been in the first stage of the campaign.

Another effect of the possession of the new base was to put the Hejaz, the original scene of the Arab revolt, into the background. In 1916 it had been hoped to capture Medina, but it was becoming less and less likely that the town, defended by a strong and well-armed force under a dour commander, would ever fall to the Arabs, who lacked the training, equipment, and resolution necessary to storm it. The most that could be expected from their pressure or the tightening of their slack blockade was that they would compel the enemy to evacuate it. That would be far from desirable unless they could cut off and capture the garrison, and there was small prospect of their doing so. The Turkish retirement northward might be seriously delayed by raids on the railway; but discipline and determination, backed by superior resources, would assuredly force a way through in the end.

Now the appearance in Palestine of the Medina garrison would have been unwelcome. To anticipate a little, it would have been most damaging in the summer of 1918, when the E.E.F. was in course of reorganization and over half its infantry was unfit to take the field. Even the wholesale capture of the Turkish forces would hardly have been advantageous, since it would have lifted from the enemy's shoulders the weight of the Hejaz. To allow the railway just, but only just, to remain working and never to frighten the enemy so seriously as to induce him to evacuate Medina was for the time being the best policy from the British point of view. That in 1917 they ever consciously acted upon that principle is improbable; at least it is not put forward in any contemporary appreciation. But the principle was followed none the less, because it represented the measure of their power and resources. In the spring of 1918, when the railway was destroyed near Ma'an so thoroughly that the Turks were unable to withdraw from Medina whether or not they desired to do so, one of the reasons for the attack was the news that Turkish G.H.Q. was seriously considering the evacuation of the Hejaz. At least it was recognized from the moment of Sir Edmund Allenby's arrival that the Hejaz was a secondary theatre of the Arab campaign.

'Aqaba was only 130 miles from the British position on the Wadi Ghazze, but it was 700 miles from Mecca; also it was to be the base for expeditions which would bring Arab forces still more closely in touch with the British and remove them still further from the control of King Hussein. The Hejaz had not only lost its early importance; its capital and government were as far from the scene of projected operations as London from Petrograd. It was therefore decided that the Emir Feisal should become, in effect, an army commander under Sir Edmund Allenby's orders. All Arab operations north of Ma'an were to be carried out by him under the direction of the British Commander-in-Chief. South of Ma'an the High Commissioner, Sir Reginald Wingate, was still to act as adviser to the Emirs Ali and Abdulla and to be responsible for their supply. In November 1917 the " Hejaz Opera-" tions Staff " was formed in Cairo, and through it was exercised the general supervision of operations and administration in both spheres. It must not be supposed, however, that the guerilla warfare on the Hejaz Railway was or could have been controlled from Cairo in the sense that British campaigns were controlled from Whitehall. That was prohibited not only by the slowness of communication, but by the nature of the fighting and of the men who were here Britain's allies. The British officers in Arabia had a general programme before them; if they could not engage the Arabs to carry it out, they endeavoured to accomplish part of it, or take some action as a substitute. Frequently there was no time or opportunity to consult Cairo; then they were thrown entirely on their own initiative. Their relation to the central authority resembled that of British commanders in " small wars " before the days of the electric telegraph, except that their position was that of advisers rather than of commanders.

The base for what was known as the Northern Army, under the Emir Feisal, was therefore shifted to 'Aqaba. Here Ja'far Pasha [1] took command of a small organized force, consisting of two partially trained infantry battalions with a small number of automatic rifles and mountain guns, and of mobile troops mounted on camels and mules. The men were for the most part either Meccans or Arab prisoners and deserters from the Turkish Army. Some of

---

[1] See Vol. I, p. 235.

the officers had actually been captured in Mesopotamia. Similar forces were formed for attachment to the commands of the Emirs Ali and Abdulla ; but, partly owing to the personality and experience of Ja'far, partly, perhaps, because he got the pick of the troops, those in the southern area never equalled his in efficiency.

An important Arab ally of the Turks had now appeared in this quarter of Arabia : Ibn Rashid,[1] the young and hotheaded Emir of Hail. In April 1917, while moving westward with a huge convoy of supplies for the use of the Turks, he had been defeated near Hanakiye, 80 miles northeast of Medina, by the Emir Zeid. The Sherifial forces took 250 prisoners, mostly Turks, four mountain guns, some three thousand camels laden with food and clothing, and three thousand sheep. Merchants from Koweit were with the convoy, which represented a vast sum of money and was a very serious loss to the enemy. Ibn Rashid with about a thousand of his followers then joined the Turks on the railway at Medain Salih, 200 miles north-west of Medina. His assistance, as head of one of the greatest ruling houses of Arabia, had some moral value, but he had lost influence in his own dominions and was from the Turkish point of view a burden rather than a source of supply. He himself became disgusted by his treatment. It is believed that he would gladly have thrown in his hand, returned to Hail, and perhaps changed sides, had not the Turks detained him as a hostage for the good behaviour of his Shammar tribesmen.

While Captain Lawrence was engaged in the capture of 'Aqaba, attacks on the railway by no means ceased. In July Lieut.-Colonel S. F. Newcombe and Major W. A. Davenport raided Qal'at Zumrud, 140 miles north of Medina, destroying three miles of line by means of explosives. This was one of the most successful raids of the whole campaign, and was carried out by detachments of Egyptians, French Algerians, and Indian cavalrymen. The Arabs co-operated at Zumrud, and also by a very spirited attack upon the station immediately north, which they captured with its garrison. A series of raids a little further south at Toweira under the orders of Major P. C. Joyce, commanding

---

[1] See Vol. I, p. 209 ; also Sketch 11 in that volume.

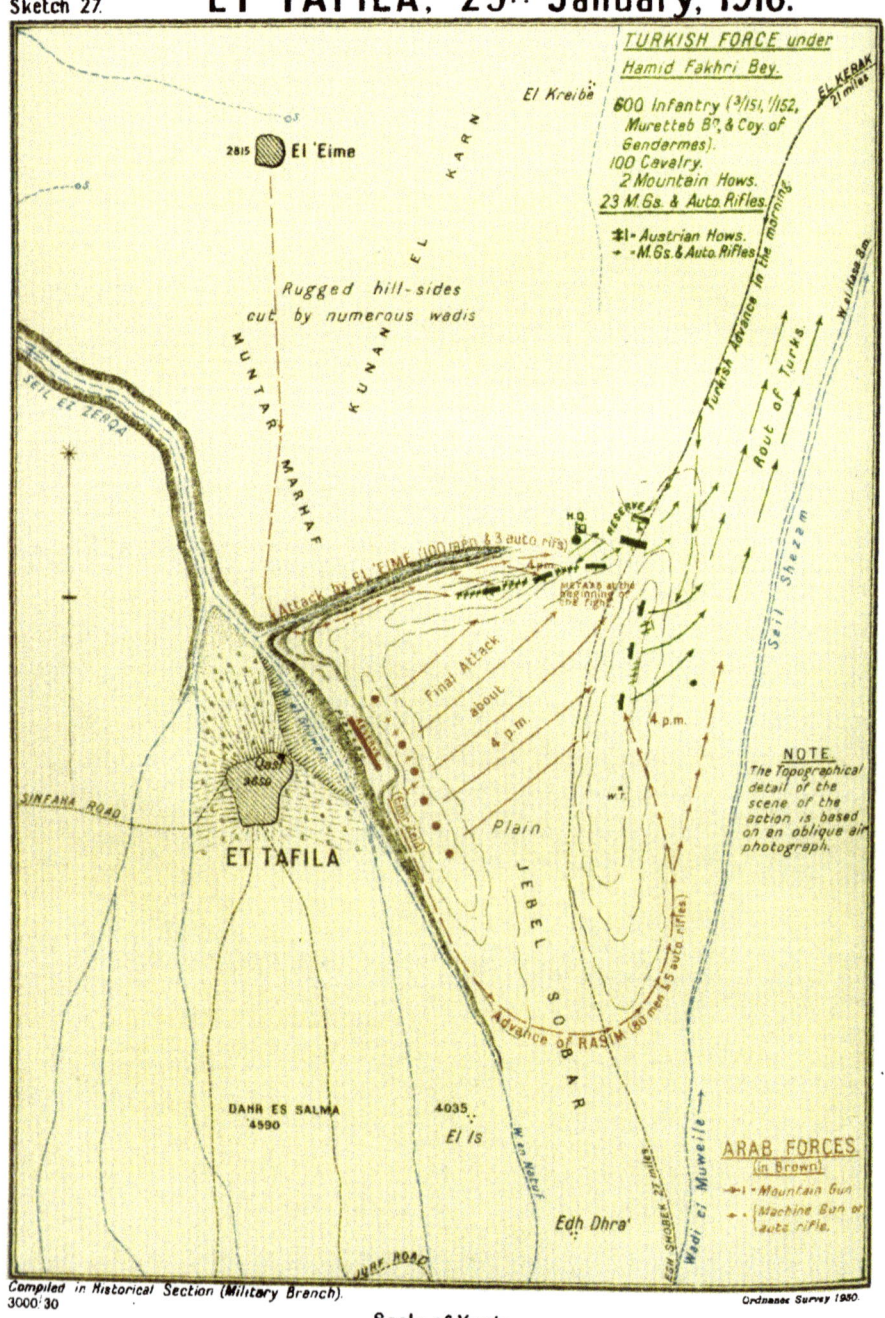

a mixed force of Egyptian troops, French Algerians, and Arabs, resulted in the destruction of 2,000 rails and several large culverts. When Captain Lawrence returned to 'Aqaba after a visit to Egypt, the raiders transferred their attentions further north to the neighbourhood of Ma'an, as the best means of preventing a Turkish counter-offensive from that quarter. By the beginning of September the enemy had a ration strength of 6,000 in Ma'an or west of it, with some sixteen guns, and was joined there by the *7th Cavalry Regiment* [1] on the 25th. He was well aware of the importance of the threat represented by the establishment of the Arab base at 'Aqaba, and had begun to make preparations to recapture that place by forming a camp at Abu el Lasan, the scene of the Arab victory on the 2nd July. This was on the best route between 'Aqaba and Ma'an, but there was another up the great Wadi el 'Araba, and thence eastward along the Wadi Musa; and this the Arabs employed to harass and threaten the garrison of Ma'an, while part of their trained force moved up to Quweira to oppose the advance of the Turks on 'Aqaba.

1917. Aug.

Little enough could they have done to stop the enemy had he come forward with determination, but so harried was he that he never could muster nerve for the attempt. The flight of the R.F.C., which had been first at Rabegh, then at Wejh, had been brought back to Egypt, owing to the severe strain imposed on both men and machines by the summer heat of Arabia; but long-distance bombing raids were possible, and a series of attacks was made on the enemy at the end of August. The machines made use of a temporary landing-place at Quntilla, 40 miles N.N.W. of 'Aqaba. Eight direct hits were obtained on the engine sheds at Ma'an on the 28th; on the following day the Turkish camp at Abu el Lasan was effectively bombed. Raids on the railway were continued under the leadership of Major H. Garland and other British officers. On the 17th September Captain Lawrence, who had with him two British sergeant-instructors from Zeitun, one with a section of Lewis guns, the other with one of Stokes mortars, carried out one of his most notable exploits near Mudauwara Station, 72 miles south-east of Ma'an. A train with two

Sept.

---

[1] See p. 12 f.n.

engines was destroyed by a mine, and about seventy Turkish soldiers who were travelling in it were killed. On the 6th October he accounted for another train near Ma'an, capturing 70 tons of food intended for Ibn Rashid at Medain Salih. Meanwhile the Bedouin cut off supply columns from Ma'an, ambushed weak parties of the enemy, and distracted him by all the means in their power.

Now the time drew near for the great British offensive. Captain Lawrence believed that he could raise all the settled Arabs about Der'a, capture the place, and leave the Turkish Armies on the Gaza–Beersheba line entirely without railway communication in face of Sir Edmund Allenby's impending blow. Yet if he did so, unless the British attack resulted in completely destroying the Turkish forces and clearing the whole of Palestine, the peasantry would be abandoned to a fearful vengeance. Even from the most selfish point of view caution was necessary; for the Hauran could be raised once only. Lawrence decided therefore that the best service he could offer at the moment was to blow up one of the bridges in the Yarmuk Valley, the deep gorge through which the railway descended from Der'a to the Ghor at Samakh on the southern shore of the Sea of Galilee. So long were some of the bridges on which the railway crossed and recrossed the river, so difficult of approach, that it was believed the destruction of one would isolate the Turks in Palestine for a fortnight. Sir Edmund Allenby agreed that this should be attempted about the 5th November, five days after the attack on Beersheba.

This extraordinarily difficult venture, beginning with a four-hundred mile camel ride from 'Aqaba, failed by a hair's breadth. The party, with its explosives, was on a hillside above the bridge, when the dropping of a single rifle alarmed a sleepy Turkish sentry, who turned out the guard.[1] The destruction by mining, on the way back, of a train between Der'a and 'Amman was small consolation. But the attempt had at least shown that the section of railway between Der'a and the Jordan Valley was highly vulnerable, and that a more thoroughly organized raid upon it had every hope of success.

Early in October the Arabs occupied Shobek, 21 miles

---

[1] "Revolt in the Desert," pp. 240–1.

TURKISH ATTACK ON PETRA

north of Ma'an; and though they held the place for a few days only, did valuable work in tearing up rails on a light line from Qal'at 'Aneiza, the second station north of Ma'an, which the Turks used to collect wood fuel for their engines. On the 27st October, three days before Captain Lawrence set out for the Yarmuk, the enemy made his first serious attempt against the regular force of Ja'far Pasha in the Wadi Musa. A detachment of four weak battalions and the *7th Cavalry Regiment*, with four guns, advanced from Ma'an against Ja'far's position at Elji, near the ruins of the famous rock city of Petra. The Arab force consisted of two companies of camel corps and two of mule-mounted infantry, with two quick-firing mountain guns and four machine-guns. Its fighting strength was about 350, with less than two hundred Bedouin auxiliaries. The Turks shelled the position for an hour, while an aeroplane dropped bombs upon it; then they advanced and carried the outer defences. Attacked in flank by the Bedouin, they drew off at evening, leaving some prisoners in the hands of the defenders. The ill-trained Arab camel-men behaved badly, but the mounted infantry under Maulud Pasha, a veteran cavalry officer of the Turkish service, was steady enough. Thereafter for some time to come intense cold with heavy falls of snow in the highlands checked the activities of both sides.

1917. Oct.

The capture of Jerusalem by the E.E.F. in early December gave prospect of closer co-operation between British and Arabs. Sir Edmund Allenby had determined to capture Jericho and drive the enemy across the Jordan; he desired that the Emir Feisal's forces should advance east of the Dead Sea until they gained touch with him in the Jordan Valley. They would occupy in the course of their movement northward between the railway and the Dead Sea country largely sown, with considerable villages or small towns such as Shobek, Tafila, Kerak, and Madeba, and of great value to the Turks as a source of supply. The task allotted to the Arabs was never completely carried out, partly because they were unable to capture Ma'an, which remained a constant threat to their communications with 'Aqaba; partly because the British did not succeed in establishing themselves permanently at Es Salt. Nevertheless, the Arab campaign of the spring of 1918 was a

Dec.

source of irritation to the enemy, and succeeded in completely cutting off the *Hejaz Expeditionary Force* at Medina from the Armies of Palestine and Trans-Jordan.

THE FIRST EIGHT MONTHS OF 1918.

Sketch 27.

Late in December 1917 Sherif Nasir with a body of Beni Sakr tribesmen and one mountain gun crossed the railway and camped in the plain of Jafr, east of Ma'an. Thence he surprised Jurf ed Derawish Station, 30 miles N.N.E. of Ma'an, capturing over 200 men and damaging two trains. Cold and lack of supplies forced him to abandon the station after three days, but he made a swift march through the snow and took Tafila, with the whole of its small garrison. He was joined here a few days later by King Hussein's youngest son, the Emir Zeid, but owing to the state of the roads the latter brought with him only about a hundred trained troops and two mountain guns. Tafila was an important centre of the corn country, and the Turks quickly made an effort to recover it. On the 23rd January a force of three weak battalions with a detachment of one hundred cavalry and two mountain howitzers moved out from Kerak, and on the following evening drove the Arab patrols from the Wadi el Hasa, 10 miles northeast of the village. Zeid evacuated the village at midnight to take up a position on the south side of the broad valley in which it stands, while the local peasantry attempted to hold up the enemy's cavalry advanced guard.

1918.
25 Jan.

Major Lawrence, who had arrived with Zeid, regretted the abandonment of Tafila, if only because it meant the loss of the villagers, sturdy fighting men, as allies. He therefore persuaded the Emir Zeid to send up a couple of light machine guns to support them on the morning of the 25th. This reinforcement had an unexpected result. The villagers drove back the Turkish cavalry screen several miles and established themselves on the edge of a plateau whence the ground dropped gradually to the wide valley of the Wadi el Hasa. Here, however, they came in contact with the main body of the Turks, just breaking camp, who opened heavy fire on them with artillery and machine guns.

Et Tafila: Looking East at the Battlefield across the Gorge. [*R.A.F. Photograph,* 1929.

ACTION AT TAFILA

1918.
25 Jan.

On going forward to the front line Major Lawrence[1] found that one machine gun had been destroyed and that the Turks were pressing rapidly forward. East of the Tafila valley was a triangular plain, its sides roughly two miles long and marked by low ridges. At the apex, which lay to the north-east, was a little pass where the road from Kerak, after climbing out of the Hasa valley, entered the plain. Along this road the enemy was advancing in strength, having already pushed a considerable number of men through the pass and along the ridge east of the plain, and the loss of the Arab position was clearly imminent. As he walked up Major Lawrence had noted that the south-western ridge above the Tafila valley—the base of the triangle—was an excellent defensive position and had ordered Zeid's bodyguard to hold it. He had also sent back urgent messages to Zeid requesting that all available men and machine guns should be moved up to this line. He now withdrew the footmen from the advanced position, directing the Motalga horsemen under their sheikh Meta'ab to hold it ten minutes longer and then to fall back. By 3 p.m. Zeid had moved up the bulk of his force from the position south of Tafila which he had originally intended to hold. He now had, with the villagers, several hundred men, 13 machine guns or automatic rifles, and a mountain gun. The advance of the Turks, whose artillery and machine guns were ill handled, was thenceforward easily checked. The Arabs then turned boldly to the offensive.

An Arab regular officer, Rasim Bey, was despatched with all the mounted men available and five automatic rifles, to work round the enemy's left flank beyond the eastern ridge. A party of about one hundred Fellahin from the neighbouring village of El 'Eime with three of Zeid's Hotchkiss rifles next crept down behind the northern ridge and reached a point within 200 yards of the Turkish machine guns unseen, the enemy's attention being distracted by a frontal demonstration across the plain of a handful of men with four machine guns. A sudden burst of fire by the left party accounted for the machine gunners

---

[1] The following account is mainly from his report sent in by express to Beersheba after the action, which is employed by him as the basis of the accounts in "The Seven Pillars of Wisdom" and "Revolt in the Desert."

on the enemy's right flank; a rush by the villagers captured the guns. Then the Arab horse charged in against the Turkish left, and the main body, with banners flying, attacked frontally across the plain. The Turks fell back in confusion, abandoning their howitzers, to the Wadi el Hasa, where their cavalry checked the Arabs. There was no pursuit by the defenders, who were wearied out and hungry, but the Bedouin of Kerak harried the fugitives all through the night. In addition to the howitzers, 16 machine guns or automatic rifles, the tents and baggage were captured, and about two hundred prisoners were taken. The enemy commander was killed.[1]

By their elementary tactics, above all by their failure to cover their flanks, the Turks played into the hands of their opponents. Nevertheless, the defence of Tafila was a brilliant feat of arms. It was followed up by another remarkable exploit on the 28th January, when a party of Bedouin under Abdulla el Feir advanced to El Mezra', on the eastern shore of the Dead Sea, seized and sank a Turkish grain fleet of one launch and six dhows, and took 60 prisoners and about ten tons of grain.

Tafila was not held for long. Fresh falls of snow immobilized the Arabs, and directly the weather improved a little Falkenhayn despatched a strong force to check their further advance.[2] This expedition was handled very differently to its predecessor. The Turks employed two columns against Tafila: one of which detrained at Jurf ed Derawish Station, 17 miles to the south-east, the other at

---

[1] The true losses of the Turks in this engagement will probably never be known. Major Lawrence believed that the enemy lost 300 killed and that only the cavalry escaped. The only Turkish report on the incident is given by Lieut.-Colonel Hussein Husni (Turkish " *Yilderim*," Part 4, Chap. V) in the following words :—" On the 26th [sic] January a detach-" ment of 600 men under Lieut.-Colonel Hamid Bey of the *48th Division* " was defeated while marching from Kerak on Tafila. Hamid Bey was " killed. Aerial reports stated that there were tents for 500 men in " Tafila. On the 27th news arrived that 21 officers and 420 men had " retired to Kerak." Steuber, still hazier regarding the date, writes (German " *Yilderim*," p. 156) :—" In mid-January the situation in " Trans-Jordan became really threatening. The disturbance spread " northward and neared the zone of operations of the *Fourth Army* at " 'Amman and Es Salt. On the 19th January part of this Army in the " neighbourhood of Tafila, south-east of the Dead Sea, suffered a serious " reverse and lost many prisoners." If 420 men out of 600 had really reached Kerak the affair would hardly have been called a serious reverse.

[2] See p. 328.

GENERAL ORGANIZATION

Qatrani, 35 miles to the north-east, thus making intelligent use of the railway. As Major Lawrence had quitted Tafila and there was no British officer with the Arabs, little is known of the engagements which followed. Liman describes them as "violent but successful." On the 6th March Zeid evacuated the village, and on the following day was defeated on the Shobek–Tafila road, but fell back to Shobek without losing guns or material. The withdrawal of the Turkish expeditionary force to 'Amman permitted the Arabs to reoccupy Tafila without fighting on the 18th March.

1918. March.

The general organization of the Arab Northern Army was now as follows, and was to be little changed during 1918.

British Section (Commander: Lieut.-Colonel P. C. Joyce)—
Hejaz Armoured Car Battery ; [1]
1 Flight of Aeroplanes ;
1 Company Egyptian Camel Corps ;
Transport Corps ;
Labour Corps ;
Wireless Station at 'Aqaba.

French Detachment (Commander: Captain Pisani)—
2 mountain guns ;
4 machine guns and 10 automatic rifles.

Arab Regular Army (Commander: Ja'far Pasha el Askeri)—
Brigade of Infantry ;
1 Battalion Camel Corps ;
1 Battalion Mule-mounted Infantry ;
About 8 guns.

The Bedouin were recruited as they were needed, tribesmen, and later settled Fellahin, being called out for service so far as possible only in the neighbourhood of their pastures or villages. The organization and co-ordination of their activities was the particular task of Major Lawrence, who employed in many of his raids a section of Indian machine gunners. No tribesmen, except a few of

---

[1] Rolls Royce light armoured battery with machine guns, and two 10-pdr. guns on Talbot lorries.

the chiefs, could be kept out for long, whatever the cause, or indeed brought out at all without high payment. For the Bedouin war was not unattractive. He had not to go far from his home, and he returned to it when he chose. The spoils were his own property. And while all the world was full of paper money, he was paid, and well paid, in chinking golden sovereigns.

The Arab movement now had a staff, transport, and an ingenious if over-imaginative intelligence service. Hitherto it had been, in Lawrence's words, " a wild-man show "; henceforth it was to be part and parcel, so far at least as the Northern Army was concerned, of Sir Edmund Allenby's fighting force. It was fortunate in having in Feisal an inspiring leader, who held together discordant elements by his prestige, charm, and tact; in Ja'far a soldier of its own race experienced in the employment of modern weapons; in Lawrence a bold and inventive partizan; and in Joyce a tireless and efficient organizer. It was still more fortunate in that the British Commander-in-Chief thoroughly understood its value to himself and therefore gave it all the support in his power. That its first attempt at direct co-operation with the E.E.F. missed complete success was due in part to the failure of the first British raid into Trans-Jordan. It will be recalled that it was Sir Edmund Allenby's intention, after cutting the Hejaz Railway at 'Amman, to leave a strong detachment at Es Salt. Lawrence, with a body of Beni Sakr tribesmen, was to ride northward to Madeba, ready to join hands with the British after their occupation of Es Salt. Meanwhile the regular troops were to be employed upon the most ambitious operation yet attempted, against the railway about Ma'an, with the object of once and for all cutting off Medina from Palestine.

Map 23.

On hearing of the evacuation of Es Salt Lawrence realized that his part of the programme must be cancelled, and accordingly turned back. The attacks on the railway at Ma'an had already begun, and were continued vigorously, despite this mischance, under the general direction of Lieut.-Colonel A. G. C. Dawnay, of the Hejaz Operations Staff. The force operated in three columns: the southern consisting of the armoured cars and Egyptian Camel Corps with some Bedouin under Lieut.-Colonel Dawnay; the

MA'AN OPERATIONS 407

central of regular troops under Maulud, with Auda's [1] 1918.
horsemen; the northern also of regular troops under Ja'far. April.
The central column began by storming Ghadir el Hajj
Station, the next south of Ma'an, on the night of the
11th April, capturing 27 prisoners and destroying about a
thousand rails. On the 13th the northern column took
Jerdun Station, north of Ma'an, and burnt it, capturing
200 prisoners and two machine guns; and destroyed three
thousand rails between Jerdun and Ma'an next day. On
the 13th also the central column, after hard fighting,
captured Jebel Semna, a hill overlooking Ma'an and the
line from the south-west, with 30 prisoners and a machine
gun. After minor operations resulting in the capture of
several Turkish outposts round Ma'an, Ja'far himself moved
down to that area to direct the final attack on the 17th.
The station was captured with 70 prisoners, but the Arabs
were driven out of it again, and fell back to Jebel Semna,
which they entrenched. The Turks from the north re-
occupied Jerdun, and managed to get a pack convoy into
Ma'an, now near to starvation.

On the 19th Lieut.-Colonel Dawnay's mobile southern
column began an attack on the railway about Tell esh
Shahin Station, captured a series of posts north of it, and
finally, by a united attack of the armoured cars, the
Egyptian Camel Corps under Captain F. G. Peake, aeroplanes, and the Bedouin, stormed the station, taking 54
prisoners. Leaving the Bedouin to loot the arms, food,
and clothing to their hearts' content, Lieut.-Colonel Dawnay
ran down next morning to Ramla Station, the next to the
south, found it abandoned, and destroyed it, spending the
rest of the day blowing up rails. But now the Bedouin,
after " the maddest looting of their history," [2] were gone.
The cars and Camel Corps, though supported by two guns,
were forced to abandon an attack on Mudauwara Station,
where the enemy's garrison had been strengthened. However, the breach was completed during the day, the whole
line with its seven stations up to Ma'an being utterly
destroyed. At a cost of 250 casualties, Medina was now
definitively cut off from the north, for the great reserves of
rails were at last used up. The line between Ma'an and

---

[1] See Vol. I, p. 239.   [2] " Revolt in the Desert," p. 314.

Mudauwara remained a ruin for the rest of the war and is a ruin to-day.

There is no need to describe in detail the events of the summer, but mention must be made of two of the most important operations of the period. The Arab regulars, aided by three British aeroplanes, again captured Jerdun on the 11th May, taking 140 prisoners. To hold it permanently was out of the question, as it was impossible to keep troops supplied at such a distance from their base. In July, as the capture of Mudauwara appeared to be beyond the power of the Arabs, Sir Edmund Allenby consented to allow it to be carried out by two of the remaining companies of the recently disbanded Camel Brigade.[1] Nos. 5 and 7 Companies, having hastily concentrated at Kubri, on the Suez Canal, marched out on the afternoon of the 24th, under the command of Major R. V. Buxton, and reached 'Aqaba on the night of the 30th. On the morning of the 8th August they stormed Mudauwara Station, taking 120 prisoners and two guns, at a cost of 17 casualties. In view of the coming British offensive it had been intended to blow up the main bridge at 'Amman if possible, and the detachment actually reached a point fifteen miles southeast of the town on the 20th. There it was discovered by hostile aircraft, and the Turks were found to be thoroughly on the alert. Surprise being out of the question, Major Buxton, in accordance with his instructions, withdrew that evening, reached Bayir, 60 miles north-east of Ma'an, on the 26th, and Beersheba on the 6th September. In 44 days the companies had marched about 700 miles.

A few figures will assist to show the value of the Arab operations to the E.E.F. after the call had come to it to send to France most of its best troops. The ration strength of the *Hejaz Expeditionary Force* in the Medina area and that of the *2nd Composite Force* with headquarters at Tebuk (which was absorbed by the *Hejaz Expeditionary Force* in April) was about 12,000, some of the battalions being good troops. This force would have been invaluable to Liman either at the moment of Sir Edmund Allenby's greatest embarrassment or that of the final offensive. Turkey's German advisers and the most enlightened Turkish officers had again and again urged the evacuation

---
[1] See Chapter XIX.

of Medina, but the authorities in Constantinople had always wavered. Strategically the city was worthless at this moment, but politically and from the religious point of view it had yet the value of its traditions and dignity. Baghdad, Mecca, Jerusalem were gone; it was hard to abandon Medina, the spot where Mohammed proclaimed the new religion, the capital of the first Khalifs. It is possible, however, that the enemy would actually have done so (for it is known that he had made preparations for retreat) if his communications had not been severed by the operations of April. After that the hazard was too great. There was only a trifling amount of rolling stock left south of Mudauwara, so that the whole evacuation would have had to be carried out by march route at least as far as Ma'an. In the Ma'an area, north of the breach in the railway, there were over 4,000 men. Another 6,000 from the whole area between Tafila and Medina were evacuated as prisoners of war to Egypt up to the end of August 1918. Deaths from sickness accounted for many more. The casualties in killed and wounded were, according to Arab claims, 5,500. Even if this last figure be heavily reduced, the fact remains that prior to the final offensive with its many thousands of prisoners, the Arab campaign killed, wounded, captured or contained well over 25,000 troops. Like the Spanish guerillas in the Peninsular War, the Arabs gave the British invaluable aid, while largely dependent upon them for their opportunities.

During all this period the Southern Armies of the Emirs Ali and Abdulla were not inactive, though their operations lacked both the zeal and the success of Feisal's forces. Numerous camel convoys making for Medina were captured by Ali; whilst Abdulla's troops made several successful raids on the railway under Major W. A. Davenport's direction, the most notable being at Bowat Station, north-west of Medina. That all was not well in this area was proved, however, by an affair at the Wadi Hamdh bridges, 80 miles north-west of Medina, in May. In order to force the ex-Turkish artillery officers to bring their guns into action the Bedouin had no other resource than in the words of Major Davenport's report, to " draw their knives " and make suggestive gestures across their throats." The infantry officers failed to go forward with the regular battalions to the attack, which naturally collapsed, though the Bedouin captured several posts on the line.

There was, in fact, a good deal of disaffection and war-weariness in the Hejaz. The Turks conducted skilful propaganda, not failing to make the most of the German successes in Europe. They themselves had been taught by the Germans to believe that if only they held firm a little longer the war would be ended on the French front, and to some extent they impressed these views upon the Arabs. Again, King Hussein now knew of the Sykes-Picot Agreement and the Balfour Declaration, both of which disquieted him. Yet another factor which caused anxiety was the growing hostility between Hussein and Ibn Sa'ud, Emir of Nejd.[1] The mission of Mr. H. St. J. Philby, I.C.S., who journeyed across Arabia, interviewing Ibn Sa'ud at Riyadh and Hussein at Jidda, failed to patch up their quarrel, which was aggravated by a controversy over the village and oasis of Kharma, about sixty miles east of Taif. The population of this oasis had long professed Wahabism, but the principal sheikh had joined Hussein's troops near Medina with a contingent. A quarrel with the Emir Abdulla led to the secession of the Kharma people, and Hussein's threats of punishment caused them to seek the protection of Ibn Sa'ud, their natural religious leader. Attacks on Kharma by Sherifial forces, which were repulsed by the natives, exacerbated both Hussein and Ibn Sa'ud, and it became clear that these chieftains would shortly be at each other's throats. It was indeed only the preoccupation of Ibn Sa'ud with his campaign against Hail which delayed the struggle between the two potentates until after the Great War was over. Britain could do no more than exhort both to keep the peace for the sake of the common cause.

Fortunately these enervating influences did not affect the Northern Army. But for the moment Feisal's mission was fulfilled. The Turks, at the expense of maintaining in Trans-Jordan a force they could ill afford to spare, had succeeded in preventing his junction with the E.E.F. There was no more for him to do until he was called upon by Sir Edmund Allenby to play his part in the offensive which brought the campaign to an end.

---

[1] See Vol. I, pp. 240–1.

CHAPTER XIX.

THE REORGANIZATION OF THE FORCE.

As has already been stated, the War Office had decided, before the German offensive was launched in France on the 21st March,[1] to despatch large numbers of Indian troops to Palestine. Its object at that time was, however, not the relief of British troops for transfer to the Western Front, but the reinforcement of Sir Edmund Allenby's Army in accordance with the proposition of General Smuts,[2] which had been generally accepted by the Government. The 7th Indian Division had arrived in Egypt by the beginning of January; and though the Government had decided against the transfer from Mesopotamia of the 13th Division, which General Smuts had suggested, they still had the intention of strengthening the E.E.F. by a second Indian division from that theatre. They had also, even before General Smuts's mission, informed the Commander-in-Chief that they would despatch to Palestine one of the two Indian cavalry divisions (which contained British regiments) in France, and subsequently determined instead to send all the Indian regiments from both divisions. Nine of these regiments were to be posted to the Yeomanry Mounted Division, 5th Mounted Brigade, and 7th Mounted Brigade in substitution for Yeomanry regiments; and one each to the 7th Mounted Brigade and the Imperial Service Cavalry Brigade, to bring them up to strength. With regard to infantry, a number of Indian battalions were to be sent from India during the spring of 1918 to replace six British battalions of the 10th Division, six of the 60th,

---

[1] See p. 350.   [2] See p. 298.

five of the 75th (which already had four Indian battalions), and two of the 53rd. Indian pioneer battalions were to be posted to the 53rd and 75th Divisions. The British units thus relieved were to be broken up, but retained in the country as reinforcements, there being as yet no intention of transferring any troops to France.

The result of these reinforcements and substitutions would have been to increase Sir Edmund Allenby's strength in mounted troops only fractionally, but to give him nine instead of seven infantry divisions. Obviously for a force of this size he required three instead of two infantry corps headquarters. The third was authorized on the 15th March, and the name of Major-General Sir G. de S. Barrow, which he submitted to the Army Council for the command, approved. However, the great German offensive of the 21st March and the consequent calls for troops for France at once put an end to the need for a third corps, and on the 29th March the Commander-in-Chief telegraphed that he no longer required it.

Mention may here be made of some important staff changes of the early months of 1918. In January Br.-General G. P. Dawnay, B.G.G.S. at G.H.Q.—whose province was the working-out in detail of all operations—was transferred to G.H.Q. in France. His post was filled first by Br.-General A. B. Robertson, and in April by Br.-General W. H. Bartholomew, hitherto B.G.G.S. of the XX Corps, who was replaced on General Chetwode's staff by Br.-General A. P. Wavell. In March Major-General W. G. B. Western succeeded Major-General Sir John Adye as Deputy Adjutant-General. In February Br.-General E. T. Humphreys, B.G.G.S. of the XXI Corps, was replaced by Br.-General H. F. Salt, and took over command of the 179th Brigade. In July Br.-General R. G. H. Howard-Vyse, B.G.G.S. Desert Mounted Corps, and Br.-General C. A. C. Godwin, commanding the 10th Cavalry Brigade, exchanged posts.

The first result of the situation in France was an order on the 23rd March to relieve one British division by the 7th Indian Division and to hold the former ready for embarkation at short notice. The 52nd Division was selected, and was ready to entrain, less artillery, at Lydda by the 4th April. As the relief of the artillery could not be carried out so quickly and was likely to strain the resources of the railway in the midst of active operations—the first raid into Trans-Jordan and the action of Berukin—permission was obtained from the War Office for the divisional artilleries of the 7th and 52nd Divisions to be exchanged. The 52nd Division, with the artillery of the 7th, sailed from Egypt during the first fortnight of April.

1918.
March.

On the 26th March Sir Edmund Allenby was ordered to send nine Yeomanry regiments, to be formed into four and a half machine-gun battalions, to France. On the following day the War Office telegraphed that the instructions he had received to take the offensive in accordance with the scheme of General Smuts were cancelled, and that the Force must for the time being fall back upon a policy of active defence. Another British division was to follow the 52nd to France, either on the arrival from Mesopotamia of the 3rd Indian Division, or earlier if he could spare it. At the same time he was asked whether he could despatch any heavy artillery, and a little later what medical units he could release in view of the reduction of his force. He selected the 74th Division, which was to be ready for entrainment at Lydda about the 15th April, and stated that it would not be necessary to await the arrival of the 3rd Indian Division before withdrawing it. He promised to send one 8-inch battery, two and a half 6-inch howitzer batteries, and two composite batteries, complete in personnel; also one general hospital, one stationary hospital, and one casualty clearing station. He subsequently stated that nine British battalions would be ready to embark in May, on relief by battalions from India. Headquarters of the 74th Division sailed from Egypt on the 1st May, while that of the 3rd Indian division arrived on the 14th April; but there was an interval of about two months between the withdrawal of the British division from the line and the arrival at the front of the Indian.

The German advance astride the Somme was brought to a halt in the first days of April; but hardly was that accomplished when another thrust had to be met, this time all too near the Channel ports. The enemy's second great offensive was launched in the valley of the Lys on the 9th, and made alarming progress. Another heavy demand upon

April.

Palestine resulted. In a telegram of the 21st April the new Chief of the Imperial General Staff, General Sir Henry Wilson, outlined the situation with extreme frankness. The casualties in France since the 21st March amounted to 225,000; to replace these there were 30,000 reinforcements in the country, while 180,000 drafts had been sent from home. For the next three or four months all that Britain would be able to find was 23,000 men per month, of whom a proportion would have to be kept in reserve owing to the prospect of renewed German attacks. It had already been necessary to reduce six divisions to cadres, and the only means of reconstituting them was to call upon the E.E.F. for more battalions. Therefore, in addition to the nine battalions mentioned above, Sir Edmund Allenby was asked if possible to release another fourteen as soon as shipping was available to transport them, without waiting for the battalions from India which the energy and organizing power of General Sir Charles Monro had provided to replace them. It was realized that this would entail loss of efficiency and a temporary reduction in strength, but, since the Germans for their part were concentrating in the West every available man, it seemed that the risk ought to be accepted.

Sir Edmund Allenby began the reorganization of the Force at once. The Yeomanry Mounted Division could be reconstituted in a short time, as the Indian regiments from France arrived together in March. The division was therefore withdrawn to Deir el Balah, near the Sinai frontier, for the purpose. At the same time the Commander-in-Chief saw his way to increasing the strength and efficiency of his new mounted force with the means at his disposal. He had, it will be recalled, two unattached brigades, the 7th Mounted and Imperial Service Cavalry. The latter was to be strengthened by having posted to it a picked Imperial Service regiment, the Jodhpore Lancers, from France. The Imperial Camel Brigade had originally been formed for service in Sinai and the Western Desert; and it had long appeared that this brigade would be more useful in Palestine if given horses. If it were reorganized as a fifth Light Horse brigade and attached to the Australian Mounted Division in place of the 5th Mounted Brigade, that division would become entirely Australian, and there would be available three brigades to form a new one; even though only a single horse artillery battery could be found for it. The War Office approved of this proposal. It suggested that the Yeomanry Mounted Division (to which the title "Yeomanry" was no longer applicable, since it was to contain only three Yeomanry regiments) should be called the "1st Mounted Division," and the new formation the "2nd Mounted Division." These titles were in use for a short time, but at Sir Edmund Allenby's request they were changed on the 23rd July to "4th Cavalry Division" and "5th Cavalry Division." As the great majority of the regiments in them were regular Indian cavalry, the Commander-in-Chief considered that these designations would give them pleasure and were their due. Major-General Sir G. de S. Barrow, previously in command of the Yeomanry Mounted Division, remained in command when it was reconstituted as the 4th Cavalry Division. Major-General H. J. M. Macandrew, who had commanded the former 5th Cavalry Division in France, took over the new formation bearing that title.

The Imperial Camel Brigade consisted of four battalions, of which the 1st and 3rd were Australian, the 2nd British, and the 4th formed of two companies of Australians and two of New Zealanders. There were also two detached British companies. From the 1st, 3rd, and 4th Battalions there was constituted at the end of June the 5th Australian Light Horse Brigade: the Australians being formed into the 14th and 15th Australian Light Horse Regiments, and the New Zealanders into the 2nd New Zealand Machine-Gun Squadron. The majority of the officers and probably well over half the men had begun their service as horsemen. The French had increased the small force which they had sent to Palestine during Sir A. Murray's command, and there was now available a complete cavalry regiment consisting of two squadrons of Spahis and two of Chasseurs d'Afrique, which was attached to the 5th L.H. Brigade as its third regiment. Lieut.-Colonel G. M. M. Onslow, formerly in command of the 7th A.L.H., was appointed to the command of the new brigade. The six British companies retained their camels for patrolling the Lines of Communication, and, as we have seen, rendered valuable service in aid of the Arabs on the Hejaz Railway.

The Desert Mounted Corps now consisted of the following :—

4th Cavalry (late Yeomanry Mounted) Division—
  10th [1] (late 6th Mounted), 11th (late 8th Mounted), 12th (late 22nd Mounted) Cavalry Brigades ;
  XX Brigade R.H.A.
5th Cavalry Division—
  13th (late 5th Mounted), 14th (late 7th Mounted), 15th (Imperial Service) Cavalry Brigades ;
  Essex Battery R.H.A.
A. & N.Z. Mounted Division (unchanged).
Australian Mounted Division (unchanged except that the 5th L.H. Brigade was substituted for the 5th Mounted Brigade).

Each brigade of the 4th and 5th Cavalry Divisions consisted of one of its original Yeomanry regiments and two of Indian Cavalry, excepting the 15th Brigade, which consisted of the Jodhpur Lancers and its original regiments, the Mysore and Hyderabad Lancers. The Yeomanry, Australian, and New Zealand regiments consisted of three squadrons, each of four troops ; the Indian regiments of four squadrons, each of three troops. The artillery of the whole Desert Mounted Corps was now equipped with the 13-pounder.

On withdrawal from the Jordan Valley for rest in August, the Australian Mounted Division was armed with the sword. When the campaign of movement came to an end early in the year Major-General Hodgson had asked for swords for his two Australian brigades, but had then been refused them. Now, however, in view of the part that the division was destined to play in the coming offensive, and of the great success which had attended the use of shock weapons by the Indian cavalry in minor affairs in the Jordan Valley, the decision was reversed. The actual training in the use of the sword was limited to two weeks. During the first, two cavalry officers on the staff of the

---

[1] In the case of the renumbered brigades the old numbering in brackets is more or less formal and official, for the sake of records, etc., though headquarters were in some cases unaltered. Actually, to take an example, the 13th Cavalry Brigade more nearly represented the former Amballa Brigade than the 5th Mounted Brigade.

division, Lieut.-Colonel R. H. Osborne and Major A. T. McMurrough-Kavanagh, taught the officers and squadron sergeant-majors; during the second the regimental officers, aided by a few British N.C.Os., taught their men. Short as was the time, it sufficed, the great majority of the men being good horsemen and all of them so keen and interested that they practised incessantly among themselves. The division had long been trained in mounted tactics, the bayonet being carried as a sword. The French regiment, which joined the 5th L.H. Brigade at the last moment before the offensive, was already armed with the sword. On the other hand, two Indian regiments of the 5th Cavalry Division, the Deccan and Poona Horse, which had been armed with the sword, were given lances at their own request when they went into the Jordan Valley; and in the opinion of Major-General Macandrew the change in weapons greatly increased their confidence and fighting value.

The infantry divisions could not be reorganized so quickly as the cavalry because the Indian battalions arrived at intervals, the first landing in February, the last in August. A camp was formed at Sarafand, near Ramle, where the Indian battalions rested after their train journey from Egypt before marching to join their brigades. The British battalions relieved then marched to the same camp, and entrained at Lydda for Qantara. But in many cases the reliefs had not arrived when the British battalions departed. Thus, when the fourteen battalions called for by the C.I.G.S. concentrated at Sarafand during the first days of June, only two Indian battalions were available to take their places. Shortly afterwards, however, Sir Edmund Allenby had completed the formation of seven new battalions by withdrawing one company from each of twenty-eight in the country.[1] Each battalion which lost a company then expanded its remaining three companies into four, and filled up to establishment with drafts from India when these arrived. Finally, during July and the early part of August ten British battalions were relieved by Indian and broken up to provide reinforcements.

---

[1] Eight battalions from the 3rd Division, which began to arrive in April, ten from the 7th Division, three from the 75th Division, and seven recently arrived battalions were thus drawn upon.

418 THE REORGANIZATION OF THE FORCE

All the seven infantry divisions in the Force, with the exception of the 54th, now consisted of three British and nine Indian battalions,[1] the so-called " Indian " divisions (3rd and 7th) being exactly the same as the others in this respect. The 54th was allowed to retain its British battalions, doubtless so that the War Office should have another complete British division on which to put its hand in case of desperate emergency. In June, to Sir Edmund Allenby's alarm, the War Cabinet decided not only to withdraw this division to France, but to take one of the mounted Australian divisions to use as drafts for the Australian infantry. Both projects were, however, dropped, though certain units of the 54th Division actually reached Qantara before the transfer of the division was cancelled.

In order to understand Sir Edmund Allenby's anxiety on this, the first and only occasion when he even hinted a remonstrance regarding the calls made on him, the composition and antecedents of the Indian battalions must be considered. Twenty-two of them (belonging to the 3rd, 7th, and 75th Divisions) had proved their value in war, but each of them had given up at least one company.[2] Ten, though composed to a great extent of men who had seen active service, had seen none as battalions. The other twenty-two had seen no service;[3] some of their commanding officers, even, were in the same case. These battalions were largely—in some instances as to one-third of their strength —made up of recruits who had done no musketry. One had never seen the service rifle, having been armed with the Ross rifle in India. They landed in Egypt with hardly any signallers, few Lewis gunners, no bombers, often no transport drivers with experience in handling animals. Their junior British officers were almost all in need of further instruction and few of them spoke Hindustani, while the Indian officers had for the most part been recently promoted. It is on record that in one battalion there were

[1] The 53rd Division, however, had one native battalion from South Africa, the 1st Cape Corps. The Order of Battle of the reorganized Force will be found in Appendix 3.
[2] The 3rd Division had undergone a similar reorganization before leaving Mesopotamia.
[3] These figures are from an official return. The question is extremely complicated, but it appears that this return overlooks the service of certain battalions in East Africa and possibly of others on the Indian Frontier.

only two British officers who could understand their men and only one Indian officer who spoke English. Intensive training was required, not only of the units as a whole, but still more of all the specialists without whom a battalion is almost useless in modern warfare. There was indeed much to be done, and for the later arrivals little time in which to do it.[1]

During the summer the French contingent, known as the Détachement Français de Palestine et de Syrie, and shortly as the " D.F.P.S.," had been considerably augmented. It now consisted of the Régiment Mixte de Tirailleurs, of two battalions; and the Régiment Légion d'Orient, of two battalions of Armenians; a Territorial battalion and another Armenian battalion; four squadrons of cavalry; three batteries; with engineers and auxiliary services. The nucleus of the Légion d'Orient was those Armenians rescued from the Turks near Alexandretta and brought to Egypt by Admiral Dartige du Fournet in 1915.[2]

---

[1] The following reports from Br.-General A. B. Robertson, in charge of training at G.H.Q., are of interest, as they show the strength and weakness of representative battalions at a date as late as the 3rd July 1918. These were two battalions out of five then in training at Tell el Kebir, the 2nd Guides being the best there, and the 2/30th Punjabis, much less advanced in training, fourth on the list.

2nd Guides Infantry.

This battalion has made great progress since its arrival in Egypt, and with another fortnight's training should be able to take its place in the front line.

The Lewis gunners are well trained, but the teams are not yet complete as regards numbers. Bombing presents some difficulties, the men not being natural throwers, but they are improving. Very few have thrown live bombs. The unit has only six trained signallers. Every man has been exercised in musketry while at Tell el Kebir. The battalion has reached a high standard in bayonet work.

2/30th Punjabis.

This battalion is progressing satisfactorily. It has 250 recruits of from three to five months' service; none of these has fired a course of musketry. Only 15 N.C.Os. have as yet been trained in Lewis gunnery, but a start is now being made to train teams. No live bombs have ye been thrown by any man, but men are being exercised with dummies and are showing signs of improvement. This battalion has very few signallers, but a class is under construction.

This unit contains good material, and in a month's time should be fit for the front line.

It is of interest to note that in the 60th Division Major-General Shea attached to each platoon of the nine Indian battalions a N.C.O. or particularly intelligent private from his three experienced London battalions. These N.C.Os. and men trained by demonstration only.

[2] Vol. I, p. 86.

As previously stated, the cavalry formed part of the 5th L.H. Brigade for active operations.

In the first volume of this history mention was made of the "Balfour Declaration," by which His Majesty's Government pledged themselves to facilitate the establishment in Palestine of a national home for the Jewish people.[1] That declaration was made in November 1917, but three months earlier it had been decided to form a Jewish Legion to serve in Palestine. It was hoped that this legion would not only rouse the enthusiasm of Jews born in Britain, but would reconcile to service the thousands of recently naturalized or still un-naturalized foreign Jews in the great cities.[2] The Jewish battalions formed part of the Royal Fusiliers. The 38th Battalion arrived in Egypt on the 1st March and the 39th at the end of April. A third battalion, the 40th, arrived subsequently, but was retained by the Force in Egypt.

To sum up, the Force could not be said to have suffered in any respect as regards its mounted arm. The Yeomanry which it had lost were indeed first-class, and some of the regiments, such as the Bucks Hussars, would doubtless not have been willingly exchanged by Major-General Barrow for any mounted troops in the world. The Indian regiments had to accustom themselves to new conditions, but this they had time to do, while both their training and their material were good. Moreover, there were now four mounted divisions instead of three; three of them cavalry divisions, armed and trained for shock tactics in pursuit, instead of one. The Desert Mounted Corps was for the Commander-in-Chief's purposes a more formidable weapon after the reorganization than before it.

The case of the infantry was very different. It had without doubt been seriously weakened in efficiency; and though the earlier arrivals among the new battalions had time and opportunity for training, the last-joined had little or none. Nevertheless, with good leadership, keenness, and a fine example set to the newcomers by the experienced

---

[1] Vol. I, p. 219.

[2] For an account of the raising and subsequent career of the Jewish battalions reference may be made to the interesting but highly controversial "With the Judæans in the Palestine Campaign," by Lieut.-Colonel J. H. Patterson, who commanded the 38/Royal Fusiliers.

troops, Indian as well as British, the infantry divisions were to prove themselves amply equal to their task.

In all Sir Edmund Allenby despatched to France two infantry divisions (with two pioneer battalions taken from other divisions [1]), nine Yeomanry regiments, five and a half siege batteries, twenty-three infantry battalions, five machine-gun companies: upwards of 60,000 officers and men. He disbanded ten infantry battalions, numbering approximately 7,000 officers and men, though these were retained as reinforcements.[2] Yet even more remarkable to contemplate than the extent of this invaluable aid to the Armies on the Western Front is the magnitude of the Empire's resources, which permitted him to maintain in these months of adversity an Army of four mounted and seven infantry divisions, fully equipped with all the material needful.

---

[1] Transferred from the 10th and 60th to the 52nd and 74th Divisions when the two latter left the country.

[2] It must be added that he sent to India one garrison battalion and three cavalry regiments, made up by withdrawing squadrons from ten different regiments of Indian Cavalry.

CHAPTER XX.

THE HOT WEATHER OF 1918.
(Maps 1, 23; Sketches 28, 29.)

SUMMER CONDITIONS ON THE FRONT.

Map 1. THE physical configuration of Palestine, with its remarkable variations in altitude and in soil, results in corresponding variations of climate. From the sea to the Jordan Valley the country is virtually without rain from at latest the middle of May to at earliest the middle of October, and months may pass in that period without the appearance of a cloud in the sky. But the temperatures of the three main topographical provinces—the coast plain, the hill range, and the Ghor—differ greatly. The sea-board is almost sub-tropical, with a mean August temperature of about 80°, though the heat is tempered by occasional cool sea-breezes. The hill country is a good deal cooler, but even on the watershed there are periods of great heat, while the variation in the course of a single day often amounts to 20°. Yet it is the heat's accompaniments, dust and insect pests, which render summer most trying in hills and plain. The malaria-carrying mosquito has been the foe of many armies campaigning in the country, but so far as the British in Palestine were concerned it was a foe which they had the means to keep in subjection. Less dangerous—though it also brings its own fever—but even more annoying was the sand-fly, against which the only protection is netting so fine as to be stifling to the sleeper.

Hills and plain, arid rocky peaks up by the Nablus road, burning dunes down by El Haram, were alike paradise to the troops by comparison with the Jordan Valley, which is tropical in heat as in vegetation, though that vegetation has not the luxuriance associated with tropical valleys. Week after week a shade temperature of 100°, rising sometimes to over 120°, is maintained. Yet the thermometer is no index to its horrors. Owing to its great depth and the enormous amount of evaporation from the Dead Sea, its air is leaden with moisture, which affected the troops, especially during the first days of their tour of duty, with an extraordinary lassitude and sense of helplessness. The hills on either side of this trench act as walls to screen it, so that its atmosphere is commonly stagnant and seethed all day in the sun's rays, though at times gusts sweep down the gullies and raise "dust devils" in the plain below. The necessary movement of the troops and their transport also stirred up the dust from a soil rendered yet more friable than usual by the incessant beating and scraping of thousands of hooves. A single column of half a dozen wagons would toss up a vast dun cloud, which would then hang for a long period like fog in the overcharged air. The insect life of the place seemed to accord with its pestiferous character. There were scorpions, six-inch centipedes, and great stinging spiders in the dry regions; mosquitoes in the marshes. No sanitary precautions could keep off swarms of flies from the horse-lines and camps.

The retention of the bridgehead over the Jordan was necessary to secure the right flank of the Force and also to maintain that threat against the Hejaz Railway which was always vital to the plans of the Commander-in-Chief. The defence of the bridgehead and of the approach to it from the hills, much the most ungrateful task which any troops in Palestine were set to perform during the hot season, was carried out at first almost entirely by the Australian Divisions and thereafter mainly by all the mounted troops in turn. If troops had to be kept in the valley, it was desirable that they should be as few as possible; and mounted men were more economical than infantry because their reserves could be more quickly moved to any threatened point. The constant employment of the Australians and New Zealanders was thus necessary while the Yeomanry Mounted Division was undergoing reorganization. But by the time conditions were at their worst the 4th and 5th Cavalry Divisions had been constituted, and the newly-arrived Indian cavalry took their turn on this heat-stricken front, finding it little easier to endure than did their fellow soldiers of European blood. The gallant veteran

General Sir Pertab Singhji, then over seventy years of age, accompanied the Jodhpore Lancers to the valley. Another formation which did regular service there was the 20th (late Imperial Service) Indian Infantry Brigade; these troops, who had seen little previous fighting though they had been in the theatre since 1914, proved themselves steady and keen. At the beginning of August the 1st and 2nd Battalions British West Indies Regiment [1] moved down to the Jordan and remained there until operations came to an end. In mid-August the first of the two Jewish battalions, the 38/Royal Fusiliers, took up a position on the Wadi Mellaha.

So far as possible brigades were relieved after about a month's duty in the valley and withdrawn to the hills for rest. The comparative cool, the lighter air, and above all the fresh, pleasant nights, which induced sleep, were welcome after the inferno down below. The food supplied had now some nourishment in it, whereas preserved meat reached the front line on the Jordan and 'Auja in a disgusting state, the tins having become so heated that their contents had melted into a mess of oil and fibre which weak stomachs could scarcely retain. Yet, despite these reliefs, the health of these troops suffered more than at any period during the campaign. Heat prevented sleep by day, needful work on the defences often made it impossible by night. Continual sweating and insufficient rest wore the men down, perhaps especially those of the A. & N.Z. Mounted Division, which had the severest campaigning record and was allotted the final spell in the valley. The horses, on the other hand, stood the heat wonderfully well. If they lost condition, the cause was rather in the quality of the forage. This was plentiful enough, but owing to the small proportion of pure grain available was too bulky, unpalatable, and lacking in nutritive value.[2]

---

[1] This regiment is not to be confused with the old West India Regiment. It was formed for service in the war, recruiting being from all the British West Indies and also British Guiana and British Honduras. Five battalions served in Egypt, but the 3rd and 4th were withdrawn to France as labour battalions. The 5th (Reserve) Battalion supplied drafts to the other two and was not employed in front line.

[2] Barley 6 lbs., gram (dried pulse) 4 lbs., tibben 12 lbs., with occasional exchange of maize for barley or gram, was an average ration. The tibben ration was too big for any horse, but there was not enough less bulky and more nourishing food to take its place.

The campaign against the anopheline mosquito was far more difficult than during the preceding summer on the Wadi Ghazze, but almost equally successful. Marshes [1] were drained or oiled and streams canalized; "diagnosis stations" established close to the front line. Yet it was impossible to prevent a certain amount of malaria in the Jordan Valley, for the enemy took few precautions or none, so that every strong breeze from his quarter blew in mosquitoes from his area. In general, however, the Force's standard of health was very high.

Few active operations of importance were conducted by the British during these hot months occupied by re-organization; and the most considerable engagement from the early days of May, when the second expedition into Trans-Jordan was withdrawn, to the final offensive in September resulted from a Turkish offensive in the Jordan Valley. There were, however, one small British attack designed to improve the front on the coast, several British raids, of which one was on a very large scale, and one minor Turkish attack in the foot-hills.

The objective of the attack on the coast, carried out by troops of the 7th Division on the morning of the 8th June, was two low hills a mile from the sea, known as "North Sister" and "South Sister." The assault was launched at 3.45 a.m., after a quarter of an hour's intense bombardment, and the hills were quickly taken by the 21st Indian Brigade (Br.-General A. G. Kemball). Recovering from their surprise, the Turks counter-attacked at 6.40, after shelling the position heavily. At North Sister they were completely repulsed by the 2/Black Watch, and, though they momentarily re-established themselves on South Sister, were again driven off it by the 1st Guides. The British casualties, chiefly as a result of the enemy's artillery fire, were 63 killed and 204 wounded; the Turks lost 110 prisoners, two heavy and five light machine guns, while a large number were killed. The two hills, which had been useful observation posts to the enemy, were

1918.
8 June

---

[1] The drainage of the Bahret Qaturiye, a marsh of some two hundred acres near the front line on the coast, appeared at first sight to present insuperable difficulties. Eventually a very ancient tunnel cut through Argyll Ridge was discovered, re-excavated, and repaired; and by this means the marsh was completely drained.

1918.
13 July.

consolidated and remained in British hands. On the 13th July the enemy made an attack on the Ra-fat salient, notable because it was preceded by one of the heaviest bombardments experienced in Palestine.[1] Br.-General Huddleston, whose brigade had previously held this part of the front, and later Br.-General Colston had been concerned by the isolation of this position, and both brigades had worked very hard to make it secure and provide its garrison with cover. It was now held by the 3/3rd Gurkhas (232nd Brigade), which owing to the reorganization in progress had not been relieved for a month. The bombardment began at 5.15 p.m. and was continued for just over an hour, during which the village was completely blotted out from sight of those in rear by a pall of smoke and dust. Fire then lifted from the village to the ridge south of the Wadi Ikba, where were battalion headquarters and the reserve company. A few minutes later sentries observed parties of the enemy advancing from north-west, north, and north-east. The Gurkhas immediately rushed to their defences and opened so hot a fire that with the aid of the artillery the attack was completely broken up, though the enemy did not desist until long after darkness had fallen. The casualties of the battalion were 52 killed or wounded by shell fire, a very small figure which paid tribute to the defensive organization of the salient.

27 July.

A successful raid was carried out on the night of the 27th July by five platoons 53rd Sikhs of the 28th Indian Brigade (Br.-General C. H. Davies) against the advanced Turkish trenches on Piffer Ridge, 3 miles east of the shore at El Haram. Two columns entered the enemy's line at different points and converged, thus preventing the escape of the garrison, which was taken by surprise. Thirty-three prisoners were brought in, the Sikhs having only four casualties. The losses of the Turks from the bombardment were apparently heavy.

On the night of the 12th August the 10th Division

---

[1] In " The Regimental History of the 3rd Queen Alexandra's Own " Gurkha Rifles," edited by Major-General Nigel G. Woodyat, is an account of this action, particularly interesting because several orders of the *Asia Corps* are given in an appendix. They show that over 3,000 artillery and 300 trench-mortar shells were allotted for the attack, which was carried out by the German *701st Battalion* and a company of the Turkish *48th Regiment*, with another Turkish battalion in reserve.

carried out a raid which far exceeded in scale anything of the sort previously attempted in Palestine. It was one of a whole series of such operations, conducted by forces from a brigade down to a platoon, and intended to be a thorough test of the Indian troops in the conditions of this theatre of war. The objective was a steep-faced ridge west of the Nablus road, four thousand yards long, of which the highest point was Kh. Gharabe.[1] It was the only part of the XX Corps front where the Turkish defences were practically continuous, and was known to be garrisoned by 600 rifles of the *33rd Regiment, 11th Division*, a good formation from which there had been little or no desertion. The whole of the 29th Brigade, under the command of Lieut.-Colonel E. H. Wildblood, 1/Leinster Regiment,[2] was withdrawn from the line by the 20th July and given three weeks' training about Janiya, nearly twenty miles from the front. The enemy's defences were reproduced as accurately as possible, and rehearsals carried out, at first by daylight, then at night, which included every detail of the attack and withdrawal. The raiders practised cutting wire with Bangalore torpedoes and crossing it on ladders.[3] Special boots with felt soles were made for the men.[4] Telephone wires were laid to the Wadi Gharib, 1,200 yards in advance of the British trenches at Kh. 'Alyata, before the attack took place. Routes were marked by tapes and luminous

---

[1] The ridge is shown on Map 19. Kh. Gharabe is not marked, but the ridge can be identified because still held by the *33rd Regiment*.

[2] Br.-General C. L. Smith, the former commander of the Camel Brigade, had succeeded Br.-General Vandeleur in June, but was on leave in the United Kingdom at this date. Major-General J. R. Longley was also on leave, the division being commanded by Br.-General E. M. Morris. The training was supervised by Major-General Shea, whose division carried out all the smaller raids.

[3] The ladder employed merits description, owing to its ingenuity and handiness. It was jointed, one section being 6 feet, the other 12 feet long; and 2 feet 6 inches in breadth. It was constructed of bamboo, and across it were fixed two thicknesses of wire netting, with rush matting in between. The long section was laid across the wire entanglement and the short lowered to the ground on the far side. Its weight was about 50 lbs.

[4] This proof of the wealth of British resources struck the imagination of the enemy Commander-in-Chief. Liman writes (pp. 327–8):—

" The Turkish troops saw with envy that the British prisoners and
" dead had felt soles nailed on to the soles of their boots so as to render
" their movements noiseless on the stony mountain ground. They them-
" selves often had only rags tied on to their feet, or at best wore ' shariks,'
" that is, hides laced up with string. In many cases even the officers
" had no other footgear."

boards; beacons were prepared to guide the attackers in their withdrawal. The 53rd Divisional Artillery (less two howitzer batteries) and the IX British Mountain Artillery Brigade were put at the disposal of the 10th Division, while 30 6-inch howitzers of the Corps Heavy Artillery were to bombard the enemy's position. In all there were employed in support of this attack and of raids and demonstrations on either flank 147 guns and howitzers.

The wire-cutting bombardment began at 9.55 p.m., by which time the attacking companies were deployed opposite their objectives: the 54th Sikhs and two companies 1/Leinster south-east of the right flank of the ridge; the 1/101st Grenadiers and two companies 1/Leinster at its western end, over two and a half miles away. The two Indian regiments advanced simultaneously with great dash, and captured the flanking works; then the Leinster companies turned inwards, a barrage moving inwards from either flank in front of them. These companies met with stiffer opposition, and there was fierce fighting at close quarters. The two left-hand companies did not reach their final objective, but otherwise the attack was completely successful. The withdrawal began about 12.15 a.m., and was conducted without hitch.

The captures in this well conceived and brilliantly executed affair amounted to 239, and the enemy's losses were estimated to be 450. Fourteen machine guns and ten ponies were brought in. The casualties of the 29th Brigade were 107. The enemy fought stoutly enough at certain points, but was hopelessly bewildered and ignorant of the real situation. As the flanking parties closed in they came on several machine-gun detachments firing away to their front, which was not threatened.

While this attack was in progress the 179th and 181st Brigades of the 60th Division carried out raids on a front of five miles east of the Nablus road, the points attacked being Keen's Knoll, Table Hill, Bidston Hill, Forfar Hill, Fife Knoll, Kh. 'Amuriye, the village of Turmus 'Aya. These raids, for the most part made without artillery support, were generally successful, and though only eight prisoners were brought in, at a cost of 57 casualties, deserters who came over subsequently stated that the Turkish losses were 120. It was also learnt that the enemy believed he

Sketch 28.

had succeeded in repelling a general attack on the whole front of nine miles between Keen's Knoll and 'Amuriye, a belief which persists in Liman's account.[1]   1918.
12 Aug.

The whole operation was a valuable test of the newly-arrived Indian troops. It proved that they could move in complete silence, manœuvre in the dark without confusion, and display determination in close fighting. So much was to be expected of old Frontier Force units like the 54th Sikhs, but the conduct of less experienced battalions was likewise admirable.

All along the front patrolling was carried out to accustom the Indian troops to the country and give them experience. Whilst acquiring it they suffered loss on several occasions, parties being ambushed by the enemy. But very few prisoners were captured by the Turks, and the Indians, gaining confidence and cunning, speedily asserted their superiority in No Man's Land. In truth the Turkish patrols now met with were generally of a quality far lower than those of the last prolonged period of trench warfare, during the summer of 1917 on the Gaza–Beersheba line. That was but one proof of the deterioration in the enemy's infantry. Equally significant was the steady trickle of deserters who came over with the likely tale that many more were only stopped from doing likewise by the risk. These men related also—and we now know there was no exaggeration in their testimony—that for every one who gave himself up to the British at least a score vanished from their units and went into hiding behind the Turkish lines.

The Affair of Abu Tulul.

On the 13th July the Jordan Valley defences were held, under the orders of the Desert Mounted Corps, by the   Sketch 28.

---

[1] Liman (p. 327). "On the 12th August from 10 p.m. onwards, "after a heavy and prolonged bombardment, the British attacked the "Turkish positions on both sides of the Jerusalem–Nablus road. The "engagement, which was very severe and resulted in many casualties, "lasted until 4 a.m. On the east of the road the enemy attack was "repulsed in front of the Turkish positions. West of the road the enemy "penetrated into the Turkish lines in places, but was driven out again "by a counter-attack, after furious fighting at close quarters. The "enemy attack east of the road was conducted by three, and west of the "road by seven British and Indian battalions. The fighting took place "near Turmus 'Aya. The entire position remained in our hands."

2nd Mounted (later the 5th Cavalry) Division [1] from the Ghoraniye bridgehead southward, and by the A. & N.Z. Mounted Division on the 'Auja and Mellaha. After a relatively cool spell about the 7th, the weather was growing steadily hotter, the maximum shade temperature on the 14th being 115°; yet greatly increased activity on the enemy's part had been noticed during the past few days, and his shelling, especially on the Abu Tulul salient, had been heavier than usual.

The capture of this salient had obvious attractions for an enemy so inferior in numbers on the whole front that he could scarcely attempt any enterprise on a great scale; for it would have shortened his line, given him good observations of the British communications with their bridgehead, and made that bridgehead useless for the purpose of another raid into Trans-Jordan. He had failed once on the 11th April, and, as was learnt from prisoners, had been about to try again on the 1st May when the capture of Es Salt by the British altered his plans. There was every likelihood that he would make another effort to force the British line back to the lower 'Auja. Little anxiety was felt for the bridgehead at Ghoraniye, which was safe against anything short of a prepared attack in greatly superior numbers, but it was recognized that the Abu Tulul salient, despite the work recently done on it, was not equally secure. Amid these tumbled hillocks, split up by rocky crevasses, the posts were necessarily isolated, while to the front of the position the broken ground afforded the enemy cover both from fire and view. In the event of attack it was hoped that the squadrons and troops in the posts would maintain themselves staunchly, even if the enemy broke through between them and entered the shallow valley which traversed the salient from north to south. In this case the attacker, galled by fire from either flank, would find him-

---

[1] The reorganization of the mounted troops had not yet been completed. The 2nd Mounted Division at this date consisted of the 7th Mounted Brigade (Sherwood Rangers, 20th Deccan Horse, 34th Poona Horse), Imperial Service Cavalry Brigade (Jodhpore, Mysore, and Hyderabad Lancers), and the Imperial Camel Brigade. The last-named had been withdrawn for reorganization as a mounted brigade. Ten days later, on the 23rd July, the 2nd Mounted Division became the 5th Cavalry Division, and at the same time the 7th and Imperial Service Brigades became respectively 14th and 15th (Imperial Service) Cavalry Brigades.

self in an ugly situation and would have difficulty in meeting the counter-stroke of the reserve.

This sector was held by the 1st L.H. Brigade. At the nose and for 2,000 yards down either side of the salient was the 2nd A.L.H., the regiment's principal posts being named "Musallabe," (four separate posts), "Maskera," "The Bluff," and "Vyse."[1] On the left and facing generally west was the 3rd A.L.H., occupying posts known as "Vale," "View," "Vaux," "Zoo," and "Zeiss." In the centre of the position, 2,500 yards south of Musallabe, was the high plateau of Abu Tulul, nearly a mile in breadth. This plateau was split into two separate positions, known as "Abu Tulul East" and "Abu Tulul West," by a gulley. The 1st A.L.H. in brigade reserve was bivouacked in the valley of the 'Auja. The artillery covering this sector consisted of the Notts Battery R.H.A., "B" Battery H.A.C., two howitzer batteries (C/301 and C/303) of the 60th Divisional Artillery, the 11th Mountain Battery, and the Hong Kong Mountain Battery. The 2nd L.H. Brigade held the line of the Wadi Mellaha, with its right on the Jordan. The New Zealand Brigade was in divisional reserve in the Wadi Nueiame, 6 miles south of Musallabe, and also held posts in the foot-hills.

The 2nd Mounted Division had under its orders two battalions of the Imperial Service Infantry Brigade, which were in the Ghoraniye bridgehead defences. The 7th Mounted Brigade was west of the Jordan. South of Ghoraniye two small bridgeheads at Makhadet Hijla and El Hinu were held by part of the Mysore Lancers, with the rest of the Imperial Service Cavalry Brigade west of the river.

The 4th L.H. Brigade, Australian Mounted Division, was in corps reserve and was bivouacked south of the 'Auja, in a position from which it could quickly move to the support of any threatened point either on the Jordan, Melhalla, or Musallabe front.

Soon after 1 a.m. on the morning of the 14th July sounds of movements were heard on the front of the 3rd A.L.H. between Vale and View Posts. The regimental commander, Lieut.-Colonel G. J. Bell, thereupon called for

---

[1] Maskera and The Bluff were on the eastern flank of the salient, Vyse on the western.

an artillery barrage in front of Vale Post. The enemy's artillery also came into action, shelling the whole position, but especially Musallabe and Abu Tulul, the highest point in the salient. About 2.30 the enemy's fire ceased, and the movements of a large body of troops were again audible, while the Australians in Vale and View Posts distinctly heard words of command given in German. Lieut.-Colonel G. H. Bourne, commanding the 2nd A.L.H., whose headquarters was just behind Vale, decided to withdraw it to Abu Tulul West. He did so only just in time, for at 3.30 a.m. a large force of German troops suddenly broke through between Vale and View and swept up the valley towards the eastern end of the Abu Tulul spur and The Bluff. The post of one troop at Vale left its position after the enemy had passed and withdrew to its second position on the western side of Abu Tulul. All the others held their ground, though heavily attacked and in some cases completely surrounded. A frontal assault on Musallabe, this time by Turkish troops, resulted in the loss of one bombing post, but it was at once retaken by Sergeant E. Carlyon and a handful of men. On the left at View Post a party of Turks scaled the cliff. A sentry, who had not seen them till they reached the top, fired, and hit a man who was evidently carrying smoke or incendiary bombs of some sort, for he at once burst into flames. By the light of this human torch the Australians shot down the rest of the party, and no man below could thereafter nerve himself to face the climb. The unremitting labour in putting up wire bore fruit, for everywhere else the enemy found it impossible to penetrate it, and suffered severely in his attempts to do so. Despite his losses, however, his main body pressed swiftly and steadily forward and established itself first on Abu Tulul East, then on The Bluff, though he captured only one Australian sangar. Vyse and all the posts on Musallabe, as well as those on The Bluff and Abu Tulul East, were now cut off and without communication with regimental or brigade headquarters. On Abu Tulul West Lieut.-Colonel Bourne's small detachment maintained its position.

At the first alarm Br.-General Cox had ordered one squadron of the 1st A.L.H. and four machine guns from brigade reserve to report to Lieut.-Colonel Bourne, and at

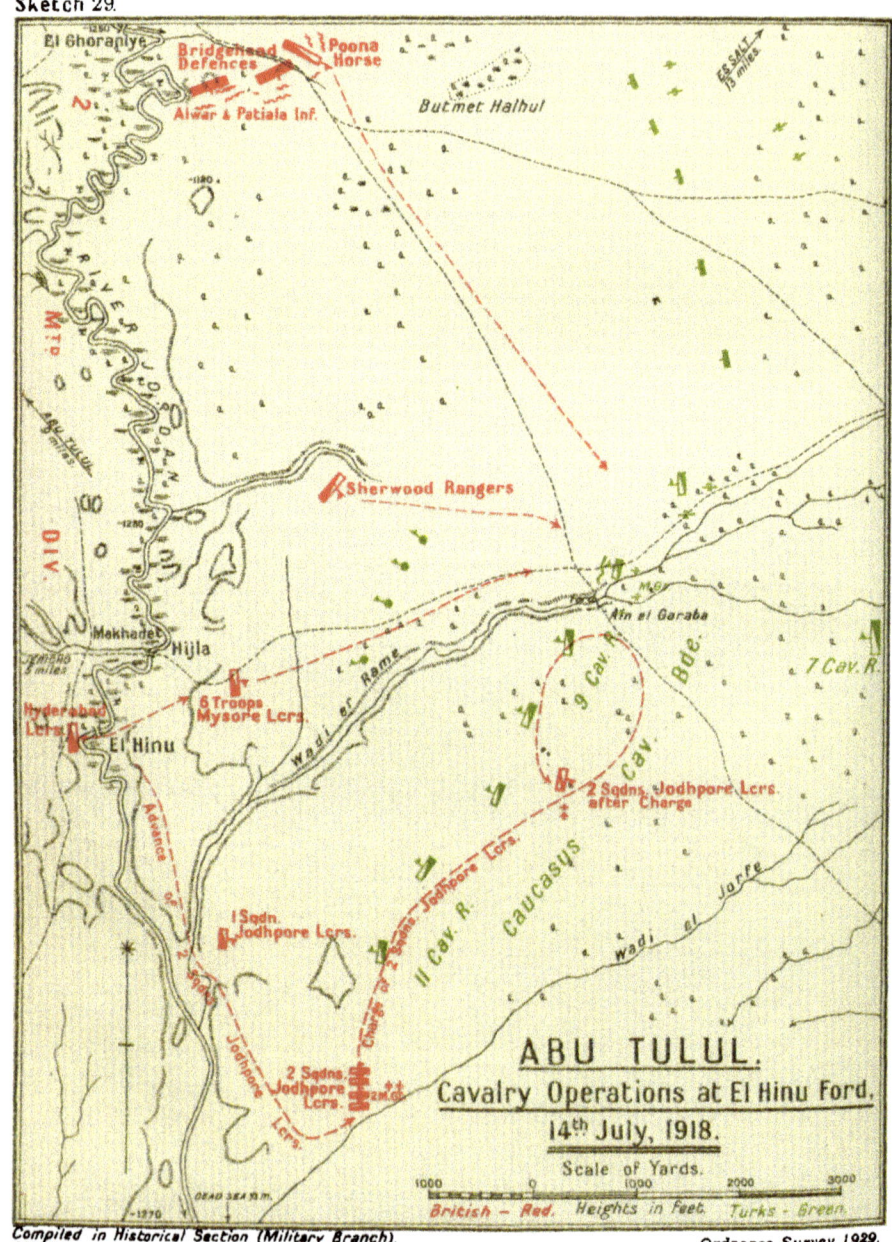

3.40 sent forward a second, under the command of Major F. J. Weir. At 5 o'clock Weir's squadron, covered by the fire of the other, attacked Abu Tulul East with the bayonet. The enemy had been prevented by the fire of the posts still holding out from consolidating the position, and was caught scattered and disorganized. He was swept clean off the hill by the charge, and retreated headlong into the valley to north of it, only to come under fresh machine-gun fire from guns on the higher ground.

1918. 14 July.

The Germans still held The Bluff, where a troop less than twenty strong, under Lieutenant L. J. Henderson, was maintaining itself against enormous odds. When at 8 a.m. this hill was retaken by the 1st A.L.H., which captured over a hundred Germans, the little post was still holding out, though only three men in the sangars were unwounded. The Wellington Regiment from reserve drove back the force still attacking Vaux, taking 61 prisoners. The whole position was now cleared, except for a number of distracted individuals who rushed wildly about, fired on from all quarters, and were only too glad to be able to surrender themselves.

On the Wadi Mellaha the enemy shelled the 2nd L.H. Brigade's posts throughout the night, and parties of infantry appeared before dawn at various points along the front, digging themselves in. One large body having established itself in front of Star Post, near the centre of the line, Lieutenant J. D. Macansh, 5th A.L.H., moved out with a party of 14 men to reconnoitre. He found the enemy 150 strong, and was forced to withdraw, after being almost surrounded. Nothing daunted, he crept out again a couple of hours later with 20 men. This time he completely surprised the enemy, capturing 26 prisoners, all Germans, one machine gun, and four automatic rifles. The remainder of the party fled at top speed towards their trenches, the Australians firing at them as they ran. After putting out flank guards, Lieutenant Macansh had actually attacked with twelve men, so that the incident proved that German troops, held in high respect upon the Palestine front, were liable like their allies to panic.

In all 448 prisoners were taken, 377 of them German; 6 machine guns, 42 automatic rifles, 185 rifles, and large quantities of ammunition. The casualties of the A. & N.Z.

Mounted Division were 108 in personnel and 101 in animals. The counter-attacks on the 1st Brigade's front had been carried out with skill and resolution, but the utter rout of the enemy's dashing attack was due above all else to the pluck, coolness, and accurate marksmanship of the garrison. The troop at Vale and the outposts at Maskera retired, as they had leave to do; one little trench on Musallabe was captured and held for a few minutes by the enemy; one sangar on Abu Tulul East, held by Lieutenant W. K. King with a troop of the 2nd A.L.H., was taken after all the garrison was killed or wounded; otherwise not a single post was ever entered. The consequence was that the Germans found themselves in a trap. Had they been fairly supported by the Turkish troops on their flanks they might have earned some reward for their boldness, but their isolated attack was almost doomed even before the launching of the British counter-attacks. The repulse of the assault confirmed the policy of preparing the posts for all-round defence and instructing them to hold out regardless of their flanks.

Sketch 29.	While the attack on the A. & N.Z. Mounted Division was in progress, large bodies of the enemy came into contact with the outposts of the Imperial Service Cavalry Brigade, on the right of the 2nd Mounted Division, and also with the Sherwood Rangers and two armoured cars, which had crossed the river. At 3.30 a.m. a squadron of the Jodhpore Lancers crossed at El Hinu and one of Mysore Lancers at Makhadet Hijla; and discovered by reconnaissance that there was a Turkish force consisting mainly of cavalry, on a frontage of two miles, its right flank being just north of the Wadi er Rame, a mile and a half east of Hijla. Br.-General C. R. Harbord, commanding the brigade, suggested to Major-General Macandrew that the remainder of the Jodhpores with two machine guns should cross at El Hinu and attack the enemy's left flank from the south, while the Mysore Lancers advanced from Hijla and attacked north of the Wadi er Rame from the west, the Sherwood Rangers of the 7th Mounted Brigade co-operating from the north-west. The divisional commander approved of this bold plan, but warned his subordinate that the Jodhpores must not allow themselves to be cut off from the crossings.

At 10.30 Major P. F. Gell, Special Service Officer,[1] was ordered to cross at El Hinu with two squadrons of the Jodhpore Lancers. The objective given to him was the ford over the Wadi er Rame at 'Ain el Garaba, $2\frac{1}{2}$ miles E.N.E. of El Hinu. He conferred with the officer commanding " A " Squadron of the Jodhpores, which was already east of the Jordan : outlining the action he was about to take and arranging for its co-operation. As soon as he was seen to charge the high ground on the enemy's left flank the Mysore Lancers and Sherwood Rangers were also to attack. " A " Squadron of the Jodhpores was to maintain its present position near the mouth of the Wadi er Rame and support the attack by Hotchkiss and rifle fire. The Mysore Lancers had meanwhile been reinforced by two troops and two machine guns.

Major Gell led his force down the Jordan behind " A " Squadron's position and under cover of the low hills, reached the mouth of the Wadi el Jorfe, which enters the Jordan about a mile north of the Dead Sea, and there turned north-eastward. The two squadrons trotted along the wadi, unobserved by the enemy, till they reached a point adjudged to be due south of the Turkish flank ; extended to an interval of two horses' length on coming under fire, swung left-handed in column of troops, and galloped due north. The machine-gun subsection came into action on their right flank to cover their advance.

Two or three troops on the enemy's left flank incontinently turned about and fled eastward toward the hills, but the Jodhpores dashed into a large body on the next ridge, spearing a number with their lances. They then advanced on the ford, capturing more prisoners ; but coming under machine-gun fire from the right bank, swung round to rally a mile to the south.

On seeing the Jodhpores charge, the Sherwoods and six troops of the Mysore Lancers likewise advanced at 1.15 p.m. The Indians alone came into contact with the enemy, who hastily retired from the open ground to the bank of the Wadi er Rame. About thirty Turks were

1918.
14 July.

---

[1] The Imperial Service regiments were commanded by their own Indian officers, but each had attached to it several British officers, known as Special Service Officers. The Senior S.S.O., always an experienced officer of Indian Cavalry, took his orders direct from the brigadier.

speared before they could reach the shelter of some scrub into which the cavalry could not penetrate. Meanwhile, however, the Jodhpore Lancers on the other side of the wadi had fallen back. Major Gell's squadrons had suffered 28 casualties out of the 125 men who rode in the charge, while they had over 50 prisoners and a large number of captured horses in their hands. Horses and men, moreover, were exhausted by the terrific midday heat. Seeing these squadrons withdraw, the Mysores likewise fell back to a position covering Hijla. This left the Sherwood Rangers strung out in a big semicircle facing 'Ain el Garaba, the right on the wadi about a mile west of it and the left flank in air. The enemy still held a trench on the north bank covering the ford with some seventy rifles and two machine guns.

At 2.30 the Poona Horse, 7th Mounted Brigade, had been ordered to move out from Ghoraniye and get touch with the Sherwoods. The regiment advanced rapidly down the track leading to 'Ain el Garaba, under considerable shell fire, but presenting such a fleeting target that it suffered few casualties. Finding that the Imperial Service Brigade had withdrawn, the commanding officer, Major G. W. C. Lucas, ordered a halt on the Sherwoods' left; but the leading troop, not receiving the message, dashed straight forward and charged the Turkish trench. The bodies of the troop leader, Lieutenant A. F. Dickson, and of six sowars were afterwards found at this point; bloody swords and lances on the trampled ground bearing witness to the desperate bravery with which they had sold their lives. An advance by the Sherwoods south of the wadi and of the Poona Horse on the north bank caused the enemy to evacuate the position at 5.30 p.m. and fall back eastward, covering his retreat with machine-gun fire.

In this mounted action it was calculated that nearly one hundred Turks were killed, a high proportion of them with the lance, though the machine-gun subsection also did much execution. Six officers, including the commander and four squadron leaders of the *11th Cavalry Regiment*, 86 other ranks, 4 machine guns, and some 40 horses were captured. The British casualties, including 9 men of the Alwar and Patiala Infantry wounded by artillery fire in the bridgehead defences, were 81. It was learnt from prisoners that there had been three cavalry regiments south of the Wadi er Rame.

1918.
14 July.

The dash displayed by his Indian cavalry in this encounter was indeed reassuring to the Commander-in-Chief.[1] Particularly gratifying was the offensive spirit of the junior Indian officers, typically exhibited by Risaldar Shaitan Singh, Jodhpore Lancers, who outpaced his troop and galloped alone into a troop of the enemy, shooting two with his revolver and unhorsing three with a loaded stick before his men came up with him. The action proved how valuable a striking force was the reconstituted Desert Corps, with its regiments of resolute and experienced Australians and New Zealanders, of well-tried and dashing Yeomanry still in the country, and of these almost over-eager Indians.[2]

Thus the Turkish offensive failed with a loss of 540 in prisoners alone and probably of well nigh a thousand all told, against a British casualty list of 189. It was, however, only when the Germans taken at Abu Tulul were examined—and in their bitter indignation at their "betrayal" they kept nothing back—that the full extent of the enemy's reverse became clear. The gallant German detachment, consisting of the *702nd* and *703rd* Battalions, one company *11th Reserve Jäger* Battalion [3], and one company *146th*

[1] He showed his appreciation by the generosity of his immediate rewards. In the Jodhpore Lancers, for example, these consisted of one D.S.O. (Major Gell), one M.C., six Indian Orders of Merit of the 2nd Class, seven Distinguished Service Medals.

[2] The account of the action east of Jordan given by General Liman von Sanders is so inaccurate that, in view of his habitual candour, it can only be supposed he was misinformed by his subordinates. He writes that the British cavalry which deployed from the bridgehead " was shot " down at close quarters," and that " the remainder of the squadron " galloped back to the Jordan bridges in disorder." The British casualty list, compared with the number of prisoners taken, is clear proof as to which side had the advantage. Liman adds that part of the *11th Cavalry Regiment*, including the regimental commander, " lost touch with the " brigade in the darkness and were taken prisoner." In fact, the Jodhpore Lancers captured all their prisoners before 1 p.m. and had returned with them hours before darkness fell. The commanders on the spot evidently prepared their reports with great care for the Marshal in distant Nazareth.

[3] The Jäger Company, the only one of its battalion remaining in the country, and consisting of the finest troops under *Yilderim's* command, went into action with a strength of 5 officers, 18 oberjäger (N.C.Os.), and 119 Jäger—a total of 142. Of these 31 escaped, for the most part telephonists, runners, and N.C.Os. carrying out liaison duties. (" Geschichte des Reserve-Jäger-Bataillons Nr. 11," by Bertram Schaefer and Heinrich Bölke.)

Regiment was in the centre of what was intended to have been a general attack on a big scale. On its right were the Turkish *163rd* and *58th Regiments*; on its left the *32nd Regiment*, which was to have attacked astride the Roman Road against the point of the salient; in support the *2nd Regiment*. The advance east of the Mellaha was carried out by two companies of the German *146th Regiment* and two Turkish battalions, with the *3rd Cavalry Division* in rear to exploit any success gained and link up with the main attack. When the German detachment broke through between Vale and View Posts, the Turkish regiments on its right halted in face of the rifle fire which broke out from the posts further south. The *32nd Regiment*, as we have seen, did a little better, but having been driven out of the single post in Musallabe which it had captured, made no further effort. Thus the Germans were left to their fate.

Not the complete failure of his scheme, not even the heavy losses of his German battalions, struck the enemy Commander-in-Chief so bitter a blow as this lamentable defection of the Turkish regiments. "Nothing," he writes, "had occurred to show me so clearly the decline in the "fighting capacity of the Turkish troops as the events of "the 14th July." The very battalions (of the *32nd* and *58th Regiments*) which had fought boldly in the open and in broad daylight three months earlier in the attack on the 4th L.H. Brigade, now could not muster resolution enough to assault a position held by widely separated posts in the dark.

THE OPPOSING FORCES.

Map 23.

This, then, was the state of the two forces facing one another as summer drew to an end and the campaigning season approached. The British cavalry was overwhelmingly superior in numbers, highly efficient, and ardent. The majority of the infantry battalions lacked training and experience, but were rapidly improving; and, after all, in the year 1918, when the troops of every combatant were suffering grievously from war-weariness, freshness was no small compensation for rawness. Above all the British Army was well fed, was supplied with every material necessity, enjoyed a reasonable amount of repose, had its health guarded by an admirable sanitary service.

Its railway communications with the Egyptian bases were now very good, the work done under the direction of Br.-General Sir G. Macauley in the course of spring and summer having provided a network of lines as efficient as those in the European theatres. The Sinai railway had been doubled to Rafah, and the down trains loaded for the front now used the new line, which was better laid than its predecessor. The average summer tonnage of supplies alone borne by it was over 2,000 a day. The railway laid from Rafah to beyond the Wadi Ghazze before the Third Battle of Gaza had been extended to Beersheba by the 3rd May, so that supplies could be transported direct from Egypt to be unloaded on the Beersheba–Jerusalem road. This line ran through Abu Irqaiyiq, on the old Turkish narrow-gauge railway, from which point that railway was relaid in the standard gauge up to Junction Station by the 8th July. The narrow-gauge line from Lydda to Jerusalem having proved insufficient, it also was relaid in the standard gauge; at first only as far as Artuf, but by the 15th June to Jerusalem. This was an extraordinarily difficult task, as much blasting was required to broaden the bed of the railway sufficiently. The section from Lydda to Jaffa, dismantled by the enemy, was likewise relaid in the standard gauge. On certain sections both gauges were in use simultaneously during the spring, and on a few occasions trains made up of the two sets of rolling stock were run, which is probably without precedent in railway history. Many light railways were laid down, the most important being one from Jerusalem to Bire. There was also one from Sarona, on the main standard-gauge line, to Jlil, which was of great assistance in supplying the XXI Corps on the coast.

The record of the development of supply is of great interest, and almost seems to demand a small volume to itself. Britain has often shown herself slow to confront a problem such as that here presented, and the early history of many of her campaigns is in consequence lamentable; but once she has set her mind resolutely upon her object she has generally displayed an unequalled power of organization. In this case the weight upon the shoulders of the administrative staff grew ever greater, until in 1918 the Deputy Quartermaster-General, Major-General Walter

Campbell, and his Director of Supplies and Transport, Br.-General G. F. Davies, became responsible not only for the supply of a quarter of a million men of various races, with a higher proportion of animals than there was in any other considerable theatre of war, but also to a large extent for the distribution of all the resources of the country.

So long as the command of the sea was not seriously threatened the problem of assembling supplies was not difficult, for Egypt itself was an ideal base. The Suez Canal and the railway along it connected Port Said, the principal coast base for Palestine, with Suez, the base for supplies arriving from the East. At Port Said cold storage for 4,500 tons of meat and a bakery [1] were established. There was good railway and canal communication between Ismailia, Cairo (where supplies from Upper Egypt and the Sudan were most conveniently assembled), and Alexandria (the main depot for supplies from the West and from Lower Egypt). Qantara, the starting-point of the Sinai Railway, had before the end of Sir A. Murray's command grown into a considerable port at which ocean-going steamers could berth and unlade. A railway bridge across the Canal was built in July 1918.

As the German submarine campaign developed, the E.E.F. was forced back to an even greater extent on local resources. Before Sir Edmund Allenby's arrival it had become clear that, since Egypt was now so vitally affected, it was necessary to give its Government a fuller share of responsibility than was represented by a single member on the Military Resources Board, which bought supplies by contract. A Supplies Control Board, consisting of both civil and military members, was therefore set up to ascertain the crops of the country, estimate and control civilian consumption, supervise exports, and hand over the surplus to the military authorities. In 1918 the Ministry of the Interior, which had direct authority over the provincial administration, was requested by the Board to undertake the work of collection. In that year the Ministry collected and handed over to the Army 30,000 tons of wheat, 30,000 tons of barley, 6,000 tons of lentils, 12,000 tons of beans, 275,000 tons of tibben, 25,000 tons of millet. The

---

[1] There were minor bakeries at Alexandria and Cairo, and also in Palestine.

Sudan Government co-operated by forwarding sheep, cattle, and gram *via* Wadi Halfa and Port Sudan. When restrictions on the export of coal from the United Kingdom made necessary the substitution of oil fuel for factories and railway engines, a military member was added to the Government Fuel Committee, which controlled the output of the Red Sea Oil Fields. A Transportation Committee held weekly meetings, at which the Chairman of the Supplies Control Board was present, to discuss the distribution and transport of the various crops. The collection of these vast supplies of food and forage was a heavy drain upon the country's resources and imposed great strain upon its means of transport.

Large industries, such as the milling of wheat, the manufacture of jam, margarine, and biscuits, the pressing of tibben into portable bales for pack transport, were carried on by the military authorities. A big fishing fleet on Lake Manzala was established under military control, and curing factories were set up at Port Said and Qantara, so that the fish surplus to the needs of the hospitals could be dried and smoked for the Army.

The sources of some of the chief supplies in 1918 were as follows:—

Supply.	Origin.	Monthly Consumption.
Frozen meat or	Australia, South Africa and Argentine	2,100 tons
Preserved meat	America and Australia	1,600 ,,
Flour	Australia, India, and Canada	2,700 ,,
Atta	India	7,000 ,,
Cheese	Australia and New Zealand	600 ,,
Tea	Ceylon	200 ,,
Sheep and goats	Sudan, Cyprus, and later Syria	9,000 head
Fuel wood	Egypt and Cyprus	7,500 tons
Potatoes	Egypt and Cyprus	750 ,,
Grain	Egypt, India, and finally the Hauran	27,000 ,,
Onions	Egypt	750 ,,

Egypt itself provided all the sugar, all the hay-stuffs, and all fresh vegetables, except for a small proportion from Palestine. The United Kingdom had almost ceased to be even an *entrepôt* of supply, so far as food and forage were concerned, though the War Office still had the responsibility of providing all supplies except those drawn from Egypt itself.

The now excellent railway system, which has been described, was able, with the aid of sea-transport to Jaffa, to keep men and horses fed adequately and with sufficient variety. Yet, as is ever the case in war, however strong are made all the links but the last in the chain of supply, that last was necessarily doubtful when subjected to unusual strain, either by reason of rapid movement during active operations or on account of the deterioration of the roads after rain. In Palestine on such occasions the strain was far greater than in France; and when, as often happened, rations were temporarily reduced to the bare issue of meat and biscuit, the troops went hungry. The Australians, who received high pay, had learnt from long experience to furnish themselves before they went into action with all sorts of extras from the canteens which they could carry on their horses, but the infantry had no such advantages. On certain sections of the front in the Judæan Hills there was at the best of times an uncomfortable shortage of water during the summer; for all the upper springs failed by the end of July. Even a brigadier, in a standing camp, was on occasion put to the shift of saving his allowance for three days to obtain enough for a bath, and perhaps keeping that precious supply for baths on the three following days. The Jordan Valley, it must be added, did not add lack of water to its other sufficient evils. The Wadis 'Auja and Nimrin were clear, pure streams which never ran dry, and even the muddy Jordan itself afforded men and horses the luxury of bathing.

None in Palestine were called upon for greater or more continuous exertions than the personnel of the mechanical transport. During the winter floods of 1917 drivers were often at the wheel for continuous periods of over fifteen hours, with perhaps intervals of lying in icy mud to repair broken chains. The terrible strain of the winter campaign was now over and the difficulties of maintenance had been eased by the opening of the port of Jaffa; but driving on the winding roads even at normal times demanded skill and physical strength, as well as strict road discipline. Hitherto the personnel had been mainly of Class " A," but in 1918 it was decided that all men of this medical category must be transferred to the fighting arm. Deprived of its fittest men the mechanical transport branch continued to meet successfully the heavy demands made upon it. Its small losses in vehicles were additional proof of its high standard of efficiency in interior economy and training.

The Ordnance Base remained at Alexandria, but a vast Advanced Field Depot with acres of offices, storehouses, magazines, and workshops had grown up at Qantara. After the autumn and winter operations of 1917 a depot was established at Lydda and a railhead post at Jerusalem. The light travelling workshops which followed the advance were for some time almost isolated, being virtually dependent upon their own resources and upon local labour and material. Useful Turkish forges and workshops were fortunately captured in Jerusalem. The reorganization of the Force in the summer of 1918 brought fresh work for the Ordnance Services, under the direction of Br.-General P: A. Bainbridge. As was the case with the Army Service Corps, the problems of the Ordnance were complicated by the heterogeneous nature of the Force and the varied nature of country and climate in Palestine.

As regards those small pleasures and comforts which afford so valuable an anodyne for soldiers undergoing the strain of prolonged warfare, the Force was not so well provided as were British troops in France, yet might count itself fortunate if it compared its lot with that of armies in former days—or even some forces in this war—campaigning in distant lands. Leave home, except on the smallest scale, was out of the question owing to the demands which it would have made on shipping and the losses which would undoubtedly have resulted from submarine attacks in the Mediterranean. Leave to Egypt was, however, fairly freely given, camps being formed for leave parties at Cairo and Alexandria. There were cinematographs and concert parties to enliven the spells of relief from the line. Sports of all kinds were organized, including numerous race-meetings. Canteens were established in all the principal towns behind the front, some of them, as at Sheikh Muwannis, Mulebbis, in the Wadi Deir Ballut, at Khirbetha Ibn Harith, Ram Allah, and Jericho, within a few miles of the outposts. A number of kiosks with soda fountains, and tobacco, sweets, and cakes (made in the Canteen Board's own bakeries) were set up, as close as possible to the line. In the whole Force, including the troops in Egypt, the canteen sales amounted to nearly £4,500,000 in the year 1918, and regimental funds were generously maintained out of a rebate of 8 per cent. on all cash sales. Rations were, as we have seen, generally sufficient; fruit, above all the finest oranges the world produces, abundant.

So, if the soldier's life was hard enough, all had been done on the British side to perfect the organization and maintain the fighting efficiency of the troops that ingenuity could suggest or money could pay for. The state of the enemy, on the other hand, had deteriorated even since the spring. In resources and communications alike Turkey was certainly at a grave disadvantage, but still more important was the fact that she no longer had her heart in the struggle and had begun to neglect the Palestine front. After the 21st March her rulers believed for some time that the war would speedily be brought to an end by an overwhelming German victory in France. At the beginning of the month the Treaty of Brest-Litovsk assured Turkey of the evacuation by the Russians of the Anatolian provinces in their hands and also of the Trans-Caucasian territory lost in 1878. Her troops, opposed only by Armenians, recaptured Erzerum on the 24th March and Van on the 5th April. The pan-Turkish ambitions with which she had entered the war had now returned to her, as dreams of infinite greatness come to a man exhausted by fever. She determined to advance, after absorbing Georgia and the mushroom Tatar Republic of Azerbaijan, into Northern Persia. Germany, however, was watching her ally with wide-open eyes, and on the 8th June concluded a treaty with the Republic of Georgia under which it was agreed that the country should be occupied by German troops.

The designs and rivalries of the two States are of interest from the point of view of this narrative merely in so far as they affected the Palestine front, so that only their repercussions in Palestine need here be noted. Not alone had *Yilderim* to go short of reinforcements to support Turkey's eastern ambitions and Germany's schemes for checkmating them, but troops were actually withdrawn in the time of its dire extremity. In the spring of 1918 there had arrived in Palestine a strong contingent of German troops, known as *Pasha II Reinforcement*, consisting of the *146th Infantry Regiment*, the *11th Reserve Jäger Battalion*, together with artillery and machine-gun detachments. Suddenly Liman von Sanders was informed that not only these, but all German troops in the country were to be withdrawn. His angry protests and threat of resignation procured the cancellation of this insane order; but the Jäger battalion, less one company, and some of his most experienced officers, Turkish and German, were taken. The Marshal's situation was indeed pathetic. That he should have been hoodwinked by the pan-Turks, who could scarcely have admitted to him that they had lost interest in Palestine and were starving it with their eyes open, was perhaps natural; but it is also apparent that the German military authorities did not keep him adequately informed of what was happening. As for Enver, he deceived even his own people, painting the situation in rosy colours to General Mustapha Kemal Pasha, when the latter was sent out in August to succeed Fevzi in command of the *Seventh Army*. The new commander, the greatest soldier and man that Turkey has produced in recent years, was indeed a pan-Turk, but wise enough to see that, while the war lasted, the retention of Palestine was a necessity. He was astounded and horrified by the state of affairs which he found on arrival.

The condition of the Armies was now deplorable. There were actually more deserters than men under arms, even though lorries with machine-gun parties patrolled the roads behind the front. The freights carried from Damascus to Der'a in August were little more than a third of those carried in May, in part owing to lack of fuel. The decision to close the Taurus tunnel for ten days in September, in order to convert the narrow gauge to standard, made it imperative to accumulate a pool of supplies south of the Cilician Gates, which meant that rations were still further diminished. The men were always under-nourished; the horses so much so that it was certain they could not pull out half the guns in the event of a hasty retreat. British propaganda, dropped from aeroplanes, sent through by agents, or tossed into the trenches, had contributed to undermine the spirit of the troops. These pamphlets had the merit, not belonging to all of their kind, of being strictly true; for, in whatever form they were written, their object was to reiterate two indubitable facts: that the Turks were being exploited by the Germans for their own purposes, and that Turkish prisoners were better fed than Turkish troops with the colours. The most dreadful of diseases associated with war, cholera and typhus, made their appearance in the enemy's ranks, though they were prevented from spreading widely by the energetic measures of German doctors. But malaria and bowel complaints due to bad and insufficient food were widespread. The severe form of influenza which swept over the world in the summer of 1918 and affected the armies of every combatant hit the Turks particularly hard, as they had not the knowledge or means to nurse the sick back to health.

Hungry, ragged, verminous, comfortless, hopeless, outnumbered, is it to be wondered that the Turkish soldiers lost heart? It is unlikely that any other troops in the world would have remained without collapse for so long a period of warfare under such conditions. And even now, though some formations almost wholly lacked their old military spirit, there were others still prepared to quit themselves, at least in a defensive battle, with the dourness and tenacity which have always characterized the Turkish race.

CHAPTER XXI

THE EVE OF MEGIDDO.

(Maps 1, 2, 19, 22; Sketches 24, 30.)

THE PROJECTED OFFENSIVE.

THE great German assaults in France had upset and brought to nothing Sir Edmund Allenby's promising plans for a renewal of the offensive. During the subsequent spring and summer he had been occupied in the reorganization of his force, which had put active operations on a large scale out of the question. His last-joined Indian battalions were incorporated in divisions no earlier than the first days of August, and some of them had then only just been formed. But he was determined upon the major offensive of which he had been baulked in March and could therefore not afford time for the seasoning of these troops. In Palestine the early rains generally come at the beginning of November. These are not, it is true, nearly so heavy as those which follow, after a short pause, about mid-December, but they are heavy enough to render the Plains of Sharon and Esdraelon impassable for transport except on two or three roads. He had therefore long decided that he would attack the enemy about the middle of September.

Maps 1, 2, 19.

The offensive was in origin and conception the result of the Commander-in-Chief's own cogitations and in no sense dictated by Whitehall, as that of the previous autumn had been. It was not until the 12th July that he informed the War Office of his hope to resume active operations that year. And even then his message was not spontaneous but in reply to a somewhat curious proposal made to him two days earlier by Sir Henry Wilson. The C.I.G.S. had telegraphed that it might be possible to lend him three or four divisions from France for the winter and asked what he could profitably undertake with this reinforcement. Sir Edmund Allenby replied that he intended to attack the enemy in mid-September and trusted to be able to reach a line from Nablus through Tul Karm to the mouth of the Nahr Iskanderune. If the troops were sent from France he might be able to continue his advance to a line from Tiberias to Acre. Beyond that he would not propose to go, as he was told that the reinforcing divisions would be withdrawn in the spring of 1919. However, the proposal came to naught. Sir Henry Wilson telegraphed on the 20th July that the divisions could not be spared, as all available troops would be required " until well into the " autumn " in an attempt to " gain more elbow-room in " front of the vital strategical objectives in France." He pointed out that Der'a was not included in either of the objectives mentioned, and that the offensive would therefore not in either case give the British control of the Hejaz Railway. In these circumstances he thought that British policy in Palestine should continue to be one of active defence. Sir Edmund Allenby answered that he hoped to gain a decisive victory with the resources already at his disposal.[1]

The Commander-in-Chief therefore turned again to his own scheme, which was to mass the greater proportion of his infantry and heavy artillery upon the eight-mile front in the plain between the railway and the sea, attack northeastward, and thus open a doorway through which his cavalry could pass to cut the enemy's communications by road and rail. The most vital point of all upon these communications, at Der'a, the junction of the Palestine railways with that to the Hejaz, was, however, out of his reach, and he proposed to allot this objective to the Arabs.

On the 1st August he issued strictly secret and personal instructions to his three corps commanders. In the first stage of the attack the XXI Corps (Lieut.-General Sir E. S. Bulfin), with five divisions, was to break through in the Plain of Sharon. Then the Desert Mounted Corps (Lieut.-General Sir H. G. Chauvel), with three cavalry

---

[1] After July there is no record of communications regarding the offensive. The reason is that, on the initiative of the C.I.G.S., a special code known as " H.W. Personal " was employed for messages passing between him and the Commander-in-Chief. These messages were not preserved at G.H.Q., and were not printed in the lists of Secret Telegrams at the War Office. Only a few of small importance have been found.

BOLDNESS OF THE SCHEME

divisions, was to advance northward in the plain through the gap opened by the infantry, to protect the left flank of the XXI Corps on a line from Tul Karm to the sea north of the Nahr Iskanderune, and to advance on Sebustiye (Samaria) by the Tul Karm–Nablus road. Here it would be astride the Turkish communications, cutting not only the railway to Nablus but the main Damascus–Tiberias–Nablus road. As soon as possible after it had carried out its first task of opening the breach, the XXI Corps was to despatch one division to support the Desert Mounted Corps in its advance on Sebustiye, and two divisions to strike the Tul Karm–Nablus road east of 'Anebta, turning the defile through which the road passes near that point. The Desert Mounted Corps was then to be ready to exploit the success, one division probably blocking the roads which converge on Nablus and the other two advancing up the plain towards Haifa. Meanwhile the XX Corps (Lieut.-General Sir P. W. Chetwode), with two divisions, was to be prepared to attack astride the Nablus road.

This scheme was but the embryo of that with which Sir Edmund Allenby startled his corps commanders after a further three weeks' consideration. On the 22nd August he informed them that he had decided to extend the scope of his operations. As before, the main attack was to be made on the enemy's right flank with the XXI Corps (3rd Indian, 7th Indian, 54th, 60th, and 75th Divisions) and Desert Mounted Corps (4th and 5th Cavalry and Australian Mounted Divisions), while the XX Corps (10th and 53rd Divisions) advanced astride the Nablus road. But now the XXI Corps, with one mounted brigade attached, was, after gaining a line from Qalqilye, on the railway 9 miles S.S.W. of Tul Karm, to the mouth of the Nahr el Faliq, to swing up its left, advance north-eastward, and take over the chief task previously allotted to the Desert Mounted Corps: that is, to advance in the direction of Nablus and Sebustiye. The Desert Mounted Corps was now given a far more distant objective. It was to advance to the Tul Karm–Haifa road between Qaqun (4 miles N.N.W. of Tul Karm) and Liktera (10 miles N.N.W. of Tul Karm) and thence march on El 'Affule, the junction of the Southern Palestine railway with that to Haifa. El 'Affule is in the Plain of Esdraelon or Megiddo, 25 miles north-east of Tul Karm and about 40 in a direct line from the British trenches in the coast sector, but Sir Edmund Allenby hoped that it would be reached by the second day. It is only 6½ miles south of Nazareth, where *Yilderim* headquarters was established, and the Commander-in-Chief subsequently directed that a detachment should be sent to this place to attempt to capture Liman von Sanders and his staff.

This scheme contrasts in boldness and grandeur very remarkably with the earlier one. In an operation of this nature, once a gap has been opened the essential factor is time. If the first plan were followed and the cavalry reached the Tul Karm–Nablus road before the retreating Turks crossed it, well and good ; the enemy was caught almost as effectively as by means of the second plan. But there was every chance that the enemy, though doubtless losing many prisoners and guns, would reach Sebustiye before the cavalry, and then retreat astride the railway line from Sebustiye to El 'Affule, with the lateral line from Beisan to Haifa behind him. Obviously the net was not cast wide enough. If the second plan were successful there was not the slightest fear of the enemy west of Jordan retreating across the Plain of Esdraelon before his road was blocked at El 'Affule. At this point, moreover, the cavalry would be within a march of Beisan in the Jordan Valley, and at Beisan it would block the other road from Nablus to Damascus, which passes through Samakh on the southern shore of the Sea of Galilee. Meanwhile if the Turkish *Fourth Army* in the Jordan Valley showed signs of evacuating its strong positions, it was to be pressed as hard as possible by the A. & N.Z. Mounted Division and certain other troops under the command of Major-General Chaytor.

The transport available would suffice to supply the Desert Mounted Corps no further north than Tul Karm, until mechanical transport could be transferred to it from the other two corps, and it had to be prepared to subsist for a time on the country after leaving the Tul Karm–Haifa road. In any case the difficulties of supply would be vastly increased by the extended scope of the plan. But with his great superiority in numbers and resources the British Commander-in-Chief felt himself justified in playing high. His first scheme would probably have led to a great but not completely decisive victory. His second gave promise

THE PLAIN OF ESDRAELON 451

of the virtual annihilation of the Turkish Armies opposed to him.

1918. Aug.

The great limestone ridge of Palestine runs at approximately even height for about 75 miles from east of Beersheba to north of Nablus. North of Jerusalem, approximately at Bethel, it becomes less regular in conformation than in the southern portion, which has a remarkably level crest-line. North of Nablus it begins to descend, and about Jenin there is a huge fault in the limestone, creating a wide, flat-bottomed valley. On the east a short spur from the ridge, known as Mount Gilboa, runs out into the plain below and overhangs the Jordan Valley. To the north-west runs a much longer spur, to end in Mount Carmel above the Bay of Acre. Some twenty miles north of Jenin the range reappears at Nazareth as the highlands of Galilee, to rise to the mountains of Lebanon. Between Jenin and Nazareth is a fertile plain, narrowing down to north-west until on the flank of Carmel it is reduced to a defile through which the River Kishon runs to the sea at Haifa. From this plain on its eastern side rise two isolated hills, the southern known as Little Hermon, the northern Mount Tabor, the latter being connected by a low col with the Hills of Galilee. Between Tabor and Gilboa deep parallel gullies, of which the southernmost and broadest is known as the Valley of Jezreel, run down to the Jordan. This is the Plain of Esdraelon or Megiddo.

The Turkish railway from Der'a followed the Valley of Jezreel from Beisan. At El 'Affule, in the centre of the Plain of Esdraelon, it branched, one line continuing across the plain to Haifa, the other running south to Sebustiye and then westward to Tul Karm. The Carmel spur was a formidable barrier between the Plains of Sharon and Esdraelon. The coast road, which passes between it and the sea, was known to be fortified and was easily defensible, besides being circuitous. There were two shorter routes across the hills further east: one starting east of Cæsarea and running into the plain at Abu Shushe on the Haifa–Jenin track; the other following the Wadi 'Ara and emerging at El Lajjun or Megiddo, $3\frac{1}{2}$ miles south-east of Abu Shushe on the same track. Neither was much more than a bridle-path, while on the second there was at Musmus a defile where a few hard-fought machine guns might delay a division for twenty-four hours or more. It will be apparent therefore that the whole plan depended upon surprise and upon both the break-through by the infantry and the advance of the cavalry being carried out with lightning speed.

The attainment of such speed was brought within the bounds of possibility by the great superiority in numbers of the British. Sir Edmund Allenby had at his disposal the equivalent of eight infantry divisions [1] and four cavalry divisions: a total strength in the fighting line of about 12,000 sabres, 57,000 rifles, and 540 guns. He estimated the strength of the *Fourth, Seventh,* and *Eighth Armies* opposed to him at no more than 3,000 sabres, 26,000 rifles, and 370 guns, including reserves as far north as Nazareth and Haifa. The garrison of Ma'an and troops on the Hejaz Railway north of it numbered another 6,000 rifles, but except for those about 'Amman they were unlikely to be able to take part in the battle. From Bozanti in the Taurus to just north of Damascus was the area of *Second Army*, consisting of only four weak divisions,[2] perhaps not more than five thousand rifles all told, with a few gendarmerie battalions. But it was unlikely that these troops could be released from their duty of watching the coast to intervene in the battle, at least until the British reached Damascus.

There has been some dispute as to the actual figures of the Turkish rifle strength. Certain of Sir Edmund Allenby's commanders considered that it was higher than he put it; Liman von Sanders suggests that it was lower. It appears probable that the British figures are approximately correct, but that, if error there be, it is on the low side rather than on the high.[3] It must be remembered

---

[1] That is, seven complete divisions, the French Detachment (approximately a brigade), the 20th Indian Brigade, and four unallotted battalions.

[2] *23rd Division* (five battalions) about Tarsus, *44th Division* about Islahiya in the Amanus, *41st Division* at Alexandretta, *43rd Division* between Tripoli and Beirut. Headquarters of the *Second Army* was at Aleppo.

[3] Among the papers taken at Nazareth was a strength return of the *XXII Corps*, dated the 12th July 1918. The ration and rifle strengths of the two divisions in the corps at that date were as follows:—

	Ration Strength.	Rifle Strength.
19th Division	6,457	2,262
20th Division	5,600	1,878

RESOURCES OF THE ENEMY

1918. Aug.

that the front had been stationary for months, that Turkish prisoners were captured constantly in raids, and that deserters entered the British lines at the rate of about seven a day.[1] British G.H.Q was therefore able to estimate with confidence the strength of the enemy opposed to it.

But what exactly does " rifle strength " mean ? It is clear that in Turkish returns it stands for infantrymen armed with rifles. Light as well as heavy machine-gunners are excluded, the two together appearing in a separate category. Now the weak Turkish divisions had each actually more heavy machine guns than the British—about 60 per division—so that west of Jordan the Turkish infantry had 600 against 350 in the possession of the British and French infantry. They were not nearly so well provided with light machine-guns, but there were about 450 west of Jordan including those of the German troops. The total machine-gun personnel of a division was approximately 800, which raises the fighting strength of the whole force very considerably. It has been pointed out that the armament of a French division in 1914 was 9,600 rifles and 24 machine guns ; in 1918 2,300 rifles, 423 light machine guns, and 72 heavy machine guns.[2] Yet the weak division of 1918 was more formidable than the strong one of 1914. It must not therefore be supposed that a Turkish division's drop in " rifle strength " to 1,646, according to British estimates, or even to 1,300, according to a statement by Liman von Sanders, represents all loss. Finally, it must be remembered that an army in retreat brings into action

---

Now in both cases the rifle strengths are considerably above the British estimates in September, which were 1,560 for the *19th Division* and 1,410 for the *20th*. Even allowing for considerable wastage not replaced in the two intervening months, it appears therefore that the British estimates were by no means exaggerated.

[1] Fifty-two deserters came over in the week ending the 19th August, 49 in the week ending the 26th August. In the latter week there were deserters from sixteen different infantry regiments, one cavalry regiment, one machine-gun company, and three batteries of artillery. During that week also 34 prisoners from six infantry regiments and two German officer airmen were captured. With such material at its disposal it is not difficult for a good intelligence service to assess the enemy's order of battle and numbers with great accuracy. The dispositions marked on British maps were proved to be absolutely correct by the prisoners taken in the offensive ; that the figures were also reliable is almost certain.

[2] " Les Étapes d'une Division d'Infanterie," by Lieut.-Colonel Laure and Commandant Jacottet. (Paris : Berger-Levrault.)

a percentage of its total strength considerably greater than that of an enemy pressing on its heels. It is an extraordinary and little-known fact that, while the total British ration strength, including troops as far distant as Sollum, and over 80,000 unattested natives in the Camel Transport and Labour Corps, was approximately 340,000, that of the Turks, including the *Second Army*, the *Hejaz Expeditionary Force*, and (presumably) also native workmen, was 247,000.[1] It was less man-power that failed the enemy than organization.

However, the fact remains that in strength—call it fighting strength or rifle strength—the British were considerably superior. In spirit and in material resources their advantage was, as has been pointed out, greater still. The enemy's powers of resistance had diminished since the previous autumn and even since the Trans-Jordan raids and the British attack at Berukin in April, in all of which his troops had shown steadiness and tenacity. His transport animals, which received only two pounds of grain a day, were generally in a wretched condition and were dying in great numbers. His railways were so overburdened that south of Riyaq they were used almost entirely for the transport of the inadequate quantities of supplies and munitions sent to the front, troops having to march. There was therefore every reason to hope, first, that the *attaque brusquée* in great strength on the coast would sweep away all opposition in a few hours, and, secondly, that the movement of such reserves as the enemy could send to his right flank either from Haifa and Nazareth or other parts of his front would be too slow to interfere with the great turning movement of the British cavalry.

Nor were the defences, hard as the enemy had worked upon them, strong enough to daunt an attacker well supplied with artillery of all calibres. It is true that between the railway and the sea, where Sir Edmund Allenby proposed to breach the Turkish line, was the only continuous series of defences upon the whole front, but that was simply

---

[1] From a captured return by the Q.M.G. of the Turkish Group of Armies, dated the 8th September 1918. The ration strength of the Turkish *Fourth*, *Seventh*, and *Eighth Armies* was 103,500, as against 140,000 of the three British corps. One ought, perhaps, to deduct a small percentage from the Turkish figures to allow for faked returns concealing the peculations of supply officers.

because the section in the plain was so much more vulnerable than that in the hills. Between Jaljulye on the railway and the shore there were two or three lines of trenches, with numerous redoubts, the whole system being from one to three miles in depth. From Et Tire, 5 miles north of Jaljulye, to the marshes of the Nahr el Faliq was a second line of defence much less formidable than the first. A third skeleton line ran from Tul Karm to near the mouth of the Nahr Iskanderune. As always, the Turks had insufficient barbed wire to make really serious obstacles.

1918. Aug.

The Plan of Attack.

The actual orders issued by the Commander-in-Chief on the 9th September need only be shortly considered, for, as had become the custom owing to the complications of modern warfare, they were but summaries of previous letters, instructions, and the decisions of conferences.[1] The XXI Corps, with the 5th L.H. Brigade attached, was to attack the enemy's right, and after capturing the trench systems between Et Tire and the Nahr el Faliq to advance eastward and drive him from the line Sebustiye–Tul Karm. As soon as the crossings of the Nahr el Faliq had been cleared, the Desert Mounted Corps, less A. & N.Z. Mounted Division and 5th L.H. Brigade, was to advance on El 'Affule and Beisan in order to cut the enemy's railway communications and block his retreat to the north and north-east. The XX Corps was to attack astride the Nablus road to gain a position from which it could co-operate with the XXI Corps and advance to the high ground north and north-east of Nablus. One division of the XXI Corps, with the 5th L.H. Brigade attached, was to advance *via* Tul Karm on 'Atara, 4 miles north-west of Sebustiye, in order to block the section of the railway between Sebustiye and Jenin as early as possible. The first objective of the Desert Mounted Corps was a line from Qaqun to Liktera. It was then to advance with utmost speed upon El 'Affule by the two hill roads already mentioned, entering the Plain of Esdraelon at El Lajjun and Abu Shushe. Then, leaving sufficient troops about

9 Sept.
Maps 1, 19, 22.
Sketch 24.

---

[1] Force Order No. 68 is given in Appendix 23.

El 'Affule, Jenin, and El Lajjun to close the Turkish lines of retreat to north and north-west, it was to push on to close the roads converging on Beisan from the Jordan Valley and Nablus. In the Jordan Valley "Chaytor's Force," consisting of the A. & N.Z. Mounted Division and attached troops, was to be responsible for the protection of the positions in the valley and of the front as far west as En Nejme, on the Wadi el 'Auja, 6½ miles south-east of Yebrud. It was to use every means to prevent the enemy from withdrawing troops to reinforce other parts of the line. If the enemy reduced his strength in the Jordan Valley this force might be required to advance as far as Jisr ed Damiye or send a detachment east of Jordan to join hands with an Arab force from the south.

Instructions issued by G.H.Q. on the 1st September assigned the great bulk of the artillery to the XXI Corps. Between Ra-fat, in the British front line 6¼ miles east of the railway, and the sea there were to be five 60-pdr. and thirteen siege batteries in addition to the artillery of five infantry divisions and of the French Detachment, and two mountain batteries. With seven R.H.A. batteries of the Desert Mounted Corps, which were to take part in the early stages of the operation and then return to their own divisions, some immobile 4·7-inch and captured Turkish guns and howitzers, the total amounted to 258 guns and 126 howitzers.[1] Of this great concentration some three-fourths were to be on the seven-mile front between the Jaffa–Tul Karm road and the sea. The orders of Br.-General H. A. D. Simpson-Baikie, G.O.C. XXI Corps Artillery, laid down that one 6-inch Mark VII gun, three batteries of siege howitzers, and two heavy batteries (60-pdrs.) would be able without moving forward to shoot on the line Et Tire to the sea; one siege battery and one heavy battery would be able to do so after moves which could be carried out in two hours; while one siege and one heavy battery could also be advanced for the purpose if required. A group consisting of one horse-drawn heavy battery and one tractor-drawn siege battery was to advance to Tul Karm, reaching that place by daybreak on the second day, and support the advance of the 60th Division

---

[1] The Counter-battery Staff estimated the Turkish artillery on the corps front to number 113 guns and howitzers.

AMMUNITION SUPPLY

on 'Anebta. The heavy artillery at the disposal of the XX Corps was to consist of four siege-howitzer and one 60-pdr. batteries, while the corps was also allotted two mountain batteries, and seven captured Turkish guns and howitzers. With the divisional artillery it had a total of 86 guns and 44 howitzers. Chaytor's Force in the Jordan Valley was to have four 60-pdrs., four 18-pdrs., twelve 2·75-inch mountain guns, four Turkish 75-mm. guns, and two Turkish 150-mm. howitzers, in addition to the twelve 13-pdrs. of the A. & N.Z. Mounted Division.

Ammunition was provided at or in front of railheads for the whole force on a great scale for all the mobile artillery: 1,100 rounds per 13-pdr., 1,000 rounds per 18-pdr. and 2·75-inch gun, 800 rounds per 3·7-inch, 4·5-inch, 6-inch howitzer and 60-pdr.; and on a considerable scale for the immobile artillery for the early stages of the operation.[1]

Owing to the nature of the country and the distance of some of their objectives, the arrangements for supply, communication, etc., were very difficult even for the infantry divisions. For example, in the XXI Corps two special water columns, each consisting of two companies of the Camel Transport Corps with 2,200 camels carrying about 44,000 gallons, had to be filled up, and the camels themselves watered, all within a few hours. It is, however, the arrangements of the Desert Mounted Corps which it is of most interest to consider in some detail.[2] The main railhead on the standard-gauge railway was to be established as soon as possible after the beginning of operations at Rantye, 4 miles south of the present front line. Stores landed at Jaffa could be railed either to this point *via* Lydda, or by the light railway to Jlil on the coast.

On the day of the attack the troops of the corps were to be furnished with that day's ration, two days' emergency

---

[1] The scale laid down for immobile guns was as follows:—

8-in. howitzer	400
6-in. Mark VII	250
60-pdrs. and 6-in. howitzers	500
150-mm. Turkish	250
105-mm. Turkish	250
French guns	700
75-mm. and 77-mm. Turkish	400
Anti-Aircraft	600

[2] For footnote [2] see page 458.

rations, and the iron ration, all on the mobile scale, carried on the horse and in the limbered wagons. A fourth day's ration was to be carried by the trains, and a fifth by a camel convoy.[1] By these means it was hoped that an ample margin of time had been given for the corps to exchange the greater part of its camel transport for lorries with the XXI Corps. But, as already stated, it was contemplated by the Commander-in-Chief that the corps might have for

[1] The allotment of transport was as follows :—

Formation.	Donkey Cos.	Camel Cos.	Tractors.	Trucks.	Lorries for Amm.	Lorries for Supplies.	Total.
Signals, G.H.Q.	—	—	3	6	—	—	—
Chaytor's Force.	300 donkeys.	—	17	34	5	15	20
D.M. Corps	—	2	—	—	30	120	150
XX Corps.	2	1	—	—	60	120	180
XXI Corps.	1	8	12	24	60	180	240
Total ..	3 Cos. & 300 donkeys.	11	32	64	155	435	590

The reason why the XX Corps was given so large a proportion of lorries was that it had the Nablus road at its disposal. With regard to the XXI Corps, the 54th Division on the right was destined to act as pivot to the attack, and the 75th Division was to be in reserve after the first day. The 3rd and 7th Indian Divisions, which had to advance over difficult country, were converted to a pack-transport basis, the supply sections of their trains being replaced by camels. Mechanical transport supply columns and camel reserve parks (carrying one day's supplies) were allotted to these two divisions, and also to the 60th Division, which was to attack on the coast and afterwards advance to 'Anebta. All transport over from these requirements was to be employed to move supplies and establish a big depot at Tul Karm at the earliest possible moment.

[1] The transport was to be divided into three echelons : " A " Echelon consisting of the fighting vehicles with ammunition, tools, and explosives, to keep up with the fighting formations ; " B " Echelon of limbered G.S. wagons, carrying a proportion of the supplies for men and horses mentioned above ; " B2 " Echelon with the heavy baggage, to be left behind. " A " and " B " echelons were to start with the formations, the trains to follow, and the camels to move in rear of the trains.

a period to live on the country. A number of engines and pumps for the development of water supply were to be carried in the advance.

The supply of gun ammunition for the corps was comparatively small in total quantity, but a large amount per gun had to be carried. Four hundred and fifty rounds per gun were to be carried by units, 150 rounds ready loaded in lorries, and another 500 rounds dumped at suitable points. Additional bridges had to be thrown across the 'Auja [1] in preparation for the advance of the corps, making a total of ten between the mouth and Ferrikhiye, seven miles inland. Of these all except two pontoon bridges (which would take 18-pdrs.) were constructed of heavy piles, for the most part imported, and would carry 60-pdrs., while a trestle bridge at Hadra would take tractors. A trestle bridge was to be carried by the engineers, and the 13th Pontoon Park was to carry pontoons and trestles in order to be able to put a bridge of each over a 30-foot span to cross the Nahr Iskanderune. Netting, timber, and billhooks were to be carried for constructing causeways over swampy places.

Effective communication was a matter of difficulty in an advance so swift as this was expected to be. Advanced corps headquarters was to be established first at Jerishe, on the Nahr el 'Auja, advancing on the evening of the day of attack to the main crossing over the Nahr Iskanderune, where all three divisions were to be connected with it by cable, and it was to be connected by cable with G.H.Q.[2] All existing Turkish air-lines had been carefully marked down by Br.-General M. G. E. Bowman-Manifold, Director of Army Signals, and instructions were given that they were to be used wherever possible to save British cable. The next move of corps headquarters would be on the second day to El Lajjun, in the Plain of Esdraelon, whence it was hoped to be able to communicate with divisions and G.H.Q. by existing wires. Divisions were ordered to erect wireless

---

[1] A bridging school had been established on the 'Auja about two months before, and bridges had on several occasions been thrown across the river, only to be dismantled within a few days. When new bridges were constructed they therefore aroused no suspicion.

[2] This cable was speedily cut by traffic, but the corps signal officer was able to use Turkish air-lines between Tul Karm and El 'Affule, and subesquently across the Plain of Esdraelon.

stations whenever possible, even when wires were working well, and also to use visual to the fullest extent. Corps headquarters and divisions were each allotted ten pigeons from the G.H.Q. loft. These birds had to be liberated within four days of receipt, but arrangements were made to maintain a daily supply of ten to each division thereafter. For despatch riding, motor cyclists were to be used when possible by day, but to be replaced by mounted men in rough country and for night work—in the latter case in pairs. One troop of cavalry was also to be employed to form a relay system on the day of attack from corps headquarters at Jerishe along the road followed by the 4th Cavalry Division to the Nahr Iskanderune, and on subsequent days as required.[1] The troops were also to communicate with the contact aeroplanes at the disposal of the corps. Two sets of an apparatus which enabled aeroplanes to pick up messages were carried by corps headquarters.

With regard to the evacuation of wounded, it was arranged that a motor ambulance convoy would run between Tul Karm and Wilhelma, where a casualty clearing station was to be established, as soon as the main road was open. All casualties sustained before the crossing of the Nahr el Faliq were to be handed over to the infantry field ambulances.

The organization of the Royal Air Force on the eve of the battle was as follows :—the 5th (Corps) Wing had its headquarters at Ramle, and its three squadrons were divided between the three corps: No. 14 Squadron to the XX Corps and stationed at Junction Station, No. 113 Squadron to the XXI Corps and operating from Sarona, No. 142 Squadron to the Desert Mounted Corps also operating from Sarona, less one flight attached to Chaytor's Force and operating from Jerusalem. It was proposed to move No. 142 Squadron to the Turkish aerodrome at Jenin when this place was captured. The corps squadrons were responsible under corps orders for co-operation with artillery, contact patrols and tactical reconnaissance, that is, reconnaissance up to ten thousand yards in advance of the XX and XXI Corps and Chaytor's Force. The 40th

---

[1] The posts were to be established approximately every two miles. In all cases the speed required—trot, canter, or gallop—was to be marked on the envelope containing the message.

SECRECY OF THE CONCENTRATION 461

(Army) Wing likewise had its headquarters at Ramle. No. 1 Squadron A.F.C. at Ramle was responsible for strategical reconnaissance and photography; No. 111 Squadron and a flight of No. 145 Squadron R.A.F., also at Ramle, for escorts and offensive patrols; and No. 144 Squadron R.A.F., at Junction Station, for bombing operations. No. 21 Balloon Company was allotted to the XXI Corps. It was impressed upon the troops that it was most important to keep Turkish landing grounds and aerodromes closed to traffic and clear of bivouacs in order that they might be taken into use if practicable.

1918. Sept.

THE CONCENTRATION.

What has been recorded above relates to preparations for the period after the attack had been launched. But there was one other problem of no less importance: to concentrate the striking-force on the coast without the enemy being made aware of the blow impending. In the first place, the greatest possible secrecy was maintained regarding future operations; so rigidly were Sir Edmund Allenby's instructions on this point enforced that their actual objectives were not explained to brigade and regimental commanders until two or three days before the attack. The Commander-in-Chief then visited each division in turn; the commanding officers were assembled and heard from his own lips an outline of his scheme. Its magnitude and the complete confidence in it displayed by the speaker made upon the minds of the listeners an unforgetable impression. It may be added that it was only the long experience of most commanders and senior staff officers in this theatre and their knowledge of the country which made it possible to keep the preparation of orders and instructions in so few hands. In the second place, elaborate measures were taken to prevent the moves from being discovered. All tents were left standing in the Jordan Valley, and a quantity of old and unserviceable tents pitched there, to make it appear that the number of troops had been increased rather than diminished. Outside the valley no fresh tentage was put up. Dummy horses of canvas took the place of the real horses of the Desert Mounted Corps when it moved west. All movement west-

Maps 2, 19. Sketch 30.

ward, whether of cavalry, artillery, or infantry, took place by night; any eastward by day, and a great parade was made of the movement of a few battalions down to the Jordan Valley. Sleighs drawn by mules raised huge clouds of dust about Jericho. Rumours were spread of a concentration near Jerusalem, new billets marked out, and the principal hotel—to-day the "Allenby"—commandeered for G H.Q. A race-meeting was announced, to be held near Jaffa on the 19th September. The fact that the front was not continuous and that spies could slip through to give information to the enemy was thus made of service instead of being a disadvantage.

Bivouacs and camps were classified as "open" or "concealed." The former were those to which the enemy was accustomed, and there was no restriction on movement about them unless they were increased in size. About concealed bivouacs there was to be no movement between 4.30 a.m. and 6.30 p.m. If it was absolutely necessary to water horses by day, this was done between 12 noon and 2 p.m., during which time the R.A.F. guaranteed to keep all enemy aircraft at a distance. No fires were lit by day or night in concealed bivouacs, any cooking necessary being done with solidified alcohol. Once bivouacked in the plain south of the 'Auja, the troops were invisible to aircraft in the thick groves, chiefly of orange trees, with which it was covered. North of the river the ground was barer, but here the camps had been increased in size two months earlier, so that it was possible to accommodate in open bivouacs twice as many troops as were normally there. Large numbers were quartered in concealed bivouacs on the shore below the cliffs, where some eighty wells had been dug by the 7th Division. Artillery and machine-gun emplacements had been begun two months earlier by the troops then in the plain. As each was completed it was temporarily occupied; an aeroplane then photographed it, and if it was visible its camouflage was improved or it was shifted to another site.

The concealment of the British movements depended, however, rather than upon any other single precautionary measure, on the activity of the Royal Air Force. The British had had definite superiority in aerial warfare for the best part of a year, but it was only during the months

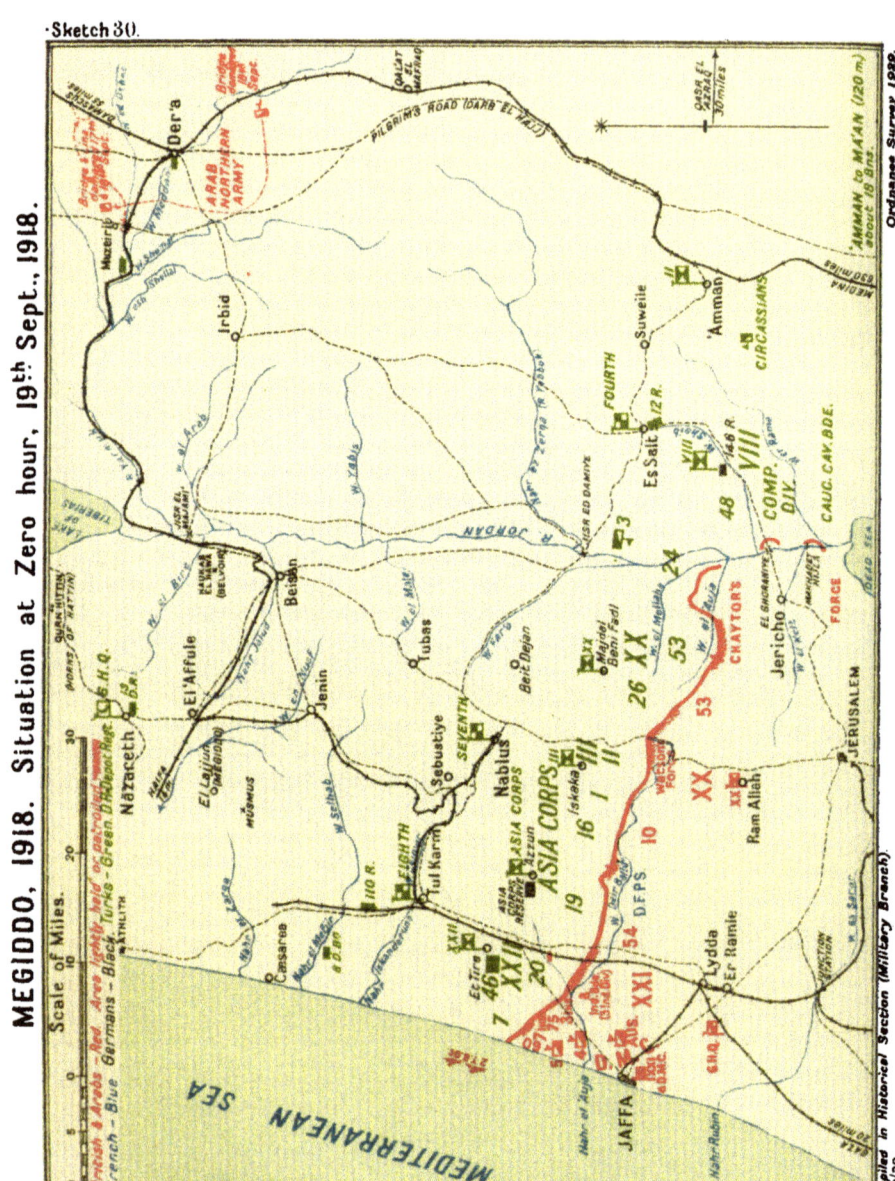

THE CAVALRY MOVES WEST 463

of July and August that the German machines were virtually driven from the skies. Only four succeeded in crossing the lines during the period of concentration, as against over one hundred which had appeared in the course of one week in June.

1918. Aug.

On the 18th August the 4th Cavalry and Australian Mounted Divisions were holding the Jordan Valley sector; the 5th Cavalry Division, recently relieved there, was moving west to the well covered area between Ramle and Deiran; the A. & N.Z. Mounted Division was moving down to the valley. On the 23rd, the relief of the Australian by the A. & N.Z. Mounted Division having been completed, Major-General Chaytor took over command of the left sector in the valley. Next came the relief of the 4th Cavalry Division in the right sector, Major-General Chaytor taking over command of the whole front on the 5th September, having at his disposal his own division, the 20th Indian Brigade, the 1st and 2nd Battalions British West Indies Regiment, and the two Jewish battalions, the 38th and 39th Royal Fusiliers.[1]

On the 16th Desert Mounted Corps headquarters closed at Tal'at ed Damm, on the Jerusalem–Jericho road, leaving its conspicuous camp standing and its wireless station working, and reopened at Jerishe on the Nahr el 'Auja. On the following morning the concentration was complete, the 4th Cavalry Division being in the orange groves east of Sarona, the 5th north-west of Sarona, and the Australian Division about Ramle. The three divisions were completely hidden from aircraft, and even the local inhabitants did not know of their arrival. The inestimable advantage of the groves was that their irrigation channels could be filled for the watering of the horses, which thus could be kept all the time under cover. By the night of the 18th the Desert Mounted Corps was assembled for the attack: 4th Cavalry Division north of Selme, to move up during the early hours of the morning until its head was about Jlil; 5th Cavalry Division in depth between the village of Jlil

18 Sept.

---

[1] The 39/R. Fusiliers did not enter the valley till the 14th September. The moves are described in outline without entering into their detail, which was somewhat complicated owing to brigades from each of the four divisions being frequently attached to others in the course of the transfer of the corps from east to west.

and the shore; Australian Division, less 5th L.H. Brigade, between Jaffa and Selme. The 5th L.H. Brigade, which was to operate under the orders of the 60th Division, moved forward during the night and was assembled by 8 a.m. on the morning of the 19th north-east of the 4th Cavalry Division at a hillock known as " The Cockshy."

Meanwhile the infantry divisions also had reached their positions of assembly. The 60th Division, transferred from the XX Corps, had moved from the Sarona area to the line on the shoreward flank by the 17th September; the 75th Division, which had been at Beit Nebala, north-east of Lydda, had entered the line between the 3rd and 7th Indian Divisions; the concentration of the heavy artillery had been completed. The dispositions of the XXI Corps were now as follows:—on the right the 54th Division, with the French Detachment on its right and under its orders, was on a front of 6 miles from Ra-fat to Ras el 'Ain on the railway, with a brigade in reserve at Muzeir'a. Next came the 3rd Indian Division, also on a wide front of $5\frac{1}{4}$ miles from Ras el 'Ain to the Et Tire road. Two of its brigades were, however, concentrated on its extreme left, the third being in reserve with the preliminary duty of watching the remaining 4 miles of the division's front. Then came the 75th Division on a front of one mile from the Et Tire road, with two brigades in line and one in reserve. The 7th Indian Division was on a front of approximately $2\frac{1}{4}$ miles from the nameless wadi running up west of Tabsor into the Zerqiye marsh, to the Wadi Hurab el Miske, with two brigades in line, closed up on the extreme right, and one in reserve south-east of Jlil. On the left was the 60th Division, echeloned in depth, with one brigade in first line, one in second about Kh. el Muntar, and the third one mile further south, concentrated east of Hill Head.

The method of concentrating the cavalry had not given complete satisfaction to General Chauvel. At a conference held at G.H.Q. on the 11th September General Bulfin had asked the Commander-in-Chief for a ruling that the troops of the Desert Mounted Corps should not pass north or east of the line of his artillery wagons until the artillery had moved forward. This would have been a matter of no great moment if both the leading cavalry divisions had used the shore route, but General Chauvel was of opinion that

the 4th Cavalry Division should use the track running past 1918.
Tabsor to the Zerqiye crossing to save time. Sir Edmund 18 Sept.
Allenby replied that personally he thought the shore route
would be the better for the two leading divisions, but that
General Chauvel could use the Zerqiye crossing if he so
desired. He considered that positions of readiness south
and west of the line suggested by General Bulfin would be
suitable in either case and should be taken up in the first
instance. For the rest, General Chauvel was held responsible that his movements in no way hindered the attack of
the XXI Corps by interfering with its supporting troops
or masking the fire of its guns. The Commander-in-Chief
would make no further restrictions.

The position was a difficult one. General Bulfin was
responsible for opening the doorway, and on the success of
his initial attack the whole operation depended. He did
not anticipate a serious counter-attack, but he realized that,
if there was one, dreadful confusion would be caused by the
cavalry interfering with the movements of his infantry and
perhaps masking his guns. It was General Chauvel's duty
to make every effort to accede to his wishes. On the other
hand Major-General Barrow, commanding the 4th Cavalry
Division, was greatly perturbed when told that his division
must be concentrated over two miles from the British front
line. His study of the employment of cavalry on this and
other fronts had taught him how fleeting is often—nay,
almost always—its opportunity, and he desired that at
least his advanced guard should be well forward so that
there should be no repetition of the distressing delays which
marred the Battle of Cambrai. Eventually it was agreed
as a compromise that the commanders of the 4th and 5th
Cavalry Divisions should have staff officers (or station
themselves) at the headquarters of the 7th and 60th Divisions, the commanders of which would inform them at the
earliest possible moment when the front was sufficiently
clear for the cavalry to go through.

On the wide, thinly-held front of the XX Corps, from
En Nejme to Ra-fat, a distance of about twenty miles, were
only two divisions, the 53rd on the right and the 10th on
the left. An attack upon the whole corps front with this
force being clearly impossible, nearly 7 miles of its centre,
from Highgate Ridge east of the Nablus road, to 'Arura,

was held by a temporary formation known as "Watson's "Force," consisting of the Corps Cavalry Regiment (Worcester Yeomanry), the two divisional pioneer battalions (1/155th and 2/155th Pioneers), and a detachment from the corps reinforcement camp, under the command of Lieut.-Colonel G. B. Watson of the 1/155th. It was General Chetwode's intention to make a converging advance with the 53rd and 10th Divisions, avoiding a direct attack on the defences astride the Nablus road, as these were stronger than on any other part of the enemy's line on the corps front, and the Turks were always on the look-out for an assault in this quarter.

From the northern end of the Dead Sea to En Nejme the Jordan Valley sector was held by Chaytor's Force, with the 2nd L.H. Brigade on the right, the 20th Indian Brigade in the Ghoraniye bridgehead, the Jewish and West Indies battalions on the northern part of the front, closely supported by the New Zealand Brigade. The 1st L.H. Brigade was in reserve north of Jericho. The urgent need for the employment of the bulk of the cavalry and infantry on the left flank had left Major-General Chaytor with a somewhat motley force at his disposal. His own division had suffered very severely in the valley; the men had had a long and severe campaign, while the horses were light in condition. These gaunt veteran troops could, however, be relied upon to fight with as much determination and skill as ever, and to go on as far as their horses would bear them. The Imperial Service Indian troops were of fair quality. The other four battalions were unknown and untried, the British West Indies personnel never having been in action, the Jewish battalions being recently formed and including Jews of many nations.

While the concentration was in progress the Turkish railway about Der'a was attacked by the R.A.F. on the 16th and 17th. On the 16th an Arab column, to which were attached British armoured cars and a French mountain battery, left Qasr el 'Azraq, 50 miles east of 'Amman, where it had assembled, and descended upon the railway, destroying a bridge and a section of the line south of Der'a. Further demolitions were carried out north and west of the junction next day. Though a few hundred troops, including some Germans, hurriedly despatched by rail from

Haifa and Damascus, then occupied Der'a and kept the traffic moving, they were unable to prevent the demolitions from continuing and seriously slowing down the movement of supplies and troops upon the Turks' one line in the days that followed.

1918.
18 Sept.

That the whole plan of the concentration had been successful was proved by an intelligence map of the 17th September captured at *Yilderim* headquarters at Nazareth. This shows Desert Mounted Corps headquarters in its old position at Tal'at ed Damm; the 4th Cavalry Division is queried at Jericho, the Australian Mounted Division shown holding the northern front of the Jordan Valley sector, the 60th Division still east of the Nablus road. There is no sign of any concentration on the coast. The enemy was thoroughly deceived, wholly unaware of the devastating blow that was about to be dealt him.

CHAPTER XXII.

THE BATTLES OF MEGIDDO: THE 19TH SEPTEMBER.
(Maps 1, 2, 19, 20; Sketches 30, 31.)

THE INFANTRY PLAN OF ATTACK.

Maps 1, 2, 20.
Sketch 30.

As darkness fell after a hot, airless day upon the great concentration of troops massed in the Plain of Sharon, there was at British G.H.Q. one anxiety overmastering all others, and shared by all except, it would seem, the Commander-in-Chief himself. Was the enemy there? Was he still holding his trenches in strength, or had he perchance taken warning and drawn back, leaving his foremost positions to be defended by mobile machine guns and skirmishers? There was no sign that he had done so, and it appeared little likely, even though he had doubtless learnt from a havildar captured on the 17th and believed to be a deserter that a great assault was to be launched. Yet there was the possibility, not pleasant to contemplate; for, though a withdrawal would have been by no means fatal to British hopes, it would have gravely increased the difficulties of the undertaking.[1] The thousands of signal rockets which soared into the air when the British bombardment began, the reports of considerable fire from the Turkish batteries, above all the swift capture of prisoners in large numbers, brought relief from this doubt; and

---

[1] The Historical Section of the Turkish General Staff states that General Jevad Pasha, the Commander of the *Eighth Army*, besought his superior, Liman von Sanders, to allow him to withdraw to the Et Tire line. The experienced commander of the *XXII Corps*, Colonel Refet Bey, states that he also begged to be allowed to withdraw his front on the coast so that the bombardment predicted by the deserter "might "uselessly exhaust itself in battering empty trenches." The Marshal believed, however, according to Refet's evidence, that the deserter was an agent "planted" on him by the British intelligence service, and refused to permit an inch of ground to be abandoned. ("Army, Navy and Air Force Gazette," 18th June 1927.)

TASK OF THE XXI CORPS

staff officers have declared that, though all was yet before them, they then felt that all was won. The enemy was there indeed, and so doomed.

1918.
19 Sept.

The task allotted to General Bulfin's XXI Corps was, first, to break through the enemy's trench system in the plain; and, secondly, to wheel right and secure positions covering the Tul Karm–Nablus road from the north, thus opening a way for the cavalry and screening its right flank during the first stage of its advance. In forming his plan he was strongly influenced by the course of the roads by which the Turks could retreat eastward after the disruption of their right flank defences. Of these there were only three of importance in the quadrilateral Qalqilye–Tul Karm–Nablus–El Lubban. The most southerly, from Qalqilye to Bidya, would be of little value to the enemy, since it would be cut by the first rush of the assault. The second ran through the middle of the quadrilateral, from Qalqilye by 'Azzun and El Funduq to Deir Sheraf on the Damascus road [1] south of Sebustiye. The third was the old main road from Tul Karm through 'Anebta to Deir Sheraf, with a branch joining the Damascus road a little higher up at El Mas'udiye. The 54th Division with the Détachement Français de Palestine et de Syrie [2] on its right and under its orders, was to attack northward in the foothills between Ra-fat and Majdal Yaba, while the remaining four divisions were to assault the enemy's trenches from the little village of Sabiye, a mile west of the railway, to the sea. As soon as the second-line Et Tire defences had been taken and a bridgehead secured across the Nahr el Faliq, the 5th L.H. Brigade was to advance with all speed to cut the road and railway east of Tul Karm and occupy the town. The way would then be open for the Desert Mounted Corps to move northward, but the infantry had still to assure its protection and to roll up the right flank of the enemy in the hills. The XXI Corps was therefore first to wheel eastwards, pivoting on Ra-fat, and to secure Bidya, Deir Sheraf, Sebustiye, 'Anebta, and possibly also Nablus;

---

[1] It will be convenient hereafter to describe the long road running from south to north, hitherto called first the " Hebron road " and later the " Nablus road," as the " Damascus road," now that we are mainly concerned with it north of Nablus.

[2] Hereafter described by the initials D.F.P.S.

after which there would be a wheel to the left, and the advance would continue northward. " Time is the enemy " rather than the Turks " was the watchword which General Bulfin had ordered should be taught to every man, Indian as well as British.

The formations taking part in the attack were, from right to left, the D.F.P.S., 54th Division, 3rd (Lahore) Division, 75th Division, 7th (Meerut)[1] Division, and 60th Division. There was no corps reserve, but substantial divisional reserves in every case. The frontages of the 54th and 3rd Divisions were very long, but on their inner flanks, from Majdal Yaba to Ferrikhiye on the 'Auja, there was a space of some five miles lightly held. The front just west of the railway was in fact only too well protected by fields of giant thistles, six or seven feet in height. There was another lightly held gap of about two miles on the left of the 7th Division. The Turkish line opposite these gaps would not, of course, be directly attacked, but during the right-handed wheel the units advancing on either side of them would close in and come into touch.

There was to be no preliminary bombardment. The opening of fire by the artillery, trench mortars, and machine guns at 4.30 a.m. was to be the signal for the infantry to advance. The time had been selected so that there should be moonlight followed by thirty-five minutes of darkness before the first signs of dawn ; this period was to be used for the deployment upon lines previously taped, in order to ensure that the troops formed up at right angles to the direction of their advance. The heavy artillery was to be devoted mainly to counter-battery work, certain guns and howitzers being employed to shell headquarters and telephone exchanges beyond the range of the field artillery, and also, if available, points holding up the infantry. The field artillery was to bombard the enemy's front line until the arrival of the infantry. Then the 18-pdrs. and R.H.A. batteries were to lift and form a creeping barrage in front

---

[1] The Lahore and Meerut Divisions had changed very much in composition since first they landed in France. The former was still officially described as " 3rd (Lahore) Division," but the latter now appeared in printed orders of battle as " 7th (Indian) Division." As the title " Meerut " was still generally used in the Army it has been retained here.

of the advancing infantry up to their extreme range, while the 4·5-inch howitzers fired on important points beyond the barrage. Two destroyers, *Druid* and *Forester*, had been detailed by Rear-Admiral T. Jackson to assist the left of the corps by fire from the sea.[1]

The attack to be carried out by General Chetwode's XX Corps in the hills was subsidiary to that of the XXI Corps. The corps commander had long decided that, if ever he should be called upon to advance on Nablus, he would, whatever the strength at his disposal, attempt a converging movement from both flanks towards the general line 'Aqrabe–Jemma'in, about 7 miles north of his present position, without attacking the enemy's defences opposite the centre of the corps. The main advantage of this plan was that his right would be moving along the watershed, and his left following the parallel spurs in a north-easterly direction, with no deep wadis to cross. A rapid advance from the flanks also afforded the prospect of capturing guns opposite the centre.

When General Chetwode learnt that he would have only two divisions on this occasion, he was more than ever convinced that his plan of action was the only one whereby he might hope to accomplish anything considerable. He had, as already stated, decided that there should be a gap of 7 miles, lightly held by " Watson's Force," between the 53rd Division on the right and the 10th on the left. The main attack of the XX Corps was not to be launched until the success of that of the XXI Corps was assured. During the previous night, however, the 53rd Division was to carry out a preliminary operation, and wheel forward the refused right flank of the corps across the Wadi Samye to the heights beyond, El Mughaiyir, Hindhead, and Nairn Ridge.[2] There was in this plan a double advantage. In the first place the Wadi Samye and its numerous tributaries cut up the ground into a maze of steep-faced gorges at various angles, with high, craggy hills between them;

---

[1] XXI Corps Order No. 42 is given in Appendix 24. The instructions referred to in the order relate to the action of artillery and aircraft, to communication, etc.; and to the plan of attack as it concerned each division, which is given in the following pages when dealing with the division's operations.

[2] XX Corps Order No. 42 is given in Appendix 25.

beyond it the right flank of the division would be on a comparatively level watershed broken by no really formidable gullies. In the second place, the preliminary wheel would secure the unlimited supply of water in the Wadi Samye—a matter of great importance in view of the reported shortage further north—and would enable a road to be made up one of the tributaries, the Forth Wadi, to join the existing road system behind the enemy's lines. This attack took place during the night of the 18th, but will be described after the main operation carried out by the XXI Corps.

THE BATTLE OF SHARON.

Maps 2, 19, 20.
Sketches 30, 31.

Disquieted by the advance of the 53rd Division east of the Damascus road, the enemy showed signs of rather more than his usual alertness that night. An increase in the number of rocket lights sent up all along his line bore witness to his nervousness. On the fronts of the 7th and 60th Divisions there were patrol encounters, which, however, caused no interference with the deployment; on that of the 75th Division there were long and heavy bursts of machine-gun fire. But only against the 54th Division was the Turkish artillery more then normally active. Here its scanty barrage was dropped on several occasions upon the British trenches and No Man's Land, the last being but a few minutes before Zero hour. At 4.30 a.m. there burst forth the terrific roar of the British bombardment, over a thousand shells a minute being thrown into the enemy's lines. The Turkish artillery replied promptly, but the intensity and accuracy of the British counter-battery fire caused its shelling to be ragged and intermittent. On the front of the 54th Division the enemy's barrage, which had already been put down and had hitherto been level, at once became wild. In many cases batteries soon ceased fire altogether, either because the guns had been destroyed or the detachments had been driven from them. The careful counter-battery study which had preceded the battle was now indeed repaid, and the British heavy artillery by its neutralizing fire gave full value for its superiority. Within a few minutes of the first discharge, while yet the earliest light of dawn had not pierced the pall of smoke and dust

LAUNCH OF THE ASSAULT 473

which overhung the lines, the assaulting infantry swarmed into the enemy's trenches.

1918.
19 Sept.

54th Division and D.F.P.S. The intention of Major-General S. W. Hare was to advance northward, the D.F.P.S. on the right, the 163rd Brigade in the centre, and the 161st Brigade on the left, pivoting on the Ra-fat salient, to a line from its apex through Crown Hill, north-east of Kufr Qasim. When this objective was reached (or sooner if the situation permitted) the 162nd Brigade was to pass through the right of the 161st, move eastward on Bidya, and secure the crossings of the Wadi Qana south of Kh. Kefar Thilth.

The D.F.P.S. (Colonel P. de Piépape) assaulted simultaneously the col west of Ra-fat from the south-east with one battalion of the Légion d'Orient, and Three Bushes and Scurry Hills with two battalions of the Régiment de Tirailleurs. The Légion d'Orient had taken its objective by 5 a.m. The more difficult attack of the Tirailleurs was carried out with great dash and skill, Three Bushes Hill being stormed in face of considerable resistance by 5.10 and Scurry Hill by 5.45. Kh. Deir el Qassis, east of Scurry Hill, was soon afterwards occupied, but had to be abandoned owing to heavy shelling by guns beyond reach of the French artillery. However, the detachment, having established itself on the western edge of the ridge, had accomplished virtually all that was required of it, and had captured 212 prisoners at light cost. During the night of the 19th it occupied 'Arara, north-east of Ra-fat.

The first phase of the attack of the 163rd Brigade (Br.-General A. J. M'Neill)[1] was to be carried out by the 5/Suffolk on the right against a spur north of the Wadi el 'Ayun, which dominated the plain and was known to be used as an observation post for three batteries, and by the 8/Hampshire on the left against Kh. ed Duweir and the high ground south-east of Kufr Qasim. The 5/Norfolk was subsequently to advance on the right of the 5/Suffolk and swing eastward against the village of Mesha, and the 4/Norfolk on the left was to be directed against the high ground west of Bidya. The approach began at 4.20 a.m. So

---

[1] Br.-General M'Neill had been ill when his brigade, the 230th, left Palestine and had afterwards been appointed to the command of the 163rd.

good was the timing that the British barrage began to move forward precisely as the infantry reached the Turkish trenches, but the first objectives were so speedily taken that companies had then to make a pause to await the next lift. The whole of the first phase was carried through without difficulty, the only critical incident being the sudden counter-attack of a fresh Turkish company against the right flank of the 5/Suffolk north of the Wadi el 'Ayun. At this moment, however, a platoon of the 7th Tirailleurs appeared on Scurry Hill and opened a devastating fire on the enemy, the survivors at once putting up their hands. A long delay now ensued owing to the 161st Brigade being checked in its advance upon the works north of Kufr Qasim, during which Br.-General M'Neill was ordered by Major-General Hare to assist an attack upon them from the southeast by clearing the enemy from the high ground at Kh. Sirisia. A detachment of the 5/Norfolk was thus engaged when at 2 p.m. the brigadier learnt that the works north of Kufr Qasim had fallen. He then ordered the 5/Norfolk to break off its engagement and move on Mesha, and the 4/Norfolk to advance on Bidya, driving the enemy off Kh. Sirisia on its way. Neither battalion met with any serious or prolonged resistance, but they were continually opposed by small parties and their progress after the fall of darkness was naturally very slow. By 3 a.m. on the following day the 5/Norfolk had occupied Mesha, while patrols of the 4th, which was on the high ground west of Bidya, had entered the village.

The 161st Brigade (Br.-General H. B. H. Orpen Palmer) was first to capture Kufr Qasim, the advance northward being carried out by the 5/Essex on the right and 4/Essex on the left. The 7th and 6th Essex were then to move through against the works running south and west of Kefar Bara. The leading battalions quickly crossed the Bureid Ridge, taking 69 prisoners, reached the Wadi Raba, where there was a quarter of an hour's pause, and stormed the high ground south of Kufr Qasim, killing or capturing all the garrison. There was now another pause of fifteen minutes to allow battalions to reorganize and the 161st Machine-Gun Company to take up positions from which it could cover the next advance by overhead fire. By 7 a.m. Kufr Qasim and Jevis Tepe to west of it were taken with little opposition. The 7th and 6th Essex then moved up to attack the next line of trenches, their right on the little wood west of Crown Hill.[1] Now for the first time there was obstinate resistance, especially on the left, but after re-bombardment by the divisional artillery the whole position was occupied. It could, indeed, have been taken earlier, but for an error committed by the headquarters of the 6/Essex, the commanding officer's messages asking for the artillery to lift not being sent off.

1918.
19 Sept.

The 162nd Brigade (Br.-General A. Mudge), less the 11/London detailed as escort to the divisional artillery and to cover the gap between the division's left and the right of the 3rd at Ras el 'Ain, concentrated at 8 a.m. south-west of Kufr Qasim, suffering somewhat severely from long-range shelling. One battery of the IX Mountain Artillery Brigade had been pushed forward to the eastern end of Bureid Ridge to support its advance eastward. On hearing that Kufr Qasim was captured, Br.-General Mudge ordered the 4/Northampton and 10/London to move up north of it and face east, and at 9.3 directed them to begin their advance. A few minutes later he received a telephone message from divisional headquarters that the 161st Brigade was in difficulties at Sivri Wood and the works to the north-west. He had just ordered his leading battalions to advance between Sivri Wood and Crown Hill, clearing the wood en route, when he learnt that the two Essex battalions had been ordered to renew their attack from the south-west, covered by a bombardment. It thus appeared that his own battalions and those of the 161st Brigade were about to assault the same objective by routes crossing almost at right angles and that the former would run into the latter's barrage. He therefore ordered the 4/Northampton and 10/London to stand fast, but his message was not received till after they had carried out the movement. Fortunately their advance began before the 161st Brigade's attack was launched, and actually passed through its right. The 5/Bedford, having followed the Northampton through Sivri Wood, came up on its left, and after a pause for reorganization the three battalions advanced steadily eastward. On reaching the south bank of the Wadi Qana the

---

[1] Known as Sivri Wood, and marked on the map, though there is no room for the name.

troops of the 10/London saw below three howitzers of two different batteries, one team being already hooked in and having reached the road. Machine-gun fire killed several of the oxen and drove away the troops about the guns with considerable loss. In face of this fire one heroic man ran back to the battery position, stooped down for a moment, and then dashed away. Soon afterwards there was a terrific explosion of the ammunition dump. The Northampton, after capturing 'Azzun Ibn 'Atme, reached Kh. es Sumra during the small hours of the morning.

The 54th Division and D.F.P.S. had thus successfully accomplished their task, having completely broken through the enemy's defences on the right, and formed the pivot for the whole offensive movement on the left. About 700 prisoners, 9 guns, and 20 machine guns had been captured at a cost of 535 casualties. Owing to the nature of the country the troops under Major-General Hare's command had had about the most difficult task of all in the early stages of the attack, but the resistance of the enemy had never been really stout.

3rd (Lahore) Division. The task set to Major-General A. R. Hoskins was to break through the Turkish defences about Sabiye; then to turn eastward, capturing Jaljulye, the work known as " Railway Redoubt," and Qalqilye, and advance on Kh. Kefar Thilth, 'Azzun, and Jiyus in the foot-hills. The 7th and 9th Brigades formed up on a frontage of about one mile, the left of the 9th on the Hadra –Et Tire road. The 8th Brigade was to be in reserve during the preliminary stages, and held a front of nearly four miles between Ras el 'Ain and Ferrikhiye.

The 7th Brigade (Br.-General S. R. Davidson), with the 2/7th Gurkhas on the right, the 27th Punjabis on the left, the 1/Connaught Rangers in rear of the left battalion, and the 91st Punjabis following in support, swept through the front-line defences. The enemy's infantry, dazed by the weight of the artillery fire and the intense overhead machine-gun barrage, made little resistance. At first the Turkish artillery fire was heavy, and though the platoon columns found gaps in the barrage, casualties would have been high on harder ground. As it was, the Turkish high-explosive shells were to a great extent smothered in the sandy soil; but even so the 27th Punjabis suffered upwards of one hundred casualties in passing through. Thereafter the worst obstacle to progress was the dense clouds of dust and smoke. Kufr Saba was captured at 7.12 a.m., and Qalqilye at 9 a.m. At 2 p.m. orders were received to support the advance eastward of the 8th Brigade, and the 91st Punjabis were accordingly directed to move on 'Azzun. The battalion did not receive this message till an hour and a half later, and the greater part of its advance was made in the dark over broken ground. It halted at midnight 2 miles west of the village.

The 9th Brigade (Br.-General C. C. Luard) moved forward at 4.27 at the rate of 100 yards a minute in a cloud so thick that the leading battalions could not see fifteen yards ahead, and after leaving the tapes stretched as far as possible into No Man's Land had to rely entirely on the compass for keeping direction. The Turkish barrage was here fairly heavy, but it was mainly of high-explosive, and there were gaps in it of which the small columns availed themselves. There was at first hardly any rifle or machine-gun fire. West of Sabiye the enemy's infantry made some attempt to hold up the advance, but the 105th Mahrattas and 2/Dorset gave him no time to collect himself. Between 5 and 5.30 a.m. the 93rd Burma Infantry and 1/1st Gurkhas passed through the leading battalions. After piercing the enemy's second line—the trench running from Tabsor to Qalqilye—the Gurkhas were to have wheeled eastward, but were threatened by a counter-attack from the north owing to the 75th Division on their left not taking part in the wheel, and compelled to push out a detachment to clear their left before bringing their left shoulders up. In this operation they captured 136 prisoners and two machine guns. The 93rd Burma Infantry advanced eastward, crossing the railway a mile north-west of Qalqilye at 9 a.m., the 105th Mahrattas now being on its right and the Gurkhas having come up on the left. Br.-General Luard, having ridden forward to ascertain the situation, which was somewhat obscure owing to the constant cutting of telephone lines and the impossibility of visual signalling in clouds of dust, ordered the advance on Jiyus to continue: 105th on the right, 93rd in the centre, Gurkhas echeloned on the left flank, Dorset in support. Progress on the left was slow, owing to the fact that the advance was now meeting opposition not from the Turkish *20th Division*, which had been completely overrun, but from the reserves of the *Asia Corps*, which had moved westward from 'Azzun. However, Jiyus was captured about nightfall by the 105th and two companies of the 93rd with 20 prisoners, including two German officers.

The two flank battalions of the 8th Brigade (Br.-General S. M. Edwardes), the 1/Manchester at Ras el 'Ain and the 2/124th Baluchis at Tell el Mukhmar, were to carry out demonstrations, the remainder of the brigade being in the wooded area on the north bank of the 'Auja, known as "Transfluvia," in divisional reserve. Owing to the thickets of thistles, movement was to be confined to the railway, the Jaffa–Qalqilye road, and a few paths cut during the preceding nights. At 4.45 a.m. a company of the Baluchis carried the trench south-west of Byar 'Adas and established in it eight machine guns to assist the attack of the 7th Brigade on the works further north. A company of the Manchester, advancing up both sides of the railway track in single file, reached the bridge over the Wadi Ishkar west of Jaljulye, bringing up two machine guns to keep the village and Railway Redoubt under fire. By 7.15 the Baluchis were in Byar 'Adas, news of their progress being received from an observation officer posted on Buttercup Hill with a telephone, and at 9.10 the 47th Sikhs moved forward to that village to assist them in the attack on Railway Redoubt. After five minutes' intense bombardment this big work was carried by the Baluchis before the Sikhs came up, a pack gun and two machine guns being captured. The 1/Manchester was then ordered to capture Jaljulye, after a bombardment beginning at 10.45, and accomplished its task without difficulty. At both points the enemy fought half-heartedly, watching over his shoulder the progress of the 7th Brigade, which threatened to cut him off. Meanwhile the 59th Rifles had begun to move across the plain by tracks cut through the thistles, turned eastward through Jaljulye, and advanced south of Hable, which was captured by the Sikhs about 1 p.m. Br.-General Edwardes was for some time unable to find the IV Brigade R.F.A., which was to support his advance eastward, but discovered at 12.30 that it had moved forward to a position south of Kufr Saba, and ordered.it to direct its fire on

ATTACK OF 75TH DIVISION

Hable to assist the Sikhs. After its capture the batteries moved eastward, and the advance was resumed at 1.45; the 59th Rifles directed on Kh. Ras et Tire and the Baluchis on Tell Manasif, the other two battalions following in close support. Both these objectives were reached about 6 p.m., as the sun was setting, and the brigade bivouacked for the night behind strong outposts.

1918.
19 Sept.

75th Division. The 75th Division was the only one in the corps which was not to take part in the general wheel eastward. Its objective was the Et Tire system and the village of that name, which it was expected would be held by the enemy's only considerable reserve on this flank, the *46th Division.* Major-General Palin had at his disposal " A " Squadron of the Corps Cavalry Regiment and the 2nd Light Armoured Motor Battery. The advance was to be carried out by the 232nd Brigade on the right and the 234th Brigade on the left, the 233rd Brigade being in divisional reserve. Two companies of the 5/Somerset Light Infantry (233rd Brigade) were attached to the 234th Brigade, to advance between the right and left battalions and capture an isolated work some six hundred yards in front of the main line, thus leaving these battalions free to move straight upon their objectives.

The 232nd Brigade (Br.-General H. J. Huddleston), with the 4/Wiltshire on the right and 2/3rd Gurkhas on the left, the leading companies in line and the remainder in artillery formation, swept through the enemy's front-line trenches, meeting with little opposition. The pack-mules carrying the signalling equipment having been stampeded by the bombardment, no information regarding progress was received by brigade headquarters till Miske was captured with over a hundred prisoners at 7 a.m., with the aid of the fire of the South African Field Artillery Brigade, which had moved forward very rapidly behind the infantry after completing its programme of bombardment. Et Tire, defended by numerous trenches and surrounded by gardens enclosed in a network of cactus hedges, was a far more formidable obstacle. It was while reconnoitring the defences of this place that Lieut.-Colonel A. Armstrong of the Wiltshire, whose leadership and personal gallantry had been of inestimable service to his battalion, was mortally wounded. The supporting battalion, the 72nd Punjabis, had now come up, and a firing line from all three battalions was established on the outskirts of the village. Then all progress ceased for some time, the troops being exhausted after their advance of over five miles, and the enemy's resistance being far more resolute than any hitherto encountered.[1] Lieut.-Colonel W. S. Prentis, commanding the Punjabis, observing that every man who exposed himself was instantly shot down, sent back a message to the brigade commander suggesting a turning movement on the right flank. The 3rd Kashmir Rifles, whose Senior Special Service Officer, Major R. A. Lyall,[2] had led the battalion up to brigade headquarters at Miske on his own initiative, received orders from Br.-General Huddleston to reinforce the attack. The armoured cars and cavalry squadron were at the same time ordered by Lieut.-Colonel G. B. Rowan-Hamilton, G.S.O.1 of the division, who had ridden forward with Major-General Palin's authority to employ them as required, to move up east of the village. Under this renewed pressure the Turks evacuated Et Tire, which was captured at 11 a.m. with the office and papers of the *XXII Corps* headquarters.[3] The cars pursued enemy cavalry and transport to the Tul Karm road and some distance up it, shooting down a number of horses.

The 234th Brigade (Br.-General C. A. H. Maclean) had an easier task. The brigade advanced in the same formation as the 232nd, the 1/152nd Infantry and 58th Rifles in first line, with the two companies of the 5/Somerset between them. These companies secured their objective with little difficulty, and remained upon it until their own brigade had moved forward. The barrage was so accurate that the leading waves were able to keep within forty yards of it, suffering only a single casualty from British fire; but its pace—fifty yards a minute—proved too slow owing to

---
[1] The *46th Division* in the Et Tire defences was commanded by Major Tiller, the stout-hearted defender of Gaza in the First Battle.

[2] The Kashmir Rifles was an Imperial Service Regiment.

[3] The corps commander, Refet Bey, appears to have been cut off from his own people, and, accompanied only by an aide-de-camp and two orderlies, to have wandered about for the best part of a week behind the British lines. Moving only by night, he was never recognized as a Turk, though more than once in touch with British troops, replying to challenges by saluting and riding slowly on. Eventually he reached Tyre, before its occupation by the British. ("Army, Navy and Air Force Gazette," 18th June 1927.)

ATTACK OF 7TH DIVISION

the weakness of the opposition. It was only when the line of the enemy's batteries was reached that there was a few minutes' hard fighting. Two or three batteries in the wadi south-west of Miske kept up fire on the 1/152nd Infantry to within 60 yards' range. The Indians then dashed at them with the bayonet, capturing three 150-mm. howitzers, seven 77-mm. guns, and the whole of their detachments. The trenches of the Et Tire line were taken soon after 8 a.m. The 21st Brigade of the 7th Division subsequently formed up east of Et Tire to continue the advance eastward, the 75th Division being thus squeezed out and coming into corps reserve. The 233rd Brigade, which had not been called upon, had moved forward to Miske. The division had suffered 518 casualties, of which 352 were in the 232nd Brigade.

1918.
19 Sept.

7th (Meerut) Division. The 7th Division, under the command of Major-General Sir V. B. Fane, was to capture the enemy's front system of defences between the nameless wadi west of Tabsor and the Wadi Hurab el Miske, this phase being carried out under an intense artillery and machine-gun bombardment and barrage moving at the rate of 100 yards a minute. It was then to break through the Et Tire defences on the left of the 75th Division, capturing the works east of the Zerqiye marsh at 'Ayun el Basse, the trench covering the Zerqiye crossing—its sole passage over the marshes—and those north of it. During this phase the divisional artillery would be moving forward, so that the attack would have the support of heavy artillery only. If, however, the opposition was so strong that the capture of the enemy's second system of defence seemed unlikely without greater artillery support, a position as close as possible to the trenches was to be occupied to cover the advance of the batteries. The attack was to be carried out by the 19th Brigade on the right and the 21st on the left. The 28th Brigade, in reserve, was to advance to Seaforth Hill, in the British front line, at 5.30, and to be prepared to carry on the attack to the east.

Br.-General G. A. Weir, commanding the 19th Brigade, had under his orders, in addition to the troops of his own brigade, two battalions—1st Guides and 20th Punjabis—of the 21st Brigade and the 134th Machine-Gun Company. The six battalions were formed up in front of the British wire in two columns, each on a frontage of one battalion. The first phase was carried out precisely according to the programme, little resistance being encountered by the 92nd and 28th Punjabis. A 150-mm. howitzer battery was captured in very gallant circumstances by a wounded N.C.O., Naik Buta Khan, of the 92nd Punjabis, and four wounded men of the 1st Guides. The naik and his party, having been bandaged, had again gone forward, but had moved to the right of the line of advance of the 92nd Punjabis. Suddenly, on topping a rise, they came on the battery, with teams of horses and bullocks moving up to hook in. Without hesitating, the naik placed his four men between the battery and its teams, went back to the top of the rise, and attracted the attention of a supporting company of his battalion, which came to his assistance. The 1/Seaforth and 125th Rifles met with more opposition on the Et Tire line, but even here the enemy surrendered tamely for the most part. The trench covering the Zerqiye crossing, for example, was taken by a party of 40 men of the 125th Rifles, who captured five times their own number of prisoners and six machine guns. Just behind this a battery of three 105-mm. howitzers in action was taken by Captain T. W. Rees and six men of the same battalion. One gun was limbered up and driven to the rear, but Captain Rees, jumping on to a captured pony, galloped after it and made the drivers turn it back. The 1/Seaforth also captured several guns as it advanced on the works at 'Ayun el Basse. Having taken these trenches, one company swung left-handed and took those covering the Zerqiye Crossing from the north.

The 21st Brigade (Br.-General A. G. Kemball) had during the first stage of the operations but two battalions, 2/Black Watch and 8th Gurkha Rifles, under its orders, and was responsible only for the capture of the front system of defence. After the Black Watch had taken those to its front the Gurkhas passed through and advanced north-westward, rolling up that part of the line not attacked frontally as far as the Wadi Hurab el Miske, and capturing nearly 350 prisoners. Br.-General Kemball rode forward at 9 a.m. to 'Ayun el Basse, where he had ordered the two battalions, as well as the 1st Guides and 20th Punjabis, now returned to his command, to concentrate. Touch could not for some time be made with the Guides, but the other three battalions, with a light trench-mortar battery, were ready by 1 p.m. to march on Et Tire, which had been for two hours in the hands of the 75th Division. By 4.30 p.m. they were concentrated east of the village. Meanwhile the 19th Brigade had also moved towards Et Tire. At 2 p.m. Lieut.-Colonel W. S. Leslie, G.S.O.1 of the division, realized that the 21st would not be ready for some time to advance into the hills, owing to the delay in collecting its scattered battalions. It was all-important that the enemy should not be permitted to form a new front. He therefore directed Br.-General Weir to push on towards El Majdal with his leading battalion, the 92nd Punjabis. The 21st Brigade advanced due eastward across the Tul Karm road at 4.30. On the right the 20th Punjabis encountered heavy machine-gun fire from the foot-hills, and was obliged to halt for the night about three-quarters of a mile short of its objective, the hamlet of Felamiye.[1] On the left the 2/Black Watch came up to the assistance of the 92nd Punjabis, which had been advancing astride the Wadi el 'Ayun in face of steady rear-guard opposition, and carried El Majdal, a hill-shrine surrounded by a few houses. The men of these two battalions were so exhausted that they could scarce climb the hillside. Both had, it will be recalled, attacked in first line, and though their task had been a light one, the moral and physical strain of " going over the top " is very severe. It was not often that a battalion which had done so was set to make another attack twelve hours later, after covering twelve miles.

The 28th Brigade (Br.-General C. H. Davies) reached a position north-east of the Zerqiye marsh at 12.30 p.m., then turned eastward and advanced with battalions in diamond formation in the direction of Et Taiyibe, east of the Tul Karm road. The 264th Brigade R.F.A. had joined it on completion of the bombardment programme. The enemy, though he had evacuated Et Tire, still held a rear-guard position on the watershed a mile and a half to the north-west with several machine guns. The advanced guard, the 56th Rifles, drove him off this ridge by 3.30, and he then established himself on a lower one 1,500 yards

---

[1] A whole German battalion had occupied Felamiye that morning to prevent an advance into the hills. See Note at end of Chapter.

further east. A company of the 2/Leicester having moved up on the right flank of the 56th Rifles and one of the 53rd Sikhs on the left, the artillery came into action, and all remaining opposition was soon at an end. Taiyibe was occupied at 6 p.m., and the brigade then bivouacked north, east, and south of the village.

60th Division. The task set to Major-General J. S. M. Shea's troops was one which made extraordinary calls upon their powers of endurance. The rôle of the division was, first, to establish a bridgehead north of the Nahr el Faliq in order to allow the 5th Cavalry Division to move north along the coast; and, secondly, to take the town of Tul Karm and cut the railway east of it. The brigade in second line which was set to capture Tul Karm was fourteen miles in a straight line from its objective and about sixteen by the route which it would have to follow. To have covered that distance in full marching order and on a hot day would have been trying enough had there been no enemy in the field. The division was to fight upon a historic battlefield. Between Arsuf and the Nahr el Faliq was decided in 1191—also upon a hot September day—one of the greatest and fiercest encounters of the Crusades; when Richard of England, against enormous odds, defeated Saladin and avenged the disaster of Hattin.

The division had been relieved by the 53rd in the hills between the 21st and 28th August and had carried out intensive training in daylight and by night in the Vale of Ajalon. Between the 15th and 18th September it had marched by Latron, Sarafand, and Sarona to the front line, moving always at night. On the evening of the 18th it was assembled in depth on the coast: the 180th Brigade in front line; the 181st in support, between Bedouin Knoll and Arsuf; the 179th in reserve about El Haram. The 5th L.H. Brigade was attached to the division, with orders to move up behind the 7th Division and advance directly upon Tul Karm, capture the town if possible, and hand it over to the troops of the 60th on their arrival. The 13th Pontoon Park was also attached. The 102nd Brigade R.G.A.[1] and 2nd Light Armoured Motor Battery were to join the division at Tul Karm.

---

[1] Its two mobile batteries, the 91st Heavy Battery (horse-drawn) and 380th Siege Battery (tractor-drawn) reached Tul Karm about 3.30 a.m. on the 20th.

ATTACK OF 60TH DIVISION

At 4.30 a.m. an intense bombardment with artillery, trench mortars, and machine guns was directed upon the enemy's front and second lines of trenches, three siege batteries carrying out neutralizing fire, while the destroyers *Druid* and *Forester* opened fire a little later on the trenches north of the Nahr el Faliq. The attack of the 180th Brigade (Br.-General C. F. Watson) was launched in two columns : the leading battalions being the 50th Kumaon Rifles on the right, east of the coast road, and the 2nd Guides on the left, with left flank on the shore. Two platoons of the right battalion were detailed to keep connection. The 2/97th Infantry (181st Brigade) was attached, with the special duty of capturing the strong Turkish redoubt below the southwest corner of the Birket Ramadan marsh. After the enemy's third line had been reached the 2/19th London was to pass through the Guides and establish the bridgehead over the Nahr el Faliq near the mouth. For all three Indian battalions of the brigade this vital assault was their baptism of fire.

At 4.40 one company of the Kumaon Rifles assaulted the outwork west of Birket 'Atife, and overran it in two minutes, capturing 110 prisoners and 8 machine guns. The remainder of the battalion passed by this work to the east, moving at the rate of 75 yards a minute behind the barrage, and took the redoubts in the two succeeding lines of trenches, with 125 prisoners and 7 machine guns. It was now only 5.50, and most of the battalion was still engaged in " mopping up " the captured position ; but, seeing the 2/19th London passing through the Guides on the left, Major A. Latham, commanding the battalion, took the half company which constituted his sole reserve and went forward half a mile on the right of the Londoners, who were in hot pursuit of the enemy west of Birket Ramadan. This party secured 69 more prisoners. The 2/97th Infantry followed the Kumaons to their second objective, when two companies turned eastward to attack the redoubt. An interesting experiment was attempted in aid of this operation. A large white arrow was placed on the ground at the point where the two companies turned eastward as a signal to an aeroplane to drop a screen of smoke bombs along the wadi east of the redoubt in order to cover the movement. However, there being some delay before the signal was seen, the redoubt was captured with 40 prisoners and 4 machine guns before the screen was put down, and the smoke caused some trouble to the troops on the right. On the left the 2nd Guides was equally successful, though it had to face a barrage which caused 54 casualties before the leading companies reached the enemy's wire. All three Turkish lines were captured, with over one hundred prisoners, by 5.40. Then the 2/19th London passed through. The only serious resistance met with by this battalion was at the bridge which carried the coast road across the river. This was captured by 7.20, and the bridgehead established, enabling the 5th Cavalry Division to pass through a few minutes later, the reserve battalion, the 2/30th Punjabis, having removed all wire entanglements from the beach. In less than three hours, therefore, the brigade had captured the enemy's front system of defence with about 600 prisoners, while one company actually crossed the Faliq, a distance of 6,000 yards from its position of assembly, $2\frac{1}{4}$ hours after Zero. Its casualties were heavy by the extraordinarily low standard of that day's fighting; for, including those of the 2/97th Infantry, they numbered 414. The Faliq was found to be carrying so little water that there was no need to employ the Pontoon Park.

At 6.15 a.m. the 181st Brigade (Br.-General E. C. Da Costa) received orders from Major-General Shea to begin its advance. The brigade moved forward, each battalion picking up a machine-gun section which had been engaged in barrage fire, and the 2/97th Infantry falling in behind. The head of the column reached the Nahr el Faliq at 8.30 and turned right-handed to cross the causeway at Kh. ez Zebabde. Here the 2/22nd London was to have advanced upon a sandy ridge running north and south about 'Ayun el Werdat. Observing, however, that the 130th Baluchis had outpaced the Londoners, Br.-General Da Costa ordered the Indian battalion to capture this objective and the 2/22nd to advance on its left, with its left flank on Umm Sir, 2 miles further north. The second objective of the two battalions was the Qalqilye–Tul Karm road, the Baluchis being ordered to take the villages of Qulunsawe and Irta on either side of it, while the Londoners moved through Burin on Tul Karm itself. The 301st Brigade R.F.A., which had crossed the Nahr el

Sketch 31. MEGIDDO, 1918. Situation at 12 m.n. 19th/20th Sept., 1918.

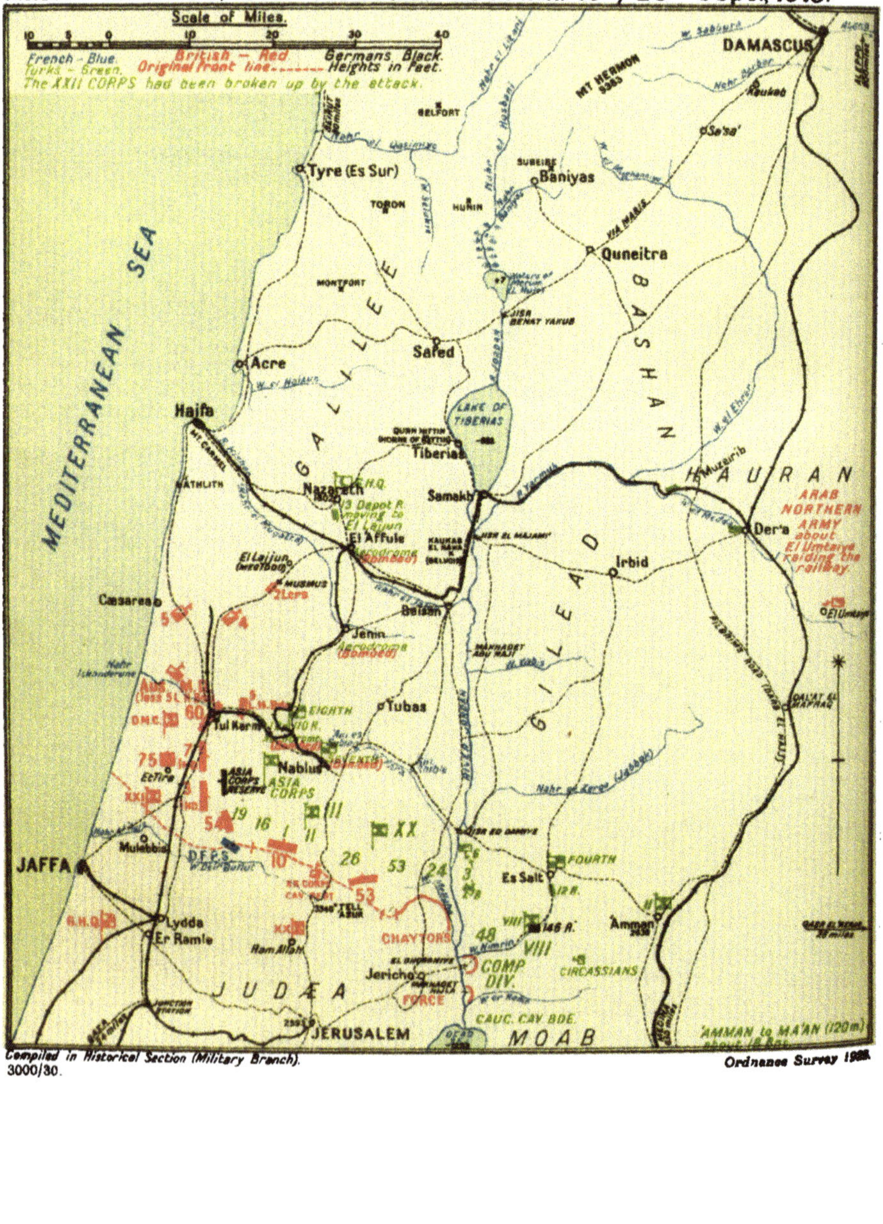

Compiled in Historical Section (Military Branch).
3000/30.

Ordnance Survey 1928.

Faliq, was ordered to detail two 18-pdr. batteries to support 1918. the advance. By 11 a.m. the first objective had been 19 Sept. gained, the only opposition coming from a small party of Turks covered by the fire of two guns.

Meanwhile the 5th L.H. Brigade had moved up to carry out its mission. Major-General Shea had instructed Br.-General G. M. M. Onslow not to concern himself with Tul Karm if there was any serious resistance, but to advance with all speed and cut the road to Nablus, leaving the town to the infantry. Swinging to the left to keep clear of the infantry battle and avoid the fire of machine guns opposing the 181st Brigade, the brigade rode north of Tul Karm. A number of British aeroplanes were now bombing the place, and the demoralization caused by this and by the appearance of the cavalry in their rear doubtless contributed to slacken the resistance of the Turks to the 2/22nd London. The Baluchis on the right meeting with much stronger opposition at Qulunsawe, were out of the hunt—the village not being occupied until 5 p.m.—and the 2/152nd Infantry was ordered up on the right of the London battalion. Tul Karm Station was carried and the town entered by the Londoners on the stroke of five o'clock. The three battalions captured about 800 prisoners and a dozen field guns, but this was far exceeded by the haul of the 5th L.H. Brigade. Sweeping down on to the Tul Karm–Nablus road, the brigade intercepted a swarm of fugitives streaming out of the town. These unfortunates made little resistance, and about two thousand prisoners, with 15 guns, were speedily rounded up. One column managed to break away from the main road and headed northward through Shuweike, but was pursued by part of the French Regiment,[1] which after a long chase returned next morning with several hundreds more of prisoners.

The Royal Air Force had contributed vastly to the day's great victory. Its reports of the advance had almost always been the first to reach the eyes of the Commander-in-Chief, but its most valuable service had been the spreading of destruction, death, and terror behind the enemy's lines. All the nerve-centres had been paralysed by constant bombing. El 'Affule, the junction in the Plain of Esdraelon,

---

[1] Régiment Mixte de Marche de Cavalerie, hereafter described by its official shortened title " R.M.M.C."

had been thrice raided, during the night, in early morning, and between 10 and 12 noon. The two Army headquarters at Tul Karm and Nablus had been bombed, and from the former the enemy never had any communication with Nazareth after the opening of the battle. Dreadful havoc had been caused upon the roads, especially that from Tul Karm through 'Anebta to Nablus, which was more than once blocked by smashed transport and dead horses. Twice the retreating enemy contrived to clear this road, but it was finally left an almost inextricable shambles. Over eleven tons of bombs had been dropped and 66,000 rounds fired from machine guns at ground targets.

The front of the XXI Corps ran at midnight just west of Bidya, Kh. Kefar Thilth, and 'Azzun, through Jiyus, west of Felamiye,[1] through Et Taiyibe, Irta and Tul Karm. The simile of a door swung back from the hinge at Ra-fat best describes the operation, for a line drawn from Ra-fat ridge to Tul Karm would have passed almost exactly through the heads of the columns. The whole Turkish system of defences was pierced, the whole of the enemy's right wing destroyed. Only about 7,000 prisoners and 100 guns had yet been captured, but such remnants of the two divisions in the Plain of Sharon as had escaped were mere bands of terrified fugitives pressing blindly northward. They also were doomed, for the British cavalry, advancing through the open doorway, was even now entering the passes over the Carmel range to sweep down upon and block their communications. Meanwhile, to complete the enemy's discomfiture, the XX Corps, with its limited means, had yet contrived to strike a powerful blow. To its operations we must now turn.

The Battle of Nablus.

Maps 2, 19, 20.
Sketches 30, 31.

53rd Division.[2] The Samye basin is a big depression, over three miles each way, on the eastern slope of the

---

[1] The Despatches give the line as Bidya–Kh. Kefar Thilth–Jiyus–Felamiye–Et Taiyibe " at dusk," but, in fact, only Jiyus and Et Taiyibe had been entered even by midnight.

[2] It is interesting to note that the confusing numbers of the new Indian infantry battalions in this division were abandoned in orders and that a return was made to the ancient custom of naming the battalions after their commanding officers, *e.g.* " Kidd's Battalion," " Withers's " Battalion." This method could not, however, be followed here.

ATTACK OF 53RD DIVISION

1918.
18 Sept.

Judæan ridge. At its eastern end is a steep gorge through which the river passes to the Jordan, being known after it has emerged from this gorge as the Wadi el 'Auja, often already mentioned. The British defences were on the southern rim, which was a precipitous cliff except near Rock Park; those of the enemy were pushed some distance forward down the northern slopes and cleverly placed to command the affluents running into the Wadi es Samye from the north and north-east. Major-General Mott's plan was to capture the basin and secure a position upon the comparatively flat watershed beyond by an encircling movement carried out by a brigade on either flank. On the right the 160th Brigade was to cross the river at dusk below the point where the Wye Wadi entered it, that is east of the gully-riven centre of the basin, and seize the works on Wye Hill, above the head of Wye Wadi. It was then to move northward over "Z" Hill, detaching a battalion to capture other Turkish works at Valley View from the rear, and finally to turn left along the northern edge of the basin through the village of El Mughaiyir. The assault on the Wye Hill works was to be preceded by an artillery bombardment, the signal for which was to be given by the officer commanding the leading battalion, and the time at which it began to be known as "Zero hour."[1] At a time to be notified by Major-General Mott, which would not be before Zero, the 159th Brigade was to advance on the western flank of the basin, capturing the heights known as Bidston Hill, Kew Hill, Deir Abu Sekub, and Nairn Ridge. On a red rocket being sent up as a signal that the 160th Brigade had completed its programme, the 159th was then to attack Hindhead, a hill 2,788 feet in height beyond the northern rim of the basin and dominating all the country round.

At 6.30 p.m. on the 18th the 160th Brigade (Br.-General V. L. N. Pearson) began to move to its assembly position half-way down the gorge of the Wadi Samye, where three of its battalions from Rock Park were joined by the 21st Punjabis from 2 miles to the south-east. So bright was the moonlight that the Hills of Moab could be distinctly

---

[1] If other methods of communication failed, a green rocket was to be fired, which was to be taken to mean: "Zero hour will be in ten minutes from now."

seen, yet for some time the long column winding its way down the pale hillside was not observed by the enemy. The advanced guard, the 17th Infantry, had attached to it a company of the 5/6th R. Welch Fusiliers (158th Brigade) which covered the left flank of the column by taking up positions on the right bank of the river, and later by crossing it and occupying Keen's Knoll and Table Hill. As the advanced guard moved up on to the ridge between Wye and Severn Wadis it met a gradually increasing machine-gun fire, and the enemy's artillery opened. A few small enemy posts were quickly overrun. The signal for Zero was sent at 9.52 p.m., and at 10.20, when the bombardment lifted, the 17th Infantry carried Wye Hill with little difficulty. The Cape Corps then captured " Z " Hill by midnight, and pushed forward to Square Hill, which was found to be strongly held. After a five minutes' bombardment it was taken at 4.45 a.m. on the 19th, just as dawn was breaking. Meanwhile the 21st Punjabis had turned westward and captured Valley View at 2.15 a.m., and the 7/R. Welch Fusiliers had taken all its objectives on the north side of the Samye basin by 3 a.m.

At 9.55 p.m. the 159th Brigade (Br.-General N. E. Money) received orders from divisional headquarters to begin its advance at 10.30. On its left the 3/153rd Infantry, detached from the 158th Brigade, had previously begun an attack on Fife Knoll from Ide Hill. This attack was repulsed with 61 casualties, but succeeded in its main object of pinning down the enemy at this point while the 159th Brigade broke through. The 1/153rd Infantry on the right and the 3/152nd Infantry on the left, which had assembled in concealed positions north-east of Cardiff Hill and east of Round Hill respectively, attacked and captured their first objectives, Bidston and Forfar Hills. In moving over the knoll at the northern end of Bidston Hill, known as Point 2430, towards Kew Hill and Deir Abu Sekub, the 1/153rd came under heavy machine-gun fire and had five of its British officers wounded. The only British company officers not hit were two subalterns who spoke no Hindustani, and the Indian officers did not know the details of the plan. The Adjutant, Captain O. D. Sutcliffe, who had himself been wounded, perceived the delay and hesitation, and swept forward two platoons which carried Deir Abu

Sekub. In the capture of Kew Hill the 4/5th Welch was called upon to assist, and this strong position was taken by 12.45 a.m. After the capture of Forfar Hill the 3/152nd advanced against the works on the southern end of Nairn Ridge. When the bombardment lifted the leading companies assaulted the hill, but were repulsed after heavy fighting with 85 casualties. On seeing the red rocket which announced the capture of all the 160th Brigade's objectives (except Square Hill) the 4/5th Welch sent two companies forward from Kew Hill against Hindhead, and took it, with two machine guns, at 4.40.

The preliminary operation—a model for staff work—had thus been completely successful except that the works on the southern end of Nairn Ridge had not been captured. Unfortunately these works prevented the making of a road which was of vital importance in linking up the British and Turkish systems to enable artillery to be moved forward. The road was to run up the Wadi el Kola and Forth Wadi and join the existing road east of Nairn Ridge. The 72nd Company Sappers and Miners, the Divisional Cyclist Company, and one battalion of the 158th Brigade had been put at the disposition of the C.R.E., Lieut.-Colonel H. Eustace, for this purpose. Two further attacks on Nairn Ridge having failed, Major-General Mott decided not to make another attempt until dusk. Meanwhile the road was made just fit for wheels up to Tower Wadi, between Forfar and Round Hills. Finally, at 7 p.m. Nairn Ridge was captured from the east by the 4/5th Welch and 2/153rd Infantry. At night [1] Major-General Mott issued orders for the advance to be continued to the line Majdal Beni Fadl–Qusra, with the object of blocking the Roman Road running from Majdal Beni Fadl to the Jordan at Mafid Jozele.

10th Division. The hour, and even the date, of the XX Corps' main attack was dependent upon the progress made by General Bulfin's troops. Soon after noon on the 19th General Chetwode received orders from G.H.Q. to launch it that night. He then issued orders to the 10th and 53rd Divisions to advance to their objective, the line 'Aqrabe–Jemma'in–Kefar Haris, at right angles to the Damascus Road. The 10th Division he directed to begin

---

[1] The time at which this order was issued is not marked upon it, nor is its receipt recorded by any of the brigades or by the C.R.A.

its attack at 7.45 p.m., but the hour of the 53rd Division's movement he left to the discretion of Major-General Mott, with whose troubles he was fully acquainted. He had previously sent the 387th Siege Battery R.G.A., which had been supporting the 53rd Division, across to Deir Ghussane to assist the 10th.

The problem which had to be faced by Major-General J. R. Longley, commanding the 10th Division, had certain peculiar difficulties. He desired to make his concentration as close as possible to his front line in order to keep his troops fresh for a long advance over very difficult country after the rupture of the Turkish position. On the other hand, he did not know previously whether they would have to remain twelve or thirty-six hours in their areas of concentration. That depended upon the success of the XXI Corps. A dump of five days' supplies had been formed in the Wadi Deir Ballut undetected by the enemy, artillery fire being employed to drown the noise of the lorries. Arrangements were made to feed the division for the first two days by pack transport, after which it was hoped the Damascus road would be available. One important road, 20 feet wide, was constructed—or improved from existing bridle-paths—from the junction of the Great North Road and North Circular Road near Deir en Nidham down the Wadi Rima to Berukin. Of this a small exposed portion south of Tin Hat Hill had to be left over until operations commenced. A large ammunition depot was also formed in the Wadi Deir Ballut in addition to the supplies in the battery positions for use during the first stage of operations.

The attack was to be divided into three phases. First, the 29th Brigade between Kufr 'Ain and Berukin was to breach the enemy's line by capturing the Furqa ridge from the west. Secondly, the breach was to be widened by the 29th Brigade continuing its advance to Selfit and the 31st Brigade pushing in on its left and despatching a detachment westward to capture Mogg Ridge. Thirdly, the whole division was to advance north-eastward to effect a junction with the 53rd Division attacking from the south-east. The troops destined to take part in the assault were closed up between Kufr 'Ain and Berukin, the remainder of the line being held by a battalion of the 29th Brigade at 'Arura, and one of the 30th on its left, on the right of the concentration; with a battalion from each of the 30th and 31st Brigades in the gap between Berukin and the French at Ra-fat. The 30th Brigade less two battalions was concentrated under the shelter of The Necklace, a hill between El Kufr and Berukin. The two battalions here (1/R. Irish and 1/Kashmiris) were, under the supervision of the C.R.E., to continue the road previously described up the Wadi el Mutwy in order to link it to the Turkish road system.

Zero was at 7.45 p.m., the artillery opening a quarter of an hour earlier to cover the noise of the deployment. Two battalions of the 29th Brigade (Br.-General C. L. Smith) advanced on either side of the Wadi Rashid, 1/Leinster on the right and 2/151st Infantry on the left. The attack was supported by the fire of medium trench mortars and of 28 machine guns. The 1/Leinster met with stout resistance at Follies Hill, on the western end of Furqa Ridge, and lost the barrage, which was therefore stopped. A message was sent back calling for a renewal of fire on the hill, and then, the leading waves having been reinforced, it was carried with the bayonet. The battalion then went forward and took the works covering Furqa, the village itself being captured by a company of the 2/151st Infantry. A risk was taken here in pushing on, for the British 6-inch howitzers were to have bombarded Furqa ten minutes later; but fortunately their fire was stopped in time. On the left the 2/151st Infantry had by midnight taken all its objectives on the north bank of the Wadi Rashid and had crossed the Wadi Selfit. This battalion had, in addition to capturing Furqa, sent a company across the Wadi el Mutwy, which took Kh. el Mutwy, likewise outside its own objective. The 1/101st Grenadiers, moving up through Qurawa Ibn Zeid, passed through the Leinster at Furqa, advancing on Selfit. The 54th Sikhs at 'Arura was ordered to move to a position north of Furqa with a view to continuing the advance next day. Owing to the Wadi Deir, up which this battalion was to have marched, being under heavy fire, it had to make a long detour through Qurawa Ibn Zeid, and its task had to be taken over by the 1/101st Grenadiers.

On the arrival of the 2/151st Infantry at Point 1722

on the right bank of the Wadi Rashid a mortar rocket—red-green-red—was sent up as a signal to the 31st Brigade (Br.-General E. M. Morris) to launch its attack. The 2/R. Irish Fusiliers followed by the 74th Punjabis then advanced up Topee Hill, east of Berukin. The leading battalion reached Point 1755 about 3 a.m. on the 20th. Meanwhile the Punjabis, after crossing the Wadi el Mutwy, turned westward, to find Kh. er Ras unoccupied by the enemy, and moved to the western end of Mogg Ridge.

The operations of the other divisions have been in general recorded up to midnight or shortly afterwards, by which time there was in most cases a pause. The troops of the 10th were, of course, less fatigued than those which had started at dawn, and now, divining that the enemy was everywhere breaking off the action, they pressed on in pursuit, and there was virtually no pause in the battle. Here, however, we must leave the account, to be continued in the following chapter, adding only that Selfit was occupied in the early hours of the morning, and that the Wadi el Mutwy road made such good progress that a cable wagon got through to Kh. el Mutwy by 6 a.m. All the artillery, except the 263rd Brigade R.F.A. at 'Arura, which was still in a position to support the infantry, was thus enabled to move forward.

On the 10th Division's front the enemy, who knew before the attack was launched that a disaster to his arms had occurred in the Plain of Sharon, had avoided the full force of the blow. He was now back upon a naturally strong, though unfortified, position from Iskaka, near the Damascus road, to the wooded hills about Kefar Haris. He did not, of course, know that the British cavalry was descending upon his communications in the Plain of Esdraelon, and believed that he might yet conduct his retreat in fair order if he held this and other rear-guard positions to the west with sufficient firmness. There was therefore every prospect that the morrow would bring stiffer fighting than had yet taken place.

NOTE.

THE ACTION OF THE ENEMY ON THE 19TH SEPTEMBER.

The only useful sources of information regarding events on the Turkish side on the 19th September are the memoirs of Liman von Sanders, and the war diary of the *Asia Corps*. The Army and corps records seem to have disappeared in the subsequent retreat.

The Commander-in-Chief was left completely in the dark as to the fate of the right flank of the *Eighth Army*. Telephonic, telegraphic, and wireless communication with Tul Karm ceased at 7 a.m. After 9 o'clock he learnt from the *Seventh Army* at Nablus, the message having come from the *Asia Corps* at 'Azzun, that the coast sector had been pierced and that British cavalry was advancing northward. He at once ordered Colonel von Oppen, commanding the *Asia Corps*—again through the medium of the *Seventh Army*—to attack in the direction of the Tul Karm road and railway. Oppen had already, at the request of the *Eighth Army*, ordered the German *701st Battalion* with the German cavalry squadron to move through Jiyus to Felamiye, and the reserve battalion of the Turkish *72nd Regiment* and the *19th Divisional Cavalry Squadron* to take up a position east of Qalqilye. A little later he had despatched a battalion of the *125th Regiment* to a position north of 'Azzun Ibn 'Atme. With the exception of the stout fight made by part of the *46th Division* in the Et Tire defences, it may be said that these three battalions caused the only serious difficulty met by the British XXI Corps that day.

Meanwhile the *19th Division* had evacuated its positions, even those about Jaljulye, which had not been attacked. Oppen despatched a German lieutenant, with clerks and orderlies from his headquarters, some transport-men, and a few machine guns to Kh. Kefar Thilth, with orders to rally the division there. He then began moving his baggage and guns back along the Deir Sheraf road to El Funduq, and at 6.30 p.m. withdrew his headquarters thither. He had previously issued orders for a withdrawal at dusk to a line from 2 miles west of 'Azzun, through Kh. Kefar Thilth, along the heights south of the Wadi Qana, through Deir Estia, to a junction with the *Seventh Army* at Kefar Haris. All the orders issued by Colonel von Oppen on the first day were typical of the coolness, skill, and determination which he displayed throughout the retreat.

The *Seventh Army* reported to the Commander-in-Chief that it had repulsed practically all attacks on its front, but was about to withdraw to its second-line position (through Kefar Haris and Iskaka) to conform with Oppen's retirement. Liman agreed to this decision, and ordered Mustapha Kemal to despatch the battalion of the *110th Regiment* at Nablus and any other troops he could spare to bar the Tul Karm–Nablus road at the easily defensible defile near 'Anebta. At 12.30 p.m. he directed Major Frey, Inspector General of Pioneers, to occupy the mouth of the Musmus Pass at El Lajjun, putting at his disposal all the best of the *13th Depot Regiment* at Nazareth and the military police on whom he could lay hands—a total of six companies and twelve machine guns. Meanwhile he had no notion of what had happened in the Plain of Sharon, and supposed that the troops of the *XXII Corps* were retiring before the British, whereas in fact they had ceased to exist.

CHAPTER XXIII.

THE BATTLES OF MEGIDDO (*continued*).

(Maps 1, 2, 19, 20; Sketches 32, 33.)

THE FINAL OPERATIONS OF THE XX CORPS.

1918.
20 Sept.
Maps 2, 19, 20.
Sketches 32, 33.

BEFORE recording the triumphant march of the Desert Mounted Corps, we will complete the account of the infantry attack which was to drive the enemy in Mount Ephraim into the arms of the cavalry, bearing in mind the fact that early on the morning of the 20th September the cavalry entered the Plain of Esdraelon and was attacking *Yilderim* headquarters in Nazareth at dawn. From now onwards the operations of the XX Corps can no longer be said to be subsidiary to those of the XXI; the battle will therefore be described from right to left after the general usage.

The progress of the 53rd Division was comparatively slow on the 20th. The main attack was to be carried out by the 158th Brigade (Br.-General H. A. Vernon), which was to advance northward from Hindhead on Kh. Birket el Qusr, due west of Dome. The 160th on the right was first to capture Kh. Jibeit and the hills to west of it, which overlooked the ground to be covered by the 158th Brigade, and then to move on Dome. The 159th Brigade, on the left of the 158th, was to assist it by capturing Ras et Tawil, south-west of Kh. Birket el Qusr.

The day began well with a very dashing bayonet attack by the Cape Corps, of the 160th Brigade, on Kh. Jibeit, which was stormed at 4.40 a.m., after ten minutes' bombardment by the 103rd Brigade R.G.A. The two companies holding the hill were, however, counter-attacked at 8 a.m. by a fresh battalion—of the Turkish *109th Regiment*, not previously identified on this front—and driven back to Square Hill with heavy loss, the battalion having had 13 officers hit out of the 21 who went into action. From 12.25 to 12.45 p.m. Kh. Jibeit was again bombarded,

Sketch 32. **MEGIDDO, 1918. Situation at 9 p.m. 20th Sept., 1918.**

and then recaptured by a brilliant assault carried out by
the 17th Infantry, who took 155 prisoners and 3 machine
guns, at a cost of 73 casualties. The 158th Brigade was to
have advanced at 7 a.m., but its concentration was delayed
till an hour later owing to work carried out by its battalions
on the Forth Wadi road having taken longer than was
anticipated. By 11 a.m. it had covered about half the
distance to its objective, having reached the Wadi Sebbas,
2,000 yards south of Kh. Birket el Qusr; but it had now
advanced beyond the support of the artillery and was
unable to make further progress in face of an obstinate
enemy rear guard, well provided with machine guns.
During the afternoon Major-General Mott decided that the
brigade should resume the attack under cover of darkness.
Meanwhile the 159th Brigade had been more successful, the
2/153rd Infantry taking Ras et Tawil at 3 p.m.

1918.
20 Sept.

Watson's Force, astride the Damascus road, had been
warned by General Chetwode on the evening of the 19th
that the enemy might retire on its front during the night.
At 5.30 a.m. a patrol from the Corps Cavalry Regiment
(Worcester Yeomanry) advanced up the road, reaching a
point west of Beacon Hill, a mile and a half beyond the
old British front line, before it was fired on. The regiment
then moved forward, brushed aside small rear guards on
Beacon Hill and on the other side of the road, and by
evening was at Es Sawiye, having covered $3\frac{1}{2}$ miles as the
crow flies but double that distance owing to the numerous
hairpin bends in the road. The two pioneer battalions of
Watson's Force—which was now broken up—set to work,
aided by the Egyptian Labour Corps, on the road, under
the direction of the Chief Engineer, Br.-General R. L.
Waller. The damage done by the retreating Turks was
less than had been anticipated, and evidence of their haste
and flurry was found in the shape of 78 unexploded mines.
The mobile 10th Heavy Battery and 205th Siege Battery
had been ordered in the morning to move as far up the
road as possible, and by evening were in action in the
neighbourhood of El Lubban and south of Es Sawiye.[1]

---

[1] These batteries had been, as we should say to-day, "mechanized,"
that is, the guns were drawn by four-wheel-drive lorries, and detachments
and ammunition carried in ordinary lorries. They could thus move on
the main road at 6 miles an hour, and were generally ahead of the field
artillery and even the mountain batteries.

On the front of the 10th Division, which we left following up the enemy to his new position from Iskaka to Haris, this line was found to be held in strength, with numerous machine guns, supported by three or four batteries. The 29th Brigade on the right attacked at 6.45 a.m. The 1/101st Grenadiers forced its way across the Selfit–Iskaka road, in face of a hot fire, and the 2/151st Infantry advanced beyond Kh. es Shejera, a mile north of Selfit, meeting with dogged resistance from German machine gunners. The 31st Brigade, delayed by road-making difficulties, began its advance at 8.45. The 2/42nd Deolis and 2/101st Grenadiers reached the wooded hills east of Haris and south of Kefar Haris, but were there held up. The Deolis made gallant and repeated attempts to capture the double-peaked ridge south-east of Kefar Haris at Deir el Jaly, but every rush was stopped by heavy machine-gun fire, and the battalion suffered over 150 casualties. At 3 p.m. the two brigades renewed their attacks, now supported by the fire of the LXVII and LXVIII Brigades R.F.A. The 54th Sikhs came up between the two battalions of the 29th, and by a brilliant and dashing attack carried the ridge between Points 2306 and 1939, which had been holding them up for several hours. A company of the 2/R. Irish Fusiliers on the front of the 31st moved forward to attack Kefar Haris from the west. The commanding officer of this battalion, Major A. H. Caldecott, had made a reconnaissance of the position during the morning's fighting and come to the conclusion that the best means of turning the position was to rush a company into the village of Haris. He addressed the men on top of Hill 1755, telling them that if they ran fast enough they might not be killed but if they were slow they certainly would be. They dashed down the hillside, swarmed up the opposite flank with very little loss, and took Haris with the bayonet. Kefar Haris was taken almost without opposition. At night the brigade's front ran approximately through Iskaka, Kefar Haris, and Haris; that is, along the line held that morning by the enemy.

The XX Corps had thus made a good deal of progress in most difficult country, but had not yet broken the resistance of the enemy rear guards. It seemed likely, however, that opposition would speedily crack when the

RETREAT OF THE ENEMY 499

Turks learnt what had happened in their rear. The Desert 1918.
Mounted Corps, having reached El 'Affule and Beisan, had 20 Sept.
blocked the roads leading northward and also that leading
down to the Jordan through Beisan. There remained open
three routes to the Jordan Valley from Nablus or south of
it: that through Majdal Beni Fadl, the old Roman Road
through Beit Furik, and—most important, as well as
hardest to reach—that from Nablus down the Wadi el
Far'a to the crossing at Jisr ed Damiye. General Chetwode
issued orders at 6.30 p.m. for the 53rd Division to press on
after dark and attempt to reach the Wadi el Far'a road,
while the 10th Division advanced on Nablus itself. He
had previously spoken to both divisional commanders on
the telephone, insisting on the need for resolute action to
brush aside resistance, and ordering them to push on without regard to the fatigue of men and animals, which he
fully realized. The moment demanded a great effort, and
hearts had to be steeled against suffering.

Major-General Mott, who had moved his headquarters
to Hindhead, ordered the 158th and 159th Brigades to
break through the enemy rear guards and advance to a
line from the 'Aqrabe–Majdal Beni Fadl road to Jurish—
a distance of $3\frac{1}{2}$ miles—thus cutting the first route to the
Jordan Valley. The 160th Brigade was to remain in its
present position, in order to guard the water in the Samiye
basin, on which the division now entirely depended, and
also because there were still unbroken troops in the Jordan
Valley on the right flank. Only pack mules were to accompany the brigades, the remainder of the first-line transport
standing ready to move at dawn.

At 1 a.m. on the 21st the 5/6th R. Welch Fusiliers 21 Sept.
occupied Kh. Birket el Qusr without opposition. General
Chetwode's anticipations had been correct; the enemy
had broken off the action. It was nearly dawn, however,
when the 158th Brigade reached the cross roads north-west
of Majdal Beni Fadl, by which hour the 4/5th Welch had
secured Jurish. Major-General Mott rode forward to the
cross roads south-east of Qusra, where a report centre was
established, saw the two brigadiers, and directed them to
continue the advance on 'Aqrabe, the 158th sending forward
one battalion to secure the heights at Kh. el Qerum to
north of the village. The 266th Brigade R.F.A., which had

reached Kh. Birket el Qusr, was ordered to move up east of Qusra to support the attack. On again unlimbering, a stream of fugitives was seen moving northward from 'Aqrabe towards Yanun, and the brigade, coming into action at about 6,000 yards' range, inflicted heavy losses upon them. The 3/154th Infantry, advancing without a pause on 'Aqrabe, found that few Turks had awaited its onslaught, and cleared the village with the grenade at 10.45. Kh. el Qerum was taken an hour later. A number of Turks escaped down the Roman Road through Beit Furik before the artillery could get within range of them. There was no further opposition, and by evening the 3/153rd Infantry of the 158th Brigade had occupied Beit Dejan, 10 miles north of its position on the Wadi Sebbas the previous day.

The 53rd Division was now ordered by General Chetwode to stand fast. There was no longer need for it to attempt to push on to the Wadi el Far'a road and intercept the stream of fugitives and transport pouring down towards the Jordan, since the first section of this road, between Nablus and 'Ain es Subian, had been brought under artillery fire at noon, and further down the Air Force had, as will presently appear, done terrible execution. The total casualties of the division amounted to 690, while it had captured 1,195 prisoners and 9 guns.

**1918.
20 Sept.**

The 10th Division's advance was resumed at 11.30 p.m. on the 20th by the 29th and 31st Brigades. The 30th Brigade was ordered to concentrate west of Selfit at that hour and to follow the 29th, with the object of passing through it when its right reached Quza on the Damascus road. The LXVII and LXVIII Brigades R.F.A. were both to march with the left column, as the route followed by the 29th and 30th Brigades was impassable for wheeled guns. The LXVIII was to rejoin the right column on reaching the Nablus road at Huwara. Meanwhile the Hong Kong Battery accompanied the 29th Brigade. Major-General Longley made a special appeal to his troops, demanding of them one great final effort to reach Nablus. He went himself to see Br.-General Greer, commanding the 30th Brigade, whose morning task was the most difficult of all, and urged him to make all possible haste, pointing out that risks could and must now be taken. The brigade was not to

Sketch 33. **MEGIDDO, 1918.** Situation at 9 p.m. 21st Sept., 1918.

delay in order to turn the enemy's rear guards off successive features, but rather, by pushing on and past them, to manœuvre him off.

1918.
20 Sept.

The 29th Brigade, moving on Quza, had difficulties owing to the very bad state of the road from Selfit as far as Iskaka, from the bed of which there were spikes of rock sticking up. The advance was, however, rapid, Quza being reached without opposition at 5.30 a.m. on the 21st, by which time the 31st Brigade had occupied Jemmai'n and was pushing on to Maza Abd el Haqq. At 7 a.m. on the 21st the 30th Brigade passed through the 29th at Quza, the leading elements of the 29th having already reached Huwara. From Quza to the north-east a prospect is obtained over a wide plain, in parts wooded, stretching away to the hills east of Nablus. Br.-General Greer, in the true spirit of his instructions, determined to swing slightly eastward, ignore long-range machine-gun fire either from Mount Gerizim or the heights east of the plain, and push straight forward in the direction of 'Azmut, due east of Nablus. Major-General Longley reached Quza about 8.30, in time to see the whole action unfolded: the 1/Royal Irish on the right and 38th Dogras on the left moving steadily across the plain, closely supported by the Hong Kong Battery, small parties of Turks rushing hither and thither, evidently surprised by the speed of the advance. " A " Battery LXVIII Brigade R.F.A. had come into action south of Huwara and was covering the left of the attack by shelling Mount Gerizim and the hills south of it, from which there was considerable but—to the good fortune of the Dogras—erratic and plunging machine-gun fire.

21 Sept.

As the 1/Royal Irish approached Rujib at 10 a.m., it was found that the place was held in some strength and with numerous automatic rifles. The position was outflanked from the east, and after a short fire fight a company charged, whereupon the enemy fled northwards. It seemed that the bulk of the terrified garrison would escape, for the men of the Royal Irish were almost dropping from fatigue and want of sleep; but at this moment the leading squadron of the Corps Cavalry Regiment appeared, and galloping in between the village and the main road, cut off and captured several hundreds of the fugitives. Meanwhile Major-General Longley had met Br.-General Greer and ordered him to march on Nabi Belan, 4 miles north-east of Nablus, as this appeared to be the most favourable position from which to block the Wadi el Far'a road, on which a stream of Turkish transport could be seen. At noon " A " Battery LXVIII Brigade R.F.A., which had trotted up from Huwara, and shortly afterwards the other batteries of the brigade and the 10th Heavy Battery, came into action at Sheikh Ghanun, south-west of Balata, against this road. At 5 p.m. the 38th Dogras, covered by the two batteries of the 103rd Brigade R.G.A., occupied Nabi Belan. Br.-General Smith, commanding the 29th Brigade, had followed the 30th on his own initiative, and had occupied Balata at 1 p.m.

The 10th Division had captured 1,223 prisoners and had suffered about 800 casualties in the course of two days' continuous fighting and marching amid the craggy hills and deep gulleys of Mount Ephraim. Its final effort had been magnificent, and in particular the march on Nablus deserves an honourable place in our military records. The Royal Irish and 1/Kashmir Rifles of the 30th Brigade had spent the whole night of the 19th with pick and shovel on the Wadi el Mutwy road, and in forty-eight hours individual men cannot have had more than five or six of uneasy sleep, snatched at intervals. In the last few miles it was only the driving force from above, through divisional commander, brigadier, and battalion commanders, and their own resolution, aided by the inspiration of victory, which had kept them on their feet.

At least they had no more to do that evening, for it was needless to take measures to secure the guns and transport on the Wadi el Far'a road. That was clearly so completely blocked that nothing could be got away. But it was not until officers rode forward next morning to view the scene in daylight that they realized its full significance. For two miles the narrow route was choked at intervals with the debris of the retreat. The aircraft had bombed the head of the column first, and, since there was not room for the vehicles behind to pass the block thus created, completely held it up. Guns, lorries, and hundreds of country carts were abandoned, some of them overturned and with stores of all kinds spilt about them. But it appeared that terror rather than the aircraft—which had a very difficult target in a road half-way down the side of a

BOMBING OF THE WADI EL FAR'A 503

ravine—had wrought most of the damage; for there were few signs of direct hits and fewer dead men than near 'Anebta. In one case lorries abandoned by their drivers in motion or out of control had evidently swept down on guns, and carried them and their teams in mad confusion into transport wagons in front, till an accumulation of smashed material and dead animals brought the avalanche to a halt. At a point where the road ran precariously along a ledge on the northern side of the wadi many guns and lorries had toppled over and crashed down to the stream below. It took several days to extricate about a hundred guns of all calibres in the column, and a great part of the vehicles had to be burned. The whole episode was an extraordinary testimony to the moral effect in pursuit of an arm which had been in its infancy when the war began, and was even now, when the war was drawing to an end, only in its early youth.

That really concluded the operations of the XX Corps, though on the 23rd and 24th the Corps Cavalry Regiment co-operated with the troops of the Desert Mounted Corps in clearing the hills between Nablus and Beisan, and captured about 1,500 prisoners. Several thousands more were taken by the infantry north of the Wadi el Far'a road within the next few days. Naught could have demonstrated more vividly the overwhelming nature of the victory than the scenes which were to be witnessed at any moment on those narrow tracks through the hills. From any valley might be seen emerging a single havildar, calmly stalking in front of a score of armed Turks who had surrendered to him. Fresh columns of abandoned transport were constantly being found. By night could be observed the silhouettes of Bedouin and their camels loaded with stacks of rifles moving down to the Jordan. The total captures of the corps were 6,851 prisoners, 140 guns, 1,345 machine guns and automatic rifles. The casualties amounted to 1,505.[1]

[1]	Killed.	Wounded.	Missing.
British Officers	9	32	—
Indian ,,	4	19	—
British Other Ranks	60	222	4
Indian ,, ,,	152	989	14

THE FINAL OPERATIONS OF THE XXI CORPS.

**1918.
20 Sept.**

At 8.45 p.m. on the 19th General Bulfin had issued orders for the advance to be resumed next morning not later than 5 a.m. with the following objectives :—54th Division, a line north and south through Bidya ; 3rd (Lahore) Division, a position through Beit Udhen and Qusein, commanding the Nablus–Deir Sheraf road ; 7th (Meerut) Division, Deir Sheraf, Sebustiye, and Burqa ; 60th Division a position facing generally north, on the north side of the Tul Karm–Deir Sheraf road, with right on Jebel Bir 'Asur, north-east of 'Anebta, and left at Shuweike, north of Tul Karm. The Corps Supply Depot had been established at Ras el 'Ain in the old front line, and that of G.H.Q. at Rantye before nightfall on the 19th ; and on the morning of the 20th the mechanical transport supply columns were able to move forward up the Tul Karm road. As, however, the Desert Mounted Corps was also based on Rantye, very careful arrangements and road discipline were necessary to control the movements of the great number of lorries working there and up to Tul Karm on all the services of the two corps. The camel reserve parks,[1] having refilled the divisional trains on the 19th, were employed on the 20th to bring supplies to the troops east of the Qalqilye–Tul Karm road from refilling points formed by the supply columns on that road.

At 2 a.m. on the 20th the 5th L.H. Brigade advanced from the neighbourhood of Tul Karm on 'Ajje, 6 miles north of Sebustiye, to cut the railway. Owing to the difficulties of the route it had to move north-eastward, through Deir el Ghusun and Ellar, at Fahme finding a good track leading down to the line a mile north of 'Ajje. Actually, however, only two squadrons of the 14th A.L.H. forming the advanced guard ever reached the line, cutting it with explosives. Br.-General Onslow had orders to move north on Jenin after carrying out this task. But the brigade was strung out over the whole of the route followed, certain units having been delayed as much as three hours by steep declivities, and it appeared impossible to assemble it before nightfall. The brigadier therefore decided to

---

[1] See p. 458, f.n. 2.

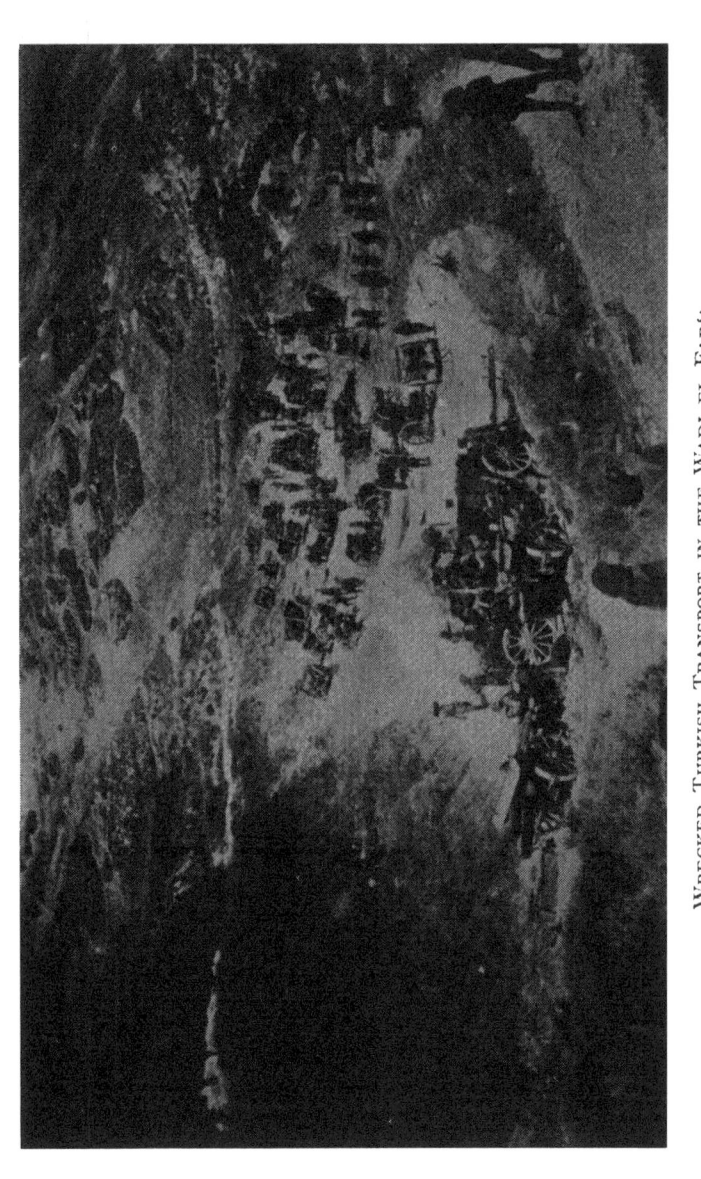

Wrecked Turkish Transport in the Wadi el Far'a.

ADVANCE INTO THE HILLS

return to Tul Karm, which he reached at 5 p.m., bringing in a number of captured stragglers.

3rd (Lahore) Division. After the 54th Division had occupied a line running from Bidya northward to the Wadi Qana and the D.F.P.S. 'Arara and Ez Zawiye on its right, the 3rd Division moved forward at 5 a.m. This division had a slice of good fortune in respect of water. There was in Hable an excellent well, on which the pump was intact, though the engine had been destroyed. A Lister engine was speedily working the German pump, enabling units to fill their camel *fanatis* at dawn, though the water did not reach the leading battalions till afternoon.

The 8th Brigade advanced astride the Wadi 'Azzun, the 1/Manchester on the south bank, the 47th Sikhs on the north, with the 59th Rifles echeloned to the right rear. Directly the piquet line was passed opposition began. The enemy had several hundred men and half a dozen machine guns south of the wadi. These troops, who were seen to be Germans, were admirably handled, and the nature of the ground suited their delaying tactics, especially as no artillery could yet support the advance. Mountain guns—even a single gun—would have been invaluable, but unfortunately the whole of the IX Mountain Artillery Brigade had been handed over to the 9th Brigade, advancing on the left through Jiyus. Progress was therefore very slow, and at 9 a.m. Br.-General Edwardes ordered the 59th Rifles to pass through the 1/Manchester and attack the ridge north-west of Kh. Kefar Thilth. 'Azzun had now been captured,[1] so that the 47th Sikhs north of the wadi were now able to give some assistance by fire, but still the enemy clung to his position, and the 59th was unable to advance beyond the line of the Manchester. Major-General Hoskins, who had ridden forward to find out the cause of the delay, sent a message to the 428th Battery, which was following the brigade, that at all costs a howitzer must be pushed forward along the Wadi 'Azzun. This howitzer first came into action a mile east of Kh. Ras et Tire, but was unable to clear the high banks of the wadi at the required range. It was then, with great boldness, brought right up along

1918
20 Sept.

---

[1] The capture of 'Azzun is claimed by both the 47th Sikhs of the 8th Brigade and the 91st Punjabis of the 7th. It appears likely that the Punjabis were first into the village.

the wadi to the left of the 59th Rifles, half-way between Kh. Kefar Thilth and 'Azzun, and came into action again at 12.30. This time the effect was instantaneous. Resistance ceased, and the advance went forward without interruption till Jinsafut was occupied at evening.

On the front of the 7th Brigade the 91st Punjabis, which had been more or less isolated since midnight, rushed before dawn a clump of trees from which desultory fire had been coming during the night, and at 5 a.m. resumed its advance on 'Azzun. The battalion was in a critical situation for nearly two hours and it was with great relief that the sound of heavy firing was heard on the right, indicating the advance of the 8th Brigade. The 27th Punjabis followed the 91st, the other two battalions moving along the Wadi 'Azzun. The 91st Punjabis entered 'Azzun at 8.10 a.m. The place had been the headquarters of the *Asia Corps*, and all about it was the camp of Colonel von Oppen's reserve. Village and camp alike had been abandoned in hot haste, and great quantities of stores of every sort were captured. A mile west of Jinsafut the 1/Connaught Rangers was ordered to pass through the 8th Brigade and secure the road junction north-east of El Funduq. Here for once the wary Oppen had not been quite quick enough, for the Connaught Rangers caught a column of artillery, held up by the fire which the 9th Brigade had brought to bear on the road further north, and captured five field guns, many horses and wagons, and some prisoners.

Meanwhile the 9th Brigade had met with little opposition, but the troops and animals suffered greatly from heat and lack of water in making their way along the rocky bed of the Wadi Sir. The broken nature of the ground and the presence of scattered bodies of Turks made necessary the protective methods of mountain warfare; and the piqueting of the heights added vastly to the fatigue of the advance. From Baqa a stream of fugitives could be seen moving along the road to Deir Sheraf. First the section of mountain artillery with the advanced guard, then the whole of the IX Mountain Artillery Brigade, came into action against this road, and with the help of machine-gun fire, completely blocked it with smashed vehicles. The 93rd Burma Infantry reached the road two miles north-east of El Funduq at 3.10 p.m. and captured about 250 prisoners,

ENEMY'S STAND AT BEIT LID

a large proportion of them Germans. A company of the 2/Dorset on the extreme left had a short engagement with a force of the enemy north of Qaryat Hajja, and captured 151 prisoners.

7th (Meerut) Division. The 7th Division advanced in two columns: on the right the 21st Brigade, with a mixed field artillery brigade of two 4·5-inch howitzer and one 18-pdr. batteries, and a machine-gun company, moving through Felamiye and Kufr Zibad; on the left the 19th Brigade, VIII Mountain Artillery Brigade, and two machine-gun companies, followed by the 28th Brigade, moving through El Majdal and Kufr Sur. The field artillery with the 21st Brigade found the track impassable beyond Kufr Zibad, and had to be sent back to rejoin the rest of the divisional artillery, which had been left at Et Tire under the orders of the 75th Division. At this point the whole brigade was compelled to halt owing to the exhaustion of the troops for lack of water. Fortunately four wells were found at Ras el Burj, where the two leading battalions, the 20th Punjabis and 1st Guides, were given a drink, the remainder of the brigade finding water at Kufr Zibad.

Meanwhile the 19th Brigade, brushing a small rear guard aside at Kufr Sur, had gone ahead, the advanced guard coming under fire at 11 a.m. a thousand yards from the village of Beit Lid. An enemy battery which shelled the column was forced by the Lewis guns of the advanced guard to limber up and withdraw, but the 125th Rifles was unable to cross the deep gully between Sefarin and Beit Lid in face of heavy machine-gun fire. Br.-General Weir was in an unpleasant quandary. His brigade had been on the move without water since 5 a.m., and only at Beit Lid could he hope to find it. He had been ordered to make El Mas'udiye Station by nightfall, and he calculated that he could only do so if he was in possession of Beit Lid by 4.30 p.m. The mountain artillery was delayed, as the mules could not be got forward till they had been watered. He decided finally to attack at 2 p.m. without awaiting the guns, under a machine-gun barrage, so that if successful he would be able to give his exhausted troops a drink and about an hour and a half's rest before continuing his advance. At that hour the attack of the 1/Seaforth was launched from the south, but was finally held up 200 yards

1918.
20 Sept.

from the village by cactus hedges, after suffering 120 casualties with a high proportion of officers. A few minutes after the beginning of the attack, Lieut.-Colonel W. S. Leslie, G.S.O.1 of the division, rode up and informed him that the 21st Brigade was approaching to co-operate against Beit Lid and that the 28th Brigade would afterwards pass through to carry out the advance on El Mas'udiye by night. He therefore had time to await the guns and to act in concert with the 21st Brigade.

Marvellous are the effects of a drink of water on parched and weary men marching beneath a hot sun. The troops of the 21st Brigade seemed to have recovered all their energy when at 1 p.m. they resumed their advance. The two brigadiers conferred at 3.45, and it was arranged that the 21st Brigade should attack Kh. ed Deir, east of Beit Lid, as the best means of assisting the 19th. The 1st Guides began their attack at 4.20, two companies quickly seizing the ridge at Kh. ed Deir and bringing Lewis-gun fire to bear on the village. At 5.30 one battery of the VIII Mountain Artillery Brigade opened fire, under cover of which the 28th Punjabis of the 19th Brigade entered Beit Lid at 6.15, clearing it with the grenade. The dogged resistance hitherto kept up in this strong position cracked immediately artillery fire—even though only of a 3·7-inch howitzer battery—was employed in support of the infantry. At 9.30 p.m. the 28th Brigade, after watering at Ras el Burj, marched out to pass through the leading brigades on its way to Mas'udiye Station and Sebustiye.

60th Division. The 179th Brigade (Br.-General E. T. Humphreys) had been, it will be remembered, in reserve on the 19th, but had not had a restful day and night. It had marched a matter of fifteen miles to Qulunsawe, where it bivouacked at 7 p.m., moved on to Tul Karm at 3 a.m., halted there for another couple of hours, and now advanced eastward on 'Anebta, with orders to seize the railway tunnel near Jebel Bir 'Asur, 2 miles north-east of the town. The 3/151st Punjab Rifles with a squadron of the Corps Cavalry Regiment, one section of machine guns, and two 4·5-inch howitzers, forming the advanced guard, speedily pushed small enemy rear guards off successive ridges, and entered 'Anebta at 11.20, capturing 66 prisoners. The 3/151st then occupied the tunnel, which was found to be intact, though preparations had been made for its demolition. The 181st Brigade had only to take up a defensive line north of the Tul Karm–'Anebta road from the right of the 179th to the village of Shuweike.

Of the 21st September there is little to be recorded. The 3rd Division continued its advance at 5 a.m., meeting with some slight opposition near Rafidia, 2,000 yards west of Nablus, and occupied a line 5½ miles long, the right near Rafidia, the left a mile and a half east of Burqa. On the front of the 7th Division the 28th Brigade, after a long march during the 20th pressed on at night, reaching the 'Anebta road near Ramin at 1.30 a.m., and capturing Mas'udiye Station at 3. The brigade pushed on in the darkness towards Sebustiye, a village on the eastern side of a table-shaped hill beneath which lie the remains of the ancient Samaria, capital of the Kings of Israel. A body of the enemy was occupying ruins excavated by archæologists before the war on the south-western slope. A company of the 53rd Sikhs, working its way up through an olive grove on the north-western side of the hill, charged this position in flank; while a platoon of the 51st Sikhs reached the crest from the south-west. The whole garrison, 181 men with 8 light and heavy machine guns, then laid down its arms. In all about 600 prisoners, two-thirds of them sick in hospital, were taken by the brigade, while at the station there were one engine and 16 trucks. The 5th Light Horse Brigade with the 2nd Light Armoured Motor Battery, moved up swiftly on the Tul Karm–Nablus road between the 7th and 60th Divisions, beat down the last resistance outside Nablus, and captured the place. The R.M.M.C., with two armoured cars, was actually the first to enter, while the 14th A.L.H. made touch with the troops of the XX Corps at Balata. The brigade then received orders to rejoin the Desert Mounted Corps at Jenin.

The XXI Corps had thus completed one of the most overwhelmingly successful operations of the war, at a cost which must, in the circumstances, be considered light. The total casualties were 3,378,[1] of whom only 446 of all

	Killed.	Wounded.	Missing.
British Officers	23	103	—
Indian ,,	11	26	—
British Other Ranks	195	876	129
Indian ,, ,,	217	1,614	184

[1] Of those reported missing it is probable that a number were evacuated

ranks were killed. The captures were about 12,000 prisoners, 149 guns, vast quantities of ammunition, countless transport wagons.[1] The whole of the Turkish *Eighth Army*, with the exception of the German and a few Turkish battalions of the *Asia Corps*, had been destroyed.

Though the resistance of the enemy had not been of the old quality, the attack remains a great achievement, whereof not the least notable aspect is the precision of the organization. The XXI Corps consisted of five strong infantry divisions and a cavalry brigade, with proportional heavy artillery, an unusually large number of troops to be fought and administered by a corps headquarters. General Bulfin in his report pays warm tribute to the capacities of the chiefs of his operations and administrative staffs, Br.-General H. F. Salt and Br.-General St. G. B. Armstrong, whose energy and accuracy had largely contributed to the victory. Not less striking is the endurance shown by the troops, perhaps especially the astonishing marching-power of the Indian infantry battalions.

Once again the supply of water had been the hinge whereon all hung. In addition to a pipe-line to Jlil, constructed before the concentration took place, a pipe 7,000 yards in length was laid by the 14th Army Troops Company R.E., working directly under the Chief Engineer of the corps, Br.-General R. P. T. Hawksley, from the mill-race near Ferrikhiye to Jaljulye, in eight and a half hours. This pipe had an output of 17,500 gallons per hour. Two water convoys, each consisting of 2,400 camels, were employed to carry water to the troops in the hills, and without them the 7th Division would not have been able to continue its advance on the 20th. Even with their aid, the leading brigade was, as we have seen, in difficulties for

---

through field ambulances without having been reported by the 22nd October, the date on which these figures were compiled.

[1] The return of prisoners and material is up to the 18th October, the date on which the 7th (Meerut) Division arrived at Beirut, and doubtless includes certain prisoners and guns taken at various points during the march north. The prisoners captured between the 19th September and the 18th October numbered 875 officers and 11,800 other ranks (a total of 12,675). One hundred and forty-nine guns, 182 machine guns, 105 automatic rifles, 11 trench mortars, 3 engines, 56 railway wagons, were taken during the same period. It is possible that in some cases prisoners taken by the three corps were counted over twice. The only completely reliable figures are the final ones furnished by G.H.Q., which will be given later.

want of water, and Beit Lid would hardly have been taken that night had not the other brigades discovered local wells.

NOTE.

THE ACTION OF THE ENEMY ON THE 20TH AND 21ST SEPTEMBER.

The attack of the British cavalry on Nazareth, which will be described in the next chapter, put Liman and the staff of *Yilderim* entirely out of action on the 20th until late in the afternoon, and left the three Army commanders without orders. Jemal, at 'Amman, lost a fair chance of escape in hopes of saving the troops of the *II Corps* at Ma'an ; the other two did all they could to extricate themselves from the net.

At 11.45 a.m. Colonel von Oppen, who had lost 'Azzun but was stubbornly disputing the progress of the British 3rd and 7th Divisions, received orders from the *Eighth Army* to fall back to a line from Beit Lid, 3½ miles W.N.W. of Deir Sheraf, to Ferata, 4¼ miles S.S.W. of Deir Sheraf. The object of taking up this position was to cover the junction of the roads from Tul Karm and El Funduq with the Damascus road as long as possible. The order went on that the retreat must be continued up the Damascus road to Silet edh Dhahr, 2½ miles north of Mas'udiye Station, that evening. The best troops were to march at the head of the column, and all baggage which could not be taken was to be destroyed. Jevad announced that he had established his headquarters at Mas'udiye Station.

Colonel von Oppen was not hopeful that he would be able to make his way up the Damascus road, as he felt pretty sure that the British would be beforehand with him. However, whichever way he went, the first part of the order must be obeyed. He therefore ordered the German troops to fall back on Deir Sheraf, leaving rear guards from the *16th* and *19th Divisions* on either side of the El Funduq–Deir Sheraf road. In the afternoon Jevad was brought round to his opinion by the advance of the British 60th Division through 'Anebta. The *Asia Corps* was now ordered to bivouac in the neighbourhood of Balata, preparatory to continuing its march down the Wadi el Far'a road next day. It was to turn north-east at 'Ain Shible, south-east of Tammun, and move on Beisan. Touch was not obtained by the Group headquarters that night with the remnants of the *16th* and *19th Divisions*. Oppen was called upon during the night to send his German troops back to Deir Sheraf to cover the *Seventh Army*, now passing northward, but with some reason refused to obey this order.

On the morning of the 21st the *Asia Corps* was reorganized. The remnants of the *702nd* and *703rd Battalions* were formed into one battalion consisting of one rifle company, one machine-gun company, and the trench-mortar detachment. The *701st Battalion* and cavalry squadron, which had suffered less, retained their individuality. Oppen discovered that the *16th* and *19th Divisions* had been placed by the direct orders of the Commander-in-Chief west of Nablus during the night and found touch with them. At 10 a.m. he learnt that the enemy was close on Nablus and that the upper part of the Wadi el Far'a road was blocked. He decided then to move by Beit Dejan, 7 miles E.S.E. of Nablus, down to the Jordan at Jisr ed Damiye, but hardly had he made up his mind to this than he found that route also cut by the advance of the British XX Corps. He was almost trapped. He now ordered the German troops to make their way north over Mount Ebal. The column came under fire from British artillery, but escaped with little loss, the German troops bivouacking that night at Tammun, and the remains of the *16th* and *19th Divisions* at Tubas. It was certainly a brilliant feat to have extricated these troops, even though all the baggage and almost all the guns were lost. Colonel von Oppen did not, however, yet realize how far he was from being out of the wood or that the British cavalry was already in Beisan.

The bulk of the *Seventh Army* appears to have taken the Wadi el Far'a road, in which it lost its guns and transport as has been recorded, and to have turned northward at 'Ain Shible, moving on Beisan by the road on which Colonel von Oppen would have followed it had he been in time to do so. It likewise suffered heavily from attacks by aircraft, and as we have seen, 1,500 stragglers were rounded up by the XX Corps Cavalry on the 23rd and 24th. Some units, perhaps the whole of the *53rd Division*, kept straight on down the Wadi el Far'a road to Jisr ed Damiye, but, as will be shown in Chapter XXV, the greater number of these were intercepted and either captured or forced to turn back by Chaytor's Force in the Jordan Valley on the 22nd. Other units, but chiefly stragglers and such remnants as there were of the *XXII Corps*, had taken the main Damascus road on the morning of the 20th, to fall into the hands of the Australian Mounted Division at Jenin that night.

CHAPTER XXIV.

THE INRUPTION OF THE DESERT MOUNTED CORPS.

(Maps 1, 2, 2A, 19, 20, 21; Sketches 30, 31, 32, 33, 34, 35, 36, 37.)

THE 4TH CAVALRY DIVISION.

THE task of the Desert Mounted Corps was, in brief, to capture El 'Affule in the Plain of Esdraelon and Beisan in the Valley of Jezreel. At El 'Affule the cavalry would cut the enemy's railway communications at the most vital point and block the Damascus road; at Beisan it would block the tracks from 'Ain es Subian and 'Ain Shible, and would also be in a position to strike at the enemy's columns if they attempted to cross the Jordan. 1918. 19 Sept. Maps 2A, 19, 20. Sketch 30.

The 4th and 5th Cavalry Divisions, as soon as the door had been opened for them by the XXI Corps, were to advance northward to a line from Qaqun and Jelame, on the Haifa road, through Tell edh Dhrur and Liktera to the sea: 4th on the right, 5th on the left. The 4th Division was then to ride through the Musmus Pass on El 'Affule, where it was to cut the railway. A detachment was to be sent to seize the bridges over the Jordan and Yarmuk at Jisr el Majami', and the main body to advance on Beisan. The 5th Cavalry Division was to march northward by way of Liktera and Zerganiya, to Abu Shushe, where it was to send a detachment to Nazareth and to be prepared to "operate towards Jenin and Beisan according to circum-"stances." The Australian Mounted Division, less the 5th L.H. Brigade, was to follow the 4th Division as corps reserve, and to be prepared to detach a brigade from El Lajjun to block the Damascus road and railway at Jenin.[1]

The 4th Cavalry Division, to which the 11th Light Armoured Motor Battery and 1st Light Car Patrol were attached, left its bivouac in the Selme–Sarona area between 4 and 4.30 a.m. At the 'Auja horses were watered, the

---

[1] Desert Mounted Corps Operation Order No. 21 is given in Appendix 26.

troughs used being afterwards packed into the wagons. The brigades then moved at a walk to their assembly positions south-east of Jlil. Here they unsaddled and fed their horses. A pioneer party furnished by the division had reached the front line at 7 a.m., and owing to the rapid progress of the 7th (Meerut) Division, was able at once to go forward to cut a gap and flag a path through the Turkish wire. Major-General Barrow, whose anxiety to obtain a quick start we have already noticed, rode into the captured position, met Major-General Fane, commanding the 7th Division, in Tabsor at 8.40, and obtained from him permission to go through. Meanwhile the 11th Cavalry Brigade (Br.-General C. L. Gregory) had moved through the British lines. The divisional commander, hastening back from Tabsor, met the head of the brigade within a hundred yards of the gap, and ordered it forward. Jacob's Horse, which formed the advanced guard, entered the gap at 8.58, followed by the whole division, the three horse artillery batteries, which had been engaged in the bombardment, joining the column as it passed.

There was no opposition. The great column streamed northward without even its vanguard being checked. For once, it seemed, the clock had been put back, and warfare had recovered in this splendid spectacle the pageantry whereof long-range weapons had robbed it. The hearts of all were high as they realized that the plan was unfolding perfectly. The two divisions were moving on parallel lines to the enemy's new flank and within a few hours would be behind him. On the right there were tempting opportunities for cavalry action, but the main objective was all that mattered now.

By 11.15 all three brigades had passed the Zerqiye crossing, and by 1 p.m. were on a line from Burj el 'Atot to Mughaiyir. After an hour's halt the division moved on, now in three brigade columns in echelon from the left: 12th Brigade (Br.-General J. T. Wigan) on the right, 10th Brigade (Br.-General R. G. Howard-Vyse) in the centre, 11th Brigade on the left. The right brigade advanced straight on Jelame; the other two crossed the edge of the Iskanderune marshes at Shellalif, being confronted soon afterwards by the rudimentary third-line of defences from Qaqun to the mouth of the Nahr Iskanderune. These trenches were garrisoned by the *Eighth Army Depot Regiment*, which may almost be excused its sudden panic at sight of the whole plain alive with cavalry twelve miles behind the Turkish line of the morning. At all events the spectacle was too much for the nerves of these troops, who fled towards Qaqun. Promptly the right flank squadron of Jacob's Horse dashed forward, and within a few minutes captured 126 prisoners. Pushing on to Tell edh Dhrur, the regiment took another 80 prisoners, and was there rejoined by the remainder of the brigade, which halted at 4.30 p.m. to water. A few minutes later the 12th Brigade reached Jelame, on the railway north of Qaqun, where water in plenty was found. The Dorset Yeomanry of the 10th Brigade had moved east of the railway to Jett, but reported that there were only a couple of small wells there. Br.-General Howard-Vyse therefore decided to ride straight on to Kerkur, $3\frac{1}{2}$ miles north-east of Tell edh Dhrur, pushing forward the 2nd Lancers as advanced guard and leaving the Dorsets to follow. He subsequently sent his brigade major to catch up the 2nd Lancers with orders for the regiment to move up the Wadi 'Ara after watering, with the 11th Light Armoured Motor Battery, and occupy Kh. 'Ara, 5 miles north-east of Kerkur and approximately a third of the way through the pass. The main body of the brigade reached Kerkur at 8.30 p.m., and began watering its horses to the north-east. The 11th Brigade arrived at Kerkur at 9.15; the 12th, which had watered at Jelame, at 10. Perhaps two-thirds of the horses had been watered since leaving the 'Auja.

At 9.40 p.m. Major-General Barrow came up to the 10th Brigade's headquarters near Kerkur. He learned from Br.-General Howard-Vyse that, owing to the very slow process of watering, the brigade was not moving on again till 11.30. He told the brigadier that, whether or not watering was completed, he must march by 11 at latest. He then decided to motor forward with his G.S.O.1, Lieut.-Colonel W. J. Foster, and direct the 2nd Lancers to push right through the pass to El Lajjun, so as to secure the division against the chance of having its progress interrupted in the reputedly difficult defiles beyond Kh. 'Ara.

*   *   *   *   *

Maps 1, 21.   The Musmus Pass follows the Wadi 'Ara up the southern flank of the Samarian Hills. The stream itself is a mere rut, but the valley is about three hundred yards in width, and at first quite smooth. Beyond Kh. 'Ara and 'Arara, which face one another from the slopes on either side of the wadi, the walls of the valley begin to draw in, though for several miles its surface is still level. By the time Musmus, near the watershed, is reached it becomes, however, very narrow; and after a descent of about a mile there is another steep ridge to be climbed. Here the path is rough and in places on naked rock, but had been improved by the enemy during the war. At El Lajjun, the mouth of the pass, hard by the mound of Tell el Mutesellim or Megiddo, a magnificent spectacle is unfolded. From this point of vantage the Plain of Esdraelon three or four hundred feet below lies like a smooth green cloth. Beyond it is the wall of the Galilean Hills, with the white houses of Nazareth, ten miles away, visible near the top. In the centre of the plain is El 'Affule, to-day with colonies sprawling out from it to draw sustenance from this rich soil. As one looks over the town to the north-east, first sharp-peaked Little Hermon, then dome-topped Tabor come into the line of the vision. Between them lies Endor with its haunted caves. Due east, on a low spur of Mount Gilboa, is Zir'in, a poor hamlet immortal as the Jezreel of Ahab, Jezebel, and Jehu.

The hill country to the north is associated with the peaceful youth of Christ, but the whole district, and especially the plain, has a long tradition of blood and battle. Skilled captains, highly-trained and well-equipped armies were matched there when Flanders, that other great cockpit of the world, was a swamp inhabited by savages. The Musmus Pass itself was used by Pharaoh Thothmes III, who won a great victory at Megiddo over the rebel King of Kadesh (Homs),[1] and by Vespasian. At Gilboa Saul was

---

[1] The strategy of Thothmes is of interest owing to a certain similarity between his situation and that of Sir Edmund Allenby nearly 3,400 years later. Thothmes, arriving at Yehem (probably in the Wadi Yahmar, about five miles east of Kerkur), held a council of war. "The wretched "enemy," he explained to his captains, "has come and has entered Megiddo; "he is there at this moment." The Syrians, in fact, lay between this place and T'ennik, 4½ miles to the south-east, in a position to move quickly to bar the King's way whether he advanced up the Plain of

Wadi 'Ara: Entrance to the Musmus Pass.

overthrown by the Philistines ; at Jezreel Jehu extinguished the House of Omri ; at Megiddo again Josiah was defeated and slain by Pharaoh-necho of Egypt. Look forward another fifteen hundred years or so, during which the plain saw the passage of many armies, and there is another battle at the same spot in 940 A.D., when the Viceroy of Egypt, Mohammed the Ikshid, was stopped on his road to recover Damascus by the rebel Ibn Raik. Two hundred and fifty years later Saladin overthrew the Army of the Latin Kingdom of Jerusalem at the Horns of Hattin, off the road from Nazareth to Tiberias. In less than another hundred years the Mongols, most terrible of all invaders, poured up the Valley of Jezreel, to be met on the eastern slope of the Jezreel spur at 'Ain Jalud by the Mameluke Sultan Kutuz, and hurled back into the Ghor. About six miles west of Mount Tabor, Kléber was completely surrounded by a Damascene Army twenty times his own strength, and formed square amid the smoke and flames of burning corn till Napoleon, hurrying up from his lines in front of Acre, fell unawares upon the attackers and routed them utterly.

Such were the memories of the region wherein the British cavalry was about to set the crown upon the latest great victory in these long records. In truth it must have

---

Dothan or by the coast road. They were also well placed to block the Musmus Pass, but apparently did not expect the King to use this track. When Thothmes told his captains that he intended to do so they were horrified. "How," they asked, "are we to advance on this narrow " path ? The enemy will await us there and can hold the pass against " a multitude. Will not horse come behind horse and man behind man " likewise ? Shall our van be fighting while our rear is still standing in " Aruna ['Arara] unable to fight ? " They urged the King to use either of the other roads, but not " this difficult path." Thothmes would not be baulked of his project, and himself led the vanguard swiftly and without opposition through the pass, though the main body was attacked by the people of 'Arara. The Syrians, like the Turks, failed to block the pass, and the King was able to draw up his army in battle array the same night. On the following day he completely routed the enemy, but his men wasted time in plundering and allowed many fugitives to be hauled up by ropes into the fortress of Megiddo. " Had not His Majesty's " soldiers given their hearts to plundering the enemy's possessions, they " would have taken Megiddo at this moment, when the wretched foe of " Kadesh and the wretched foe of this town were being hauled up in " haste in order to bring them into this city." Criticism so strong is not always permitted to official historians. However, the place was invested, and finally surrendered, the booty including 924 chariots, some of them wrought with gold, and large herds of animals. (From " Ancient History of the Near East," by H. R. Hall.)

seemed to the imaginative that the ghosts of many warriors accompanied them on their ride that night and next morning. The most dramatic of all the scenes, though it was not that of a battle, appealed with particular force at this moment to a great English poet, Thomas Hardy, who painted it a few days later with appropriate grimness.

Did they catch as it were in a Vision at shut of the day—
  When their cavalry smote through the ancient Esdraelon Plain,
And they crossed where the Tishbite stood forth in his enemy's way—
  His gaunt mournful Shade as he bade the King haste off amain?

On war-men at this end of time—even on Englishmen's eyes—
  Who slay with their arms of new might in that long-ago place,
Flashed he who drove furiously? . . . Ah, did the phantom arise
  Of that queen, of that proud Tyrian woman who painted her face?

Faintly marked they the words "Throw her down!" rise from Night eerily,
  Spectre-spots of the blood of her body on some rotten wall?
And the thin note of pity that came: "A king's daughter is she,"
  As they passed where she trodden was once by the chargers' footfall?

Could such be the hauntings of men of to-day, at the cease
  Of pursuit, at the dusk-hour, ere slumber their senses could seal?
Enghosted seers, kings,—one on horseback who asked "Is it peace?" . . .
  Yea, strange things and spectral may men have beheld in Jezreel!

* * * * *

Maps 2A, 21. Sketches 31, 32.

The 2nd Lancers, marching without piqueting the heights, reached Kh. 'Ara at 11 p.m., having met with no opposition, but having overtaken and stopped a long column of Turkish transport and captured about two hundred unresisting men. As Major-General Barrow passed up he saw the horses and bullocks still standing patiently in the traces. He reached the advanced guard at 11.45 and ordered Captain D. S. Davison, commanding the Lancers,[1] to push on forthwith to El Lajjun. The light armoured cars in front, the advance was continued without opposition and El Lajjun reached at 3.30 a.m. on the 20th. About a hundred Turks, possibly the advanced guard to the force sent to hold the mouth of the pass, were found sitting round fires, with arms piled.

Major-General Barrow meanwhile went back down the valley to meet the main body of the 10th Brigade, but on reaching the exit found to his consternation that there

---

[1] Captain Davison was in command owing to the illness of Lieut.-Colonel G. Knowles and Major K. Robertson. Major G. Gould joined from the United Kingdom on the 23rd and took over command.

ACTION OF 2ND LANCERS

was no sign of it. Being informed that it had missed its 1918. way, he despatched Lieut.-Colonel Foster in the car to find 19 Sept. it. After what seemed to the divisional commander an interminable delay his staff officer came back on horseback to report that the brigade was now swinging eastward to reach the pass, but that it had moved some five miles due northward on the wrong road, followed by the 11th Brigade. Lieut.-Colonel Foster was so exhausted that Major-General Barrow had to leave him to recover and take his horse.

The general rode back alone, met the 12th Brigade— which was to have been the rear brigade through the pass— and ordered it to take the place of the 10th, at the same time putting the 2nd Lancers under the orders of Br.-General Wigan. The 10th Brigade's guide had in fact failed it, and it had gone astray.[1]

It was 1.10 a.m. on the 20th when the 6th Cavalry, 20 Sept. advanced guard to the 12th Brigade, moved out from Kerkur, the delay thus being two hours and ten minutes.[2] The advanced guard, trotting twenty minutes, walking twenty, and halting five, arrived at El Lajjun at 4.5 a.m., the remainder of the brigade soon afterwards. At 5.30 the 2nd Lancers, which had meanwhile watered, fed, and breakfasted, advanced on El 'Affule on a three-squadron front, followed by the 11th Light Armoured Car Battery and a subsection of the 17th Machine-Gun Squadron. Within about ten minutes the centre squadron came under fire, and it was evident that a considerable enemy force, having failed to reach the Musmus Pass in time, had taken up a position in the plain and intended to prevent the cavalry from debouching. Captain Davison directed this squadron with the machine guns and armoured cars to engage the enemy frontally, and sent the reserve squadron round to

---

[1] The lesson of this incident, by no means new, is that connecting files are a better assurance than guides. On the other hand the officer commanding the 2nd Lancers no doubt held himself absolved from the responsibility of dropping files to guide the brigade, as he had been told that it would not leave Kerkur until his report from Kh. 'Ara was received, and so might hold that his regiment was acting temporarily as a detachment. But it may perhaps be said that no precautions which can be taken in such a case are superfluous.

[2] That is, from the hour at which the divisional commander had ordered the 10th Brigade to march, which order, of course, cancelled the arrangement that the brigade should await the report of the 2nd Lancers before moving.

the right where it had the advantage of a slight depression, to charge him in flank. While it was making its detour the officer commanding the squadron originally on the right saw what was happening and at once decided to co-operate with it. It was fortunate that he did so, for the enemy was found to be in two lines, one behind the other, which were attacked almost simultaneously by the two squadrons. The enemy kept three machine guns in action until the last moment, but the men serving them were unnerved by the pace of the cavalry, and their fire was high. The charge was driven home, and resulted in the complete rout of the Turks. Forty-six were speared and the remaining 470 captured, hardly a single man escaping. The Lancers had only one man wounded and twelve horses killed. The Turkish force was the *13th Depot Regiment* which Marshal Liman had ordered out from Nazareth at 12.30 p.m. on the 19th to occupy the pass. From Nazareth to El Lajjun is 15 miles by road, so that the delay of this force was as incomprehensible as disastrous.[1]

Within forty minutes of the opening of this brilliant if fortunate little operation the Lancers were on the move again. At 7.45 a.m. they came under fire from El 'Affule at a range of half a mile, but by the time the left-flank squadron had swung round the village and galloped in from the north, resistance had ceased, the station having been already taken by the Deccan Horse of the 5th Cavalry Division and the road to Nazareth seized by the Poona Horse. About 75 Germans and 200 Turks were taken here, while there were ten engines and fifty trucks in the sidings. Three aeroplanes were captured on the aerodrome, a fourth rising just in time to escape. A little later another machine landed. Suddenly realizing that the place was occupied by the British, the pilot and observer opened fire, but were at once shot down, and the machine taken intact with its cargo of mailbags from the north. The armoured cars pursued a dozen German lorries towards Beisan and captured them all. The railway lines running south and east from El 'Affule were then cut, that running west having

---

[1] Liman, to his great and justifiable surprise, found Major Frey, the commander of the detachment, in Samakh on the evening of the 20th, and was informed by him that the British cavalry had reached the mouth of the pass before he could occupy it. (Liman, p. 349.)

The Valley of Jezreel from Zir'in: Gilboa in Foreground.

been cut at 3 a.m. by the 13th Cavalry Brigade of the 5th Cavalry Division.

After allowing time for the remainder of the fighting troops to reach El 'Affule, Major-General Barrow gave orders for the advance to continue on Beisan. The 19th Lancers of the 12th Brigade was left at El 'Affule with orders to march that evening on Jisr el Majami', 9 miles N.N.E. of Beisan, seize the railway bridges, and prepare them for demolition.

The division moved out from El 'Affule at 1 p.m., led by the 10th Cavalry Brigade, of which Lieut.-Colonel W. G. K. Green, Jacob's Horse, had now assumed command. On the march to Beisan some hundreds of prisoners, the first trickle of the great stream of fugitives making its way north from Mount Ephraim, were captured. Only a show of opposition was met as the column moved down the railway line, through Shatta, into Beisan, where about a hundred prisoners and three 150-mm. howitzers—their muzzles turned *eastward*, it may be noted—were taken. The division was concentrated here by 6 p.m., and a line of piquets was put out as far as El 'Affule. Another 700 prisoners were rounded up during the night.

The 4th Cavalry Division after five night approach marches had covered 70 miles in 34 hours.[1] Only 26 horses had been lost, but all were now somewhat distressed, those of the batteries—which had started with the heavy pedrails on the gun-wheels but had abandoned them before reaching the Musmus Pass—in particular. Had any exertion equal to that of the last two been called for on the following day, doubtless a great number would have been foundered. But for this there was fortunately no need. The task originally set to the division was fulfilled, and the road north denied to the enemy. Except those of the 19th Lancers, the horses now had a chance to rest. The transport was over fifty miles behind. " A " and " B " Echelons, the Train, and Ammunition Column bivouacked on the night of the 19th with the Rear headquarters at Shellalif or further

---

[1] The divisional records give the distance as greater. It is important to risk no exaggeration on a point so interesting and vital as the marching powers of a cavalry division. The distance has been measured with a wheel and a small allowance made for windings in the tracks not shown on comparatively small-scale maps. The calculation agrees with that made by Colonel Rex Osborne in the " Cavalry Journal."

south. The special camel convoy¹ could not keep up, and its rations were returned for use elsewhere. By the evening of the 20th "A" Echelon and the Ammunition Column were at Kerkur, "B" Echelon and the Train at Qaqun. Rations were delivered by motor lorry at El 'Affule *via* the Musmus Pass on the evening of the 20th; but, as it was unsafe to send the lorries on to Beisan and the division had no means of collecting these supplies, the second of the two days' special emergency ration carried in a sandbag on each man's saddle was consumed. The lorries were able to deliver to Beisan on the 21st.

The 19th Lancers, with a section of the 18th Machine-Gun Company and a party of the 4th Field Squadron R.E., moved out from El 'Affule at 7.30 p.m., and after a very arduous all-night march of about twenty miles over rough and stony country reached Jisr el Majami' at 5 a.m. on the 21st. The few troops holding the railway at this point decamped in haste. Charges were placed in the bridge over the Jordan and also in that over the Yarmuk to the north, but were not exploded, as the line might soon be required by the British. Rails were picked up on the left bank of the Jordan and the right bank of the Yarmuk, and the detachment sat down to block the one communication between the Hejaz Railway and the Palestine system.

THE 5TH CAVALRY DIVISION.

1918.
19 Sept.
Maps 2A,
19, 20.
Sketch 30.

The 5th Cavalry Division, with " B " Battery H.A.C.,² the 12th Light Armoured Motor Battery, and 7th Light Car Patrol attached, had not so much ground to cover before entering the Turkish lines as the 4th, because it had marched to its position of readiness after dusk on the 18th. The head of the advanced guard, which consisted of the 13th Brigade (Br.-General P. J. V. Kelly) and the armoured car battery, was just south of Arsuf, on the beach. Major-General Macandrew was informed at 7 a.m. by Major-General Shea, commanding the 60th Division, that there

---

¹ For the proportions of supplies carried by " B " Echelon, the Train, and the camel convoy, see footnote, p. 458.

² It will be recalled that on formation there was only one battery, the Essex, to allot to this division. " B " Battery H.A.C. had accordingly been detached from the Australian Mounted Division.

ADVANCE TO NAHR ISKANDERUNE

was no longer any shelling on the beach south of the Nahr el Faliq, and that in his opinion the cavalry could now move up to the river.

Hodson's Horse, the leading regiment of the 13th Brigade, went forward at the trot along the beach and reached the Nahr el Faliq an hour later, the horses being somewhat blown by their rapid progress through the soft sand. Brushing aside a small party of the enemy, the regiment wheeled right-handed to the coast road. At this moment an aeroplane of No. 113 Squadron R.A.F. dropped a message that the large orchard east of Basse el Hindi appeared to be held by about two hundred infantry. The leading squadron, without waiting for covering fire, attacked at once, was met by wild fire, and captured the orchard, with about sixty prisoners, two guns, and a dozen wagons, for a loss of two men wounded and one man killed. Another isolated machine gun in action was captured a little further north. On approaching Mukhalid, a Turkish troop was seen to occupy some trenches on a hill 300 yards north of the village. The leading troop of Hodson's Horse kept straight on to outflank the position; two troops shook out and charged it; and the Turks promptly put up their hands. Another enemy troop holding the crossing of the Nahr Iskanderune took to flight when outflanked, and the regiment rode over the river at 10.15 a.m. Liktera was reached at 11, about fifty prisoners being taken here.

The brigade had now covered upwards of twenty-five miles, and was an hour ahead of its time-table. It would seem that the pace set by Hodson's Horse had been unduly hot, and that, though the eagerness which produced it was comprehensible, greater consideration for the horses would at this early stage have been advisable. At all events, the horses of the regiment were already fatigued, and a number of them—for the most part remounts recently issued—unfit for further use. Those of the remainder of the brigade had suffered less, but were also showing signs of distress.[1]

---

[1] Before the 13th Brigade moved on again the 18th Lancers destroyed five horses, and had to leave behind ten others. The number left behind by Hodson's Horse is not recorded, but was almost certainly greater than this. Major-General Macandrew watched the start of the brigade, and when he saw how fast it was going galloped after it in hopes of steadying it, but was unable to catch it.

Major-General Macandrew reported to General Chauvel that he did not propose to march again until 6.15 p.m. The division closed up on Liktera, where there were fairly good wells, watered, and fed. Orders were issued for the 13th and 14th Brigades to resume the advance at the hour mentioned, without wheeled vehicles. The 15th Brigade was to bring on the artillery and " fighting wheels " next morning; while the Mysore Lancers was to await the arrival of the remaining transport, which was in difficulties several miles in rear.

The 13th Brigade, with the 18th Lancers now acting as advanced guard, followed a fair road northward to Ez Zerganiya, 3½ miles north-west of Kerkur, then turned off on to a track which led into the pass following the bed of the Wadi Qudrah. North of the village of Subbarin in the hills, it turned eastward from Napoleon's route, which it had so far followed, moved along the Wadi el Fuwar, and reached J'ara, on the northern side of the watershed, at 1 a.m. on the 20th. Br.-General Kelly, who spoke Arabic, himself led the vanguard. He had picked up a native who knew something of the country and got further information from others met on his way. The tracks followed were bad at best, and at worst almost indistinguishable even in the bright moonlight. The greater part of the ride through the hills was carried out in single file. Silent and gaping with astonishment, a few villagers watched the long column pass. At J'ara two squadrons of Hodson's Horse were dropped to prevent the enemy sending down troops from the direction of Haifa to block the passage of the 4th Cavalry Division through the Musmus Pass. It would perhaps have been a better arrangement to have found this protective detachment from the 14th Brigade in rear, for, as was soon to be proved, the 13th Brigade had need of every man.

The head of the brigade reached Abu Shushe at 2.15 a.m. So far, not a Turk had been seen since reaching Liktera but for a party of nine men surprised and captured at Subarin. There was a short halt in the Plain of Esdraelon to allow the column to close up; then it moved on, and at 3 reached the Haifa–El 'Affule railway, in which the field squadron R.E. blew a breach one hundred yards long north-west of El Waraqani. Half an hour later the 18th

ATTACK ON NAZARETH

Lancers approached a village which the guide declared to be Nazareth. The brigadier was doubtful whether this was so, but ordered the place to be seized. The 18th Lancers quickly rounded up some two hundred sleeping Turks without loss.

1918. 20 Sept.

Before the village had been cleared Br.-General Kelly realized that this could not possibly be Nazareth. It was, in fact, El Mujeidil, 3½ miles as the crow flies to the south-west. The Gloucester Hussars, which had been somewhat delayed by losing touch with the tail of the leading regiment in the darkness, was ordered to move on Nazareth as advanced guard to the brigade. The horses, after their tremendous exertions, showed their endurance and staunchness by going forward at a sharp trot. The regiment was followed by one squadron and three troops of the 18th Lancers—the remainder being still engaged in collecting prisoners at El Mujeidil—and one squadron of Hodson's Horse, the fourth squadron of this regiment having also gone astray in the darkness. Two more troops of the Lancers stopped to clear the village of Yafa. It was therefore a weak as well as a very weary brigade which reached the outskirts of the town at 4.30 a.m. The 14th Cavalry Brigade, which followed it, got astride the El 'Affule–Nazareth road about an hour later, and at 7.15 the Deccan Horse, after charging a body of the enemy, took El 'Affule Station with nearly three hundred prisoners.

Nazareth has a population of 15,000 and is for its size probably the best-built town in Palestine. It lies at the bottom and on the sides of a cup-like depression in the hills, these sides being so steep that in places the roofs of the houses seem to form a giant stairway. The whole town is dominated by several buildings on the top of the hill to the north-west. The roads from El 'Affule and Haifa, which wind up the hillside in fantastic and dangerous loops, join three-quarters of a mile south of the town proper, but from about this point houses run almost continuously along both sides of the road. There is a large tourist hotel, then known as the Hotel Germania, on the left of the road, and five hundred yards further on, facing the great Latin Monastery, is the Casa Nuova, a hospice in which the main offices of G.H.Q. were established.

The leading troop of the Gloucester Hussars drew

swords and galloped straight up the main road, looking for the house of Marshal Liman von Sanders. Unfortunately, although Br.-General Kelly had made urgent application for a guide who knew the town, none had been found for him. The inhabitants, recalling grisly tales of British sympathizers strung up in rows after the evacuation of Es Salt, were terrified to be seen speaking to the assailants, and would give no reliable information. Several houses were visited, but the Commander-in-Chief was not found, and an erroneous report was received that he had left the place the previous night. At the Hotel Germania, the *casino* or mess of headquarters and the sleeping-place of many officers and clerks, a great number of prisoners were taken. A mass of documents was found in neighbouring houses used as offices, but the general staff office in the Casa Nuova was never reached. It is, indeed, owing to the fact that the enemy burned the majority of his papers in this place that the history of the campaign from his side is so difficult to reconstruct.

Within a few minutes street fighting began. Machine guns opened from the buildings on the high ground, while German clerks and orderlies boldly fired down upon the troops from balconies and windows. It was extraordinarily difficult to move in the roadway, choked by a column of German lorries, which had been parked about the road junction facing southward and had been captured while trying to turn, and by a mob of prisoners, who had to be disarmed and passed back down the hill. Br.-General Kelly's object was to force his way either through or round the town in order to block the Acre and Tiberias roads on the northern side. The Gloucester Hussars had driven the enemy off the hill north-west of the cross roads, but, far from making further progress, had now some difficulty in holding its own. At 8 a.m. a squadron and a troop of the 18th Lancers came up on the left of the Yeomanry, and a little later this position was strengthened by the squadron of Hodson's Horse. The enemy counter-attacked boldly, and a body of German clerks displayed a desperate bravery which won the admiration of the British, being almost annihilated by machine-gun fire before it would desist from its attacks. All the efforts of the enemy— urged on, as we now know, by the Commander-in-Chief himself [1]—were without avail, but, on the other hand, no further advance was made by the British.

1918.
20 Sept.

At 6.50 a.m. Br.-General Kelly had sent off a message to divisional headquarters, stating that he had in his hands many prisoners and much material, but that Liman was reported to have left the town on the evening of the 19th. He added that he hoped that the 14th Brigade would be sent up to his assistance. But at 10.55 a message came back from Major-General Macandrew that the state of the horses precluded him from despatching the 14th Brigade to the assistance of the 13th, and ordering the brigadier to withdraw to north of El 'Affule. The retirement was carried out in good order and very gradually, the Gloucester Hussars holding the high ground at Junjar, 3½ miles southwest of Nazareth, until the remainder of the brigade reached El 'Affule. Counting those taken at El Mujeidel and Yafa, 1,250 prisoners were captured in the raid, a large proportion of them Germans. The casualties of the Gloucester Hussars were 13 and of Hodson's Horse 9, those of the Lancers not being recorded. The Gloucesters had 28 horses killed.

The attack on Nazareth had not succeeded in capturing the Marshal, but it had completely broken up and disorganized his headquarters. It was as a fugitive, without a staff, that Liman, accompanied only by General Kiazim and the German orderly officers Major Prigge and Rittmeister Hecker, reached Tiberias that afternoon. Nevertheless, it was a bitter disappointment that the dramatic coup had just missed complete success, and that the enemy's Commander-in-Chief had not been taken, as Guy King of Jerusalem was taken by Saladin at Hattin, 11 miles away. There is a splendid simplicity in riding straight upon the enemy's headquarters and capturing his leader which would have appealed not only to the Army but to the whole world.

Here, as in most affairs of the sort, there were several

---

[1] Liman was awakened by the shots fired in the southern portion of the town. According to his housekeeper's account, he first of all motored north in sleeping-clothes, but finding that the situation was not so bad as appeared at first sight, returned to dress. This incident he does not himself confirm, but states that he later went up to the French school on the western heights and organized the defence of the remaining troops of the *13th Depot Regiment*. He left Nazareth at 1.15 p.m., after ordering the rear guard to withdraw to Tiberias. (Liman, pp. 354–8.)

causes contributory to the failure. The chief was the weakness and fatigue of the force which actually reached Nazareth. Secondly, Hodson's Horse had been the regiment originally selected to lead the attack; but it had been ridden out, and another, the headquarters of which had given less study to the question, had taken its place. It would probably have been advisable not to have employed Hodson's Horse for advanced-guard duties in the first stage of the march. Finally, there was the lack of a guide. But for the secrecy with which the forthcoming operations had been enshrouded, G.H.Q. would have been able to find a reliable agent who could not only have pointed out Liman's house, but—what was more important still—have led the brigade, or a portion of it, up from Yafa by a path which would have enabled it to encircle the town and cut the Tiberias road before giving the alarm. In that case not a man could have escaped. It is useless to speculate whether, with affairs as they were, the support of the 14th Brigade would have enabled the whole town to be taken; but it must be recalled that the message that Liman had left Nazareth probably influenced Major-General Macandrew in refusing to send it forward, and also that it was advisable to keep a brigade in hand in case he were directed to advance on Jenin and Beisan, as the orders of the Desert Mounted Corps foreshadowed.

As with the 4th Cavalry Division, the special camel convoy fell so far behind that it was unable to fulfil its appointed rôle, which was to issue supplies to the troops at Liktera in replacement of those consumed there by horses and men.[1] It was therefore sent back to Ras el 'Ain. The motor convoy, of which mention has been made in the account of the 4th Cavalry Division, delivered a day's supplies at El 'Affule on the evening of the 20th. The transport of the division did not reach Liktera until 9 a.m. on the 20th, having had great difficulties in the heavy sand at Arsuf and also at the Nahr Iskanderune. A request was made to the Desert Mounted Corps that, owing to the nature of the Abu Shushe track, the transport might use the Musmus Pass. When General Chauvel reached Liktera after midnight on the 19th he ordered the 15th Brigade to

---

[1] A fair quantity of tibben and barley was, however, found at this place by the brigades.

take the guns *via* J'ara and Abu Shushe, leaving the transport to be escorted over the Musmus Pass by the Australian Mounted Division. The 15th Brigade and the artillery reached Abu Shushe at 3 p.m., rejoining the division at El 'Affule during the night. The batteries had extraordinary difficulties in making their way, even by daylight, over tracks which are described in their reports as "non-existent." The Train, moving by Musmus and El Lajjun, did not reach El 'Affule till noon on the 21st.

1918.
20 Sept.

THE AUSTRALIAN MOUNTED DIVISION.

The Australian Mounted Division (less 5th L.H. Brigade) moved out from its assembly area south-east of Jaffa at 8.45 on the morning of the 19th, and bivouacked that evening, after a march of 28 miles, on the right bank of the Nahr Iskanderune. Advanced corps headquarters, which had found some difficulty in bringing its cars over the sandy ground, opened for the night on the southern side of the river. On arrival General Chauvel ordered Major-General Hodgson to resume his march through the Musmus Pass to El Lajjun, leaving one regiment of the 4th L.H. Brigade as escort to corps headquarters. The 11th A.L.H. had already been detailed as escort to the divisional transport, and soon after midnight the remainder of the brigade was ordered to find the transport of the 5th Cavalry Division and convoy it through the Musmus Pass.

1918.
19 Sept.
Maps 2A, 20, 21.
Sketches 31, 32.

When, therefore, he marched at 1 a.m. on the 20th Major-General Hodgson had with him only the 3rd L.H. Brigade and divisional troops. He halted for an hour at Kh. 'Ara in the pass, where horses were fed and the troops breakfasted. The 3rd L.H. Brigade then pushed forward rapidly to El Lajjun, where the division was rejoined by advanced corps headquarters at noon. At 2.45 p.m. General Chauvel received a report from the air that the enemy was retiring northward in large numbers from Jenin. He first of all ordered Major-General Hodgson to send officers' patrols, supported by a single squadron, in the direction of the town to make touch with the 5th L.H. Brigade, which he supposed was advancing northward up the Damascus road. As we know, the brigade had in

20 Sept.

fact returned to Tul Karm after cutting the railway.[1] At 3.35, however, Major-General Hodgson, on General Chauvel's direction, ordered the 3rd L.H. Brigade, leaving one regiment at El Lajjun, to march with one battery on Jenin, occupy it, " and capture the hostile fugitives now " retreating north and north-east of that place."

The 3rd L.H. Brigade (Br.-General L. C. Wilson), leaving the 8th A.L.H. at El. Lajjun, moved out at 4.30 p.m., accompanied by the Notts Battery R.H.A. and the 11th Light Armoured Motor Battery.[2] The 10th A.L.H., with six machine guns, formed the advanced guard. The movement began at the trot, but Lieut.-Colonel A. C. N. Olden, commanding the 10th A.L.H., anxious to get astride the road north of the town before dusk, increased the pace to a gallop and the regiment covered 11 miles in 70 minutes. Approaching Kufr Adan, 3 miles north-west of Jenin, a body of over a thousand Turks was seen in a grove near the village. 2nd Lieutenant P. W. K. Doig, commanding the right flank troop of the vanguard, instantly deployed and galloped straight at the enemy. The Turks seem to have been taken completely by surprise, not looking for any attack from this quarter, and surrendered immediately. Upwards of 1,800 men, including a number of Germans, and 400 animals were captured here.

The advanced guard pushed on swiftly, one squadron racing for the road from Jenin to Zir'in, up which a column of Turks was retiring. Both this and the direct road to El 'Affule and Nazareth having been closed, the 10th A.L.H. turned south and advanced on the town itself. All troops in the open surrendered, but a party of Germans for a time held up the Australians by machine-gun fire from windows. Hard pressed, this stout-hearted body of men tried to fight its way out, but was finally hemmed in and captured.

Pandemonium broke out in the town. Screaming " Arab ! Arab ! " as if this were a pass-word with the Australians to allow them to loot, men, women, and children threw themselves on the immense stores of food, clothing, and equipment stacked in sheds or piled on the transport which was blocked in the narrow street. Hampered by

---

[1] See p. 504.
[2] This unit had come directly under the orders of corps headquarters, and was handed over to the 3rd L.H. Brigade.

prisoners greatly exceeding their own numbers—for some 1918. 3,000 had now been captured—the Australians could do little to stop the orgy of pillage save by firing over the people's heads, and many thousands of pounds worth of stores were stolen or destroyed before order was restored. A bullion wagon was, however, rescued—to be found of great value later on for purchasing necessary supplies—and officers of the 9th A.L.H. had the presence of mind to put an armed guard over 120 cases of German champagne, "some of which was later distributed to the troops." Dumps at the station and elsewhere had been set alight before the arrival of the brigade, and were burning too fiercely to be saved. As darkness fell the place was lit up by their glare, and the moon rose upon a scene of frenzy like one of the sacks of German towns in the Thirty Years' War—save that here the peaceful inhabitants played the part of despoilers instead of that of victims.

Meanwhile part of the 10th A.L.H. had been ordered to move up the road towards the pass through which it issues from the Judæan Hills about a mile south of Jenin, in order that there should be no chance of retreating columns dispersing into the plain under cover of darkness. Lieutenant R. R. W. Patterson with a subsection of machine guns was sent to its support, but in the darkness got ahead of it and struck the road further south. At 9 p.m. a long column of the enemy was seen approaching. Lce-Corporal T. B. George suggested to his leader that it might be induced by bluff to surrender, and Lieutenant Patterson agreed, though his total strength was 23. Machine-gun fire was opened over the heads of the enemy, who was at that moment in the narrowest part of the defile, and he was summoned to surrender. A short parley took place, Patterson's statement that there was a strong force behind him being interpreted by a German nursing-sister walking at the head of the column. Then the whole body, 2,800 strong, with four guns, surrendered. By morning nearly 8,000 prisoners 21 Sept. had been taken by the 3rd L.H. Brigade, which was almost overwhelmed by the task of rounding up and keeping together this horde in the darkness. In response to urgent messages Major-General Hodgson ordered the 4th L.H. Brigade, which had now reached El Lajjun, to move to its assistance next morning.

So far, all that the Commander-in-Chief had asked of his troops they had accomplished. The net had been drawn and the prey was in it. Something like 25,000 prisoners were already in British hands, and the Turkish *Eighth Army*, with the exception of the troops under the command of Colonel von Oppen, had ceased to exist. The *Seventh* was in little better case; for if the greater part of its troops were still in the hill country between Nablus and Beisan, they had lost most of their transport and were grievously disorganized. For them also, as we shall presently see, destruction was impending.

The Capture of Haifa and the Actions at the Jordan Fords.

Maps 2A, 21.
Sketches 33, 34.

The Desert Mounted Corps had but one urgent task for the 21st. This was the occupation of Nazareth, and was accomplished without opposition by the 13th Brigade, the enemy having withdrawn towards Tiberias. Patrols advanced as far as Kufr Kenna (" Cana of Galilee "), 4 miles along the Tiberias road, without making contact with him.

The 3rd L.H. Brigade at Jenin was relieved from the embarrassment of looking after its haul of prisoners by the arrival of the 4th L.H. Brigade—less the 4th A.L.H., acting as escort to corps headquarters at El Lajjun—and of the 14th Cavalry Brigade, the latter being withdrawn to El 'Affule at night after order had been restored and the prisoners disposed of. A great column of 7,000 marched out at 9 a.m. under the escort of the 8th A.L.H. for El Lajjun, but owing to their exhaustion the prisoners did not arrive until 7 p.m. The Germans, marching at the head of the column out of the dust and evidently far better nourished, kept their discipline and goose-stepped when a general's car passed them. Two squadrons of the escorting regiment remained to guard the compound, which now contained nearly 14,000 men. The feeding of this host was carried out by lorries which came from Tul Karm through the Musmus Pass. Eight thousand were evacuated through the pass to Kerkur on the 22nd, under the escort of the Hyderabad Lancers.

Sketch 34.

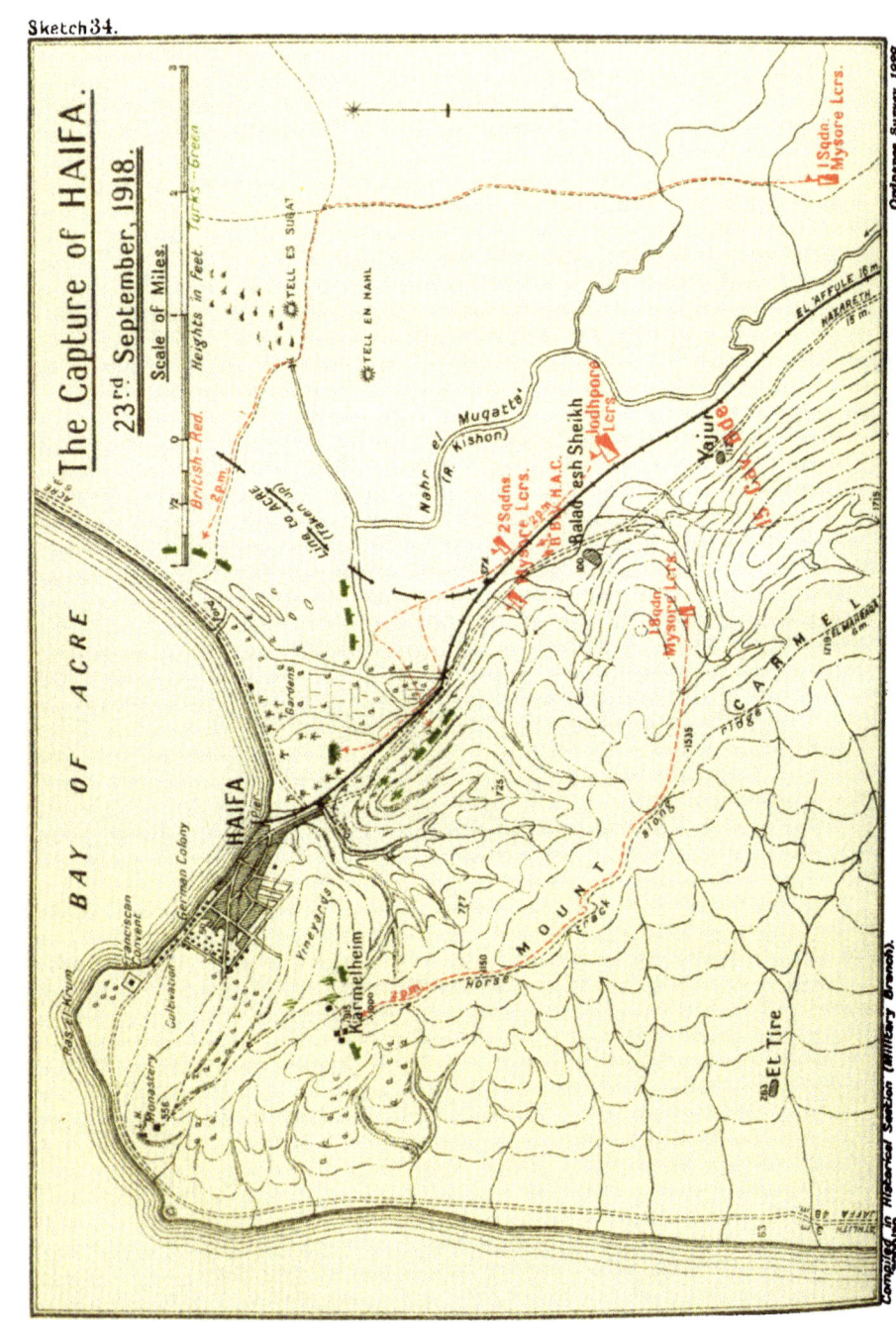

The 4th Cavalry Division piqueted the Beisan–El 'Affule road from the Jordan to Shatta Station, half-way between the two towns, in order to intercept the Turkish columns which had fled down the Wadi el Far'a road from the British infantry and were now making their way through the block of hills between the wadi and the Valley of Jezreel. These fugitives were, however, for the moment swallowed up in this bleak and inhospitable country, and it was not until after dark that the first formed body, about two hundred strong, approached the outposts of the 10th Cavalry Brigade. This detachment made a bold attempt to break through to the north, but a few rounds from the Hants Battery brought it to a halt and a charge in the moonlight by a handful of men of the Central India Horse against the head of the column induced it to surrender. That was only the beginning, but there was no more fighting. All through the early hours of the morning and until well after daylight on the 22nd the Turks came marching blindly forward on Beisan, stupefied by fatigue, surrendering without question at the first challenge. The musicians of one regimental band came in carrying their instruments. By evening over 4,000 prisoners had been rounded up. Had any organization or power of command been retained by this large body of troops the chances are that at least a proportion of them would have burst a way through.

During the night of the 21st the 18th Lancers of the 13th Cavalry Brigade, holding the hills north of Nazareth, had a brisk action with a strong body of the enemy which attacked from the north. The alarm was given by a small Turkish patrol blundering into the regiment's outposts. As it seemed that the enemy was about to deliver an assault, three troops moved out on the right to take him in flank. This counter-attack proved to have been perfectly timed; for it was found that the Turks, advancing in two waves, were within thirty yards of the piquet line. Having given the counter-attack time to develop, the whole line went forward, and after some close fighting completely routed the enemy, who streamed away in confusion. Over two hundred prisoners were captured, and about forty dead found on the field when light appeared. The captured Turks gave no very clear account of what they had intended, but it seemed probable that they represented part of the

1918.
21 Sept.

Haifa garrison which was attempting to break through by the main road to Tiberias.

**1918.
22 Sept.** On the morning of the 22nd orders were issued by General Chauvel for the capture of Haifa and Acre by the 5th Cavalry Division next day; but, on a report being received from the air that Haifa was being evacuated, G.H.Q. directed that an attempt should be made to occupy it that afternoon by the 12th Light Armoured Motor Battery and 7th Light Car Patrol. Br.-General A. D'A. King, G.O.C.R.A. Desert Mounted Corps, was put in command of the detachment and was to become Military Governor of the town. The result was a failure, though of slight importance. The column, following the main road from Nazareth, encountered a body of the enemy at the railway bridge 8 miles south-east of the town. This party, 69 strong, surrendered at once, but proved that Haifa was still held. Br.-General King nevertheless determined to go on, trusting that the demoralization of the enemy would have spread to the garrison, though it had not yet been engaged. Three miles short of Haifa, however, near the village of Balad esh Sheikh, the column came under artillery fire, and machine guns opened upon it from the hills. Several tyres were burst, the commander's touring car was damaged, and he was obliged to enter one of the armoured cars. There was nothing for it but to turn back, but this was a matter of difficulty under heavy fire. Eventually, after a critical few moments, the column extricated itself and returned to El Lajjun.

23 Sept. It was necessary, therefore, to carry out an attack in force against Haifa on the 23rd, and this operation was the task of the 5th Cavalry Division, which was simultaneously to occupy Acre, where less opposition was expected. The 5th L.H. Brigade had arrived at Jenin over night from Nablus, rejoining the Australian Mounted Division for the first time since the beginning of the battle. The 3rd L.H. Brigade had at once marched to El 'Affule to relieve the 5th Cavalry Division, and was followed on the morning of the 23rd by the 4th L.H. Brigade. The 8th A.L.H. took over the defence of Nazareth at 5 a.m. The 5th L.H. Brigade remained at Jenin, the Australian Mounted Division being now responsible for the piqueting of the line Shatta–Zir'in–El 'Affule.

The 5th Cavalry Division advanced in two columns: 1918. the right, consisting of the 13th Cavalry Brigade Group 23 Sept. (less " B " Battery H.A.C.) with the 11th Light Armoured Motor Battery moving on Acre by way of Saffurye and Shafa 'Amr; the left, consisting of the remainder of the division, the 15th Cavalry Brigade (Br.-General C. R. Harbord), less Hyderabad Lancers, with " B " Battery H.A.C., and the 1st Light Car Patrol as advanced guard, by the main road on Haifa. The right column met with but trifling opposition, and the renowned fortress of Acre, which had defied Simon Maccabæus, Baldwin I (though he later took it with the aid of the Genoese fleet), and Napoleon, and had cost the Crusaders 60,000 men when they captured it in 1191, now fell into British hands almost without resistance.

Haifa, a town with a less eventful history than most of its neighbours, has a splendid site at the foot of Mount Carmel on the southern shore of the Bay of Acre. Though it is very open to attack from the sea, the approach to it from the Plain of Esdraelon is easily defensible; for the road is commanded from the south by Carmel, while to the north the country is broken by the swift and swampy Nahr el Muqatta', or River Kishon, and its tributaries. Carmel is a long, narrow ridge, running from the coast to the south-east. Its beauty, lauded by Isaiah and in the Song of Solomon, is indeed striking, above all in spring, when the wild fruit-trees which mingle with its oaks and pines are in blossom; but perhaps it is its never-failing verdure, preserved by heavy dews, which has made so strong an impression upon dwellers in a land generally baked brown in summer and won it a large share of its paradisical fame. It gives its name to one of the greatest of monastic orders, which still owns a monastery and hospice overlooking the sea. Another prominent building is a religious pension, known as the *Karmelheim*, on the crest overlooking Haifa.

The 15th Cavalry Brigade met with no opposition until the leading squadron of the Mysore Lancers passed through Balad esh Sheikh at 10 a.m. and came under fire from machine guns on the heights west of the village and from guns near the *Karmelheim*. More Turkish artillery opened fire from the eastern end of Haifa, and an aeroplane dropped a message that the place was strongly held. One squadron was then despatched up the road to Tell es Subat, 4½ miles east of Haifa, with orders to advance on the town from the north-east. A second squadron, with two machine guns, climbed up on to Carmel from a point south of Balad esh Sheikh with the object of advancing along the track following the crest-line against the guns at the *Karmelheim*. " B " Battery H.A.C. came into action, and the Jodhpore Lancers halted in the open east of Balad esh Sheikh with orders to advance mounted.

At 11.54 the Sherwood Rangers (14th Cavalry Brigade) joined the brigade, and one squadron was ordered to move up and assist the Mysore squadron on Carmel. Br.-General Harbord postponed the mounted attack until 2 p.m. in hopes that the force on the hill would by then be ready to attack the guns simultaneously. The interval of waiting was utilized to despatch several patrols to reconnoitre the ground and locate the enemy's position, but they were prevented by machine-gun fire from examining the bank of the Kishon west of the Acre railway, where it was intended that the Jodhpore Lancers should cross in order to attack the enemy on the far bank. One patrol of the Mysore Lancers did reach the river, but the horses were bogged and drowned.

At the appointed hour the Jodhpores trotted forward in column of squadrons in line of troop column, their advance being covered by the H.A.C. Battery, four machine guns, and the two remaining squadrons of the Mysore Lancers. As they crossed the Acre railway the enemy's fire increased, but they quickened their pace and suffered little loss, riding straight for the Kishon. As they neared the bank it was seen that it was precipitous ; but a worse obstacle still was immediately disclosed, when the two ground scouts in the van, forcing their horses down to the water, were swallowed up in a quicksand. It was only too clear that no crossing was possible.[1]

Lieut.-Colonel H. N. Holden, the Senior Special Service Officer, ordered the regiment to swing left-handed, cross

---

[1] It may be noted that on the map of Haifa in the secret pre-war military report on Syria this stretch of the river is marked " unfordable." As so often happens in military affairs, this information was not available at the right moment to those most closely concerned. The fate of Sisera's host in these very waters might also have been remembered.

Sketch 35. MEGIDDO, 1918. Situation at 9 p.m., 24th Sept., 1918.

the narrower wadi beside the El 'Affule–Haifa railway, and charge the machine guns on the lower slopes of Carmel. It was a most critical moment, for the regiment was being raked by fire from front and flank, and horses were falling fast. But the leading squadron, swiftly rallied and turned, got among the machine guns and speared the detachments, thus opening the defile through which ran the main road into Haifa. The second squadron thereupon galloped up the road, wheeled half-right, and charged a mount east of the road, on which it captured two more machine guns. Lieut.-Colonel Holden then led the two remaining squadrons straight into the town. Here and there shots were fired from the houses, and a few Turks were actually ridden down in the streets; but the passage of the defile had practically decided the issue, and there was little left to do but round up prisoners. The two Mysore squadrons which had supported the advance mounted as soon as the Jodhpores masked their fire, and followed them into Haifa.

1918.
23 Sept.

Almost at the same instant as the main attack was launched the left detached squadron of the Mysores charged the enemy's guns south of the *Karmelheim*. In the course of the very difficult ascent there had been some casualties, and a number of this squadron's horses had dropped out exhausted or lamed, so that after the Hotchkiss rifles and a party to cover the two machine guns supporting the attack from a flank had been dropped, only about fifteen men were left for the actual charge. Nevertheless, it was completely successful and broke through the enemy position. About half the squadron of Sherwood Rangers arrived in time to follow up the charge and prevent the enemy rallying. One 150-mm. naval gun, two mountain guns, and 78 prisoners were taken. The right squadron of the Mysores, which had been held up by fire $2\frac{1}{2}$ miles north-east of Haifa, mounted and advanced as soon as the Jodhpore attack was seen. A strong body of Turks near the mouth of the Nahr el Muqatta' was charged and dispersed, two more guns and over a hundred prisoners being taken.

The total captures were 25 officers and 664 other ranks (exclusive of a number of sick in hospital), 16 guns, 10 machine guns. The British casualties were 3 killed and 34 wounded, and if the loss in horses was fairly heavy— 60 killed and 83 wounded—it was made up from some unexpectedly good ones captured. No more remarkable cavalry action of its scale was fought in the whole course of the campaign. The position was naturally formidable, with a precipitous hill and an impassable river on either side of a defile; it was held by a well-armed force about a thousand strong which had not yet been engaged, though doubtless in some degree affected by news of the general rout; it was taken in a few hours by a cavalry brigade of two weak regiments and a single 13-pdr. battery. Undoubtedly only the boldness and dash of the cavalry, combined with the skilful flanking movements, made success possible, and there is little likelihood that a dismounted attack by a force of this strength would have had equal fortune. The check on the river bank, which might well have been disastrous, was nullified by the speed and good order in which the leading squadron of the Jodhpore Lancers changed direction and charged the enemy on the slopes of Carmel. Machine-gun bullets over and over again failed to stop the galloping horses, even though many of these succumbed afterwards to their injuries.

Maps 21.
Sketches
35, 36.

Chaytor's Force had, as will be recorded in the next chapter, captured Jisr ed Damiye on the 22nd, thus barring to the enemy escape by the Wadi el Far'a road. The 4th Cavalry Division held the Jordan crossings east and south-east of Beisan. But from Beisan to Jisr ed Damiye was a distance of 25 miles, and it was suddenly realized on the afternoon of the 22nd that this constituted a serious hole in the net. The failure to close it by a movement southward along the Jordan on the part of the 4th Cavalry Division simultaneous with the approach of Chaytor's Force to Jisr ed Damiye was, in fact, the sole blot on an operation the main lines of which had hitherto been perfection itself. It must be remembered, however, that the division had had to piquet the road from Beisan half-way to El 'Affule, that it had been encumbered with prisoners, and that rations had not been delivered at Beisan till the 21st.

General Chauvel learnt from the air on the afternoon of the 22nd that, despite the great numbers of Turks who had marched northward, heads down, to fall into the hands of the 4th Cavalry Division at Beisan, large formed bodies, whose commanders had better realized the situation, had

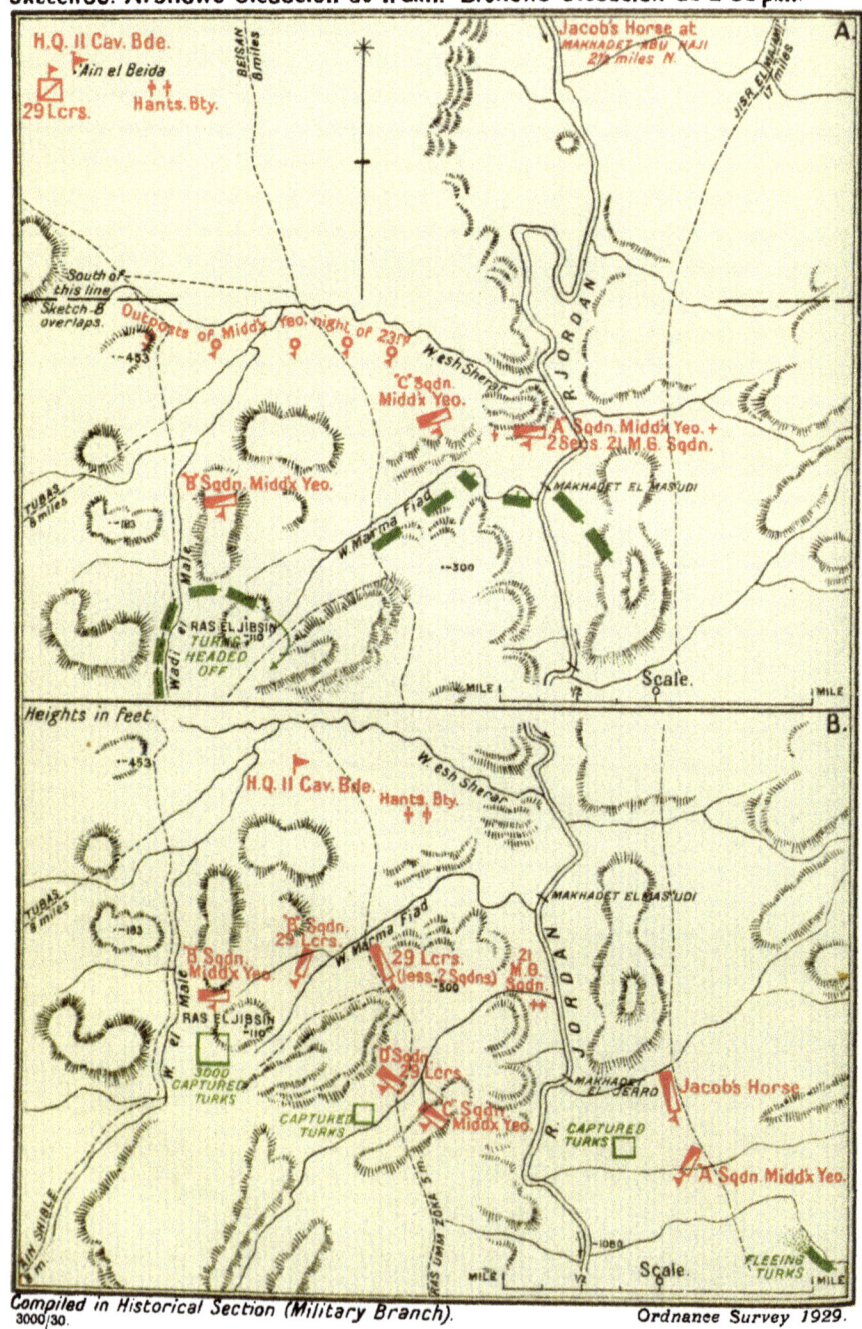

Action at MAKHADET EL MAS'UDI: 24th Sept. 1918.
Sketch 36. A. shows Situation at 11 a.m. B. shows Situation at 2·30 p.m.

turned eastward and were crossing the Jordan further south. Nothing could be done that evening, but the 4th Cavalry Division was ordered to move down on either bank of the river next morning and intercept the retreating enemy. Major-General Barrow ordered the 11th Cavalry Brigade to carry out this operation, and if possible to make touch with the XX Corps Cavalry Regiment, which was harrying the rear of a Turkish column south-east of Tubas.

1918.
23 Sept.

The brigade marched at 6 a.m., with Jacob's Horse on the east bank. While the main guard, consisting of the 29th Lancers, was halted at Kh. es Samriye, $4\frac{1}{2}$ miles south of Beisan, the advanced squadron sent in a report that it had been fired on by the enemy south-east of the village. Two squadrons, under Captain M. H. Jackson, at once moved forward and discovered that a large body of Turks was attempting to cross the river by the ford at Makhadet Abu Naji under cover of a rear guard holding a position facing northward, with a hillock in the centre. Placing his Hotchkiss rifles on a small mound 800 yards west of the position, Captain Jackson ordered one squadron to attack the left flank of the enemy, while the second made a wide enveloping movement and took him in the rear. The flank attack was checked by heavy fire, but the other squadron swept right through the enemy's position and broke up the defenders in hopeless rout. Eight hundred prisoners, including Rushdi Bey, commander of the *16th Division*, and 18 machine guns were captured.[1]

Meanwhile the Middlesex Yeomanry had been ordered by Br.-General Gregory to attack a body of Turks moving on the river a mile further south, and a message had been sent for the Hants Battery R.H.A., which had been left in position at Beisan, to move down at once to the brigade's support, as the enemy was in great numbers and had already repulsed two attacks by Jacob's Horse on the east bank. The battery, which had saddled up in anticipation of being called upon, set off at once, trotted the whole six miles, and arrived at 11 a.m., men and horses alike smothered in dust and sweat. At its very first shot from a position in

---

[1] This force was the rear guard of Colonel von Oppen's *Asia Corps* (see Note at end of Chapter). The diary of that formation records that the commander of the *19th Division* was also missing. As there is no record of his capture by the British, he was probably killed.

the open 4,000 yards west of the ford, the enemy disclosed two batteries [1] on the east bank, and opened so accurate a fire that within a few minutes three guns were hit by splinters and it was necessary temporarily to withdraw the detachments. Yet the check was very short. The Middlesex Yeomanry had driven the body of Turks against which it had been directed across the river, had pushed a squadron on their heels over the ford by which they had escaped, and had begun an attack on the two Turkish batteries. The gunners did not await the mounted assault, but immediately abandoned their pieces, of which the Yeomanry destroyed the breech-blocks. Then, from both sides of the river, the British mounted troops closed in upon the ford. In a few minutes all was over. Four thousand prisoners were captured, and the Turkish losses in killed must have been heavy, for the banks were bestrewn with dead.

The day had been intensely hot, the ground was rough and dusty, and the horses had been without water since leaving Beisan. The brigade therefore went into bivouac at 'Ain el Beida, 4 miles south-west of Makhadet Abu Naji, with the Middlesex Yeomanry holding outposts to the south and Jacob's Horse still on the east bank.

1918.
24 Sept.

Early on the morning of the 24th Br.-General Gregory issued orders for the sweep to be continued southward as soon as rations, which were being sent by a pack column, had arrived from Beisan. At 10.35 Lieut-Colonel E. F. Lawson, commanding the Middlesex Yeomanry, learnt from one of his observation posts that a body of Turks, which had advanced up the 'Ain Shible–Beisan road, parallel to the Jordan, had turned eastward and was making for a ford at Makhadet el Mas'udi. He ordered " A " Squadron to gallop for the ford and forestall the enemy. An exciting race followed, but the cavalry was hampered by broken ground, and the Turkish advanced guard arrived first. It at once brought its machine guns into action and also lined the bank of the little Wadi Marma Fiad, running down to the Jordan near Makhadet el Mas'udi, to cover the escape of a larger body which attempted to reach another

---

[1] These batteries belonged not to the *Seventh Army*, which was endeavouring to retire over the Jordan, but to the *Fourth*, and had been moved northward on the east bank.

ACTIONS AT JORDAN FORDS

ford a mile further south. Uncertain how long it would take the remainder of the brigade to advance to his support, Lieut.-Colonel Lawson decided to head off the main body. " B " Squadron came into action dismounted against a great column, marching six abreast, opened a devastating fire upon its head, and forced it to turn away south-eastward. " A " Squadron, which had attempted to cut off the Turkish advanced guard moving on Makhadet el Mas'udi, launched an attack on the ford, and after a sharp action captured it at 12.30 p.m., with the aid of " C " Squadron, which engaged the enemy on the Marma Fiad.

Meanwhile Br.-General Gregory, having received from Lieut.-Colonel Lawson a message outlining the situation, had ordered forward the 29th Lancers and a section of the Hants Battery. Lieut.-Colonel P. B. Sangster, commanding the 29th, saw the head of the column which had been turned off by the Middlesex squadron and brought the two guns into action against it. The second section came into action a few minutes later, and the Turks fled southward in confusion, pursued by the 29th Lancers. Some three thousand prisoners were quickly rounded up, the battery then directing its fire against the troops which had already crossed the river. Jacob's Horse, on the east bank, had been delayed by the mistake of an Indian officer who had had the rations sent round by the bridge at Jisr esh Sheikh Husein, east of Beisan, but now moved south at top speed, joined hands with " A " Squadron Middlesex Yeomanry, which had crossed at Makhadet el Mas'udi, and completed the rout of the Turks beyond the Jordan. Only a comparatively small body escaped to the hills in wild disorder. Five thousand prisoners were captured, and the two fords, with their approaches on either side of the river, were shambles.

The brigade now advanced six miles southward to Ras Umm Zoka, without encountering any further bodies of the enemy. The XX Corps Cavalry Regiment had reached 'Ain Male, 7· miles east of Tubas, and had rounded up several thousand prisoners. A patrol of the 29th Lancers, despatched the previous day to find touch with it, had done so, and returned to its brigade on the night of the 24th after a remarkable march through these almost unmapped hills. It brought news that, but for a few terrified fugitives skulking here and there in rocky gullies, not a Turk now remained west of Jordan between the Dead Sea and the Lake of Tiberias. The 11th Cavalry Brigade therefore, after camping that night at Ras Umm Zoka, returned on the 25th to Beisan. Only one small formed body, consisting mainly of the German troops of the *Asia Corps*, had escaped the brigade in the two days' fighting, thanks to having crossed the Jordan before the attack of the 23rd had fully developed, though considerable numbers had got over before it appeared on the scene. The operations may stand as a pattern to cavalry upon the flank of a beaten and demoralized foe.

The Capture of Samakh and Tiberias.

Maps 1, 2A, 21.
Sketch 36.

While the 4th Cavalry Division was intercepting the enemy who had endeavoured to escape over Jordan, the Australian Mounted Division had been ordered by General Chauvel to despatch a brigade to capture Samakh, on the southern shore of the Lake of Tiberias. It was reported from the air that this place was held by a comparatively small body of the enemy, which was evacuating stores by boat across the lake. The tiny village was, however, of no small account at this moment. Liman obviously hoped to establish a rear-guard position from Der'a along the Yarmuk and between the western shores of the Lake of Tiberias and Lake Hule ("The Waters of Merom") in order to win time to organize the defence of Damascus. Samakh was the weak link between the two halves of this position, and the Marshal, passing through after his escape from Nazareth, had ordered it to be held to the last man. From the British point of view it was also important to secure the Yarmuk bridges.

The 4th L.H. Brigade (Br.-General W. Grant)[1] reached Beisan at 1.45 p.m. on the 24th September, and after some hours' rest arrived at Jisr el Majami', still held by a regiment (now the Central India Horse) of the 4th Cavalry Division, at 9 p.m. The 4th A.L.H. was still detached from the brigade, and five troops of the 12th A.L.H. were also on escort duty. Br.-General Grant was given the choice of

---

[1] Br.-General Grant had hastened out of hospital on the 21st to take over command of his brigade from Lieut.-Colonel M. W. J. Bourchier.

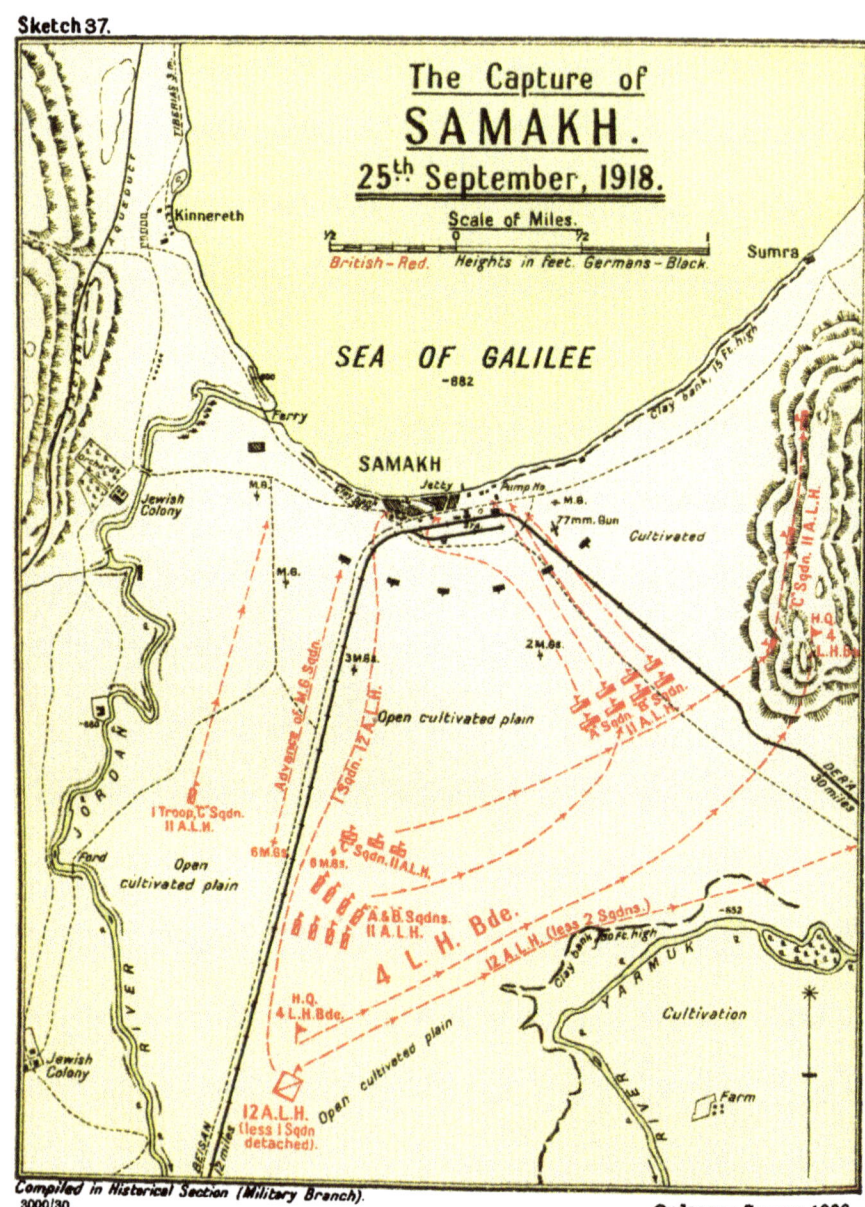

awaiting the return of the latter detachment, or going on without it. He decided not to waste time by waiting, as he had been informed that the garrison of Samakh was weak and that the 3rd L.H. Brigade would be advancing on the morrow directly on Tiberias from Nazareth.

1918.
25 Sept.

The brigade crossed the Jordan and Yarmuk at Jisr el Majami' at 2.30 a.m. on the 25th so as to arrive in front of Samakh at dawn, and advanced up the railway line. No reconnaissance in the darkness was possible, but Br.-General Grant had learnt from the officers of the Central India Horse (a squadron of which had attempted on the 24th to blow up a culvert east of the village and had been beaten off) that the village and station buildings lay at the end of a plain 2½ miles wide, flat as a carpet and without cover of any sort, but also without other obstacles to mounted action than patches of big thistles. His orders in the circumstances were of the simplest: that the 11th A.L.H. should attack mounted from the south-east at dawn, supported by the fire of the machine guns from due south on the railway.

At 4.25 a.m., while it was still quite dark, intense machine-gun and rifle fire burst out on a front of half a mile on either side of the railway. Lieut.-Colonel J. W. Parsons immediately swung the 11th A.L.H. to the right, and all twelve guns of the machine-gun squadron came into action, firing at the flashes in front. Having trotted north-eastward till they reached the railway from Samakh to Der'a, " A " and " B " Squadrons of the 11th A.L.H. charged on either side of the line. The men yelled as they rode, to warn the machine-gunners of their progress, for day was only now breaking. Probably the dim light favoured them; at any rate they broke clear through the left flank, though a number of horses fell into pits dug by the enemy to cover his position. They rode on to the east side of the station buildings, with the exception of two troops of " A " Squadron, which swung to the west of the station and entered the village. The station buildings being strongly held, the two squadrons dismounted, left their horses in a gulley near the pump-house, and attacked the position with the bayonet. " C " Squadron had meanwhile moved to cover the right of the attack, taking up a position on Hill 377 east of Samakh, which commanded the railway to Der'a and the road running up the eastern side of the lake. As soon as the charge was driven home the machine guns concentrated on machine guns on the enemy's right, put them out of action, and were then galloped forward to the west end of the village.

Dawn came up on one of the hottest and most fiercely contested fights of the whole campaign as the two Australian squadrons assaulted the station buildings. The enemy lined a stout stone wall, fired automatic rifles from the windows, hurled bombs. Several parties had established themselves in engines and tenders in the sidings. The struggle raged a full hour, quarter being neither asked nor given, until every man of the defenders had been killed or wounded. In the village itself, where a squadron of the 12th A.L.H. took part, afterwards moving on for the final stages of the battle at the station, the fighting was less severe, and here a number of prisoners were taken.† By 5.30 all was over. As they made their way through the captured buildings the Australians noted that there were numerous empty spirit-bottles scattered about. Two motor-boats lying at the jetty made off in the midst of the action but one was caught by a burst of fire from a Hotchkiss rifle, broke into flames, and sank.

About one hundred dead Germans were found, and the prisoners numbered 364. It appears, however, that over two hundred Turks among these had taken little part in the defence, which had fallen almost entirely upon the Germans. One field gun and seven machine guns were captured, as well as an aeroplane and a quantity of rolling-stock. The Australian casualties numbered 78, mostly suffered in the dismounted fighting, and about one hundred horses. Had the attack, unsupported by artillery fire, been made by daylight, its losses would certainly have been more severe; indeed it may be doubted whether it would have succeeded at all against defenders prepared to resist to the last.

Directly the firing had died down Br.-General Grant, who had taken up his position on Hill 377, ordered the 12th A.L.H. to move eastward along the railway line up the Yarmuk. The regiment had secured the first bridge when a message was received from Major-General Hodgson that it was to advance no farther, as the whole division was to move up the west side of the lake.[1] Br.-General Grant now ordered a squadron of the 12th A.L.H. to move on towards Tiberias, on the western shore. This squadron found touch with one of the 8th A.L.H. (3rd L.H. Brigade) and the 12th Light Armoured Motor Battery, which were reconnoitring towards Tiberias from the direction of Nazareth. As it was seen that the place was being evacuated, the two squadrons and the armoured cars pushed on and occupied it during the afternoon after slight opposition, taking nearly one hundred prisoners and 13 machine guns.

1918.
25 Sept.

The hope of making a serious stand on the line of the Yarmuk or between the two lakes had thus been denied to the enemy commander.

NOTE.

THE ACTION OF THE ENEMY FROM THE 22ND TO THE 25TH SEPTEMBER.

The movements of the Turks and the orders issued by *Yilderim* have been briefly outlined in Notes to Chapters XXII and XXIII up to the evening of the 21st, when Colonel von Oppen's detachment escaped over Mount Ebal; and Liman's departure from Nazareth has been described in this chapter in a footnote. The Commander-in-Chief drove first to Tiberias, then down to Samakh. He hoped to reach Beisan, but finding that it was in British hands, left at midnight on the 20th for Der'a.

"It was clear," he writes, "that only one course remained open to me. The Tiberias sector from Lake Hule to Samakh must be held with all the means at our disposal to prevent the pursuit overtaking us, whilst the formations retiring along the River Jordan and east of Jordan to the Yarmuk Valley sector, from Samakh to Der'a, must form front for at least the time being."[2]

Der'a he found fairly secure, owing to the energetic action of the commandant, Major Willmer (of Suvla fame), who was keeping the Arabs at a distance. From here he issued orders to the *Fourth Army* to retire to the Yarmuk. He put Major Willmer temporarily in command of the whole front from Der'a to Samakh. On the evening of the 21st he had an interview with the sheikhs of the Druses, who rode into Der'a with several thousand armed men. They had not made up their minds which side to back, as they had small love for the Arabs, and were not indisposed to help him if he would send troops to support them at Busra, in Jebel ed Druz. This he was unable to promise, but they nevertheless agreed at least to remain neutral.

It was on the 22nd that he received a delightful telegram from the Military Mission, which is worth mentioning because it shows how little

---

[1] It was perhaps unfortunate that the brigade was not allowed to capture the second bridge, which was covered by a small redoubt, for the enemy blew it up later and its repair took many weeks. Major-General Hodgson had understood from corps headquarters that the 4th Cavalry Division was to secure the Yarmuk bridges.

[2] Liman, p. 360.

the situation was understood in Constantinople, even though Turkish headquarters had been constantly informed of what was happening. He was asked to offer a prize for the sack-race at the military sports shortly to be held. Liman remarks that he took no interest at that moment in sports, and least of all in a sack-race, which was a painful reminder of his own position.

Colonel von Oppen, with his faithful detachment, the fighting strength of which was now 700 Germans and 1,300 Turks of the *16th* and *19th Divisions*, was meanwhile making his way northward from Tubas towards Beisan. Learning that the place was held by British cavalry, he formed the bold design of breaking through during the night of the 22nd, and marching straight on Samakh, where he rightly guessed Liman would endeavour to make a stand. Ten minutes after he had issued his orders he was summoned to report to Jevad Pasha, the commander of the *Eighth Army*, in the Wadi Shubash, which enters the Jordan near the ford of Makhadet Abu Naji. Jevad directed him to cross the Jordan that night. He moved down at once, and had got all his German troops and a small proportion of the Turkish over when the 11th Cavalry Brigade attacked. The remainder of the Turks and a flood of fugitives from other formations which attempted to follow, were captured as we have seen. Liman comments very adversely upon Jevad's intervention and points out that his scheme of fighting a delaying action at Samakh would have been possible had Colonel von Oppen reached the place. The answer to that is that to do so he had to break through at Beisan, and that a whole cavalry division could have been assembled at any point to bar his march. The troops intercepted on the 24th by the 11th Cavalry Brigade formed the rear of the *Seventh Army*, and it is believed that Mustapha Kemal Pasha himself only just escaped. This Army had apparently passed a fair proportion of its troops across during the previous night and the early morning, and moved on Irbid, while Colonel von Oppen marched to Der'a across its front. The *Fourth Army* also was now retiring on Der'a.

Liman, who had already sent back his staff to Damascus, arrived there himself on the evening of the 23rd. He requested the commander of the *Second Army*, the skeleton force holding Northern Syria, to put at his disposal in Damascus as many troops as possible, but only a few battalions, chiefly of Arabs, could be spared.

CHAPTER XXV.

THE OPERATIONS OF CHAYTOR'S FORCE.
(Map 22; Sketches 24, 35).

THE CAPTURE OF THE JORDAN CROSSINGS.

CHAYTOR'S Force [1] in the Jordan Valley was in the first place responsible for the defence of the British right flank from the northern end of the Dead Sea, through the Ghoraniye and 'Auja bridgeheads, to a point in the hills 8 miles north-west of Jericho, where it was in touch with the XX Corps. Major-General Chaytor had a difficult part to play; for his action depended entirely upon the enemy's movements, and a good deal was necessarily left to his own good sense and initiative. If the attack of the XXI Corps and the flanking ride of the Desert Mounted Corps on the coast met with success, it was certain that the Turkish *Fourth Army* would withdraw northward along the Hejaz Railway. Until it began its retreat Major-General Chaytor could do little more than demonstrate against it. But when that moment came he would have an opportunity to harry it, to cut off its rear guards and baggage, and above all to capture the Jordan crossing at Jisr ed Damiye. He would also have the chance of intercepting its detachment down the railway at Ma'an; for that would hardly be able to rejoin in time for the move north unless the main body waited so long as to ensure its own destruction.

1918.
Sept.
Map 22.
Sketch 24.

The Turks had improved their defences since the second British raid into Trans-Jordan. The line of the foot-hills from opposite Makhadet Hijla to about four miles north of the main Jericho–Es Salt road was strongly entrenched and in places wired, with advanced posts, also wired, on the left flank at Qabr Said, Kh. el Kufrein, and Qabr Mujahid. From the right flank in the foot-hills a line of

---
[1] The composition of the force is given on p. 466.

redoubts and trenches ran across the floor of the valley to the Jordan south of Umm esh Shert. This line was being hastily wired in mid-September. West of Jordan it was continued along the left or northern bank of the Mellaha, consisting here of wired-in redoubts with good fields of fire. The line then ran south-west to Bakr Ridge, west of the British salient at El Musallabe, with an advanced post on Grant Hill, facing the point of the salient. The chief formation of the *Fourth Army* was the *VIII Corps*, consisting of the *48th Division* and the *Composite Division*, the dividing line of these divisions being apparently the Jericho–Es Salt road. On the left of the *VIII Corps* the *Caucasus Cavalry Brigade* and the *Mule-mounted Infantry Regiment* held the outposts on that flank and watched the country to the northern end of the Dead Sea. On the right the *24th* and *3rd Cavalry Divisions* were astride the Jordan, the right boundary of the *Fourth Army* being at El Baghalat, 6 miles W.N.W. of Umm esh Shert; so that Chaytor's Force was also faced by the greater part of the *53rd Division*, in the *Seventh Army* area. The local reserve, in addition to the *3rd Cavalry Division*, which had few if any troops in the trenches, consisted of part of the *12th Regiment* at Es Salt and the German *146th Regiment*. The troops protecting the railway were under the command of the *II Corps*,[1] which appears to have been responsible for its defence for some two hundred miles. The strongest detachment was that at Ma'an, consisting of about seven battalions; between Ma'an and 'Amman there were about eight. Between Der'a and Damascus was the *Hauran Detachment* of one regiment and irregulars, also under the command of the *II Corps*; but they were no concern of Chaytor's Force. There were also the Circassian irregulars, who were not altogether to be despised, because they knew that the expulsion of their Turkish patrons would permit the local inhabitants to settle old scores.

The British front was divided, as it had been all the summer, into two sectors, the boundary between them being just north of El 'Auja on the Jordan. The right was now commanded by Br.-General G. de L. Ryrie, who had under

---

[1] It is not quite certain whether the headquarters of this formation was at 'Amman or Der'a. It has been placed at the first-named town on the situation maps.

PROBING THE ENEMY'S POSITION 549

his command, in addition to his own 2nd L.H. Brigade, the 20th Indian Brigade. The left was under the orders of Br.-General W. Meldrum, and was held by the 38/R. Fusiliers and the 1st and 2nd Battalions British West Indies Regiment,[1] with the New Zealand Brigade and 39/R. Fusiliers in reserve. The 1st L.H. Brigade was in Force reserve.

During the 17th and 18th September vigorous patrolling was carried out by the mounted troops. The enemy was quiet, but a well-known heavy high-velocity gun near Shunet Nimrin caused some trouble and loss by shelling Jericho and Major-General Chaytor's headquarters in the Wadi Nueiame north of the town. On the afternoon of the 19th it was learnt that the 160th Brigade in the hills had made good progress and that a mountain battery under its orders was in a position to shell Bakr Ridge. The 2/B.W.I. was therefore ordered to test the enemy's strength at this point, and to occupy the ridge if he had withdrawn. Three companies advanced with great dash in face of heavy artillery and machine-gun fire and, driving in the enemy's outposts, captured the ridge south of Bakr Ridge, overlooking the Wadi Bakr, at a cost of 35 casualties. The Turks were evidently still holding Bakr Ridge in strength, so no more was attempted that evening.

Before morning light on the 20th, however, the battalion seized Bakr Ridge, and, as the dawn came up, it was seen that the enemy was evacuating Chalk Ridge to the north. This position was occupied by 9.30 a.m. Meanwhile the 1/B.W.I. had seized Grant Hill and Baghalat, where it dug in under considerable shell fire. Fighting patrols of the 38/R. Fusiliers found the enemy still holding his trenches north of the Mellaha and were driven back by machine-gun fire. East of Jordan a force consisting of the 6th and 7th A.L.H. and a company of the Patiala Infantry demonstrated against the posts on the enemy's left flank and found these likewise strongly held. It was only to be expected, however, that the Turks would cling to the Mellaha bank, and still more to their positions east of Jordan, until they had withdrawn their right. Major-General Chaytor was convinced that they were about to

---

[1] Hereafter described for brevity's sake as "1/B.W.I." and "2/B.W.I."

do this, and that the moment had come to press forward to the crossing at Jisr ed Damiye. He therefore gave orders to Br.-General Meldrum to seize Kh. Fasail, 2 miles north of Baghalat on the track to Jisr ed Damiye, before dawn on the 21st.

1918. 21 Sept.

The Auckland Regiment, brushing through a weak rear guard, occupied this objective at 4 a.m., capturing 26 prisoners. Its patrols soon afterwards discovered the enemy upon a line from Mafid Jozele on the Jordan to El Musettera, $3\frac{1}{2}$ miles to the north-west, that is, disposed to cover Jisr ed Damiye, to which a portion of the *Seventh Army* was moving by the Wadi el Far'a in an endeavour to escape over Jordan.[1] At 4.15 p.m. Major-General Chaytor received a message from the Auckland Regiment that the Turks appeared to be leaving Mafid Jozele. He issued orders for the remainder of the New Zealand Brigade, with the two West Indies battalions, the Inverness Battery R.H.A., and the 29th Indian Mountain Battery to join the Auckland Regiment at Kh. Fasail. The movement could only be carried out under cover of darkness, since it was across the front of the Turkish trenches on the upper Mellaha and in full view of the enemy. As soon as Br.-General Meldrum had concentrated his force at Kh. Fasail he was to attack Jisr ed Damiye. The 1st L.H. Brigade was to take over his old position at Musallabe.

The column moved out at 9 p.m., the mounted troops reaching Kh. Fasail at 11.30 and the 2/B.W.I. at midnight.

22 Sept.

Leaving this battalion to cover his right by holding the track to Mafid Jozele, Br.-General Meldrum, after only a few minutes' halt, began his advance on Jisr ed Damiye down the Roman Road. On reaching the cross roads north of Meteil edh Dhib the Auckland Regiment was directed to follow the track to 'Ain Jozele, one mile north-west of Jisr ed Damiye, cut the Wadi el Far'a road, and secure the crossing. The Wellington Regiment was to seize El Makhruk, a little higher up the Wadi el Far'a road, whence another track ran northwards along the valley.

'Ain Jozele was reached just as a considerable Turkish column had passed through and was in the act of crossing the Jordan. The leading squadron of the Aucklands made

---

[1] See p. 512.

CAPTURE OF JISR ED DAMIYE 551

a dash for the bank, but the enemy, now with his back to the wall, counter-attacked fiercely and drove the New Zealanders back some hundred yards. A second squadron moved up, but the enemy was likewise reinforced, and endeavoured to turn the right flank of the Aucklands.

1918.
22 Sept.

The 1/B.W.I. had not reached Kh. Fasail till 1.30 a.m. There Lieut.-Colonel C. Wood-Hill received an urgent message from Br.-General Meldrum to move on at once towards Jisr ed Damiye. Dumping his kits and blankets in order to march light, he arrived south of 'Ain Jozele at 5 a.m. The Wellington Regiment had meanwhile seized El Makhruk, just as another column reached it, and captured here several hundred prisoners, including the commander of the *53rd Division*—the second occasion in the war on which a commander of this division was taken by troops of the A. & N.Z. Mounted Division, the first being at Gaza in March 1917. A third column, five hundred strong, with two mountain guns, was seen at 7 a.m. advancing down the Wadi el Far'a road. Before it came within range another body of the enemy east of Red Hill began moving back on Mafid Jozele, apparently tempted by the prospect of cutting off Br.-General Meldrum's force while it was still hotly engaged at Jisr ed Damiye and threatened on the other flank by the Wadi el Far'a column. The situation of the New Zealanders was for the moment anxious.

The 1st L. H. Brigade (Br.-General C. F. Cox) had meanwhile marched to Kh. Fasail. Here at 8.15 a.m. it received orders from Major-general Chaytor to clear the broken ground west of Mafid Jozele. Its rear thus covered, Br.-General Meldrum's force speedily disposed of the threat to either flank. On the left the Wellington Regiment, supported by a squadron of the Canterbury, drove the Wadi el Far'a column back into the hills. On the right a general advance on Jisr ed Damiye, covered by the fire of the two batteries, began at 10.50, and a dashing bayonet attack by the Auckland, a squadron of the Canterbury, and a company of the 1/B.W.I., broke right through the enemy's rear guard. A troop of the Auckland, which was standing by its horses awaiting this moment, galloped straight to the bridge and captured a number of fleeing Turks. At Mafid Jozele the 2/B.W.I., supported by the 3rd A.L.H., drove in the enemy's rear guard covering this crossing-place and captured 37 prisoners, though bodies of Turks maintained themselves west of the Jordan until nightfall. Early in the morning the 38/R. Fusiliers had found the enemy's resistance weakening on the Mellaha, had pushed back his rear guard, and secured the crossing at Umm esh Shert. The last of the enemy's defences west of Jordan had now fallen, and he had lost 786 prisoners, 6 guns, and 9 machine guns. From the reports of the R.A.F. it appeared that only about six hundred men had escaped across the Jordan at Jisr ed Damiye before the bridge was secured. These belonged to the *Seventh Army*, and probably for the most part to the *53rd Division*. At Mafid Jozele and Umm esh Shert the greater part of the troops opposed to Major-General Chaytor had been able to cross. There were indications that the *Fourth Army*, having waited as long as Jemal Pasha dared in the hopes of saving the troops south of 'Amman on the Hejaz Railway, was now about to begin a general retreat.

THE CAPTURE OF 'AMMAN AND INTERCEPTION OF THE MA'AN GARRISON.

Map 22.
Sketches
24, 35.

Before midnight Major-General Chaytor issued orders to his troops to press hard upon the enemy's heels and inflict all the damage possible upon him next day. The 2nd L.H. Brigade was to advance against Qabr Said and Qabr Mujahid. The mobile portion of the 20th Indian Brigade [1] was to move straight up the main Es Salt road on Shunet Nimrin. It was to be accompanied by A/263 Battery and to have the support of all the heavy artillery if required. The 1st L.H. Brigade was to drive back the enemy opposite Mafid Jozele into the foot-hills. The New Zealand Brigade, leaving one squadron and the 1/B.W.I. at Jisr ed Damiye, was to cross the Jordan there, followed by the 1/B.W.I., and if possible capture Es Salt, moving by the Damiye track. The two Jewish battalions, now placed under the senior commanding officer, Lieut.-Colonel

---

[1] In order to make the eight infantry battalions sufficiently mobile for a possible advance to 'Amman, it had been necessary to withdraw the equivalent of a company from each and a certain number of machine guns and Lewis guns. The immobile portion was to remain in the defences. The mobile strength of the 20th Brigade was 1,500 rifles, 3 sections of machine guns, and 40 Lewis guns.

J. H. Patterson, as " Patterson's Column," were to concentrate at the 'Auja bridgehead in readiness to follow the 20th Indian Brigade.

1918.
23 Sept.

The 23rd September was an inspiring day for Chaytor's Force. Directly the sun was up it became clear that the enemy would make no stand in the valley; before darkness fell it was shown that he dared not fight even upon the eastern scarp. By that time the four columns had all entered the hills on a frontage of nearly fifteen miles. Patrols of the 2nd L.H. Brigade found first Qabr Mujahid, and at 11.40 a.m. El Helali, 2 miles to the north-east, unoccupied. The 20th Brigade, with a squadron of the 2nd L.H. Brigade as advanced guard, reached Tell el Mistah in the foot-hills at 6.30 p.m., having the pleasure of seeing "Jericho Jane," the 150-mm. gun which had caused so much annoyance, lying abandoned in a gully by the roadside. The 1st L.H. Brigade crossed at Umm esh Shert and made its way without opposition up the Wadi Abu Turra track, leaving its transport to follow by the main road. The New Zealand Brigade alone met with some resistance as it wound its way up the Damiye track, but the advanced guard of the Canterbury Regiment was scarcely checked. A strongly-held redoubt a mile west of Es Salt was skilfully outflanked, and promptly surrendered, 169 prisoners being taken. At 4.20 p.m. the leading regiment rode into Es Salt, this being the third occasion in six months that the town had been captured by the British. Over five hundred prisoners, mostly stragglers and administrative troops, three guns, and large quantities of stores were found in it. The 1st L.H. Brigade arrived at midnight, but Patterson's Column, which had had exhausting work clearing the banks of the Jordan, was not ready to cross the river until after that hour. In each column a day's rations on the emergency scale were carried by the troops, as all wheeled vehicles had to concentrate that night at Shunet Nimrin.

During the night Major-General Chaytor received orders from G.H.Q. to continue his pressure and endeavour to cut off the enemy's retreat northward from 'Amman. He had, however, some difficulty in getting his supplies through on the 24th, the main road having been badly damaged with explosives by the retreating Turks. The 2nd L.H. Brigade, marching by the very difficult track

24 Sept.

up the Wadis Jeri'a and Sir, reached 'Ain Hummar, on the main road 5 miles east of Es Salt, in the afternoon, where it joined the 1st L.H. Brigade. The New Zealanders had meanwhile moved forward and occupied Suweile, whence a party of one hundred men of the Auckland Regiment, with picked horses, was sent forward to cut the railway 5 miles north of 'Amman. The detachment accomplished its mission and was back within eleven hours, having covered 20 miles of trackless country.

1918.
25 Sept.

At 6 a.m. on the 25th the mounted troops advanced on 'Amman. On the right was the 2nd L.H. Brigade; on the left the New Zealand Brigade; in reserve the 1st L.H. Brigade, which also had instructions to watch the left flank. The 2nd L.H. Brigade was for some time held up by Turkish posts 4 miles west of 'Amman, but drove them in by a vigorous attack. As the leading troops pressed in on the town resistance stiffened. At 10.40 a.m. an aeroplane dropped a message that the enemy was evacuating 'Amman, but his rear guard was still fighting stoutly enough, and the lack of any artillery other than the two mountain batteries which had accompanied the mounted troops was a severe handicap in face of hot machine-gun fire. The Canterbury Regiment made an attempt to advance mounted, but, being checked by the Citadel, attacked it on foot and carried it with the bayonet, capturing 119 prisoners and 6 machine guns. The 1st L.H. Brigade had meanwhile despatched the 1st A.L.H. round the left flank of the New Zealanders, and this regiment advanced on the railway. At the same time a squadron of the 7th A.L.H. carried some Turkish sangars on the right of the 5th, the leading regiment of the 2nd L.H. Brigade. The defence cracked suddenly. At 1.30 p.m. the 5th A.L.H. entered the southern part of the town. There was some street fighting, but the enemy was speedily driven out. The local authorities and notabilities met Br.-General Ryrie with a white flag and handed over the town to him. Meanwhile troops of the Canterbury Regiment had galloped in, followed shortly afterwards by the remainder of the regiment, which made for the station. A general advance all along the front followed, and all was quickly over. The captures were 2,563 prisoners, 10 guns, numerous machine guns, and 300 horses. Considerable quantities of forage were fortunately found in the place, and it was possible to buy from the inhabitants some food, including livestock, though at exorbitant prices.

1918.
25 Sept.

The attack had thus succeeded in cutting off the Turkish rear guard at 'Amman. The remainder of the garrison, and also apparently the troops from Qatrani, had escaped northward, the last trains having left the station on the night of the 24th just before the line was cut. There were, however, breaches further north made by the Arabs, so that the retreating Turks would soon be forced to detrain. Major-General Chaytor's task was not to pursue them but, in accordance with orders received from G.H.Q. on the 25th, to bar the road to the troops from Ma'an, reported from the air to be moving up the railway. He ordered the 20th Indian Brigade to move on from Es Salt, which it was to hand over to the 39/R. Fusiliers, and take over the defence of 'Amman. In case the enemy attempted to advance north between 'Amman and the Jordan, he gave orders to Lieut.-Colonel Patterson that Shunet Nimrin, Es Salt, and Suweile were to be entrenched, and directed the 2nd L.H. Brigade to watch the Madeba–Na'ur–'Ain Hummar road across the plateau. His troops, now some three thousand feet above sea level after having been for long a thousand feet below it, were suffering from cold at night and already beginning to go down rapidly to attacks of malaria, which were to cripple the force completely after the fight was won.

On the 26th the 1st L.H. Brigade, after a short action at Qal'at ez Zerqa Station, 12 miles north-east of 'Amman, captured 105 prisoners and a gun. On the following days patrols were despatched northward along the line, a troop of the 1st A.L.H. actually reaching Qal'at el Mafraq, 30 miles as the crow flies N.N.E. of 'Amman, on the 28th, where several trains with ammunition and one Red Crescent train full of wounded were found. South of 'Amman the 2nd L.H. Brigade came in contact with Turkish troops near Libban Station on the 27th, and captured a prisoner who declared that the Ma'an garrison was moving up the line and that its head had reached El Qastal, a few miles further south. The brigade had already damaged the railway in this neighbourhood. On the 28th the force was located by an aeroplane. The pilot dropped a message to its commander that all water which he could possibly reach was

26 Sept.

27 Sept.

28 Sept.

in British hands, and that if he did not surrender his force would be bombed next day.

1918. 29 Sept.

Early on the morning of the 29th the 5th A.L.H., less one squadron, advanced down the railway to establish contact with the enemy. At Libban natives reported that there were no troops in Qastal, but that Ziza, 3 miles south of it, was held in strength. The regiment halted 700 yards north of the Turkish position. On the hills east and west of the railway station hundreds of men, mounted on horses and camels, could be seen: their patient, watchful attitude suggesting the spectacle of vultures attending on a dying man.

At 10.30 a trolley, flying a white flag, ran up the line. An officer, who had been driven up on it, handed to Lieut.-Colonel D. C. Cameron a letter from the Turkish commandant, who desired to see him. Before this could be arranged, however, another message came from the Turk that he wanted to surrender, but was afraid to lay down his arms, since he did not think the Australian force was strong enough to protect him from those menacing onlookers on the sky-line. Lieut.-Colonel Cameron then sent Captain J. M. Boyd to interview the commandant, and his representative returned with the following formal surrender:—

"I hereby surrender unconditionally all my force, "guns, ammunition, stores, etc., at Ziza under my command, "and in so doing claim your protection for the safety of "my soldiers, wounded, and sick."

The commandant made, however, the reasonable request that the British squadrons should not enter the position until reinforcements arrived to protect the garrison from the Bedouin. These were now gathering in force on every hand, and launching attacks upon the Turks from east, south, and west, while to the north the Australians stood quietly to their arms. The signallers had repaired the telephone line along the railway, which had been cut in several places, and Chaytor's Force had been informed of what was happening. But at 2.45 p.m. Lieut.-Colonel Cameron learnt that it was not certain whether the message sent off to cancel the bombing attack had reached the Air Force in time. With great presence of mind he sent into the Turkish position the ground-sign employed to indicate the position of his regimental report-centre to.

A GRIM COMEDY

aircraft, and had it spread out behind the trenches. The Turkish commander was informed of the situation and advised to put his men under cover. Colonel Ali Bey was deeply grateful for this chivalrous action, but did not blench at the prospect of the raid. If it came, he said resignedly, it would be the will of God.

1918. 29 Sept.

Three-quarters of an hour later Cameron, to his great relief, received a message from Major-General Chaytor's chief staff officer, Lieut.-Colonel J. G. Browne, that the raid had been cancelled. He still had cause for anxiety while awaiting reinforcements, and finally despatched another message to the Turks that if these did not arrive before dark they must keep their trenches manned all night. The spectacle before him furnished a grim proof of the havoc played by fatigue and the depression of defeat upon the nerves of good troops. The Turks, superior in discipline, training, equipment, and probably even in numbers, to the aggressors, were terror-stricken. They knew that the regular Arab troops behind them had occupied Ma'an and Jerdun, so that there was no turning back. They feared that the Australians might abandon them to the wild desert men gathered about them, and this dread almost paralysed them. Stragglers, pounced upon by little groups of Bedouin, made no effort to use their arms, but were borne away screaming. Cameron had several interviews with the sheikhs, who offered to assist him in an assault, but maintained that if the enemy had surrendered they should be allowed to go in and take the arms. He replied that he intended to protect the Turks, who had given themselves up to him, and at last declared roundly to the Arabs that if they persisted in their attacks he would be forced to fire on them. The threat had a good effect, though there were some critical moments thereafter.

About 5 p.m. Major-General Chaytor arrived from 'Amman. As he drove up, the Turkish Chief of the Staff was coming out under a white flag. Major-General Chaytor informed him that as reinforcements could not arrive before the fall of darkness the Turks might hold their trenches all night. In the morning they must lay down their arms, which were not to be damaged. If these terms were accepted the commandant was to come out as a hostage. The general's A.D.C. then drove Lieut.-Colonel Cameron and the

Turkish officer into Ziza to bring Colonel Ali Bey to him. The commander of the force was very reluctant to quit his troops and showed great concern for their safety, and particularly for the fate of the numerous sick. A few minutes later Br.-General Ryrie came up at a gallop, having ridden on ahead of the other two regiments of the 2nd L.H. Brigade, and was left in charge by Major-General Chaytor, who drove back to 'Amman with Colonel Ali Bey.

Br.-General Ryrie, after a conference with the Turkish officers at Ziza, placed parties of the 5th and 7th A.L.H. in position at intervals in the Turkish line. To the Australian troopers the grim humour of the situation appealed forcibly, and they sat round their bivouac fires greeting every burst of fire from the machine guns of the nervous Turks with cheers and laughter. In the morning the Turks were concentrated at the station, where the bolts were taken from their rifles. The two best battalions, of Anatolian Turks, were, however, ordered by Br.-General Ryrie to keep their bolts and full bandoliers, in case of a Bedouin attack on the march. The arrival of these fine troops, fully armed, in 'Amman caused, as can well be imagined, no small sensation. All the most seriously wounded and sick were put on the camel *cacolets* of the 2nd L.H. Field Ambulance, the remainder being left to be brought to 'Amman, as soon as the line could be repaired, by the railway trains which had accompanied the Turkish force. The New Zealand Brigade, which arrived at 5.30 a.m., took over the protection of the station, the sick, and the stores. Then the 5th A.L.H. marched northward with 4,068 prisoners, leaving 534 sick for the trains. In addition to these 4,602 prisoners[1] there were 14 guns, 35 machine guns, 3 engines, 25 trucks, and considerable quantities of ammunition and stores. The captures by Chaytor's Force for the whole period of operations were 10,322 prisoners, 57 guns, 132 machine guns, 11 engines, 106 railway trucks and carriages. Large numbers of lorries rendered useless by the enemy were also taken, and

---

[1] This did not represent anything like the strength of the force. A great number, possibly some thousands, of local men slipped away in the night. A few days afterwards a deputation came to Major-General Chaytor to inquire what these men's position was. It was overjoyed to be told that the war here was over and that if they remained quietly at home they should not be interfered with.

huge stocks of ammunition. The casualties, from first to last, were 139. The heaviest loss in any unit was 41 in the 2/B.W.I.

Thus the force, at very light cost, had carried out its mission with astounding success. Cool and skilful direction, careful staff work had advanced it step by step on the enemy's heels; every move had inflicted the maximum of damage on the Turks with the minimum of risk to itself. The resistance of the enemy had nowhere been serious, except at Jisr ed Damiye and for an hour or two at 'Amman, but the whole operation would not have had a tithe of the results which it achieved without clever handling, good timing, and the determination of the troops.

CHAPTER XXVI.

THE PURSUIT THROUGH SYRIA AND CAPTURE OF DAMASCUS.

(Maps 1, 2A, 3, 21, 23; Sketches 35, 38, 39, 40.)

ORDERS FOR A NEW ADVANCE.

Maps 1, 21. Sketch 35. THE plan which the British Commander-in-Chief had already unfolded had been as extensive as it was bold. It had involved the complete rupture of the Turkish front by his infantry and a great flank march by his cavalry, ending in the destruction of the two enemy Armies west of Jordan. The objective had been distant enough to call for a mighty physical effort on the part of troops and horses, and to impose severe strain upon administrative and transport services. What more was in Sir Edmund Allenby's mind he had kept to himself, not diverting men's thoughts to a second spring while spirits and bodies were braced for the first. To General Chauvel he had said not a word regarding an advance on Damascus.

Now all that he had asked of his commanders and troops had been rendered to him. The objective was taken; the two Turkish Armies were virtually destroyed, for nothing was left of them but a couple of weak columns, almost without artillery or transport, struggling northward beyond Jordan. The *Fourth Army*, though in far greater numbers and unbroken, was likewise in full retreat and had suffered heavily. Thanks to the cutting of the railway by the Arabs south of Der'a, it was compelled to march. It would have difficulty in reaching Damascus before the British cavalry, and if it were caught upon the road its doom was inevitable. There had been time to move up detachments of infantry from the XX and XXI Corps to take over the advanced positions in the Plain of Esdraelon and at Nazareth held by the cavalry, and so free the latter for a fresh task; time also to transfer a proportion of the transport originally employed

by General Bulfin to the service of General Chauvel. There
was no longer any serious obstacle to the capture of the
famous and ancient Syrian capital.

*1918.
22 Sept.*

On the 22nd September Sir Edmund Allenby had visited the advanced headquarters of the Desert Mounted Corps at El Lajjun and then for the first time mentioned to General Chauvel his new design. At that moment he gave no instructions. The *Fourth Army* was not yet manœuvred out of its fortifications at 'Amman; Haifa, which was to provide a new landing-place for supplies, was not yet captured; the enemy's rear-guard position at Samakh and Tiberias was still unbroken. General Chauvel, however, was thus given an opportunity to prepare his plans. It was not until the 25th that Br.-General Bartholomew was sent from G.H.Q. to explain to the staffs of the Desert Mounted and XXI Corps the Commander-in-Chief's intentions. On the 26th, he himself held a corps commanders' conference at Jenin, and on the same day his orders for the advance were issued. On the capture of Haifa, the 7th Division of the XXI Corps had been directed to despatch a brigade group to that town to relieve the 5th Cavalry Division there. The 2/Leicester of the 28th Brigade was sent on ahead in lorries with six days' supplies on the 24th, arriving next morning. The 21st Brigade marched up the coast, and, after great difficulties with its transport, reached Haifa on the 27th. The remainder of the 7th Division was ordered to follow. The 7th Brigade of the 3rd Division, put at the disposal of the Desert Mounted Corps, moved up *via* Jenin to Nazareth and, leaving one battalion there, on to Samakh on the 28th. On the 26th the Inspector-General of the Lines of Communication took over control of all the country south of a line from Jisr ed Damiye on the Jordan to the mouth of the Nahr el Faliq on the Mediterranean.

26 Sept.

Sir Edmund Allenby's order began with the statement that he intended to advance to Damascus and Beirut, employing the Desert Mounted Corps and two divisions of the XXI Corps. The cavalry was to set out for Damascus at once, two divisions west of the Sea of Galilee, the third moving in the first instance to Der'a, and after disposing of the retreating *Fourth Army*, rejoining the remainder of the corps. One division of the XXI Corps was to advance from Haifa and Acre to Beirut, and was to be followed by a second when it was possible to provide for its maintenance. General Chauvel at once issued his orders by telegram. The Australian Mounted and 5th Cavalry Divisions, now concentrated about Tiberias and Nazareth respectively, were to march across the Jordan at Jisr Benat Yakub, on the southern shore of Lake Hule, through El Quneitra, where the Australian Division was to arrive on the morning of the 28th. On reaching Damascus a defensive position was to be taken up on high ground commanding the city, and all approaches covered.[1] The 4th Cavalry Division had already received instructions to march on Der'a and co-operate with the Arab forces which were attacking the railway, and was afterwards to advance northward by the Darb el Hajj, or Pilgrims' Road, through Es Sanamein and Kiswe to Damascus.

The problem of supplying the mounted troops was even more difficult than it had been during the first advance. The arrangement made by Br.-General E. F. Trew, D.A. & Q.M.G. of the Desert Mounted Corps, was that the troops should march with two days' supplies for themselves and at least one for their horses. As horsed transport would be unable to keep up, he proposed to assemble an echelon of lorries at El 'Affule to follow the 5th Cavalry and Australian Mounted Divisions, up the fair road through Quneitra along which they were to march. For the 4th Cavalry Division, which was moving *via* Der'a, he hoped to employ the captured Turkish railway, which had been put in order from Haifa to Samakh by the 27th; but this part of the programme broke down, owing to the insufficiency of the captured rolling stock and the damage it had suffered. Three companies of the Camel Transport Corps, which were moved to Jisr el Majami' to feed the 4th Cavalry Division, proved too slow for the purpose, and the supply situation became at one moment very serious. The 4th Cavalry Division was obliged to requisition meat and forage on its march, and even then the troops had finished their iron rations when they reached Damascus. It was only for the march, however, and perhaps for a few days afterwards, that Br.-General Trew expected much trouble. The landing of supplies from the sea had begun at Haifa on the 27th. He hoped shortly

---

[1] Desert Corps G.A. 72 is given in Appendix 27.

Sketch 38.

Arab Raids against the Railway: 16th–27th September, 1918, & March of 4th CAVALRY DIVISION, 28th–29th Sept, 1918.

to be able to move these by rail to El 'Affule, and later perhaps to Samakh, and to take them on thence to Damascus by lorry. The British railway had now reached Ras el 'Ain and was being pushed forward towards Tul Karm on the Turkish permanent way, reaching that town on the 15th October. It did not, however, reach Haifa until January 1919.

With regard to the XXI Corps, the 7th Division and 102nd Brigade R.G.A. were concentrated at Haifa, with the Corps Cavalry Regiment at Acre, by the 29th. The 54th Division was ordered to take its place as soon as it began its march up the coast to Beirut, but owing to the difficulty of supplying the two divisions so far from railhead the two rear brigade groups of the 54th were considerably delayed. The 7th Division was ordered to resume its advance on the 3rd October.

The Arab Northern Army.

So far, all that has been recorded of the Arabs is that Sketch 38. they had begun to attack the railway in the neighbourhood of Der'a and between that station and 'Amman before the launching of the British attack. We have mentioned, however, in Chapter XVIII the attempt by Major Buxton's column of Camel Corps to destroy the main bridge at 'Amman. That had failed, but its failure was not of grave consequence and had small effect upon the general plan of operations evolved by Lieut.-Colonel Lawrence at Sir Edmund Allenby's request. The Commander-in-Chief wished the Arabs to begin their attacks on the line about Der'a not more than four or less than two days before the opening of his offensive on the 19th September. He asked chiefly for moral effect. He hoped, indeed, that this might be combined with some material damage which would hinder the working of the railway, but his first demand was that the nerves of the Turks should be stretched and the attention of their command turned to the Trans-Jordan front. The British officers with the Arabs were confident that they could give him what he wanted; but Lieut.-Colonel Lawrence at least was determined that in this, probably the last task of the war, the Arabs should pull their weight, that, for the sake of their self-respect and political future, they should contribute grandly to the coming victory.

The plan was to march a mobile column, of about 450 regular Sherifial Camel Corps with 20 Hotchkiss guns, the French mountain battery under Captain Pisani, two armoured cars, a party of Egyptian Camel Corps for demolitions, a detachment of Gurkhas with 4 machine guns, to Qasr el 'Azraq, a Roman fort in the desert, with large pools of pure water and the shelter of palms, 60 miles south-east of Der'a. A landing ground was to be prepared for two aeroplanes provided by the R.A.F. Nuri esh Shalaan,[1] the greatest desert chieftain of this region, who had at last burned his boats by bringing out his tribesmen against the Turks, was to join the force here with his camel-mounted men; Auda Abu Tayi was to come with his Howeitat, Talal el Hareidhin with the villagers of the Hauran who gave him allegiance. The so-called "Hejaz Revolt" had spread to new ground, and at this moment there was scarcely a Hejazi in the mobile column but Sherif Nasir, Feisal's friend, who had seen almost every action since the outbreak of the revolt more than two years ago. With this force, which might amount to five thousand, Der'a was to be enveloped on the 16th September, and the railway lines north, west, and south of it cut.

The remainder of the Arab Northern Army under Ja'far Pasha was to hold its ground, ready to occupy Ma'an if the Turks abandoned it, while a detachment prepared to cause a diversion by an attack upon Madeba. That plan was foiled by the enemy, who suddenly, after the 'Azraq expedition had marched, advanced from the railway and again occupied Tafila. However, naught could have been more fortunate than this move of the Turks, who were marching south as their attackers marched north and playing into the hands of British and Arabs by still further dispersing their force.

A petty dispute between King Hussein and the Arab officers, due to the King's temper and obstinacy, almost wrecked the plan and slightly delayed its operation. However, the troops were sent forward from Abu el Lasan to 'Azraq, and Lawrence, who had remained to patch up the

---

[1] See Vol. I, p. 239.

ARAB ATTACKS ON RAILWAY

quarrel, started north by car with Sherif Nasir and Major Lord Winterton on the 4th September, and caught them up. The whole force was concentrated at 'Azraq by the 12th, the bulk of it then moving on to El Umtaiye, a village 15 miles south-east of Der'a, but only 5 miles east of the railway at the bridges near Jabir. An attack was carried out on the 16th with the aid of the armoured cars, the blockhouse covering the bridges captured, and one of them destroyed. Next day came the turn of the line north of Der'a. The redoubt on Tell 'Arar was taken by 200 Arab regulars, covered by the fire of the French battery, and extensive demolitions carried out. While the action here was in progress a strong detachment moved on Muzeirib, the junction with the old French line to Damascus, took the station, and again damaged the line. It was decided not to attack Der'a itself, which was strongly reinforced on the 17th by German troops from El 'Affule, but another bridge was destroyed at Nasib, the first station to the south, on the 18th, and on the 19th Captain Peake cut the line north of Mafraq, about half-way between 'Amman and Der'a.

The Arabs were playing a dangerous game, however, in thus sitting down in front of the railway junction. Fairly safe from attack by ground troops owing to their mobility and the enemy's lack of cavalry, they were on several occasions bombed by aircraft, of which there were about nine at Der'a aerodrome. Of the two British machines at 'Azraq, one had been put out of action, though its adversary had fallen in flames; the other was a B.E.12, no match for the German scouts. On the 20th Lawrence motored to 'Azraq, met an aeroplane which bore him news of the British victory, and flew in it back to Palestine. At G.H.Q. Major-General Salmond, commanding Middle East R.A.F., agreed to send him two Bristol Fighters, and, in order to supply them with petrol, promised to despatch the great Handley Page bomber, the only one in Palestine, if it could land. Captain Ross Smith,[1] No. 1 Squadron Australian Air Force, the pilot of the Handley Page, flew over with the Bristols to Umm es Surab, whither the Arabs had shifted camp to avoid the bombing and the fire of a gun on the railway, and found that it was quite possible for the giant machine to land.

---
[1] Later Sir Ross Smith, who made the first flight from England to Australia in 1919 and was killed in an aeroplane accident in 1922.

He duly returned and brought it over, but it was scarcely required except as an exhibition of British might; for before its arrival the Der'a squadron had been practically accounted for by the Bristols. The Arabs were thenceforth unmolested, and the British machines shortly afterwards returned to Palestine.

1918.
23 Sept.
On the 23rd the Arabs made a new descent upon the railway at Jabir and burned the wooden bridge which the Turks were throwing in place of that destroyed a week earlier. The enemy made no further effort to mend this line, but the energy of the Germans had restored communication between Der'a and Samakh, and also north of Der'a. Another attack on the line near Mafraq was beaten off by German machine gunners. The *Fourth Army* was at last on the move north, a column of between two and three hundred having reached Mafraq on the night of the 24th. The Air Force promptly bombed the station and set it afire, so that it burned fiercely all the following day.

Now had come the great moment which the Arabs were awaiting. Chaytor's Force had entered 'Amman on the afternoon of the 25th, and that same morning the Australians had stormed Samakh. The *Fourth Army* was streaming northward. The British cavalry was about to begin its advance on Damascus. Before the astonished eyes of the Arabs the Turkish Syrian Empire was tumbling down. They saw their old enemy reeling to destruction; they saw a vision of freedom and, nearer at hand, a vision of loot. Their passion for both flamed up and possessed them.

Hitherto Nuri esh Shalaan's wild camel-men had been kept at 'Azraq as doubtful bed-fellows and allies to the Fellahin of the Hauran villages. Now Feisal decided to bring them up, thus raising the total strength of his force to 4,000, three-fourths of whom were irregulars. The whole column made a forced night march northward, crossed the railway north of Der'a, again tearing up rails to check the resumed stream of traffic, and arrived at Sheikh Sa'd,
27 Sept. 15 miles N.N.W. of Der'a, at dawn on the 27th. Breaking off from the line of march, Auda Abu Tayi captured a train and 200 prisoners at Ghazale Station; Talal took Izra', a few miles further north, with rich booty. Between noon on the 26th and noon on the 27th two thousand prisoners were captured. At dusk a party of Anazeh tribesmen burst

THE ADVANCE BEGINS

into Der'a, which had been abandoned by the main body of its garrison but was still held by a rear guard, and spent the night in killing, in burning and looting the station and the camps about it. On the morning of the 28th touch was obtained with the 4th Cavalry Division.

1918.
27 Sept.

THE ADVANCE ON DAMASCUS.

When, in the record of a great engagement, operations are described in detail for the sake of their tactical incidents, it inevitably befalls that events closely connected by time, by their influence one upon another, perhaps even by space, become widely separated in the narrative. Let us therefore restore perspective by a bird's-eye view of the battlefield at the beginning of the British advance to Damascus.

Maps 2A, 3.
Sketches 38, 39, 40.

On the 27th September, when that advance began, the bulk of the Turkish *Fourth Army* and what of the other two had escaped destruction were either at or north of Der'a and Muzeirib, which towns the tails of their straggling columns were just quitting. Some units had got through by train and were thus beyond reach of pursuit. But the greater number, already exhausted by forced marches, by lack of food and of sleep, with hearts broken by dread of mounted pursuit and of the yet swifter enemy in the skies above, with boots worn to ribbons, had about seventy-five miles to cover afoot before they could reach the city. On their flank were the Arabs at Sheikh Sa'd, terrible foes to a beaten and retreating army, above all to one conscious of misdeeds and cruelties crying aloud for retribution. From Beisan the 4th Cavalry Division was moving eastward on Der'a, there to turn northward and pursue them up the Pilgrims' Road. On the other road, from Tiberias through Quneitra, the Australian and 5th Cavalry Divisions were preparing to race these unhappy fugitives to Damascus.

Australian Mounted Division. The Australian Mounted Division marched out from Tiberias at 6 a.m. on the morning of the 27th, followed by the 5th Cavalry Division, which had concentrated at Kufr Kenna the previous day, and corps headquarters. The Australians, as well as their horses, had benefited by a short rest on the shores of the Sea of Galilee, and rejoiced to find themselves once more in the van. It was known that the beautiful four-arch bridge at Jisr Benat

Yakub (Bridge of the Daughters of Jacob), which dated from the fourteenth century, had been broken by the enemy, and the 3rd L.H. Brigade had orders to seek for fords in its neighbourhood. The 9th A.L.H., sent forward to reconnoitre, discovered the enemy holding the left bank of the river from the bridge to Lake Hule. Major-General Hodgson sent orders to the 3rd Brigade to engage the Turks south of the lake, and if possible find a crossing near it, so as to work round their right flank. The 5th Brigade was to advance on the Jordan on the right of the 3rd, hold the enemy to his ground opposite the bridge with one regiment, and force a crossing at El Min, a mile and a half further south. The 4th A.L.H. temporarily attached to the 5th Brigade, forded the river here without great opposition, followed by the 14th A.L.H., but all the efforts of the 3rd L.H. Brigade on the left were unavailing while daylight lasted. In the twilight a crossing was effected here also by the 10th A.L.H., and a squadron captured a strong enemy post after hot close fighting, taking 50 prisoners and three guns which had previously been put out of action by the Notts Battery. The 4th A.L.H. after crossing the river advanced about a mile and a half eastward to Ed Dora, but there Lieut.-Colonel Bourchier decided to halt owing to the roughness of the ground. The envelopment of the enemy, for which Major-General Hodgson had hoped, was therefore not completed, and the rear guard was able to withdraw in motor-lorries. Though the 3rd L.H. Brigade struck the road at Deir es Saras, 4 miles up, by midnight, it had then already passed that point and escaped.

**1918.
28 Sept.**

The Corps Bridging Train, which had been obliged to dump its heavy trestle-bridge material, but had collected timber at El 'Affule, had been sent forward in motor lorries, and in five hours put up a high trestle bridge to span the demolished arch of the old stone bridge. Meanwhile the engineers of the divisional squadron had improved the neighbouring fords. Soon after 7 a.m. on the 28th the advance was resumed, the 3rd L.H. Brigade in the van. There was some trouble from bombing by enemy aircraft, but few casualties resulted. At 1 p.m., the leading troops, brushing aside the resistance of a weak rear guard, entered Quneitra, where water was found in plenty; and at dusk the division bivouacked there, with the 3rd L.H. Brigade

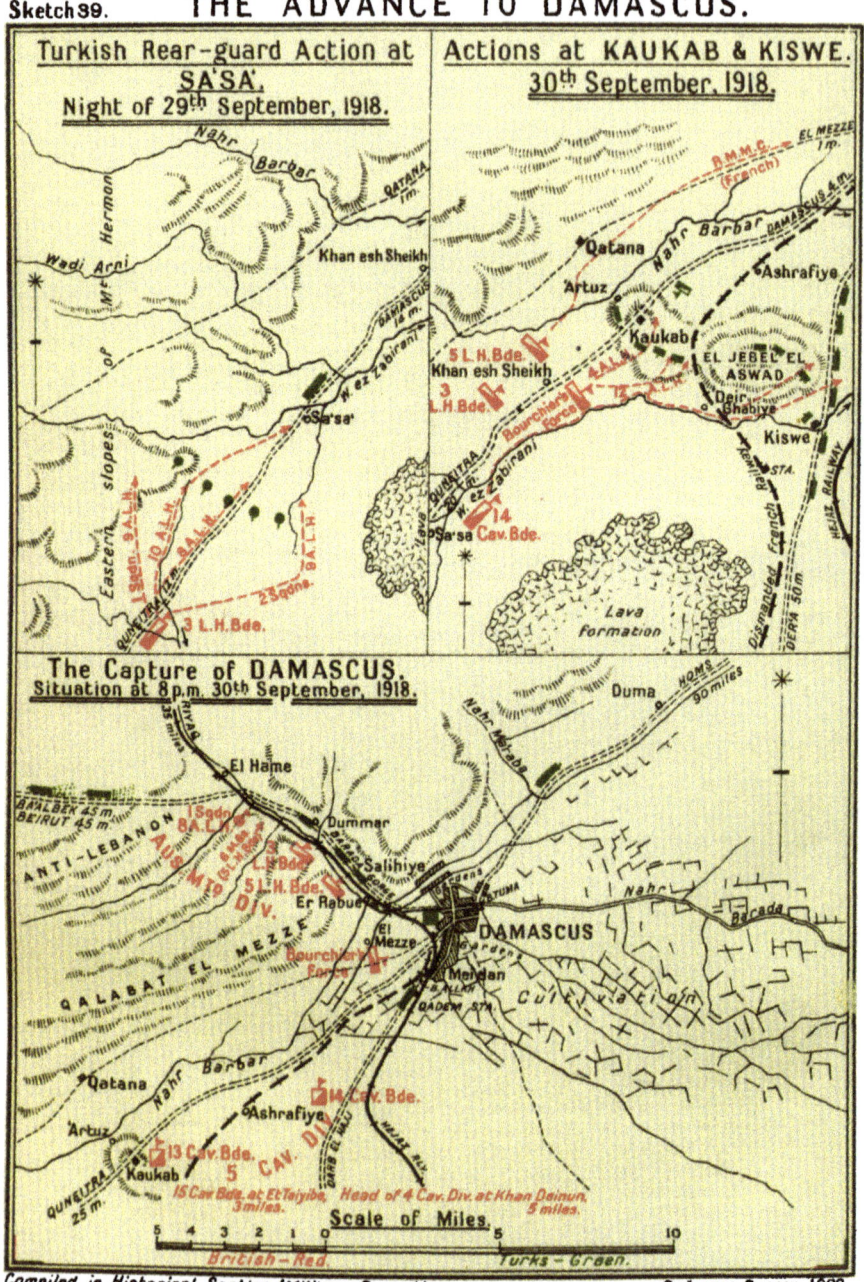

ACTION AT SA'SA'

about three miles along the Damascus road. By this time **1918.** all fighting troops of the 5th Cavalry Division were also **28 Sept.** across the Jordan. Some delay was caused by a lorry breaking the temporary arch of the bridge, but it was again speedily repaired.

General Chauvel considered it necessary owing to the hostile attitude of local Circassians to drop a strong force, with headquarters and the bulk of its troops at Quneitra, to guard and organize his lines of communication from Safed, 9 miles south-west of Jisr Benat Yakub, onwards. Br.-General Grant was given the command with four regiments under his orders: the 11th A.L.H. of his own brigade, the 15th A.L.H. of the 5th L.H. Brigade, the Sherwood Rangers and Hyderabad Lancers of the 5th Cavalry Division. The 14th A.L.H. and Sherwood Rangers were, however, to be held in reserve and sent on to Damascus if required. In addition, all men dismounted or whose horses were flagging were formed into six brigade groups and left at Quneitra under Br.-General Grant's orders. The remaining regiments of the 4th L.H. Brigade (the 4th and 12th A.L.H.) were placed under the command of Lieut.-Colonel M. W. J. Bourchier and henceforth known as " Bourchier's " Force."

While Major-General Hodgson was making these **29 Sept.** arrangements, resting his troops, and awaiting his transport, the cars of the 11th Light Armoured Motor Battery drew fire from a force of all arms posted astride the road 3 miles south-west of Sa'sa', which lies 20 miles beyond Quneitra. At 2 p.m. on the 29th orders were issued for the advance to be continued. Major-General Hodgson intended, first, to move rapidly forward to the Wadi ez Zabirani—perhaps the Pharpar of Naaman the Syrian—which crossed the road beyond Sa'sa', there to halt and push out reconnaissances towards Kaukab and Qatana, two villages lying some ten miles south-west of Damascus; secondly, to break or pass round the right flank of a trench system reported to run through Kaukab across the high ground east of it, and to cut the Aleppo and Homs roads north of the city. From the rear guard south of Sa'sa' he expected little resistance.

When the 9th A.L.H., advanced guard to the 3rd L.H. Brigade, attempted to approach the enemy's position in front of Sa'sa' it was found that the problem was not so simple as had appeared, especially in view of the late start made by the British. The opposing force held slightly rising ground bestrewn with boulders, and its left flank rested upon a rough lava formation. Heavy machine-gun fire was directed down the road, and, the guns having been laid by daylight, lost nothing of its accuracy as dusk began to fall. At 8.30 p.m. two squadrons of the 9th A.L.H. moved out eastward to outflank the enemy, with orders to light a green flare when the hill on his extreme left had been gained. In the darkness they found themselves floundering across eight-foot crevasses, but reached the objective by 10. The third squadron had at the same time been ordered to clear the hill on the enemy's right, and the 10th A.L.H. was subsequently directed to support it. The action, however, went slowly, the Turks and Germans being very difficult to shift from their positions amid the rocks. At 2 a.m. on the 30th, just as the flanking attacks were beginning to dislodge the enemy, Br.-General Wilson ordered a frontal attack astride the road to be carried out by the 8th A.L.H. This was attended by instant success. The regiment, advancing dismounted and guided by the flashes of the enemy's guns, captured the position at 3.15 a.m., taking seven machine guns. It must be added that the defenders were, according to the evidence of prisoners, unsteadied by sight of the flares sent up by the squadrons of the 9th A.L.H., which proved that they had been outflanked. This rear guard, the actual fighting portion of which must have been very small in numbers,[1] again escaped in motor lorries, pursued by the 10th A.L.H.

The 10th A.L.H. advanced to Sa'sa' and there halted. At 5 a.m. Bourchier's Force passed through, and, riding quickly forward, espied as day broke a disorganized body of the enemy, which had evidently halted for the night behind the Sa'sa' position, making its way towards Kaukab. The 4th A.L.H. at once pursued, one troop under Lieutenant G. R. Bingham charging into a column and cutting off 180 men. Spreading out across the plain, now covered with

---

[1] It was apparently divided into two wings, of which the left consisted of 50 Germans, 70 Turks, 6 machine guns manned by Germans, and 4 guns, which were useless, as their mechanism was not understood. (Liman, p. 376.) On the small-scale sketch illustrating this action the width of the flanking movements and of the Turkish rear-guard position are exaggerated.

THE TURKS PREPARE TO STAND 571

fugitives, the regiment continued to harry them, groups of three or four horsemen riding at bodies of Turks ten times their own strength and calling upon them to surrender. On reaching Khan esh Sheikh, 3 miles from Kaukab, a halt was called to breathe the exhausted horses and collect the prisoners, who numbered 350, with a field gun and several machine guns.

The 4th A.L.H. then despatched patrols to the north-westward to discover whether the Nahr Barbar could be forded. While they were out, a strong column of the enemy was seen swinging westward across the front from the Pilgrims' Road and taking up a position from Kaukab eastward along the high ground of Jebel el Aswad. Leaving the remainder of the division to water and feed horses at the Wadi ez Zabirani, Major-General Hodgson went forward to Khan esh Sheikh with the brigade commanders and gave them their instructions. While Bourchier's Force, to which the two batteries were to be attached, pinned down the hostile flank at Kaukab, the 5th L.H. Brigade was to cross the Nahr Barbar and advance rapidly between the villages of 'Artuz and Qatana upon El Mezze, on the south-western outskirts of Damascus. The enemy's position was, indeed, not well chosen for defence unless its right flank were effectively covered by artillery, and this arm the Turkish force seemed to lack. The plain wherein lie Damascus, its gardens, and the highly-cultivated land to the east of it, is cut off from the plain of the Hauran by the volcanic ridge of El Jebel el Aswad; but between Kaukab, on the western edge of this ridge, and the slopes of Mount Hermon is a valley two miles broad through which runs the Nahr Barbar. On the left bank of the river the valley was undefended, and there was no sign of troops at Qatana, at the foot of the hills on the other side. There was thus admirable opportunity for turning the enemy's right flank.

Near Khan esh Sheikh the whole division deployed. Bourchier's Force was on the right, the 5th L.H. Brigade on the left, the 3rd L.H. Brigade immediately in rear : each in column of squadrons in lines of troop columns. The grey Barbs and Arabs, the picturesque uniforms of the Spahis and Chasseurs d'Afrique on the left front, added to the magnificence of the spectacle : one rare in modern warfare and which will never again be seen, unless, as here had happened, the aircraft of the enemy have been driven from the skies.

While Bourchier's Force advanced against the Kaukab line the R.M.M.C. trotted up the valley, swinging westward near 'Artuz to get beyond reach of fire from the high ground at Kaukab, and was soon well behind the enemy's right, doubtless contributing to the panic which followed. Since the Turks had no guns, " A " Battery H.A.C. and the Notts Battery were able to advance to the crown of a hillock 2,500 yards from their line and to fire upon them over open sights. The shelling of the horse artillery batteries at this short range was very effective, and devastating at least to the nerves of the wearied and demoralized troops upon which it was directed. Large numbers were seen to run back into the thickly-wooded gardens behind the ridge. Lieut.-Colonel Bourchier therefore determined to attack mounted, despite the roughness of the ground and the great numerical superiority of the enemy. At 11.15 a.m. the two regiments trotted into the slight valley between the opposing forces, and charged up the slope. The blast of machine-gun fire that might have been expected did not come. At sight of the advancing horsemen the enemy, almost as one man, broke and fled into the gardens at his rear, a squadron of Turkish cavalry galloping wildly up the road towards Damascus. Only about twenty prisoners were taken, but a dozen machine guns, abandoned in the rout, were found upon the position.

Meanwhile the French regiment had reached the Baniyas–Damascus road beyond Qatana and ridden forward some five miles, till it came under heavy machine-gun fire south-west of El Mezze. Commandant Lebon decided not to risk a charge along the narrow corridor between the enclosed gardens on the right and the hills of the Anti-Lebanon on the left. The regiment dismounted and, followed by a squadron of the 14th A.L.H., made its way along the ridge known as Qalabat el Mezze which ran parallel to the road. At first very slow progress was made, but when the horse artillery batteries, their work at Kaukab finished, advanced up the main road at 1 p.m. and came into action, the fire of the Turkish machine-guns slackened and presently ceased altogether. Br.-General Onslow then rode up the hill to Commandant Lebon and at 3 p.m. ordered him to

SCENE IN THE BARADA GORGE, 1ST OCTOBER 1918.

Imperial War Museum Photograph.

BLOCKING OF BARADA GORGE 573

press forward and cut off the fugitives making for Ba'albek. Scrambling over the rough ground with all haste, the force in the hills reached a point above the Barada Gorge, west of Er Rabue soon after 4.30 p.m., or nearly an hour before sunset. The remainder of the 14th A.L.H. had kept up steady pressure all the while, and now, as the Turkish resistance cracked, it advanced rapidly on the lower ground.

1918.
30 Sept.

The Barada Gorge, winding through the rocky hills north-west of Damascus, carries not only the turbulent river—Naaman's Abana—but also the road and the railway to Beirut and Ba'albek. It was by this road that the Turks were retreating, since that running north-eastward to Homs was almost waterless. As the R.M.M.C., with six machine guns of the 2nd New Zealand Machine-Gun Squadron, reached the edge of the gorge, not only the troops retreating before the 14th A.L.H. but a great proportion of those in the city were struggling through. From the top, fire was opened on the head of a long column with terrible effect. The wretched Turks, seeing that to go forward meant complete destruction, turned back, only to fall into the hands of the 14th A.L.H. About four thousand prisoners were taken here. Six machine guns of the brigade squadron reached the gorge higher up, south-east of El Hame, and shot down a number of Turks.

The 3rd L.H. Brigade had followed the 5th, with orders to cross, without entering Damascus, from the Beirut road to that leading to Homs and to block it also. The leading squadron of the 9th A.L.H. arrived at a point above the Barada Gorge overlooking the village of Dummar about two miles west of that occupied by the R.M.M.C. and apparently only a few minutes after it. Here also was found an amazing target in a packed column moving along the road below. The enemy, or at least the Germans in his ranks, attempted resistance, but his situation was hopeless. Some struggled through, others turned back, while the Australians fired and fired till the road was littered with the bodies of men and animals and the wreckage of transport wagons. Four hundred dead were later found on the road, and it took several days to burn the vehicles in order to clear the pass.[1]

---

[1] Liman pretends (pp. 381–2) that the Barada Gorge was never seriously blocked, and gives as evidence to support his argument the fact that one train managed to pass through in the darkness. He is quite in

Br.-General Wilson had now decided that it was impossible for him to carry out the instructions he had received to avoid Damascus. The only route to the Homs road was through the city. Major-General Hodgson ordered him to remain where he was for the night, rest his troops as far as possible, and start off at 5 a.m. next day to fulfil the latter part of his mission. All night long the Australians on the heights saw the glare of flames and heard terrific explosions as great dumps of munitions and oil were destroyed in the plain below.

5th Cavalry Division. The 5th Cavalry Division had been ordered to march in rear of the Australian Mounted Division at 6 p.m. on the 29th, but had been held up for several hours by the fight at Sa'sa'. Its head reached that village at 8.30 a.m. on the 30th. It could, in fact, have been there by that hour if it had remained in its bivouac at Quneitra until about 3 a.m., in which case the troops would have been spared a cold and miserable night halted or crawling along the road. A few minutes after reaching Sa'sa' Major-General Macandrew received orders from General Chauvel to intercept a force of 2,000 Turks reported by an aeroplane to be retiring on Damascus by the Pilgrims' Road, here about nine miles east of that which the division was following. He at once ordered his leading brigade to move eastward and endeavour to cut off this column. The Essex Battery R.H.A. was to follow at the best possible pace.

The 14th Cavalry Brigade (Br.-General G. V. Clarke) consisted at the moment of two Indian regiments only, the Sherwood Rangers having been left at Haifa and being now on the corps lines of communication at Quneitra. By the fortune of war it was the only brigade in the Desert Mounted Corps which had not yet been seriously engaged. It now made the best of its opportunity by advancing with great speed, though checked by patches of standing maize, along the left bank of the Wadi ez Zabirani on Kiswe, a village on the Pilgrims' Road 9 miles south of Damascus. As it approached the place, patrols came in to report that it was

---

error. No troops could have faced the fire of machine guns and Hotchkiss rifles which were got into position while it was yet light enough to see the road, though it was possible for a train, with luck on its side, to pass through afterwards. It may be added that other trains found it impossible to run the gauntlet, and backed into Damascus.

ACTION OF 14TH CAV. BRIGADE

strongly held, that the enemy was established also on the hills of El Jebel el Aswad to the north, and that the road was packed with troops and transport. Two squadrons of the Deccan Horse were ordered to seize the nearest point on the hills above the road; the remainder of the brigade moved on to a pass through which it ran, half a mile nearer Damascus. Both sides of this pass were found to be held by the enemy, and between them a close-packed column, transport of all sorts, troops marching six or eight abreast, was retreating northward. Higher up the road great numbers could be seen already nearing Damascus. Attacking dismounted, the Deccan Horse established itself in a position covering the road. On its left the Poona Horse was faced by a body of the enemy in a large stone sangar. The Essex Battery had now arrived, and with its support one squadron attacked mounted. The enemy, who had been firing hotly until this moment, broke and fled at sight of the charge. The great Turkish column was now split in two. Large numbers further down the road had already left it and streamed away eastward, but a party of about two thousand was established at Kiswe, and checked by machine-gun fire all attempts to approach the village.

Major-General Macandrew, who had been fretting at the delay all through the night and had now been halted again for two hours, despatched Major G. B. H. Wheler, attached to his headquarters, with a verbal message to Br.-General Clarke, bidding him not to trouble about the Turks coming up from the south but to turn and make for Damascus. The message was welcome to the brigadier, who preferred not to attack Kiswe with only two regiments. Sending his divisional commander a request that another brigade might be despatched against Kiswe, he concentrated his troops at noon and moved off north against a body of Turks on a ridge 3 miles nearer Damascus, leaving a squadron of the Deccan Horse to watch the enemy force in the village. The Essex Battery quickly silenced a single Turkish gun, and a mounted attack on the right of the Turkish position by two squadrons of the Deccan Horse caused the enemy to flee before the cavalry was within half a mile of him. In the neighbouring gardens 40 officers and 150 men, the headquarters and all that remained of one regiment of the *3rd Cavalry Division*, were rounded up and captured. The

1918.
30 Sept.

horses were now, by 3 p.m., very exhausted, having been on the move for 21 hours. Touch had not been established with the Australians, nor did Br.-General Clarke know the position of the rest of his own division. Not feeling himself strong enough to enter Damascus unsupported, he ordered his brigade to bivouac for the night on the ridge which it occupied, the last feature in front of Damascus. In the course of the day it had taken 594 prisoners, its own casualties being 5 killed and 4 wounded.

On receiving Br.-General Clarke's message at 2.30 p.m., the divisional commander ordered the 13th Brigade, which had now reached Kaukab, to advance on Kiswe. Just before 4.30 p.m. the brigade arrived at the village of Deir Ghabiye, on the French railway, and appears to have temporarily mistaken it for Kiswe. While it was searching the place and the neighbouring groves, a message arrived ordering Br.-General Kelly to withdraw. General Chauvel, who had reached Kaukab, desired the brigade to bivouac there, in order to move into Damascus next morning by the Quneitra road. The Turkish troops at Kiswe, with the 14th Cavalry Brigade between them and Damascus, and the 4th Cavalry Division in their rear, need not, he thought, be taken into account. Meanwhile, however, one squadron of Hodson's Horse under Major M. D. Vigors, which was acting as vanguard, had pursued a body of Turks, who fell back upon a party about three hundred strong. Dropping his Vickers subsection, his Hotchkiss rifles, and one troop for dismounted action, Major Vigors sent one troop against either flank of the enemy. The two troops wheeled inwards and charged, but the Turks put up their hands before the Indians got among them. An amazing incident followed. Risaldar Nur Ahmad, accompanied at first only by his orderly, until his troop had handed over its prisoners, rode on into Kiswe, and found the streets full of Turks. He shot down one man who fired at him, and shouted to the rest to surrender. So abject was their demoralization that nearly three hundred gave themselves up.

Meanwhile Major Vigors had caught sight of a column, which he estimated to be about 1,500 strong, moving up from the south and about three-quarters of a mile east of the road. He sent off a galloper with the news, but the latter, as happened on a famous occasion at Quatre Bras,

Sketch 40.

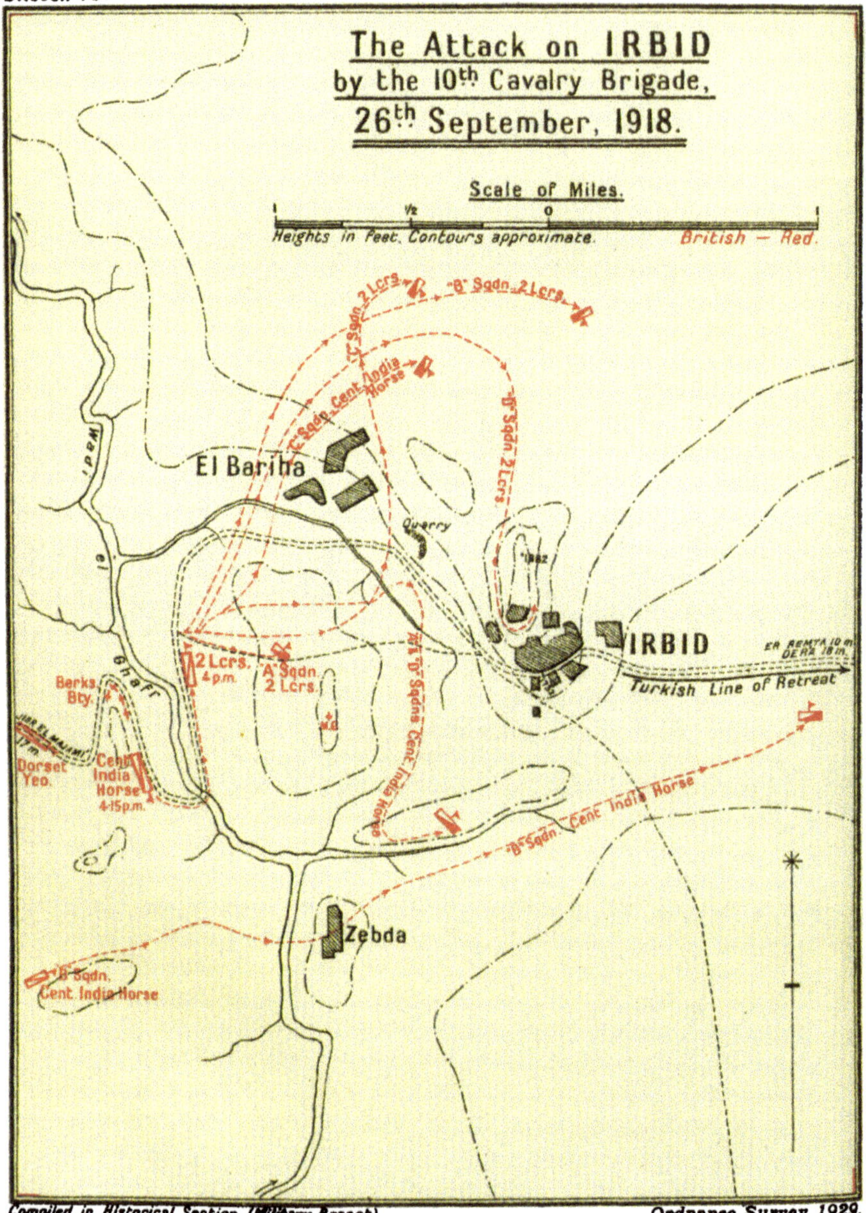

Compiled in Historical Section (Military Branch).
3000/30.

Ordnance Survey 1929.

fell into a gully and did not arrive until it was too late. Sending back his 700 prisoners escorted by two troops, Major Vigors then led forward the remaining troop with the machine guns and Hotchkiss rifles at a gallop to head the enemy, trusting that the brigade would move to his support and take the Turkish column in flank. Alone, his tiny force was helpless, and he had some difficulty in extricating it under cover of the fire of his Hotchkiss rifles. He lost several horses and had to abandon one Hotchkiss, but suffered no casualties to personnel. As the action was broken off, shells from the guns of the 4th Cavalry Division were seen bursting in the midst of the Turkish column.

1918.
30 Sept.

Half an hour before the 13th Cavalry Brigade moved on Kiswe a troop of the Gloucester Hussars with a Hotchkiss-rifle section was ordered to reconnoitre the wireless station at Qadem and if possible save it from destruction. As the patrol advanced, the wireless mast was seen to be surrounded by thick smoke and presently to fall. The patrol pushed on, capturing a number of Turks, whom it disarmed but could not afford to send back. Entering the close country west of Qadem it was seen that both railway and wireless stations were in flames, and the commander, Captain Lord Apsley, was told by natives that five hundred Turks and Germans were destroying them. He would not be satisfied till he had charged a large body of the enemy and got close enough to see for himself that there was nothing left to save. Then, again charging the enemy and killing a number with the sword, he withdrew and reached the headquarters of the Australian Mounted Division after dark. He had had but a single casualty.

4th Cavalry Division. At midnight on the 25th September the 4th Cavalry Division was concentrated at Beisan with the 10th Cavalry Brigade at Jisr el Majami'. The 10th Brigade marched at 8 a.m. on the 26th with orders to reach Irbid and if possible find touch with the Arabs that night. It was greatly delayed by the state of the road, which wound its way up a steep gradient, was carpeted with sharp stones, and generally prevented movement at a pace faster than a walk. Three miles west of Irbid the 2nd Lancers, which had been urged forward with the object of reaching that place before darkness fell, encountered a difficult defile in the gorge of the Wadi el Ghafr, after crossing which its patrols

26 Sept.

came under fire from the plateau above. Major G. Gould, fearing that darkness would descend with Irbid still in the enemy's hands and the brigade without water for the night, determined to attack at once. He ordered one squadron to move through the village of Bariha (already seized by a troop of the regiment), a mile north-west of Irbid, and make its way east of the latter village. A second squadron was to follow and attack mounted from the north, and a third to attack simultaneously from the south. The attached subsection of the machine-gun squadron was to support the advance by firing on any Turkish machine guns which came into action.

"B" Squadron failed to get round by the north owing to machine-gun fire. It therefore took up a position 1,200 yards north of Irbid and opened Hotchkiss-rifle fire in support of "D" Squadron's attack. This squadron, which was only 48 strong after dropping its Hotchkiss troop to give covering fire, likewise came under heavy fire from a hill on the northern outskirts of the village. When some two hundred yards short of the position the squadron leader, Captain E. W. D. Vaughan, realized that the ground was too rough and the hill too steep to be galloped over in face of the enemy's fire. He accordingly swung the squadron west of the hill, and dashed into the village at the north-western corner. The leading troop, however, galloped straight up to the hill and was shot down almost to a man. Wounded in the knee and on a mortally wounded horse, Captain Vaughan now found himself with only eight N.C.O's. and men, the remainder having been killed or wounded outside the village. Seeing that his situation was hopeless, he ordered a retirement, in the course of which he was wounded twice more and was carried out of action with great devotion under heavy fire by his Indian orderly. "C" Squadron mistook Bariha for Irbid and, not discovering its error until Captain Vaughan's attack had failed, swung round Bariha and took up a position to the north.

Br.-General Green rode up on to the plateau just after the attack had begun. He saw that it was of urgent importance to get the Berks Battery R.H.A. into action as quickly as possible; but the battery was moving through the defile in rear of the Central India Horse, so that it was after 5 p.m. when it opened fire—too late to assist the 2nd Lancers. Meanwhile the Central India Horse (less a squadron acting as right flank guard, which was then approaching Zebda, a mile south-west of Irbid) reached the plateau, to be met by a galloper from Br.-General Green with the verbal message, as recorded by the commanding officer, Major J. R. Hutchison :—" Your orders are to follow " the squadron of the 2nd Lancers down the valley [*i.e.* that "running south-east from Bariha past the outskirts of Irbid] "at once." Major Hutchison felt that, as the light was failing, he had no time to gallop to Br.-General Green for further instructions. Had he done so, he would have found that the brigadier had no intention of confining him to the valley, but desired him to move south and east to cut the Der'a road beyond Irbid. Hearing heavy firing, he started his regiment off in squadron columns at the gallop. The leading squadron (" C "), catching sight of " C " Squadron of the 2nd Lancers, which it had been ordered to support, advancing—in error as we have seen—north of Bariha, followed it, and so became useless. " A " Squadron, met by a blast of machine-gun fire, swung left-handed and took cover in a wadi west of the village. Major Hutchison stopped " D " Squadron, and ordered the two to work round the enemy's left flank and get behind Irbid. They struggled across the rough ground and eventually reached a hill due south of the village, where darkness prevented further movement. " B " Squadron, the right flank-guard, which had seen the action from west of Zebda, pressed on to aid the attack, charged through Zebda, where it captured a machine gun, and approached the Der'a road a mile west of Irbid. It was now quite dark, and every effort to reach the road, along which the Turks were retreating on Der'a, was foiled by machine-gun fire.

With some difficulty the brigadier established touch in the darkness with his scattered squadrons. The night passed quietly, and when at dawn patrols approached Irbid, it was found clear of the enemy. The inhabitants declared that the Turkish force had been at least five thousand strong, and that it had commenced its retreat, leaving a strong rear guard to hold the village, directly the British cavalry appeared.

This action was the first check that the 4th Cavalry

Division had met with since it rode through the Turkish trenches on the morning of the 19th. Comparison with other mounted attacks, even those apparently most temerarious, will afford some clues to the failure. Haste to force the issue before dark, allied with the confidence born of many victorious actions, had caused the usual precautions to go by the board. It was not alone that there had been little or no reconnaissance of the ground; no one had any idea of the strength of the enemy force. And these troops of the *Fourth Army*, weary and dispirited as they were, had not been defeated or broken by infantry. Major Gould's situation was indeed a difficult one. With the wisdom which comes after the event it can be seen that he would have done better to have awaited the arrival of the Central India Horse and of the battery, but it is comprehensible that at the moment any delay should have seemed to him to risk the loss of a golden opportunity. Had he done so and occupied in reconnaissance the time thus spent, his brigadier would at least have had better information to work upon by the time the main body arrived. Seeing one regiment committed to the attack, Br.-General Green had little choice but to order a second to support it at once; and even then all might have gone well but for some confusion either in the delivery or in the interpretation of his verbal orders. The casualties of the brigade were only 46, the great bulk being in Captain Vaughan's squadron of the 2nd Lancers; but a considerable number of horses were killed. And for this light loss it undoubtedly had above all to thank the very bad marksmanship of the Turks.

The 12th Cavalry Brigade bivouacked on the night of the 26th at Esh Shuni, 2½ miles east of the Jordan; divisional headquarters and the 11th Brigade at Jisr el Majami'. Major-General Barrow, who had no news from the 10th Brigade at Irbid[1], ordered the 12th Brigade to march at 6 a.m. to rejoin it at the Wadi esh Shelale, west of Er

---

[1] It is of interest to record that the staff of the 10th Brigade passed a great proportion of the night in coding a long message describing its situation, for transmission by wireless. This message was despatched all in one piece, and naturally took a long time to decode when received. Had it even been transmitted by sections, time would have been saved; but it would seem that in the circumstances large portions might without great risk have been sent in clear.

Remta. To the 10th Brigade he sent a message which arrived before dawn, ordering it to move on Er Remta, but if strong opposition were encountered to await the arrival of the 12th Brigade at the wadi.

1918. 27 Sept.

The Dorset Yeomanry with a subsection of the machine-gun squadron marched at 7.15 as advanced guard, and got a long start owing to the rest of the brigade having to water its horses at small and scattered wells. The unmetalled track was wide and level, a most welcome relief to the horses after the last day's stony surface. The regiment had crossed the Wadi Shelale and advanced two miles beyond it to cover the passage of the brigade when a British aeroplane dropped a message that Er Remta was clear of the enemy. Lieut.-Colonel G. K. M. Mason then ordered two troops to reconnoitre the place and establish themselves beyond it if it were found to be indeed unoccupied. The leading troop was met by heavy machine-gun fire at a range of a thousand yards from the village, and withdrew to the cover of a ridge to the south-west, where it dismounted. Immediately a body of three hundred Turks moved out of the village and deployed, two-thirds of the force with four machine guns taking up a fire position, while the remainder advanced to the attack. About fifty men boldly made their way across a small wadi in front of the ridge and got into dead ground below it. By this time the whole of the regiment had assembled behind the ridge. A mounted attack by three troops, which swung in from the right, resulted in the killing or capture of all those men who had crossed the wadi, and the remainder fell back on the village. The place was seized a few minutes later by the Yeomanry after hand-to-hand fighting among the houses.

Br.-General Green, on learning of the counter-attack, ordered a squadron of the Central India Horse to move to the support of the Dorset Yeomanry and directed the remainder of the Indian regiment to advance eastward, under cover of the high ground north of Er Remta, in order to intercept the enemy reported to be making off in the direction of Der'a. The Central India Horse went forward in column of squadrons in extended order, and on crossing the Wadi Ratam caught sight of about one hundred and fifty of the enemy—doubtless the party which had retreated from the Dorset Yeomanry—in the plain to the south-east.

Major J. R. Hutchison ordered two squadrons to form line, a wide front being necessary owing to the scattered formation of the enemy, and charge. The long line swept down upon the Turks, who were taken by surprise ; and though they contrived to bring into action two machine guns carried on pack-ponies, they had small chance to fire before they were attacked with the lance. Four machine guns and 60 prisoners were taken. As the charge began, Major Hutchison noticed a movement on the edge of the ridge above the plain, where the Der'a road wound its way into the hills, and at once divined that the enemy was in the act of abandoning a rear-guard position here. He ordered the third squadron with him to gallop to the shoulder of this ridge and if possible cut off fugitives in the defile below. The movement, carried out with dash, was attended with success, another 90 prisoners and four machine guns being taken.

The action was over by noon, but the divisional commander, who now arrived, ordered Br.-General Green to bivouac. The brigade had reached the furthest objective set to it, and both men and horses were fatigued. The 12th Cavalry Brigade arrived in the evening. The 2nd Lancers, sent forward before darkness fell to the edge of the hills overlooking Der'a, saw the buildings and sidings swarming like an ants' nest. The observers took all this bustle to be that of the retiring Turkish *Fourth Army* ; it was, in fact, the Arab irregulars and half the local countryside engaged in looting the abandoned station.

**1918.
28 Sept.**

Major-General Barrow ordered the 10th Cavalry Brigade to push forward patrols in the morning in order to discover whether Der'a was held by the enemy, but not to enter the place before 7 a.m., in case British aeroplanes should bomb it. At 4.30 on the 28th the brigade took up a position to cover the assembly of the division (of which the 11th Brigade was moving up from Irbid) east of Er Remta. It could now be seen that the station buildings, intact on the previous evening, were in flames, that trucks in the sidings were smouldering, and that the roof of the big hospital had fallen in. Bursts of musketry fire could be heard, but it still remained uncertain whether or not the place was occupied by the Turks. At 7 a.m. the brigade advanced, and on the eastern edge of the hills above the station Br.-General Green encountered Lieut.-Colonel T. E.

SCENES AT DER'A

Lawrence, from whom he learnt that the Sherifial irregulars had entered Der'a the previous afternoon.

1918.
28 Sept.

A grim spectacle was needed to shock the troops of a cavalry division which for ten days had been harrying the retreat of a routed army; but the sight of Der'a Station and its encampments that met the 10th Cavalry Brigade as it rode in that morning was ghastly beyond aught that any man there had yet witnessed. Everywhere there were dead Turks, but they were the fortunate; for the wounded lay scattered about, despoiled and in agony, amid a litter of packages, half looted, half burnt, of torn documents, and smashed machinery. A hospital train stood in the station; the driver and fireman were still in their cab, still alive, but mortally wounded; the sick and wounded in the train had been stripped of every rag of clothing. " In the whole "course of this war," writes Major-General Barrow, " in " France and in Palestine, I have never seen such a sight of " dreadful misery." Lieut.-Colonel Lawrence, who had hurried back from the main body of the Sherifial Army to meet Major-General Barrow, probably looked upon it with different feelings, for he had come from the scene of far more appalling excesses by the enemy. It is a terrible passage in his book which describes the slaughter of women and children, carried out with every bestial device by the Turkish rear guard at Tafas the day before.[1]

After arranging with Colonel Nuri Bey, Feisal's Chief Staff officer, that the Arabs should cover his right flank during his march north on the morrow, Major-General Barrow directed the 11th and 12th Brigades, with divisional troops, to move to Muzeirib, as the watering facilities at Der'a were insufficient. The 10th Brigade piqueted the station, collected and dressed the Turkish wounded, and buried the dead, afterwards bivouacking on a comparatively clean open space near the station. This was its first real night's rest since leaving Beisan, some squadrons having had their saddles off for only two hours between Jisr el Majami' and Der'a.

The division marched up the Pilgrims' Road on the morning of the 29th, halting at Sheikh Miskin, 13 miles north-east of Muzeirib, at 2 p.m. Here it was rejoined by

29 Sept.

---

[1] " Revolt in the Desert," pp. 409-10.

the 10th Cavalry Brigade from Der'a, less a squadron left there to protect the wounded and what rolling stock had been saved. In hope of striking another blow at the retreating *Fourth Army*, Major-General Barrow decided to move on to Dilli, five miles further north, where the division bivouacked that night. By now it was beginning to feel the pinch of hunger. Nine tons of barley, with a small herd of cattle, sheep, and goats, had been captured at Irbid and brought on; and at Der'a the supply officer of the 10th Cavalry Brigade had requisitioned goats for the Indian troops and tibben for the horses. At Muzeirib the last rations carried by the Train had been issued, with the exception of the loads of 13 G.S. wagons. These marched out with it from Dilli on the 30th, the remainder of the Train waiting there until 4 p.m. in the hope of the lorries arriving from Samakh. No lorries were, however, to be seen until after the capture of Damascus, and the troops were henceforth wholly dependent upon requisitioning. Fortunately, a fair amount of food and forage was obtained in this way. Another difficulty with which the division was faced was that it was no longer possible to evacuate sick and wounded, who had to be carried on to Damascus by the field ambulances. Wounded there were few, but there were now many men suffering from malaria and influenza who had to ride their horses with the medical units. The ambulances also picked up such sick Turks as they had room for to save them from slaughter by the peasantry and Bedouin, but many hundreds along the line of march had to be left to their fate.[1]

1918.
30 Sept.

On the 30th the division set out for Kiswe, a march of about 30 miles. In its course, however, Major-General Barrow decided that the distance was too great for his

---

[1] The work of the little column of *cacolet* camels belonging to the 10th Cavalry Brigade Field Ambulance deserves mention. The only British rank with the party was Private R. A. Gibbs, R.A.M.C., the remaining personnel being Egyptians of the Camel Transport Corps. On the morning of the 30th it left Er Remta for Irbid with 30 patients. Next day it returned to Er Remta, picked up some sick Turks, and took them on to Der'a. On the 2nd October it set out to rejoin the division at Damascus. Private Gibbs was unarmed, and had neither map nor compass. He was continually threatened by marauding Arabs, and on one occasion beat off an attack with a Turkish rifle. When supplies ran short he took boots and equipment from dead Turks on the road and bartered them for tibben, milk, and eggs in the Hauran villages. Including its journeys to and fro, his column travelled 150 miles, and for whole days was without sight of British troops. He rejoined at Damascus on the 4th October.

horses, owing to the fatigue caused by the stony ground, especially to protective troops. The main body halted at Zeraqiye at 4.30 p.m., the 11th Cavalry Brigade pushing on towards Khiara, 6 miles further north. At about 4.45 p.m. the advanced guard reported that there was a big column on the hills to the right of the road, near Deir 'Ali. It was thought at first that this was the Sherifial Army, but a few minutes later Lieut.-Colonel Lawrence arrived to inform Br.-General Gregory that it was the rear guard of the Turkish *Fourth Army*, which the Arabs were endeavouring to check. On the 27th they had sighted two columns, one some five thousand strong marching north from Der'a; the other about two thousand strong, moving out from Muzeirib on the Pilgrims' Road. It was decided to let the greater column go by and attack the smaller. This passed through Tafas, there committing the atrocities of which mention has been made, and was attacked by the Arab regulars, Auda's horsemen, and the peasantry, who were swiftly arming themselves with captured rifles. The Turkish force was gradually split up. One section, consisting chiefly of German machine gunners, beat off all attacks; the others broke up, probably rather from fatigue than as a result of the Arab attacks, into smaller fragments, and the greater part of them was eventually engulfed by their pursuers. Then the Arabs fastened themselves on to the big Der'a column, and harried it all through the 29th. Without venturing to press home an attack in face of its mountain artillery and machine guns, they cut off hundreds of stragglers. They now called upon the 11th Cavalry Brigade for assistance.

The Hants Battery was at once sent forward, over very bad ground, and came into action, firing upon the Turks over open sights, though actually outranged by their screw-guns, until it was too dark to see them. The 29th Lancers, which advanced in an attempt to head off the enemy, was forced to return, as it found movement impossible after dark. What damage was done to the Turks it was difficult to see, but it appeared that they headed north-east across the heights of Jebel Mani' in some confusion. According to Lieut.-Colonel Lawrence's account, the column was practically destroyed by Auda Abu Tayi before the next day broke. " In that night of his last battle the old man killed and "killed, plundered and captured, till dawn showed him the "end."[1]

The Capture of Damascus.

Map 3.
Sketch 39.

Thus, at midnight on the 30th September the Desert Mounted Corps was at the gates of Damascus. The Australian Mounted Division was at El Mezze, 2 miles to the west, with the 3rd and 5th L.H. Brigades commanding the whole length of the Barada Gorge; the 5th Cavalry Division was at Kaukab, with the 14th Cavalry Brigade on the hills east of Ashrafiye; the 4th Cavalry Division was at Zeraqiye on the Pilgrims' Road, with the 11th Cavalry Brigade 7 miles nearer the city at Khan Deinun. The Arab forces were to the north-east of the 14th Cavalry Brigade. General Chauvel had issued orders to encircle the place on the morrow: the Australian Mounted Division maintaining its position, the 5th Cavalry Division taking up one on the east of the city by 9 a.m., the 4th Cavalry Division advancing to the southern outskirts astride the Pilgrims' Road.

While Damascus awaited capture the commander of its defences was enjoying the hospitality of Major-General Barrow. General Ali Riza Pasha el Rikabi, a soldier of some forty years' service in the Turkish Army but of Arab birth, had galloped out to meet the British the previous afternoon. He was in high spirits over his escape and the tricks he had played upon his masters. As the headquarters of the 4th Cavalry Division sat down to breakfast at 2 a.m. next morning, he laughed so heartily at his own story of how he had selected heavy-artillery positions which could not be occupied for lack of water that he tripped over the table in the darkness and upset the scrambled eggs and cocoa. The incident was typical enough of the spirit in which the Turks had been served by many of their Arab soldiers and officials.

Vaster in size, more ancient in days, richer in wealth, more blessed with the kindly fruits of the earth than Jeru-

---

[1] "Revolt in the Desert," p. 422. British patrols afterwards in fact found hundreds of dead in the Jebel Mani', and doubtless terrible execution was done by the Arab partizan. It is, however, probable that it was the remains of this column, then under 1,600 strong, which was cut off by the 9th A.L.H. on the 2nd October, as will be recorded later. It was, of course, the head of this column that had been attacked by Major Vigors.

salem, Damascus lacks the Jewish city's quality of fortress-capital; and therefore, though its annals contain even more mighty names, lacks its heroic past. If Jerusalem is a city of soldiers and priests, Damascus is a city of merchants and shopkeepers. It might on occasion become a capital of warrior princes, as in the days of the Ommayyad Khalifs and of Saladin; it could never be their refuge in adversity. Its defenders had to meet their foes in open country. If they suffered defeat, the city was inevitably captured and almost always sacked. In consequence it has to-day comparatively few memorials of its teeming history in the form of ancient buildings. The most famous which remain, though they are of no great antiquity by the standards of Syria, are the Citadel and the vast Ommayyad Mosque, in the precincts whereof is the tomb of Saladin.

The site of Damascus was determined by the movement of trade as surely as were those of Venice and Marseilles; it is a port of the desert as they are ports of the sea. The city lies on a plateau between desert and mountain, upon the most important ancient trade route between Syria and Mesopotamia, and therefore, over long periods, between Europe and Asia. Watered by many rivers which bring down the rains and melting snow of the Anti-Lebanon and run away into the sand some twenty miles east of the city, where they form a chain of huge swamps, this site was the natural port and depot for the merchant navigators of the desert—the nomad tribes—steering whether from Babylon or Baghdad. A halting-place, a place of exchange or bazaar, a settlement, a city: such were the stages in the growth of Damascus—stages of very long ago, for it has some claim to be the oldest inhabited city known to man. Its reputation is founded in part upon the contrast of its verdure and its abundant waters to the bleakness of the country through which the west-bound traveller approached it, a contrast that gladdened his eyes and made it appear a paradise of wealth and luxury. Even the European must admire its surrounding gardens in the season when mile on mile of fruit trees are in bloom, and find beauty, as well as evidences of a high civilization, in its courts where fountains play upon gaily-coloured paving-stones, in the mosaics and stained glass of its mosques, in the craft of its goldsmiths, silk-weavers, engravers, and inlayers.

In Damascus there had been days of turmoil to mark the end of Turkish rule. Bedouin had ridden about the streets firing rifles in the air under the eyes of Marshal Liman. During the afternoon of the 30th bold spirits had hoisted the Sherifial flag over the Town Hall, and the Turks marching past had not attempted to pull it down. Not even for gold could the retreating troops get food. All day long their columns had been passing, friendless and unsuccoured, through the false haven which they had endured so much to reach; and at night, after the Barada Gorge had been closed, though some had headed northward by the bare mountain road to Homs, far greater numbers had abandoned hope of escape and phlegmatically awaited their fate.

1918.
1 Oct.

Of the state of affairs in the city Br.-General Wilson knew little or nothing when at 5 a.m. on the 1st October the 3rd L.H. Brigade began its advance through the shambles of the Barada Gorge. His decision, therefore, to make a dash through the northern part of the city, as the only way of carrying out his orders to reach the Homs road, was bold in the extreme. The 10th A.L.H., moving as advanced guard, first descended by a steep slope to the bottom of the gorge and reached Dummar Station, where there was standing a train, loaded with troops but without an engine. As the leading squadron rode up, not only the men in the train but a party several hundreds strong drawn up outside the station threw down their arms. After crossing the Barada there was a delay because the road was completely blocked by transport wagons and by the bodies of men and animals, including a whole flock of sheep, mown down by the machine-gun fire of the previous night. One squadron dismounted and had three-quarters of an hour's gruesome work before the way was sufficiently clear for the advance to continue. On emerging from the gorge, Major A. C. N. Olden, second-in-command of the regiment, who was riding with the advanced-guard squadron, ordered it to enter the city at the gallop. On the outskirts it swept past the great barracks, where thousands of Turkish soldiers could be seen. Not a shot was fired by the enemy, and the Australians, who had another quarry, did not check their pace.

Once in the streets the horsemen were compelled to pull up to a walk, for they found themselves surrounded by a population gone mad with joy. Rifles were fired off in the air about them; women leaned from windows to spill perfumes and scatter rose-leaves and confetti upon their heads; men risked going down beneath their horses' feet by pressing forward to offer them fruit and cigarettes. Major Olden dismounted for a few minutes at the Serai or Town Hall, where he found sitting a committee, under Mohammed Said, a descendant of Abd el Kader, the famous Algerian opponent of the French, who declared that he had been installed by Jemal Pasha as Governor the previous afternoon, and formally surrendered the city to him. With some difficulty persuading the committee of his haste and that he wanted no entertainment, Major Olden obtained a guide to lead him through the streets.

On leaving the city by the Bab Tuma, a report was received from natives that the enemy was holding the Nahr Ma'raba, which crosses the Homs road 5 miles to the northeast. The leading squadron came into action here, and was quickly joined by the remainder of the regiment. A brisk engagement against a rear guard of German machine gunners followed, but the enemy abandoned his ground when he saw that the attack was about to be pressed home. This stand by his rear guard availed him little; for a squadron, passing round his right flank, reached Duma, 4 miles further on, and captured some five hundred prisoners, with no less than 37 machine guns. The prisoners were sent to the rear under the escort of a single troop, and the machine guns destroyed. At Khan el Quseir,[1] a couple of miles beyond Duma, the enemy made another attempt to hold up the light horsemen, but was hustled out of this position with a loss of 50 prisoners, mainly Germans. A column some 1,500 strong was now seen ahead, nearing the pass by which the road mounted into the hills; but though a determined effort was made by the Australians to close with it, a strong rear guard with a score of machine guns foiled them. They had, in fact, encountered troops of different quality to those overtaken on the march to Damascus—the German *146th Regiment* of the *Fourth Army*, which was acting as rear guard to the retreat on Homs.[2] They hung on to the column as long as possible, however, inflicting loss upon it before

---

[1] Khan Kusseir on Map 3.   [2] Liman, pp. 283—4.

it disappeared into the hills, then returning to bivouac at Duma, where rations and forage were requisitioned for hungry men and horses.

1918.
2 Oct.
The last of the fighting near Damascus took place the following morning. This little engagement was also the last fought by Australian troops, and was a fitting end to their long service, which dated from the opening of hostilities in this theatre. At 6.15 a.m. on the 2nd it was reported that a long column, which had evidently avoided Damascus and had been concealed in the close country east of the Homs road, was moving northward and making for the pass by which the *146th Regiment* had escaped the previous afternoon. If once it reached the hills it was safe, provided it showed the smallest energy in defending itself. At 6.45 the 9th A.L.H. moved out and advanced along the road at a sharp trot. The enemy column having now reached the road ahead, the regiment quitted it and made its way through the vineyards on the left. It gained rapidly on the Turks, who pushed out several small parties with machine guns in an endeavour to delay the pursuit, but without avail. Having got level with the centre of the column, Lieut.-Colonel W. H. Scott ordered two squadrons to gallop for Khan Ayash, just below the entrance to the pass. The Turks opened fire with several machine guns, but at a range of nearly a mile it was innocuous. As soon as he observed that the leading squadrons had reached the road and cut off the main column, Lieut.-Colonel Scott ordered his third squadron to charge it in flank. The Turks threw down their arms before the charge was driven home. Their advanced guard, consisting of cavalry, had meanwhile surrendered to the leading squadrons on the road near Khan Ayash. The total force thus cut off consisted of 91 officers, including a divisional commander, 318 cavalry, 1,072 infantry, 3 guns, and 26 machine guns. Its capture had been effected within an hour of the time when the 9th A.L.H. left its bivouac.

1 Oct.
To return now to the events of the 1st October at Damascus, at 6.40 a.m. Lieut.-Colonel Bourchier received orders from Major-General Hodgson to send forward patrols to the western outskirts south of the Barada. A squadron of the 4th A.L.H. approached the barracks, and, finding them swarming with troops, awaited the rest of the regiment, though the enemy made little show of resistance beyond

firing a few shots. On reinforcements coming up, the Turks were challenged, and instantly surrendered. Their captors were astounded by their numbers when they were marshalled on the parade ground. There were 265 officers and 10,481 rank and file who, though in many cases sick or wounded and in almost every case exhausted, half-starved, and filthy, were yet capable of walking to a concentration camp hurriedly established outside the city. There were about another six hundred unable to be moved from the dormitories. Lieut.-Colonel Bourchier discovered 1,800 more sick in three other hospitals, in a state of appalling misery and destitution. In some cases those that had died had lain three days on the floors of the wards amidst the living. He then posted guards upon the principal public buildings and the Consulates, which remained until the following afternoon, when they were relieved by Sherifial troops.

1918.
1 Oct.

Major-General Macandrew had meanwhile joined the 14th Cavalry Brigade, and at 10.30 a.m. entered Damascus from the south at its head. He also was welcomed with frantic joy by the populace in the southern part of the city, few of whom can have seen the Australians pass through the northern part earlier that morning. The brigade emerged by the Bab Tuma, and put out posts to find touch with the 13th Cavalry Brigade, which had moved up east of the city.

Lieut.-Colonel Lawrence drove in about 7.30 a.m., and went straight to the Town Hall, whither Sherif Nasir and Nuri esh Shalaan had preceded him on horseback. The committee which Major Olden had interviewed was still sitting,[1] but after a stormy scene Lawrence ordered the deposition of the Algerian brothers Abd el Kader and Mohammed Said, as hostile to Feisal, and in the Emir's name appointed a local notable Shukri Pasha, to be Military Governor.

To explain this proceeding we must look back to the negotiations of 1915 and early 1916 which were described at some length in the previous volume.[2] By the Sykes-Picot

---

[1] There has been some controversy as to which troops were the first to enter Damascus. It seems clear that a number of Sherifial irregulars were in the city by midnight on the 30th September. They did not, however, venture to attack the Turks, to whom they were indistinguishable from the local Bedouin who had been demonstrating for some days. The advanced guard of the 3rd L.H. Brigade entered the city before 6.30 a.m. on the 1st October. [2] Vol. I, pp. 217—9.

Agreement, Syria and Mesopotamia had been divided into four zones, known as " A," " B," the " Blue," and the " Red." " A " and the " Blue " zones were both within the French spheres of influence, but the character of their respective administrations was to be quite different. While in the " Blue " zone, which represented Syria north of Acre and west of Damascus and Aleppo, France was to establish such administration as seemed suitable after consultation with the future Arab state or confederation of states, in " A " she was pledged to uphold an independent Arab state. Now " A " was, roughly speaking, a triangle from Aleppo, down to Lake Tiberias, and across the desert to Rowanduz, and it included the city of Damascus, as well as Homs and Aleppo. Damascus was the obvious capital of this new Arab state. While, therefore, Sir Edmund Allenby had instructions to allow the French to take over control of the " Blue " zone, of which the chief town was Beirut, as soon as the situation permitted, he was to recognize the authority of friendly or allied Arabs in the " A " zone, and also in the " B," which lay east of the Dead Sea and Jordan Valley. The only difference between the two zones was that, if the Arabs asked for the assistance or advice of European functionaries, these would have to be British in the " B " zone, and French in the " A " zone. No military control, it was obvious, could be delegated to French or Arabs while the war lasted. On the 3rd the Commander-in-Chief had an interview with the Emir Feisal at which he informed him that he was prepared to recognize the Arab administration of enemy territory east of the Jordan from Ma'an to Damascus inclusive. He also stated that he would appoint two liaison officers, one British and the other French, who would communicate with him through his chief political officer regarding the affairs of the Arab administration.

Political affairs properly find a place in military history only when they are the cause of, or have an effect upon, military operations. The thorny questions concerning French and Arab claims, complicated by the imprudent steps of Arab committees in the " Blue " zone, which aroused in French breasts a distrust of Feisal fatal to his future, come under neither head, though they occupied henceforth a great part of the Commander-in-Chief's time. They may therefore be passed over, though we shall have to mention them again in the following chapter when the arrangements made after a further advance had taken place are discussed. It need only be added that the first Arab Administration broke down within a few days, and that Shukri Pasha resigned, to be succeeded by Ali Riza Pasha el Rikabi.

On the 2nd October Lieut.-General Chauvel, Major-Generals Barrow, Macandrew, and Hodgson, each with representatives of their staffs, one squadron from each regiment, one battery from each division, and a section of the 2nd New Zealand Machine-Gun Squadron (5th L.H. Brigade), marched through Damascus, the detachment forming up on the Pilgrims' Road south of the suburb of Meidan. The great procession was thus composed of British Yeomen, Australian Light Horse, New Zealand Machine Gunners, Indian Cavalry, French Chasseurs d'Afrique and Spahis, British Territorial Royal Horse Artillery. The A. & N.Z. Mounted Division was represented by a squadron of the 2nd L.H. Brigade acting as the corps commander's bodyguard. The 3rd L.H. Brigade was, as we have seen, in action many miles from Damascus, but its triumphal entry of the day before had been far more dramatic and memorable, so that it could well resign itself to missing this ceremony. The march had an extraordinary effect upon the excited and unruly populace. There had been some looting by local Bedouin, but this now ceased, and Damascus at once returned to business, so far as the conditions allowed, speedily recouping herself for recent losses by a thriving trade with the British troops.

The prisoners captured by the Desert Mounted Corps at Damascus and during the advance on the city, that is, from the 26th September, numbered 662 officers and 19,205 other ranks, bringing the total taken by it since the commencement of operations to over 47,000. There appears to have been no separate record made of the guns captured by the corps, for it had other duties to perform which prevented it from enumerating them, but it is known that 360 fell into the hands of the E.E.F. With these there were, in the words of Sir Edmund Allenby's final Despatch, " the " transport and equipment of three Turkish Armies." The losses to be set against this vast haul of prisoners and material were mainly from sickness, of which we shall speak later. The actual battle casualties of the Desert Mounted Corps from the 19th September were little more than five hundred.[1]

The British Commander-in-Chief estimated that when the pursuit began there were upwards of 40,000 Turks, including, of course, men of auxiliary services and non-combatants, retreating on Damascus or already there. Disorganized and broken as they were, these men would have formed the material out of which the enemy commanders could have created a force to oppose the British cavalry in the difficult country ahead. At a blow, the pursuit and capture of Damascus had halved their numbers and driven the remainder, of which only a few thousand were effective rifles, northward as an uncontrolled mob. It is not too much to say that only the two German detachments, Colonel von Oppen's force which had passed through by train to Riyaq before the Barada Gorge was closed, and the *146th Regiment*, which had marched to Homs, were at the moment disciplined formations upon which their commanders could rely. This great cavalry operation in effect finally decided the fortune of the campaign.

NOTE.

THE ACTION OF THE ENEMY FROM THE 26TH SEPTEMBER TO THE 1ST OCTOBER.

After the loss of Samakh and Tiberias the remnants of the garrisons, known temporarily as the *Tiberias Group*, fell back towards Quneitra, leaving rear guards to hold the Jordan south of Lake Hule. The group was reinforced at Quneitra by all available troops from Damascus. On the 26th Colonel von Oppen reached Der'a, his German troops of the *Asia Corps* consisting of 700 men, including the *205th Pioniere Company*. After their great marches these troops, inspired by the energy and personal bravery of their commander, were still in good spirits and fighting fit. The other German formation, the *146th Regiment*, under Lieut.-Colonel Freiherr von Hammerstein-Gesmold, reached Er Remta on the same date. Three hundred men of the Haifa garrison, mainly Germans and Austrians, reached Beirut and were despatched to Riyaq.

Liman, who had sent his staff back to Aleppo on the 25th, had now given up hopes of making a serious stand south of Damascus, but he

---

[1]

	Killed.	Wounded.	Missing.
British Officers	11	36	1
Indian Officers	5	12	—
British Other Ranks	51	200	15
Indian Other Ranks	58	117	27

Of the comparatively few missing several were found in hospital at Damascus, together with a few men missing in former engagements.

realized that unless the *Tiberias Group* retired stubbornly, disputing the ground step by step along the Tiberias road, the *Fourth* and *Seventh Armies* would not escape the British pursuit. He issued orders that the group should resist vigorously, and, as we have seen, they were, considering the circumstances, well fulfilled. The next line of defence was to be Riyaq, whither he ordered Colonel von Oppen to withdraw by train from Der'a at 5.30 a.m. on the 27th. Nine hours' work was needed to repair a breach in the line 500 yards long, 30 miles north of the station, but the train reached Damascus next morning and went straight through to Riyaq.

Liman transferred his headquarters to Ba'albek on the 29th. On this date Mustapha Kemal Pasha arrived at Kiswe with the leading troops of the *Seventh Army*, and was ordered to proceed to Riyaq and take over command of that front. Jevad Pasha and the staff of the *Eighth Army* had been sent back to Constantinople, and Jemal Pasha, in whom the Commander-in-Chief seems to have placed great reliance, took over the *Tiberias Group* defending Damascus, while retaining command of the *Fourth Army*.

On the 30th the *146th Regiment*, fired at from the houses, was the last formation to leave the town. Hearing that the Barada Gorge was closed, Lieut.-Colonel von Hammerstein took the Homs road, along which he had been preceded by the scanty remnants of the *III Corps*, the *24th Division*, and the *3rd Cavalry Division*.

All through the 30th a mob of refugees streamed through the outposts of Colonel von Oppen at Riyaq, even the companies of the *43rd Division* of the *Second Army*, which had not been engaged, having been infected with panic.

It is quite clear from Liman's account that, had the British pursuit closed upon Damascus twenty-four hours later, the majority of the Turkish troops in the city would have escaped. Even after the British had blocked the Barada Gorge the Homs road lay open, and Br.-General Wilson's bold march through the streets to close it was a brilliant and decisive stroke. Liman had seen his troops win the race to Damascus, only to drop at the post from complete exhaustion. For their own sakes as well as for the convenience of the British administration it was as well that they fell into the hands of their pursuers in the city rather than upon the road.

CHAPTER XXVII.

THE END OF THE CAMPAIGN.

(Maps 3, 23; Sketches 41, 42, 43.)

The Occupation of Riyaq and Beirut.

Map 3.
Sketch 41.

The capture of Damascus was the climax of the campaign. To us, who look back across the years upon the successive episodes of this great victory, what remains to be recorded must seem of minor interest and importance. The last heavy blow has been struck; the end of the drama is approaching. To commanders and troops, however, no such aspect of the operations can have appeared. They realized the fullness of their success, and perhaps guessed that no big battle remained to be fought in Syria; that, though progress might be slow, they could now go forward, based upon the Syrian ports, and that till they reached the mountain masses of Taurus and Amanus no barrier could long check their march. Yet the very distances now stretching before them, so much greater even than those traversed between Jaffa and Damascus, were impressive. The resources of Turkey were believed to be nearly exhausted, but the best information on this matter could only be vague. What effort the enemy would make to replace the armies which they had destroyed was uncertain. At the moment, therefore, the capture of Damascus brought no feeling that strenuous exertions were nearly at an end or that demands for sacrifice were soon to cease.

Meanwhile ill-health was cause enough for anxiety, and the death in hospital of many officers and men who had passed unscathed through fight after fight was depressing to their comrades. Viewing the situation of his troops at the beginning of October, the Commander-in-Chief could congratulate himself upon the small number of battle casualties which his victory had entailed; yet the length

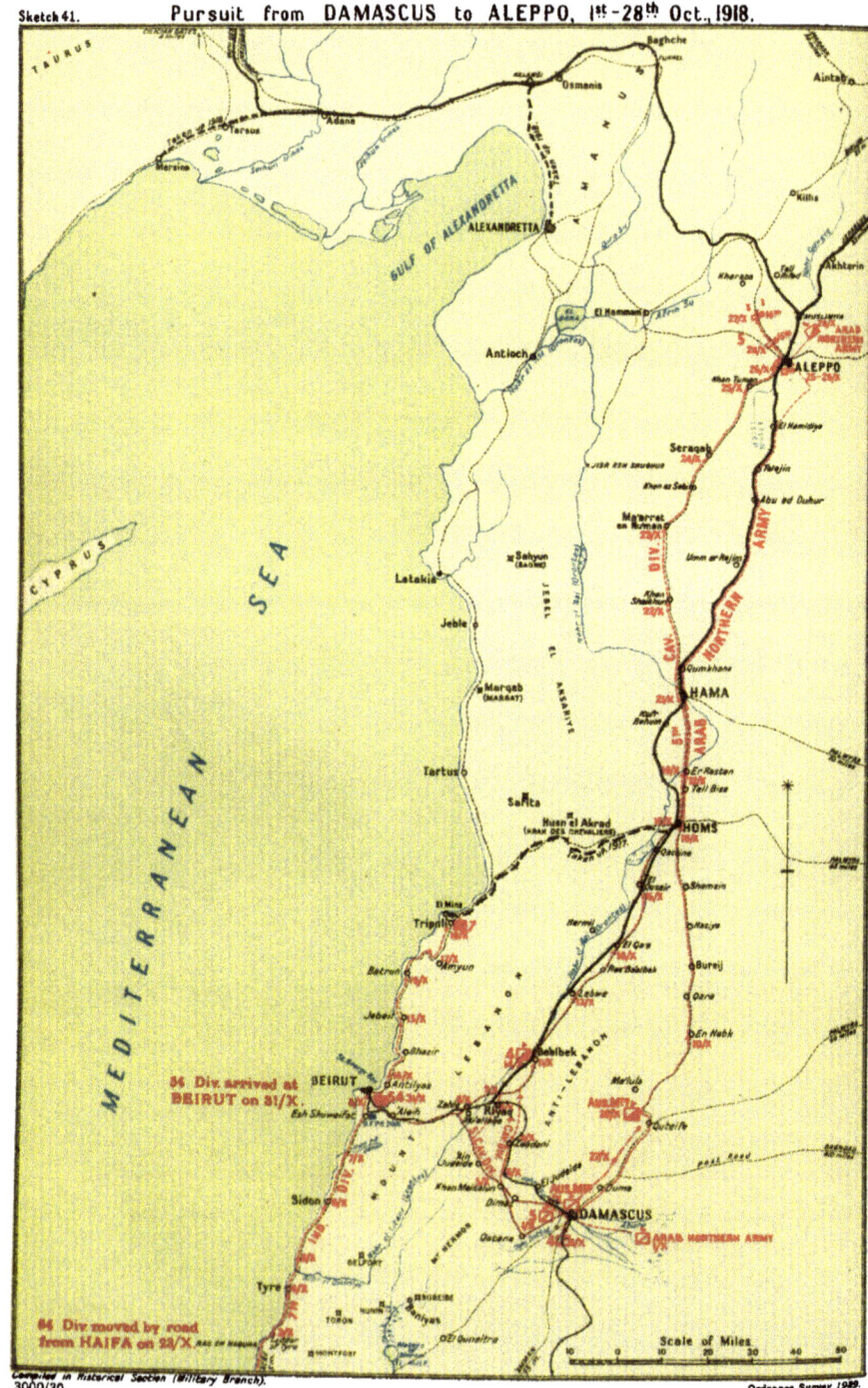

of the daily lists showing the wastage from disease and the speed with which they mounted up made him realize that he had to bring his campaign to a close with a force crippled by sickness. The losses from this cause in the two infantry corps, and still more in Chaytor's Force, were high; but those troops, with the exception of the 7th Division which was marching on Beirut, were not to be called upon for any further considerable effort, and their sick were generally close to the railheads and hospitals. The bulk of the infantry, too, could now be brought back to the old camping-grounds previously cleared of mosquitoes. It was in the three divisions now forming the Desert Mounted Corps, which had to finish the work, that the progress of disease was most alarming.

The causes were very simple. The British had advanced from an area wherein every precaution known to science had been taken, straight into one in which little or nothing had been done to fight the mosquito. As a result, from the date of the capture of Damascus the admissions to hospital from the E.E.F. of men suffering from malaria, fairly high in the month preceding the attack, were doubled at a bound, rising from 2·85 to 5·51 per cent. The disease was, moreover, for the most part of a malignant type. The Desert Mounted Corps suffered particularly, owing to its sojourn in the Jordan Valley and the days it had spent in the Plain of Esdraelon; the 4th Cavalry Division most of all, since it had not only had a very long spell in the Jordan Valley, but had been stationed for several days at Beisan, one of the unhealthiest spots in Palestine. That, however, was only the beginning. About the 6th October came the wave of influenza which was experienced in every theatre and indeed all over the world. At once the hospitals and receiving stations established in Damascus were filled to overflowing with patients suffering from this scourge, which could not at first be clinically differentiated from the malignant malaria. The Indian troops were affected only slightly less than those of European blood. Admissions to hospital from the Desert Mounted Corps, 1,246 for the week ending on the 5th October, rose to 3,109 for that ending on the 12th. The inevitable attacks of pneumonia followed. The death rate was not high, yet nearly four times as many men of the corps died in Damascus as had been killed between the opening of the offensive and the capture of the city. In the course of October and November there were 479 deaths in hospital, of which perhaps not a score were due to wounds. That it was no higher was due to the energy and devotion of the medical services, themselves much affected by sickness. The evacuation of the sick then, and still more after the advance into Northern Syria, was a matter of great difficulty. It was carried out chiefly by hospital ships from the ports successively occupied, the sick being brought down by motor convoys to the coast.

It was, however, the dreadful state of the Turkish prisoners, the necessity of succouring them which common humanity dictated, and above all the urgent need of preventing their more serious ills from spreading to British troops and perhaps incapacitating the whole force, which caused most work and anxiety. The Turks were suffering from almost all the diseases which warfare brings in its train. Cholera, the worst of all, was fortunately absent, owing it would seem to a great extent to Falkenhayn's chief medical officer, Obergeneralarzt Steuber, who had insisted upon the isolation of units which arrived in Palestine with the disease in their ranks. There were a few cases among the civilian population of Tiberias, but it was quickly stamped out, and only one British soldier was affected. Typhus, enteric, relapsing fever, ophthalmia, were prevalent among the prisoners, as well as the universal malaria and influenza. A little-known disease called pellagra[1] caused many deaths, though not a single man of the British troops developed it. Syphilis, always widely spread in the Turkish Army and having apparently little effect upon the general health of the men when they were otherwise normally fit, played havoc with constitutions weakened by want of nourishment and over-exertion. The number of sick and wounded prisoners of war admitted into the Desert Mounted Corps field ambulances was over 2,000; the number admitted into the Turkish hospitals in Damascus after its capture was 8,250.

The Turks actually in hospital were not the only ones

---

[1] Pellagra is an intestinal and cutaneous disease of which certainly one, and possibly the chief, cause is lack of protein in diet. There is no evidence that it is infectious. There were a good many cases also among Egyptians of the Labour Corps.

in need of attention. Ten thousand prisoners in a compound at Kaukab, which was later on swelled by some thousands more from the advanced compound at El Mezze, were also in a deplorable condition. They had expended all their energies, physical and moral, in the supreme effort to reach Damascus, and now they were worn out, their spirits so broken that they could not struggle even against death. For some time they died at the rate of seventy a day. This compound was put in charge of Lieut.-Colonel T. J. Todd, 10th A.L.H., and at once the regeneration of the prisoners began. Himself ruined in health, he devoted all his remaining strength to improving their lot. The weakest men were transferred to houses in the village; blankets were obtained by threats and cajolery from the Arab authorities at Damascus; Syrian doctors were set to work in the camp and ordered to enforce sanitary precautions; sheep and cattle from the countryside, grain concealed in Damascus, were requisitioned; the men were organized into companies under their own officers. The death-rate fell suddenly to fifteen a day, and the health of the remainder improved wonderfully. Like Lieut.-Colonel A. M. McLaurin of the 8th A.L.H., like their gallant opponent Oberst von Oppen, Lieut.-Colonel Todd was himself to die from disease and exhaustion soon after the Armistice; but his last work was an example of the chivalry and spirit of compassion which adorn the finest martial characters.

Once again the horses had wonderfully withstood their tremendous exertions. The admissions to veterinary hospitals and mobile veterinary sections from the 15th September to the 5th October were 3,245 [1] out of a total strength of 25,618, but of these 904 were re-issued as cured during the period, and of those evacuated the greater part could be again made fit for service. Those which were killed in action, died, or were destroyed, numbered only 1,021—less than 4 per cent.—while there were 259 missing. The chief causes of wastage were galls, debility or fever, and bowel complaints such as colic or diarrhœa. The value

---

[1] It is rather unfortunate that statistics were compiled from week to week instead of from the 19th September. This figure of 3,245 undoubtedly includes a good number got rid of before the operations began because they were unlikely to stand the work. The result is that a worse complexion is put on the casualty list.

of seasoning was made plainly apparent. The horses which had been long with their units and sometimes appeared distressingly light in condition at the start withstood the marches well and picked up rapidly afterwards. The newly-acquired remounts, apparently in good condition, rarely reached Damascus, and if they did were useless for a long period. There had often been shortage of water, but on the whole the area was much better watered than that traversed by the corps in the latter stages of the Third Battle of Gaza. The excellence of the horsemastership throughout the corps is proved by the comparatively small wastage, especially when it is recalled that the mount of the average Australian and Yeoman, with kit, arms, and rations, carried not far short of twenty stone, and that of the Indian, with a lance added, probably not more than a stone less. The horsemastership of the 4th Cavalry Division, which had much the lowest wastage in the corps, was outstanding. "A" Squadron 19th Lancers (Sikhs), commanded by Captain G. M. Fitzgerald, reached Damascus without having lost a horse.

Immediately after the capture of Damascus the three divisions were concentrated south of the city, between it and Kaukab, for convenience of supply. The new sea base at Haifa was now in full working order, an average of nearly a thousand tons a day being landed there during the first week of October. Even then the strain was severe, for lorries from Haifa had to cover 85 miles and those from El 'Affule 73 miles. As soon as possible a depot for the whole corps was formed at Samakh, which then became the railhead whence supplies were borne by lorry to Damascus; but fresh meat was requisitioned locally, as well as all supplies, except groceries for the Australian Mounted Division while it remained in the Damascus area. Not until the 26th October, owing to the delay caused by the destruction of a long bridge in the Yarmuk Valley, could supplies be sent right through to Damascus by rail, and then they were limited in quantity by shortage of rolling stock for the old Turkish line. Local purchase for the troops and the 20,000 prisoners was a business demanding patience and an admixture of firmness and tact, owing to the rawness of the Arab administration and the slack business methods of merchants and farmers. When the advance of the 4th and 5th Cavalry

Divisions and the occupation of Beirut by the 7th Division, both of which we are about to record, had taken place, the Damascus–Beirut line was put into working order from Damascus to Mu'allaqa, at the foot of Lebanon. Supplies were landed at Beirut, and from the 19th October railed to Mu'allaqa and carried by lorries to Damascus, and also to Ba'albek for the two cavalry divisions. These divisions had hitherto been living on the country, entirely so far as forage was concerned, and to a large extent as regards bread and meat.

On the 3rd October General Chauvel, who had established his headquarters south-west of the suburb of Salahiye, in a building recently occupied by *Yilderim*, was visited by the Commander-in-Chief and instructed to capture Riyaq as soon as possible. Riyaq lay 30 miles north-west of Damascus, in the valley of the Nahr el Litani, which separated the ranges of Lebanon and Anti-Lebanon, and was the terminus of the standard-gauge line from Constantinople. It had been heavily bombed on the 2nd by the R.A.F., which had reported it to be held by several thousand troops. As we have seen, the *Asia Corps* and troops from Haifa and Acre had been withdrawn there by train.[1] The 7th Division was moving along the coast to Beirut, where it was reported that there were few if any Turkish troops, and reached Tyre on the 4th. General Chauvel ordered the 5th Cavalry Division, followed by the 4th, to march on the 5th October and seize both Riyaq and Zahle, a considerable Christian town on the eastern slope of the Lebanon.

The 5th Cavalry Division marched from its bivouac on the Tiberias road, through Qatana and El Mezze, by a track across the hills to Khan Dimas,[2] on the Beirut road, and bivouacked at Khan Meisalun, 15 miles W.N.W. of Damascus. Here it was rejoined by the wheeled transport and guns which had moved through Damascus and by the Sherwood Rangers from Quneitra. The 12th Light Armoured Motor Battery and 7th Light Car Patrol also reported to Major-General Macandrew at this point. Having received information that munition depots and rolling stock were being destroyed at Riyaq, Major-General Macandrew issued orders for the 14th Cavalry Brigade to push on during the night with the armoured cars and stop the enemy doing further

1918.
5 Oct.

---

[1] See p. 595.   [2] Khan Dimez on Map 3.

damage. Learning a little later that the Turks had gone, he decided that the night march would exhaust troops and horses to no useful end, and cancelled it. The brigade reached Riyaq at 2 p.m. on the 6th. The place was in confusion, with many Turkish dead lying about to bear witness to the effect of the air raid; but though much had been destroyed, it contained valuable booty in the shape of engineers' stores, several locomotives, and many trucks of both the broad and narrow gauge. Stragglers and sick numbering 177 were captured here and at Zahle. The remains of thirty aeroplanes, burnt by the enemy, were found on Riyaq aerodrome. On the following day the armoured cars carried out a reconnaissance across the Lebanon to Beirut, which was found unoccupied.

The 7th Division marched up the coast in three columns, of which the leading one consisted only of the Corps Cavalry Regiment, one company of infantry, and the 2nd Light Armoured Motor Battery. With the second column were the 3rd and 4th Companies Sappers and Miners, and the 121st Pioneers, which on the 2nd October marched from Acre to Kh. el Musheirefe, 12 miles along the coast, and with the assistance of the 53rd Sikhs and 2/Leicester set about the task of preparing the road for the advance of the division, under the supervision of the C.R.E., Lieut.-Colonel E. F. J. Hill. The road here bends towards the shore and mounts the white rocks of Ras en Naqura. This promontory is distant from Tyre about thirteen miles as the crow flies, and for the first six or seven miles the road rarely quits the shore. It was then a rocky track, in places only six feet wide, with gradients of one in five. The whole stretch from Ras en Naqura to 6½ miles south of Tyre is sometimes known as "The Ladder of Tyre," but this title belongs more properly to a portion rather over a mile long, beginning at Kh. Iskanderune. Here, before the work of the 7th Division had been accomplished, to stand perhaps for all time, the term "ladder" was indeed fitting, for the path was cut from solid rock in the shape of great steps, and ran along the face of steep cliffs. General Bulfin, who had established his advanced headquarters at the *Karmelheim* and gone forward to look at the road, was told by Lieut.-Colonel Hill that extensive blasting was necessary to make the Ladder fit for wheels, including those of a 60-pdr. battery moving with the rearmost column, and that there was a risk of the whole shelf slipping into the sea. The chances seemed in favour of a successful outcome, but success could not be guaranteed. There was no other route northward for many miles inland, and if the Ladder were destroyed the division's progress would be blocked. General Bulfin demanded " time for a couple of cigarettes " in which to consider the problem ; then ordered the attempt to be made. It was completely successful. The whole length of the cliff road was made practicable for wheeled transport in the course of three days.

1918.
2 Oct.

Without waiting for this work to be completed, the Corps Cavalry Regiment advanced on the 4th October and in the early afternoon entered Es Sur, or Tyre, the renowned Phœnician capital and mother of Carthage, but now a small and unimportant town. Here three days' supplies were put ashore, and picked up by successive columns as they passed through. On the 6th the advanced troops entered Saida, or Sidon, once Tyre's lesser rival, but now, when both are in eclipse, much the larger town. Further supplies were landed here from the sea. On the evening of the 8th the head of the division reached the city of Beirut, to be received with acclamation by the inhabitants, who handed over about six hundred Turks to the British.

4 Oct.

8 Oct.

Beirut, the second city of Syria, is the most largely Christian, the various creeds of that faith having numbered nearly two-thirds of its pre-war population of 190,000. It is mentioned in the Tell el 'Amarna letters, but did not rise to importance until Roman times. Under the Crusaders it was the capital of a fief of the Kingdom of Jerusalem. A great port with a noble site, and the healthiest and most intellectual city of Syria, it contains few antiquities of interest ; but in its neighbourhood is an impressive record of Syrian history. Seven miles to the north-west the Nahr el Kelb, or Dog River, runs to the sea through a narrow ravine. Here are inscriptions of successive conquerors upon panels in the rock. Rameses II is followed by a number of Assyrians, from the bloody Ashur-nasir-pal to Sennacherib and Esarhaddon. The Ottoman conquest of the sixteenth century A.D. is commemorated by the name of Sultan Selim. Fittingly, a British inscription has been added to the list.

General Bulfin established his headquarters at the principal hotel, the Deutscherhof, the same day. French military governors were appointed at Beirut, Sidon, and Tyre, Colonel de Piépape, commander of the D.F.P.S., being given this important position at Beirut. Small detachments of French troops were brought by trawlers from Haifa to take over the policing of the three towns, in which there was a certain unrest created by adherents of the Sherifial cause. French destroyers had entered the harbour before the arrival of the British troops.

The Occupation of Homs and Tripoli.

The country which the advanced troops were now penetrating far exceeds in beauty and grandeur that which they had known for the past year. South of the Amanus and separated from it by the valley of the Orontes is a hundred-mile chain of hills of moderate height—none much exceeding 3,000 feet—known as Jebel en Nuseiriye or Jebel el Ansariye. This range ends abruptly in a broad gap connecting the coast plain and that to the east. South of this valley rises the Lebanon, and 20 miles to the east, from the Plain of Hama, the Anti-Lebanon. These two ranges run parallel to one another from north-east to south-west, separated by the Nahr el Litani, or Leontes, which enters the sea between Tyre and Sidon. The great heights and majestic contours of their peaks, the fertility of their slopes—whereon vines in places are found nearly 5,000 feet up—give to this land a splendour that nothing in Palestine can match. The highest points are on the northern half of the Lebanon, where the Dahr el Qadib raises its snow-clad head well over 10,000 feet above the sea. This peak is moreover famous because of the group of ancient cedars which stand upon its flank, over 6,000 feet above sea-level. The Anti-Lebanon, however, must claim in Mount Hermon (9,383 feet), the most impressive and beautiful mountain in Syria.

Such being the conformation of the country, it can be imagined that communication from east to west is difficult. It may be said, in fact, that the road from Damascus to Beirut was the only one of importance which crossed the Anti-Lebanon and Lebanon. The next great route was from

Homs, and ran through the gap between the Lebanon and Ansariye ranges, of which mention has been made, to Tripoli. Railways also connected Damascus with Beirut, and Homs with Tripoli; but on the line to Beirut the rack-and-pinion system had to be employed for twenty miles in the Lebanon.[1] The produce of the old Damascus and Beirut *Vilayets* is vastly greater than that of Palestine, barley and wheat being grown in great quantities, though oats only begin further north. Cattle, sheep, and goats, especially the two last, were plentiful, though their numbers had naturally been diminished by the needs of the Turkish Army.

The enemy, after hastily evacuating Riyaq, had retired by way of Ba'albek on Homs. So hopelessly disorganized, however, were the Turkish troops that Liman had no hope of making a real stand short of Aleppo. Thither he had despatched the *Asia Corps* under Colonel von Oppen, and had ordered Mustapha Kemal Pasha with the headquarters of the *Seventh Army* to proceed there and undertake the work of reconstruction. The remains of the *Fourth Army*, under Jemal Pasha, were to remain as long as possible at Homs in the hope of gaining time to organize south of Aleppo the final defence of Syria.

On the 9th October Sir Edmund Allenby issued orders for the occupation of Homs by the Desert Mounted Corps and of Tripoli by the 7th Division. The rate of progress, he informed Generals Bulfin and Chauvel, would have to depend upon supply and could not be exactly foreseen, but he desired that the troops of both corps should advance as soon as possible and carry out the movement as fast as they could be fed. The Commander-in-Chief accepted the offer of the Emir Feisal to send a body of 1,500 cavalry and camel-men northward by the Damascus–Homs road to operate between Hama and Aleppo against the Turkish communications.

On the 10th October the armoured cars attached to the 5th Cavalry Division found Ba'albek, famous for its ancient Acropolis whereon are the ruins of two colossal second-century temples, unoccupied. General Chauvel was perturbed by the sickness in the 4th Cavalry Division and

---

[1] It was lack of the special engines that prevented supplies being railed all the way from Beirut to Damascus. (See p. 601.) The Homs-Tripoli line had been dismantled by the Turks.

suggested that it should be relieved by the Australian Mounted Division and withdrawn to Damascus to rest. The Commander-in-Chief, however, decided that this exchange would take too long and directed him to push on at once from Ba'albek towards Homs with the 5th Cavalry Division, the 4th following. Both divisions had established temporary hospitals for light cases, the 4th at Bludan,[1] 20 miles north-west of Damascus, the 5th at the pleasant little town of Mu'allaqa. General Chauvel ordered the 5th Cavalry Division to reach Homs by the 16th, and requested Feisal to instruct his lieutenant, Nuri Bey, to cover its right flank by moving parallel to it along the main Damascus–Homs road.

Sketches 41, 42.

Major-General Macandrew decided to advance on Homs in two columns, headquarters moving with the leading one, which consisted of the 13th Cavalry Brigade (Br.-General G. A. Weir),[2] " B " Battery H.A.C., and armoured cars. The rear column, consisting of the remainder of the division, was to follow, a day's march behind. On the 13th October the 13th Cavalry Brigade reached Lebwe (17 miles), on the 14th El Qa'a (12 miles), on the 15th El Quseir (15 miles). Somewhat surprisingly, it was discovered that food was fairly plentiful, and that there was no great difficulty in requisitioning a day's supply of bread, fresh meat, and grain at each place. It had for some days been reported that the enemy had evacuated Homs, and this proved to be the case.

1918. 16 Oct.

The leading column reached this town of 70,000 inhabitants, lying in the centre of the fertile plain of the Orontes, on the 16th. Here the troops had a most enthusiastic reception, and a banquet was given to Major-General Macandrew by the authorities, at which he spoke of the traditional friendship of the noble enemies, Richard of England and Saladin. The division then closed up and enjoyed three days of rest. The 4th Cavalry Division had halted at Ba'albek, with one brigade at Lebwe. Generals Allenby and Chauvel visited this division, remaining some days in the area.

On the 11th October General Bulfin issued orders for

---

[1] Bludein on Map 3.
[2] Br.-General Weir, formerly, it will be recalled, in command of the 19th Infantry Brigade, had succeeded Br.-General P. J. V. Kelly in the command of the 13th Cavalry Brigade. His successor in the command of the 19th Infantry Brigade was Br.-General W. S. Leslie, late G.S.O.1 of the 7th Division.

Sketch 42.

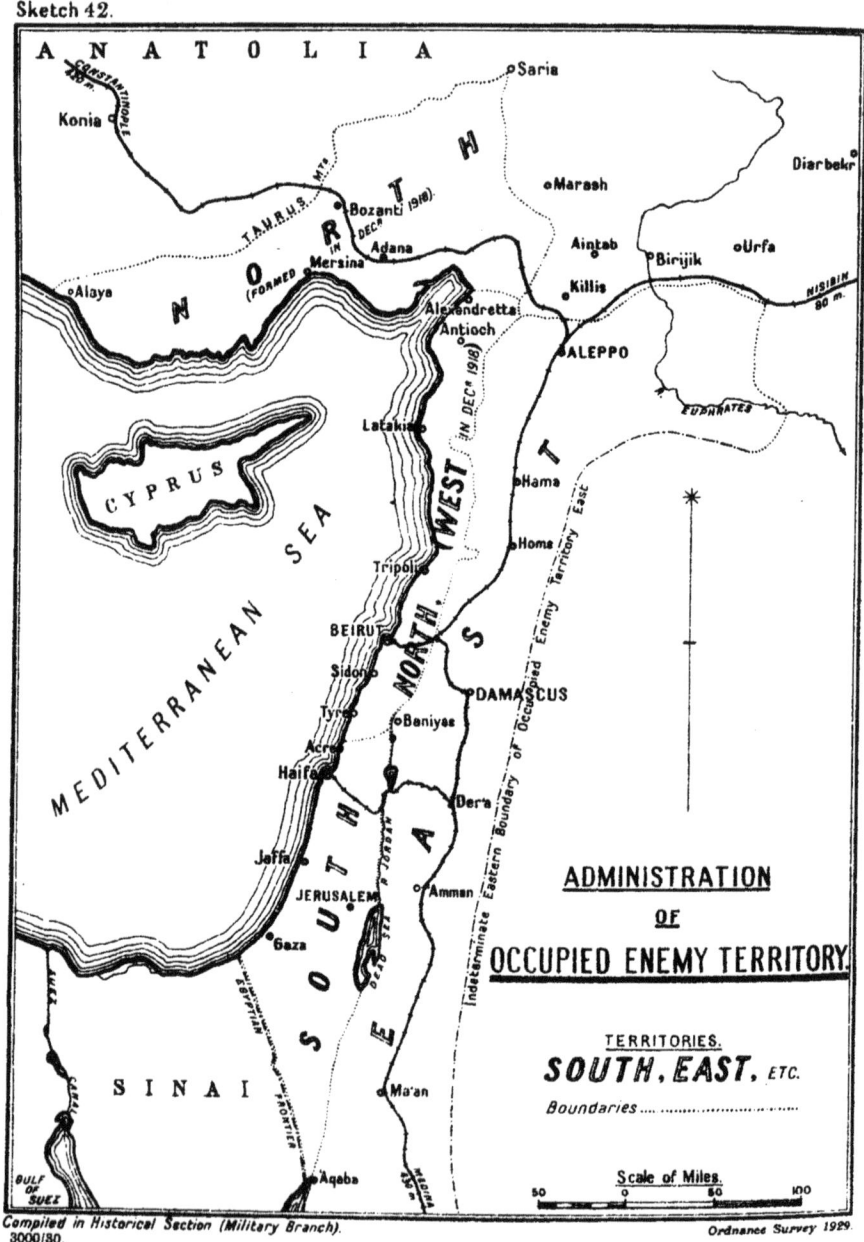

ADMINISTRATION OF SYRIA

the XXI Corps Cavalry Regiment and the 2nd Light Armoured Motor Battery to advance to Tripoli and its port of El Mina. The detachment arrived on the 13th. The 19th Infantry Brigade Group (Br.-General W. S. Leslie), marching from Beirut on the 14th, reached Tripoli on the 18th, the remainder of the division closing up on the town. Meanwhile the 54th Division was marching on Beirut, which was reached by the leading brigade on the 31st October. The D.F.P.S. had also been transferred to that city and had arrived on the 20th. On the 24th it was rejoined by the French R.M.M.C., which had been attached to the 5th L.H. Brigade throughout the operations.

On the 23rd October Sir Edmund Allenby reported to the War Office that he had issued fresh instructions for the military administration of enemy territory in Syria and Palestine already in his hands or likely to be occupied in the near future. There were to be three administrative areas, known as Occupied Enemy Territory South, Occupied Enemy Territory North, and Occupied Enemy Territory East. The first two comprised respectively the "Red" and "Blue" zones of the Sykes-Picot Agreement; the third such portions of Zones "A" and "B" of that agreement as came under the control of the Commander-in-Chief. Occupied Enemy Territory South—Palestine, in short—was to have a British chief administrator, Major-General Sir A. W. Money, who had hitherto held that appointment in the portion of Palestine occupied prior to the last offensive. Occupied Enemy Territory North, the future French Zone, from north of Acre to Alexandretta, was to be administered by Colonel de Piépape. Occupied Enemy Territory East was to be administered by General Ali Pasha el Rikabi. The three zones cannot be described by boundaries without a knowledge of the old Turkish administrative areas being presumed in the reader and are therefore shown on the attached sketch. It must be added that Occupied Enemy Territory North differed from the "Blue Zone" of the Sykes-Picot Agreement in that the *Qazas*[1] of Ba'albek, Hasbeya, and Rasheiya (37 and 34 miles respectively southeast of Beirut) were, in deference to Arab susceptibilities,

---

[1] *Qaza* is a small Turkish administrative district which may be compared with the French "arrondissement."

attached, pending a final settlement of the whole question, to Occupied Enemy Territory East.

Occupied Enemy Territory East, that is, the portion of Zones " A " and " B " under Sir Edmund Allenby's control, was for the time being formed into one area, instead of being divided at Lake Tiberias in accordance with the Sykes-Picot map, for two reasons. The first was the convenience of military administration. The second was more important and complex. Since the signature of the Sykes-Picot Agreement a great wave of what may be described as democratic nationalism had swept over the Old World. The entry of America into the war and the collapse of Russia had both helped to raise it, but it sprang from a deep-seated sentiment in the bosoms of oppressed peoples which diplomacy could not ignore, and which British diplomacy, at least, did not desire to ignore. This sentiment had a very important effect upon the political situation in the Middle East, in that it seemed to clash with the provisions of the Sykes-Picot Agreement. Its force was recognized by both France and Great Britain in a declaration dated the 7th November 1918, and telegraphed in French by the Foreign Office to Sir Reginald Wingate, High Commissioner in Egypt, for transmission to King Hussein and for circulation in the native Press, of which the following is a translation :—

" The goal aimed at by France and Great Britain in
" their conduct in the East of a war unchained by German
" ambition is the complete and definite freedom of the peoples
" so long oppressed by the Turks, and the establishment of
" national governments and administrations deriving their
" authority from the initiative and free choice of the native
" population.

" In order to fulfil these intentions, France and Great
" Britain are agreed in the desire to encourage and assist in
" the establishment of native governments and administra-
" tions in Syria and Mesopotamia, at this moment freed
" by the Allies, and in the territories of which they are
" attempting the liberation, and on the recognition of these
" as soon as they are effectively established. Far from
" wishing to impose on the populations of these regions such
" or such institutions, they have no other care than to assure
" by their support and practical aid the normal working of
" the governments and institutions which these populations

" have freely set up. To ensure equal and impartial justice
" for all, to aid the economic development of the country by
" inspiring and encouraging local initiative, to facilitate the
" spread of education, to put an end to the divisions too
" long exploited by Turkish policy—such is the rôle which
" the two Governments proclaim in the liberated territories."

Great Britain had virtually no direct political interests in Syria beyond the desire to see that country settled and contented under a friendly government. She was not hostile to French aspirations save in so far as they might contain the seeds of future unrest. But she did not desire to be a party to any measures conflicting with the declaration set out above or with the spirit which gave birth to it. To have established at Damascus a French sphere of influence would have had this effect. Even to have included the *Qazas* of Ba'albek, Hasbeya, and Rasheiya in the French " Blue " Zone would probably have resulted in the resignation of the Emir Feisal, which in its turn might have let loose anarchy in the newly-occupied regions. It was for these reasons that Great Britain was averse to a strict and immediate enforcement of the provisions of the Sykes-Picot Agreement. She could, however, only put forward to France her point of view; if France demanded that she should stand by the letter of that agreement, she had no choice but to do so. As is well known, France did make this demand at Versailles, and Britain complied with it. The Arab zone was divided into two, the southern of which became, and remains to-day, the mandated territory of Trans-Jordan, under the rule of Abdulla, Hussein's second son. At Damascus the experiment was tried of a French-protected State under Feisal, but it speedily failed. Feisal was ejected by the French in July 1920, and Zone " A " linked with the " Blue " Zone under a common administration. The subsequent history of French Syria is a matter of public knowledge.

THE CAPTURE OF ALEPPO AND THE AFFAIR OF HARITAN.

The Commander-in-Chief had now determined upon the occupation of Aleppo, the chief city of northern Syria. Immediately after the successful opening of his attack of the 19th September the C.I.G.S. had suggested to him a

Map 23.
Sketches 41, 43.

cavalry raid on Aleppo and informed him that the War Cabinet was prepared to accept the risks involved in the enterprise. But he would then have nothing to do with the scheme. Unless the War Cabinet was prepared to undertake a combined operation on a large scale at Alexandretta—a project thrice before discussed and now once again being examined—he was convinced that the only sound policy was to advance by stages. At that time the first stage, the advance to Damascus and Beirut, was only about to begin.

1918.
18 Oct.

Now the situation was altogether changed. The march on Damascus had almost destroyed the Turkish Armies, and, so far as he could judge, the anticipated enemy reinforcements were not appearing in numbers worth consideration. He learnt that the Turks were evacuating Aleppo as fast as they could collect trains. Hama, 27 miles north of Homs, was reported by the R.A.F. to be clear of enemy troops on the 17th October. On the following day he ordered General Chauvel, by telegram and also by means of a letter carried by air, to make preparations for the 5th Cavalry Division to continue its advance on the 20th, so as to reach Aleppo by the 26th. The 4th Cavalry Division was to move to Homs. He informed General Chauvel that he had directed the XXI Corps to despatch the 2nd Light Car Patrol and 2nd Light Armoured Motor Battery to join the 5th Cavalry Division at Homs. This reinforcement gave Major-General Macandrew the strongest column of light armoured motor batteries and light car patrols yet employed in the theatre, viz. 2nd, 11th, and 12th Light Armoured Motor Batteries and 1st (Australian), 2nd,[1] and 7th Light Car Patrols. Sir Edmund Allenby also directed General Chauvel to find out from the Emir Feisal how far his forces could co-operate. On the 20th General Chauvel stated that the 5th Cavalry Division, which now had a fighting strength of 2,500, was leaving Homs that day. The 4th Cavalry Division, on the other hand, had been reduced

---

[1] The 2nd Light Car Patrol left Sollum, in Libya, on the 11th October and on the 13th entrained at El Hamman on the Khedivial Railway to Alexandria. It reached Lydda on the 15th, unloaded, and went by road to Tul Karm on the 16th, Acre on the 17th, Beirut on the 18th, Homs on the 20th. On the 21st it was in action many miles north of Hama. It had then covered about 1,200 miles, half by road.

by sickness to 1,200, and it seemed likely that any further exertion at this moment might put it *hors de combat* for many weeks to come. Feisal had promised to despatch 1,500 troops from Homs under Sherif Nasir, and hoped to raise some thousands more of local Arabs on his march.

The news regarding the 4th Cavalry Division was disquieting. Aleppo was 120 miles from Homs, and it appeared that the 4th Division was actually unable to advance to the latter town, still less to support the 5th in case of need at Aleppo. That division and the car column would therefore, it seemed, be in grave risk from an attack, should the Turks have sufficient strength and energy to make one. Their troops remaining in Aleppo had had time for a certain measure of reorganization. The Commander-in-Chief therefore cancelled the advance, ordering the 5th Cavalry Division to go no further for the present than Hama.

General Chauvel then ordered the postponement of all moves until further notice. The message reached Major-General Macandrew on the night of the 20th, after his first day's march toward Hama, and was little to the liking of that vigorous and headstrong commander. Hama was already in the hands of the Arabs. He did not expect any serious resistance at Aleppo and was confident that the enemy, in whatever strength, had not mobility enough to endanger the safety of his division. He telegraphed [1] that he was on the move and proposed to go straight on to Aleppo. General Chauvel asked G.H.Q. whether the 5th Cavalry Division should be allowed to push on without awaiting support if the situation permitted, and received the Commander-in-Chief's assent. Sir Edmund Allenby was not the man to baulk a divisional commander in whom he had confidence, and whose object was so fully in accord with his own wishes.[2]

---

[1] Throughout the advance from Damascus the Signal Troop R.E. had comparatively small difficulty in maintaining telegraphic communication with corps headquarters. The wires along the railway were seldom cut and the posts were all standing.

[2] The following are the telegrams on this subject :—

Adv. Descorps.
G.A. 248.   20th.   In reply to G.A. 585.

Not understood. Troops far in advance, and I propose advancing with armoured cars to Aleppo. Believe the railway road avoids all blown bridges. Shall be in Hama by midday to-morrow, which is already

On the 19th October the 15th Cavalry Brigade had marched to Er Rastan, 10 miles north of Homs, accompanied by the 5th Field Squadron R.E., with material in lorries to repair the bridge over the Orontes. The Turks had had ample time to demolish it, yet in their flurry had blown out only one of the eight brick arches, though some of the piers were badly shaken. Work began at 8 p.m. that night and was completed by 6 a.m. on the 21st. That afternoon the cars, the 15th Cavalry Brigade and divisional headquarters, reached Hama, an ancient town of about 60,000 inhabitants. On the 22nd the car column went forward to gain touch with the enemy. At Ma'arret en Nu'man, 35 miles north of Hama, the inhabitants declared that there was a Turkish rear guard at Khan es Sebil, another 9 miles up the Aleppo road. That point was reached at 2.30 p.m., but it was found that the Turkish detachment had hastily made off in half a dozen lorries, an armoured car bringing up the rear. The leading British cars went forward at full speed and within a mile caught up and captured the armoured car. The pursuit was continued, and eventually the rearmost lorry broke down, the troops in it making for the hills under heavy machine-gun fire. Altogether 24 Turks were killed and 5 captured. Two German aeroplanes which appeared in the course of the pursuit swooped down and opened machine-gun fire on the Turkish lorries. The car column bivouacked that night at Seraqab, 18 miles from Ma'arret el Nu'man and only 30 miles from Aleppo. It had, of course, far outdistanced the cavalry, of which the leading column was two marches behind. On the 23rd, while awaiting the

---

occupied. No opposition worth thinking of expected at Aleppo. Hoped advance may secure engines and rolling stock.

Fivecav., 10.15 p.m.

C.G.S., G.H.Q.   21st.

To-day 5th Division will be in Hama with Hejaz troops pushing forward. Should 5th Division push on without awaiting support if situation should permit of this?

Descorps, 9 a.m.

Adv. Descorps.
O.A.M. 80.   21st.

Yes. It is the wish of the C.-in-C. that Aleppo be taken as soon as possible. Please own receipt.

G.H.Q.

(Paraphrased after deciphering.)

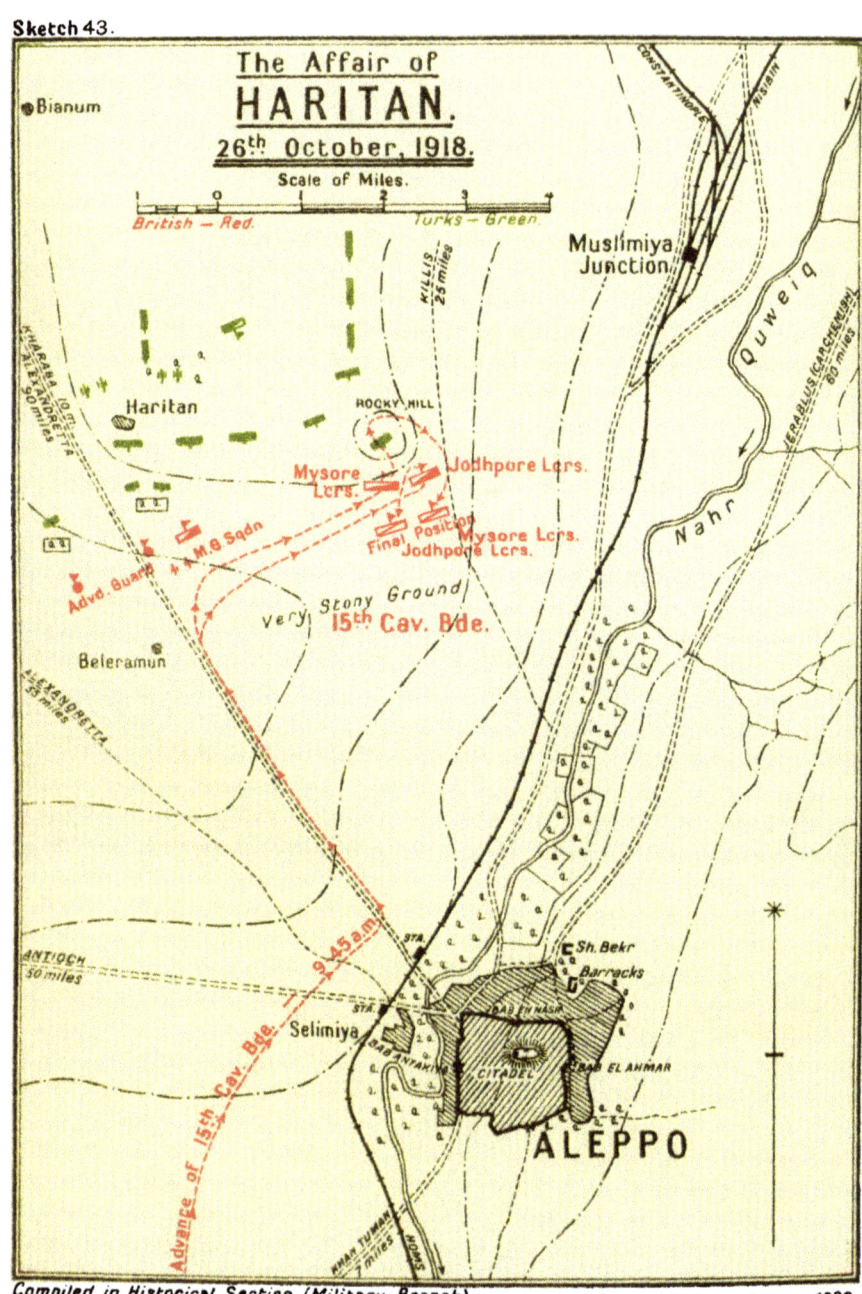

15th Cavalry Brigade, it carried out reconnaissances towards 1918. Aleppo and discovered the enemy, some two or three 23 Oct. thousand strong, holding a position in short lengths of trench astride the road 3 miles south of the city. Captain R. H. M. McIntyre, commanding the 7th Light Car Patrol, was sent in under a flag of truce by Major-General Macandrew's orders to demand the surrender of Aleppo. He was courteously treated by the Turks, but the written message from Mustapha Kemal's chief staff officer which he brought back was stiff and laconic. It ran :—" The " Commander of the Turkish Garrison of Aleppo does not " find it necessary to reply to your note."

On the 25th October the 15th Cavalry Brigade joined 25 Oct. the car column at Zi'bre, 13 miles south-west of Aleppo. The Arabs were advancing along the railway on the British right flank, and Colonel Nuri Bey promised to move up east of Aleppo to co-operate in the attack. He was even better than his word. In the afternoon he launched an assault on the Turkish position south of Aleppo. This was repulsed, but towards evening a body of 1,500 Bedouin forced its way into the city from the east. Street fighting followed. The Bedouin appear at one moment to have entered the Citadel and to have captured the government buildings. According to Liman's account, they were then ejected, yet the Turks immediately withdrew not only what troops they had in the city but also the two strong divisions holding the road to the south.[1]

At 7 a.m. on the 26th October the 15th Cavalry Brigade 26 Oct. moved forward to clear the ridge west of the city and get astride the Alexandretta road. The brigade was still without the Hyderabad Lancers, on the Lines of Communication, and had no battery attached—indeed, none could have

---

[1] These two divisions were the fruit of the organizing power of Mustapha Kemal. They had been numbered the *1st* and *11th*, and constituted the new *XX Corps*, under the command of Major-General Ali Fuad Pasha.

Liman, who was apparently at Adana on this date, gives (pp. 396–7) an extraordinarily inaccurate account of events, doubtless because he was misinformed by his subordinates. He states that " the British had brought " up infantry in a great number of motor lorries to reinforce their cavalry." Perhaps it was thought that a lorry column, actually bringing up supplies from Tripoli through Homs, was carrying troops. It must be remembered also that the armoured and light cars, with maintenance cars, made up a very big column.

accompanied it by the route which it took that morning. Br.-General Harbord found the ridge unoccupied and was told by Arabs that Aleppo was evacuated by the enemy; but he felt by no means sure that this was the case. The only other information he had was an air report that there was a body of 300 cavalry on the Alexandretta road 8 miles to the north-west. The brigade reached the road at its exit from Aleppo at 9.45 and halted for a quarter of an hour. Soon after resuming his advance Br.-General Harbord received a verbal message—which was apparently founded on an air report—that a body of about a thousand Turks, with two small guns, had left Aleppo at 7.30 in a northerly direction. The advanced guard, two squadrons of the Jodhpore Lancers and a subsection of the 15th Machine-Gun Squadron, pushed forward at a trot. Topping the ridge overlooking Haritan, 8 miles north-west of Aleppo, at 11 a.m., it suddenly came under machine-gun fire from the right side of the road. It thereupon fell back 400 yards, dismounted, and took up a position astride the road, with the machine guns on the right.

So far all that had actually been seen of the enemy was a body of a couple of hundred in an enclosed garden south of Haritan. Br.-General Harbord, in view of the information he had received, decided to attack at once. He ordered the Mysore Lancers to move round the eastern end of the ridge and charge the enemy. The remaining two squadrons of the Jodhpore Lancers were to follow, while the rest of the machine-gun squadron[1] reinforced the advanced guard, which was to support the attack by fire. The 12th Light Armoured Motor Battery, having passed through Aleppo, reported to him at 11.30 and was ordered to advance along the road. Its support was of no value, however, for the cars at once ran into heavy fire, had several tyres burst, and turned back.

Meanwhile the Mysore Lancers was advancing north-

---

[1] This machine-gun squadron was on a special establishment. All the others consisted of British personnel, but this was made up of Imperial Service personnel from the three States represented in the brigade. The Mysore and Hyderabad Lancers had always had machine-gun subsections, and one had been formed also from the Jodhpore Lancers by permission of the Commander-in-Chief in India at Sir Edmund Allenby's request. The Jodhpore subsection, which did good work on this occasion, had not previously been in action.

15TH CAV. BRIGADE AT HARITAN   615

eastward. Major W. J. Lambert, the Senior Special Service **1918.**
Officer, made a personal reconnaissance and discovered that **26 Oct.**
the enemy's flank was on a rocky knoll, further east than had
been supposed and unfortunately beyond the range of the
British machine guns. Nevertheless, he ordered the regiment
to charge the knoll. In this, the last engagement of the
campaign, the Mysore Lancers advanced with great dash in
face of artillery and subsequently rifle fire, three squadrons
in line of squadron columns, the fourth in support. The
position, held by a party of 150 Turks, was carried, about
fifty of the enemy being speared and twenty prisoners
taken. The Turks now disclosed far greater strength than
had been anticipated, and the regiment, coming under heavy
fire, fell back from the ridge. Lieut.-Colonel Holden, who
had halted the two Jodhpore squadrons in a fold of the
ground in rear, sent to Major Lambert for news. He was
informed that the Mysores would charge again and was
requested to move forward to cover them while they rallied.
He thereupon advanced to a position about half a mile
south-east of the knoll, and the Mysores, who were momentarily shaken, rallied a thousand yards in his rear. The
Jodhpores in their turn, however, came under heavy fire;
Lieut.-Colonel Holden was shot dead at close range; and
the two squadrons likewise began to fall back in some
confusion. Then Captain H. P. Hornsby rallied the leading
squadron and turned about to charge, Major P. F. Gell
promptly swinging round the second squadron and following
him. A moment later Captain Hornsby was shot through
the neck,[1] and the Indian squadron commander, seeing large
numbers of Turkish reinforcements moving up, wisely
wheeled the squadron about. Major Gell then decided to
take up his position on the left of the Mysores. The enemy
had now disclosed a strength of at least three thousand, and
for a few moments threatened to counter-attack, but then
hesitated and began to dig in. The situation of the two
Indian regiments was, however, precarious until the 14th
Cavalry Brigade came up about 11 p.m. By midnight it
appeared that the enemy had withdrawn.

The check which had been sustained was not a very
serious one, the total British casualties being only 80, and

---
[1] Left for dead, he recovered consciousness and crawled back through the Turkish lines after dark.

its causes were pretty clear. The Turkish troops encountered may have been mainly fugitives who had been reorganized, but they had been rested, fed, re-equipped, formed into new units, and were now fighting in a strong position under the eye of a most resolute commander.[1] That they should have held up two weak regiments, unsupported by artillery, is not to be wondered at; indeed, it was probably only the great boldness of the 15th Cavalry Brigade which saved it from a heavy counter-attack. The action also served as a warning of the danger of trusting to reports from the air regarding the position and numbers of hostile troops without verifying them by ground reconnaissance.

At 10 a.m. on the 26th, an hour before this action began, Major-General Macandrew entered Aleppo with the armoured cars and was given a reception as enthusiastic as had greeted the British at any point hitherto.

Aleppo, the last city captured in the course of the campaign, had a population at the outbreak of war of about 150,000. It is of vast antiquity, perhaps a Hittite foundation, and appears in the second millenium B.C. as "Halab," which is its Arabic name to-day. Captured by the Arabs in A.D. 646, it changed hands several times before falling into those of the Seljuk Turks in 1085. It was the capital of Nur-ed-Din's Syrian dominions, and then possessed by his former Egyptian viceroy, the famous Saladin. The Crusaders frequently reached its gates, but never conquered it. In 1516 it fell to the Ottoman Turks, to remain in their possession for just over four hundred years, with a break of nine years from 1831, when they were expelled by Ibrahim Pasha. The Citadel, standing on a natural mound with artificially steepened sides, is one of the most splendid monuments of Arabic military architecture. Though its origin and its foundations are far more ancient, it dates in its present form from the reign of Saladin's son, Maliq ez Zabir; and his inscriptions are still to be seen upon its gateway, the most perfect of its kind in the East. The Ottomans allowed it to fall into decay, and though without it appears little damaged, within it is a hollow shell.

---

[1] An Arab officer, now in Trans-Jordan, records that he fought a machine gun in this action, and that fire was controlled and directed by Mustapha Kemal Pasha in person.

CAPTURE OF MUSLIMIYA JUNCTION 617

On the morning of the 27th it was discovered by reconnaissance that the enemy was holding a ridge north of Bianum, 3½ miles N.N.W. of Haritan. The 13th and 14th Cavalry Brigades relieved the 15th, which withdrew to the neighbourhood of Aleppo. Ample stores of grain and meat were found in the city. On the 28th the armoured cars reported that the Turks had fallen back another five miles to Deir el Jemal. Next day the Sherifial Arabs occupied Muslimiya Station, the junction of the Baghdad and Syrian railways, thus cutting rail communication between Constantinople and the Turkish troops in Mesopotamia. The station had been destroyed, but a certain amount of rolling stock was undamaged. On the 30th the enemy's outposts were still at Deir el Jemal. Some four miles in rear of their outposts the Turks held a line 25 miles long, crossing in two places the Alexandretta road, which here makes a great curve to the south-westward.

1918.
27 Oct.

29 Oct.

30 Oct.

Major-General Macandrew's boldness and the timely vigour of his Arab allies had been rewarded by the capture of Aleppo, but even he did not venture to attack the new Turkish position without further support. The Turks, over-extended as was their line, must have outnumbered his division by at least six to one,[1] so that all he could do was to keep them under observation while awaiting the arrival of the Australian Mounted Division. That division marched out from Damascus on the 27th October, but it never reached Aleppo. Before it arrived at Homs the last shot of the campaign had been fired.

The thoroughness of the Turkish defeat is almost without a parallel in modern military history. It may be said that their armies had been completely destroyed, for,

[1] The Turkish position was held, from right to left, by the *24th Division*, the *XX Corps* (*1st* and *11th Divisions*), and the *43rd Division*, all under the command of Mustapha Kemal Pasha, with headquarters at Katma. The two divisions of the *XX Corps* had been brought up to a strength of 2–3,000 rifles apiece by drafts and a reinforcement of one complete regiment from Turkey; the other two were weaker. In rear there still existed the weak *41st Division* at Alexandretta and the *44th* north of the Gulf of Iskanderun. The *23rd* was apparently further along the coast at Tarsus, and the *47th* may also have been in this area. The German troops had been concentrated near Tarsus, but, as will presently be explained, were about to return home. The *3rd Cavalry, 7th, 16th, 19th, 20th, 26th, 46th, 48th, 53rd,* and *Composite Divisions* had all been either completely destroyed or subsequently dissolved. The *Fourth Army* headquarters had been broken up.

praiseworthy as were Mustapha Kemal's attempts at reorganization, the force he now commanded would have met the fate of the rest within a few weeks, when a frontal attack would have been combined with a landing at Alexandretta. It was saved from that fate only by the Armistice. Practically all the warlike stores of the enemy had been taken. The prisoners captured by the British numbered over 75,000, of whom about 200 officers and 3,500 rank and file were Germans and Austrians. In addition, 360 guns, 800 machine guns, 210 motor lorries, 89 railway engines, 468 railway carriages and trucks fell into the hands of the victors. No transport beyond repair was included in Sir Edmund Allenby's report, so to these figures has to be added a vast quantity destroyed by aircraft or burnt in the retreat.

The losses of the British were incurred, as might be expected, chiefly in the preliminary operation which broke the enemy's front and opened the gateway to the cavalry. The casualties from the 19th September to the 31st October were 71 officers killed, 249 wounded, 3 missing; 782 other ranks killed, 4,179 wounded, 382 missing; a total of 5,666, of which the Desert Mounted Corps had only 650.[1]

THE ARMISTICE WITH TURKEY.

Meanwhile the Allies were advancing in all the other main theatres of war. On no single front had they yet dealt a knock-out blow in more than four years of warfare; now they struck almost simultaneously, and almost simultaneously their enemies crumpled everywhere. In France the Hindenburg Line was broken in the latter part of September, and on the 4th October Germany sent her proposals for an armistice to the President of the United States. In Italy the Battle of Vittorio Veneto began on the 24th October, and within three days the Austrian Government—which had approached President Wilson at the same time as the German—was suing for an armistice with Italy. In Mesopotamia the British, after long inaction, attacked at Sharqat, and were now preparing to march on Mosul. It was, however, the Allied victory in the Balkans that had most effect upon the theatre with which we are concerned. Here the Battle of Monastir–Doiran, begun on the 18th September, resulted

---

[1] The battle casualties from January 1915 amounted to 51,451.

PLIGHT OF TURKEY 619

in the complete rupture of the Bulgarian front and the speedy dissolution of the Bulgarian Armies. The Allies advanced swiftly into the heart of the enemy's country, and on the 30th September an armistice between Bulgaria and the Entente Powers was signed at the headquarters of General Franchet d'Espérey. The Bulgarian Government agreed to demobilize their forces, to open their ports and hand over their railways for the military purposes of the Allies.

Austria-Hungary, and through her Germany, were hard hit by this surrender, but Turkey was still more seriously affected. In her present desperate situation she was cut off from Germany. The effect was immediate. It was not merely that German aid could no longer reach her, for this had already of late diminished; German pressure, exerted through Enver, which had so largely contributed to keep her fighting, instantly slackened, and Germany's chief desire became to bring her own troops safely home. It was as though a jockey, on a flagging horse, had lost his whip at the most critical moment of the race. Yet the Bulgarian surrender probably hastened by only a few weeks at most the final collapse of Turkey. That nation had now in the field on all fronts, including Thrace and Macedonia, 560,000 men, with a fighting strength of 100,000. This was all that remained of upwards of three million men called to the colours since 1914. She had lost 325,000 killed, 240,000 from disease, and, it is said, over a million and a half from desertion.[1] Her man-power was not exhausted, as was to be proved in the years to come, but her present rulers could draw no further upon it, for the enormous numbers of deserters were beyond their control. And these rulers were now universally execrated. In the eyes of their countrymen they bore the responsibility for defeat, loss of life and of territory, financial disaster, and the general misery of Turkey. The Talaat–Enver ministry fell in early October, and the Sultan appointed to the post of Grand Vizier, Marshal Izzet Pasha, a soldier who commanded general respect.

The British Government had already realized that Turkey was on the point of surrender. As soon as they had news of the Bulgarian Armistice, the negotiations for which had been conducted entirely by the French, they instructed

[1] Larcher: "La Guerre Turque dans la Guerre Mondiale," p. 540.

the Admiralty to prepare the naval conditions of one with Turkey. On the 7th October the Council of Allied Premiers at Versailles decided that the British Salonika Army should march eastward into Thrace in the direction of Constantinople. Vice-Admiral the Hon. Sir S. A. Gough-Calthorpe, the British Commander-in-Chief in the Mediterranean, was directed to go to Mudros, where he was senior to the French commander, Vice-Admiral Amet. Great Britain, having borne the brunt of the war against Turkey, was determined that on this occasion the armistice negotiations should be the work of her representative, and that when the Allied Fleet entered the Black Sea it should be under the command of a British Admiral.

Admiral Calthorpe arrived at Mudros on the 12th. On the morning of the 20th Major-General C. V. F. Townshend, accompanied by an aide-de-camp of the new Turkish Minister of Marine, was conducted by the Turks to Mytilene, and came on to Mudros that afternoon. He had been a prisoner of war since the fall of Kut, but had been allowed an extraordinary measure of liberty and had many acquaintances among the governing classes in Constantinople. He was now sent by Izzet Pasha to inform Admiral Calthorpe that Turkey was prepared to conclude a separate peace. This news having been sent to Whitehall, the Admiral was instructed to inform the Turkish Government that he was empowered to sign an armistice, and a message to this effect was sent by the Turkish aide-de-camp by telegraph through Smyrna. On the 26th three Turkish envoys, of whom the senior was Raouf Bey, the Minister of Marine, were picked up by a British warship off Mytilene and transported to Mudros Harbour. There, in the battleship *Agamemnon*, after four days of arduous and at times very painful discussion, the Armistice was signed at 9.40 p.m. on the 30th October. The four signatures were those of the Admiral and of the Turkish Envoys, Raouf Bey, Hikmet Bey, and Colonel Saadullah Bey. The most important of its terms were the opening of the Dardenelles and Bosporus and the Allied occupation of their forts ;[1] the immediate

---

[1] This clause was particularly wounding to Turkish pride. To soften it, Admiral Calthorpe gave a pledge, not embodied in the terms, that the occupation should be carried out by troops of Britain and France only, the two foes whom the Turks most respected.

THE ARMISTICE CONCLUDED

demobilization of the Turkish Army, except for such troops as were required for the surveillance of frontiers and the maintenance of internal order ; the evacuation of Cilicia ; the surrender of all war vessels in Turkish waters ; the right of the Allies to occupy any strategic points which they considered necessary ; the evacuation from Turkish dominions of all Germans and Austrians ; the obligation of Turkey to cease all relations with the Central Powers. The final clause stipulated that hostilities between the Allies and Turkey should cease from noon, local time, on Thursday, the 31st October 1918.[1] This final clause alone was circulated by wireless, and reached the 5th Cavalry Division at Aleppo two hours before it came into force.

One immediate effect of the Armistice was the departure of Liman von Sanders. The Marshal, who was prepared for what was coming, handed over the supreme command to General Mustapha Kemal Pasha at Adana on the morning of the 31st and at once left by train for Constantinople. The German troops were ready to move, and were transported by train to Haidar Pasha Station. For some time their evacuation to Germany was carried out by boat to Odessa and thence through the Ukraine, but for various reasons, including the unrest in that area and the troops' lack of winter clothing, it was finally decided to send them home through the Mediterranean to the North Sea ports. Including those in Constantinople, those from Mesopotamia, and the various detachments scattered about the Middle East, there were 10,000 Germans repatriated.

British and French warships entered the Gulf of Iskanderun on the 9th November, and on the 14th a French battalion was landed at Alexandretta. The Turkish garrison only quitted the town after a threat that a landing would be made by force if it did not instantly withdraw. On the 12th November, the day after the Armistice with Germany came into force, the Allied Fleets, under the command of Admiral Calthorpe, passed through the Dardanelles.

---

[1] The terms are given in full in the Note at end of Chapter.

THE OCCUPATION OF NORTHERN SYRIA.

Map 23. Sketches 41, 42.

After the signing of the Armistice the Commander-in-Chief of the E.E.F. was confronted by a host of problems, not all of them strictly military in nature, apart from that of the withdrawal of the Turkish Armies. The country just wrested from the Turks was in chaos. Large numbers of the poorer classes were on the verge of starvation; thousands of refugees were awaiting repatriation; records of accounts and title-deeds had been destroyed; currency was depreciated. Prisoners of war, chiefly British and Indian, often in an appalling state of misery, had to be taken over from the Turks and evacuated.

General Mustapha Kemal Pasha proved difficult to deal with, and his successor, General Nihad Pasha, commanding the *Second Army*, was a master of the arts of obstruction and procrastination. He at first pretended ignorance of the terms of the Armistice, then tried to evade them by leaving behind in the areas evacuated large numbers of troops in the guise of gendarmerie. By the 26th December, however, Sir Edmund Allenby's firmness had induced him to withdraw the whole of the *Second Army* westward of Bozanti, in the Cilician Gates. These troops were then gradually demobilized. Two Armenian battalions of the Légion d'Orient were landed at Mersina, and with the one which had been previously landed at Alexandretta were established in posts along the Baghdad Railway from Bozanti to Islahiya near the Baghche Tunnel in the Amanus. These troops were employed in accordance with French wishes, but their presence increased the hostility between the Turkish and Armenian populations, and frequent collisions occurred. Sir Edmund Allenby was finally compelled to relieve the Légion d'Orient in Cilicia by British troops, the Armenian battalions being then concentrated at central points.

The Turkish *Sixth Army* had retired from Mesopotamia to the area north-east of Aleppo, with headquarters at Nisibin on the railway. With the commander of this Army, Ali Ihsan Pasha, Sir Edmund Allenby had still greater difficulties. The Turkish general not only played the same game as had his colleague by maintaining large bodies of soldiers as gendarmerie; he also delayed his withdrawal until the route through Diarbekr was made almost impassable by winter weather, and then demanded that his troops should be evacuated by rail through Aleppo. His request was refused. His headquarters also conducted active anti-British and anti-Armenian propaganda in districts not occupied by British troops. It seemed likely that fresh massacres of Armenians would occur as a result of these activities and of the general spirit displayed by the Turks. Sir Edmund Allenby therefore ordered the occupation of Killis, Birijik, Aintab, and Urfa, towns lying just north of the Baghdad Railway, and of Marash, 100 miles W.N.W. of Aleppo. For this purpose he placed the 28th Indian Brigade at the disposal of the Desert Mounted Corps. Killis and Aintab were occupied on the 24th December; Marash and Birijik at the end of February 1919; but the supply situation did not admit of troops being maintained at Urfa till the third week of March. In February Sir Edmund Allenby visited Constantinople to expostulate with the Turkish Government regarding the many infractions of the terms of the Armistice and to demand the withdrawal of Ali Ihsan. The supersession of that officer brought about a change for the better, and thenceforth the demobilization of the *Sixth Army* about Nisibin was conducted quietly.

After the occupation of Cilicia it was necessary to form a new area of Occupied Enemy Territory, consisting of the greater part of the Turkish *Vilayet* of Adana. A French officer, Colonel E. Brémond, formerly head of the French Military Mission in Arabia,[1] was appointed Chief Administrator of this area. The country east of the Adana *Vilayet* was left in the hands of the Turkish officials, who carried out its administration under the general control of the G.O.C. Desert Mounted Corps.

By the end of 1918 the headquarters of the XX Corps with the 10th, 53rd, 54th, 60th, and 75th Divisions had been moved to Egypt. It was decided that, pending the decisions of the Peace Conference with regard to Palestine and Syria, an Army of Occupation should be maintained consisting of the Desert Mounted Corps (4th and 5th Cavalry Divisions) and the 3rd and 7th Indian Divisions in Palestine and Syria, one British brigade in Egypt, and the 75th Division at Qantara as general reserve. The Australian and New Zealand

---

[1] See Vol. I, p. 236.

troops were to be transferred to Egypt preparatory to returning home. The Army was in the midst of demobilization and reorganization when the process was rudely interrupted by a serious political conflagration in Egypt in March 1919, and the troops were called upon for the unpleasant task of stamping it out.

At Medina the Turkish garrison under General Fakhri Pasha resolutely refused to surrender. A month before the Armistice General Sir Reginald Wingate had sent the Turkish commander an offer of honourable terms, including safe conduct for himself and his troops to Egypt, and had received the typical reply :—" I have received your letter. " I am a Mohammedan. I am an Osmanli. I am the son of " Bali Bey. I am a soldier.—Fakhri Pasha ed Din, Com- "manding Forces, Medina." The Emir Abdulla wished to avoid bloodshed, and was moreover distracted by the dispute between his father and Ibn Sa'ud over Kharma,[1] which had now grown acute and had already involved some fighting. He therefore contented himself with maintaining the blockade of Medina. Whether Fakhri would ever have surrendered is doubtful; but at last, in early January, the problem was solved by his officers, overcome by want, seizing the fierce veteran on a bed of sickness and handing him over to the Arabs. The garrison was in a state of destitution, and over a thousand men had died in the past few months of influenza. Four hundred and ninety-one officers and 7,545 rank and file were evacuated to Egypt, but a considerable number of Syrians and Arabs volunteered to remain and serve the new régime.

In July the masterful and energetic soldier who had led the 5th Cavalry Division to Aleppo died there as the result of an accident. Major-General Macandrew had lived to see his theories and the results of his life's work put into practice, and left behind him a record of achievement hardly equalled by any cavalryman of modern times.

* * * * * *

As, after battle, the battlefield has to be cleared, so, after war, work of similar nature, but on a far greater scale and extending to the political and moral spheres, has to be accomplished. The settlement of the problems created by

---

[1] See p. 410.

this vast struggle lies outside the scope of the present work, especially since that settlement is scarcely yet complete. Were an attempt to describe it called for, were that description confined merely to the direct concerns of Britain, Turkey, and the portions of the latter's empire wrested from her as a result of the war, it would be necessary to embark upon another volume of this history. The conclusion of peace with Turkey by the Treaty of Lausanne actually took four years and nine months, which was nine months longer than the war had lasted.[1] The years since the war have witnessed many changes and shifts of fortune. Feisal's kingdom at Damascus has collapsed, and he is now King of Iraq. The Sherifial State in the Hejaz has been overthrown by Ibn Sa'ud and his Wahabis. There has been a bloody revolt against the French in Syria and lesser but still considerable disturbances in Iraq. While the British mandates for Palestine and Trans-Jordan have been successful and by comparison peaceful, the early days of Zionism have not been easy, and the events of 1929 are proof that the country's problems are by no means solved. Above all, in Turkey a new flame has been kindled by the breath of Mustapha Kemal from the ashes of defeat.

These events have here no place. They belong to the troublous yet hopeful infancy of a new age, which is indeed the child of Mars: heir to his passions, fretted by the maladies of his blood, but, as we are now beginning to see, imbued also with his courage and his daring.

NOTE.

THE TERMS OF THE ARMISTICE WITH TURKEY.

Conditions of an Armistice agreed to and concluded between—

Vice-Admiral the Honourable Sir Somerset Arthur Gough-Calthorpe, British Commander-in-Chief of the Mediterranean Station, acting under authority from the British Government, in agreement with their Allies,

and

His Excellency Raouf Bey, Turkish Minister of Marine; His Excellency Rechad Hikmet Bey, Turkish Under-Secretary for Foreign Affairs; Lieutenant-Colonel Saadullah Bey, Turkish General Staff; acting under authority from the Turkish Government.

---

[1] The British Ambassador at Constantinople demanded his passports on the 30th October 1914 (see Vol. I, pp. 15–16); the Armistice was signed on the 30th October 1918; the Treaty of Lausanne—replacing the Treaty of Sèvres, which was never operative—was signed on the 24th July 1923. Even then the problem of Mosul was left unsettled.

1. Opening of Dardanelles and Bosporus and secure access to the Black Sea. Allied occupation of Dardanelles and Bosporus forts.

2. Positions of all minefields, torpedo-tubes, and other obstructions in Turkish waters to be indicated, and assistance given to sweep or remove them as may be required.

3. All available information as to mines in the Black Sea to be communicated.

4. All Allied prisoners of war and Armenian interned persons and prisoners to be collected in Constantinople and handed over unconditionally to the Allies.

5. Immediate demobilization of the Turkish Army, except for such troops as are required for surveillance of frontiers and for the maintenance of internal order. Number of effectives and their disposition to be determined later by the Allies after consultation with the Turkish Government.

6. Surrender of all war vessels in Turkish waters, or in waters occupied by Turkey. These ships to be interned at such Turkish port or ports as may be directed, except such small vessels as are required for police or similar purposes in Turkish territorial waters.

7. The Allies to have the right to occupy any strategic points in the event of any situation arising which threatens the security of the Allies.

8. Free use by Allied ships of all ports and anchorages now in Turkish occupation, and denial of their use by enemy. Similar conditions to apply to Turkish mercantile shipping in Turkish waters for purposes of trade and demobilization of the Army.

9. Use of all ship repair facilities at all Turkish ports and arsenals.

10. Allied occupation of the Taurus tunnel system.

11. Immediate withdrawal of Turkish troops from North-west Persia to behind the pre-war frontier has already been ordered, and will be carried out. Part of Trans-Caucasia has already been ordered to be evacuated by Turkish troops; the remainder to be evacuated if required by the Allies after they have studied the situation there.

12. Wireless-telegraph and cable stations to be controlled by the Allies, Turkish Government messages excepted.

13. Prohibition to destroy any naval, military, or commercial material.

14. Facilities to be given for the purchase of coal, oil-fuel, and naval material from Turkish sources after the requirements of the country have been met. None of the above material to be exported.

15. Allied Control Officers to be placed on all railways, including such portions of Trans-Caucasian railways now under Turkish control, which must be placed at the free and complete disposal of the Allied authorities, due consideration being given to the needs of the population. This clause to include Allied occupation of Batum. Turkey will raise no objection to the occupation of Baku by the Allies.

16. The surrender of all garrisons in Hejaz, Assir, Yemen, Syria, and Mesopotamia to the nearest Allied Commander and the withdrawal of troops from Cilicia, except those necessary to maintain order, as will be determined under Clause 5.

17. Surrender of all Turkish officers in Tripolitania and Cyrenaica to the nearest Italian garrison. Turkey guarantees to stop supplies and communication with these officers if they do not obey the order to surrender.

18. Surrender of all ports occupied in Tripolitania and Cyrenaica, including Misurata, to the nearest Allied garrison.

19. All Germans and Austrians, naval, military and civilian, to be evacuated within one month from Turkish dominions. Those in remote districts as soon after as may be possible.

20. Compliance with such orders as may be conveyed for the disposal of the equipment, arms, and ammunition, including transport, of that portion of the Turkish Army which is demobilized under Clause 5.

21. An Allied representative to be attached to the Turkish Ministry of Supplies in order to safeguard Allied interests. This representative to be furnished with all information necessary for this purpose.

22. Turkish prisoners to be kept at the disposal of the Allied Powers. The release of Turkish civilian prisoners and prisoners over military age to be considered.

23. Obligation on the part of Turkey to cease all relations with the Central Powers.

24. In case of disorder in the six Armenian vilayets the Allies reserve to themselves the right to occupy any part of them.

25. Hostilities between the Allies and Turkey shall cease from noon, local time, on Thursday, 31st October 1918.

Signed in duplicate on board His Britannic Majesty's ship *Agamemnon*, at Port Mudros, Lemnos, the 30th October 1918.

CHAPTER XXVIII.

EPILOGUE.

The Policy of the Campaign.

The lessons to be learnt from the campaigns in Sinai, Palestine, and Syria are many and valuable, but like those of all historical events they are broad and general in character. History does not repeat itself exactly on the field of battle any more than in the council-chamber, and it is seldom possible to draw from it precise deductions such as the mathematician, the chemist, and even to some extent the philosopher, present to us. The problems of military history, or of political, or of economic, are to this extent in the air, that we cannot keep all the factors simultaneously pinned down while we examine them. We can say that if Alexander the Great had not been cut off in young manhood by disease the world's future would probably have been vastly changed; but the effect that his survival would have had upon the nascent empire of Rome and the whole of Mediterranean civilization is impossible to estimate. We can say—to consider a smaller point—that if Grouchy had not been a headstrong cavalryman disinclined to take advice from an infantry soldier, he would probably have marched to the sound of the guns at Waterloo, as Gerard entreated him to do, and that if he could have reached the ground in time (which is a matter of dispute) Napoleon might have won the battle; but it is fruitless to speculate upon what would have followed. In concluding this record with a short review of the policy, strategy, and tactics of the campaign, we shall therefore constantly ask questions which cannot be answered with certainty. (This will be the case most with policy and least with tactics, because in descending from one to the other we move from the vaguer to the more precise and tangible.) Yet the review is worth

DEVELOPMENT OF POLICY 629

making. Though we must not allow ourselves to entertain the false notion that military history will provide us with a series of formulas for every eventuality, neither must we fail to draw upon its deep wells of experience.

At the end of the previous volume the curious beginnings of the campaign were discussed.[1] It was shown that the sole function of the forces under the command, first of Sir John Maxwell, then of Sir Archibald Murray, was the defence of the Suez Canal. The first stage of the advance across Sinai and the occupation of the Qatiya basin had no other object, and was carried out to deny to an enemy advancing against the Canal the water in that area. The second stage, the advance to El Arish, was carried out still with the same purpose, it being considered by Sir A. Murray that he could most safely and economically defend the Suez Canal at that point. It was not until after the First Battle of Gaza had been fought in March 1917 that the Government contemplated the invasion of Palestine, and informed Sir A. Murray that his " immediate objective " should be the defeat of the Turkish forces south of Jeru- " salem and the occupation of that town." The reverse suffered in the Second Battle of Gaza did nothing to change their determination ; rather was it a spur to greater endeavour. The new Commander-in-Chief, Sir Edmund Allenby, was promised before he left London that he should receive all the reinforcements he considered necessary. He did in fact receive two infantry divisions (the 10th and 60th) from Salonika, and was given the means to form a third (the 75th) in the country. His aircraft, heavy artillery, and transport were enormously increased, so that his Army at the Third Battle of Gaza was at least twice as strong in all respects as that which had suffered defeat six months before.

Thereafter it was not the Government's policy but their resources which varied. They adhered until the end of the campaign to their design of completely defeating the Turk in Palestine and Syria, in the hope that this would result in eliminating Turkey from the war. But the German offensive on the Western Front robbed them of the means for the time being ; for they were compelled to denude the Army of British troops and to replace them with Indian.

---

[1] See Vol. I, pp. 368—70.

The result was that the second great offensive in Palestine was delayed until the tide of victory had begun to flow almost everywhere else, and that Turkey's elimination did not take place until all Britain's other foes were on the high road to being eliminated also.

Two schools have joined issue over this policy. The "Westerner" has begun his attack with the argument that the war-time phrase, "knocking out the props," was meaningless where Palestine was concerned and should have been replaced by "lopping off the limbs."[1] The Turkish Armies in Syria and Palestine were indeed to a very small extent a "prop" to Germany. The Gallipoli campaign had represented a blow at the heart of the Turkish Empire, with direct repercussions upon Germany; the Palestine and Mesopotamian campaigns were attacks upon that Empire's most distant outskirts. The "Westerner" has gone on to point out that in Palestine, as in Mesopotamia and Macedonia, the Allies were compelled to maintain forces greater in numbers, and also in resources—which means in expense—than those to which they were opposed. He has enlarged upon the risk and strain entailed by the maintenance of the E.E.F. at the strength required for a successful offensive, and the vast demands made upon shipping in the submarine-infested Mediterranean at a time when the United Kingdom was short of food and it was urgently necessary to transport as many American troops as possible to Europe. He has been presented with an easy debating point by a false argument of his opponent, who has sometimes compared the Palestine campaign to the "Spanish "Ulcer" so fatal to Napoleon. The facts that it was first-class French troops which were destroyed in the Peninsular War and that France touched Spain, so that she could be (as she eventually was) invaded from that country, make this comparison of small value; and he has retorted that the whole of the Near East was in fact an "ulcer" to the Allies. Finally, he has declared that British policy should have been throughout to keep open the Suez Canal. Nothing else that could be achieved was worth the cost or the risk.

The "Easterner" has replied that in Palestine Britain

---

[1] This phrase is used by Colonel A. P. Wavell in "The Palestine Campaigns" (p. 176). He is there outlining the rival opinions, not speaking as either a "Westerner" or an "Easterner" himself.

pursued her traditional policy, the policy of a maritime nation. He has argued that all attempts to breach the German line in France had failed, and that if the Germans were going to breach our line in that theatre a couple of divisions from Palestine would not prevent them. In Palestine, on the other hand, there was a chance to accomplish something. Even the capture of Jerusalem, though its only effect upon Germany was to induce her to despatch an extra infantry regiment and auxiliary troops to Palestine, had heartening moral results. Turkey was, without doubt, the weakest and weariest of our enemies. Was it not worth while to force her to surrender, and perhaps thereby bring about the surrender of Bulgaria, who was almost equally weary of the war? The cost of the experiment might be great in money, but it would be comparatively small in human life, which was more than could be said for the experiments of the Western Front.

Two problems emerge from these conflicting theses. Turkey was not, as we have seen, forced out of the war by action in Palestine alone, for her defeat there was only one of a series of defeats inflicted almost simultaneously upon her and her Allies. Could she have been? That problem we have already touched upon,[1] but it is one to which no definite solution can be found. That Sir Edmund Allenby would have inflicted a heavy defeat upon the Turks in Palestine about the month of May 1918 if he had had available all his original formations is almost certain. It is far less certain that he could have thereby brought about Turkey's defection from the cause of the Central Powers; and the question is too hypothetical to be worth detailed discussion. The other problem is simpler. Was there a half-way house between the Canal and Aleppo, and, if so, where was it? The answer is that there is no reason to doubt the ability of the British to have held the position in front of Gaza occupied before the offensive of the 31st October 1917 for the rest of the war with four, or at most five, infantry divisions and two mounted divisions, thus setting free for France two or three infantry divisions and one mounted division. But it must be recognized that, against this advantage to the Western Front, inactivity in

---

[1] See p. 295.

the Palestine theatre might have resulted in the appearance of more Turkish troops in Mesopotamia and in the eastern European theatres of war. It may also be argued that the reinforcement of the Western Front would not have compensated for the blow struck at Gaza, the capture of Jerusalem, and the subsequent prospects thereby unfolded.

These arguments apply only to Sir Edmund Allenby's first offensive. The " Easterner " has it all his own way with regard to the second. In the spring of 1918 the E.E.F. made almost[1] all the sacrifices possible in any event to the Western Front. It was then brought up to strength with Indian troops, to whom the climate and conditions of Palestine and Syria were much more favourable than were those of France. These troops could be found, and it was obviously good policy to employ them to inflict decisive defeat upon the Turkish Armies. The decision taken as a result of the visit of General Smuts—though actually reached before the German offensive and the withdrawal of British troops from Palestine—to stand on the defensive in Mesopotamia and attack in Palestine was also certainly correct. After March 1918 there can be no question that British policy in Palestine was the best that could have been adopted. It must, however, be added that the project of lending divisions to Palestine from France for an autumn campaign, of which mention has been made,[2] is difficult to understand, even though it may have appeared that the campaign in France would last until the spring of 1919.

In Sir Edmund Allenby's despatch dated the 28th June 1919, which recounts events subsequent to the Armistice with Turkey and summarizes the whole campaign, there is the following passage :—

" The course of the campaigns in this theatre followed " closely the course of events in the main Western theatre.

" Thus, the first period, the defence of the Canal, " corresponded to the first check of the enemy's onrush in " France and Belgium ; the period of the advance through " the Sinai desert, to the general development of the Allied

---

[1] We say "almost" because the 54th Division, the only infantry division to be maintained as wholly British, was at one time under orders for France. As events turned out it could probably have been spared, but that could not have been anticipated.

[2] See p. 447.

"strength and the building up of a secure battle line along "the whole front; the 1917 advance, to the period of "increased Allied pressure which exhausted the enemy's "reserves; while the last advance coincided with the "final Allied counter-offensive."

These words are manifestly true, and their effect is damaging to the more extreme claims of the "Easterner." They show that, while the operations of the E.E.F. were not isolated from those in the main theatre, yet they did not effect a decision which could not be effected there—and to do so was the object of the confirmed "Easterner." Throughout the war the Western theatre called the tune. This fact the enemy recognized clearly. From March to August 1918 the Turks in Palestine were confident that the war would shortly be ended by an overwhelming German victory in France, and knew that, if it were, Germany and her Allies would have all they wanted everywhere. This confidence was actually of value to the British, because it tended to induce the enemy to neglect the Palestine front, so that when fortune ceased to smile upon Germany the Turks suffered disastrous defeat.

As for the final surrender of Turkey, the immediate cause of that was clearly the success of the Allies in Macedonia and the defection of Bulgaria, which were in turn largely influenced by the victories of the Allies on the Western Front. But the victory of the E.E.F. in Palestine and the capture of Damascus—which took place the morning after the conclusion of the Bulgarian Armistice—were undoubtedly a powerful contributory cause. And, as we have said, even without the Salonika offensive, it is probable that Turkey would have thrown up the sponge as a result of her defeats in Syria and Mesopotamia and her general exhaustion, soon afterwards.

To sum up, then, the E.E.F. had no direct effect upon the decision in the main theatre. It was not primarily responsible for driving Turkey out of the war, but it contributed notably to that end. It deprived the British forces in France of two or three divisions which might have been spared before the German offensive. After the German offensive it contributed largely to the needs of the Western Front by the despatch of troops which, it might be argued, were actually more valuable then than they would have been in March. Thereafter it achieved final victory mainly with troops not required on the Western Front. Its operations enhanced British prestige. Their moral effect upon Britain's position in the world of Islam, their material effect in her control of the aerial routes to the east, both still endure.

The Strategy of the Campaign.

Sir Edmund Allenby possessed many advantages over the enemy. He had the greater numbers and resources, including heavy artillery, for the sudden breaching of the enemy's front, and aircraft, which provided him with information, denied information to the enemy, and paralysed the enemy's means of intercommunication. His transport was larger in quantity, even in proportion to his greater strength, better in quality and organization, thus giving him mobility in attack. He had vast superiority in mounted troops with which he could exploit success. He had behind him naval power—a command of the sea not indeed absolute, but never seriously challenged by the enemy's submarines— which assured his communications on his seaward flank while keeping his opponents in constant anxiety for theirs, and permitted him to victual his troops from successive landing-places as he advanced. He had the means to create better railway communications. Though when he assumed command the Turks were still flushed by victory and the British to some extent depressed, yet his own qualities of leadership and the reinforcements in men and material which he received speedily gave him an advantage in morale ; and this had become immense before the launching of his final offensive. He led troops whose intelligence was in general on a very high level against an army of Eastern European or Asiatic peasants, unable to make full use of the up-to-date material provided by their German mentors.

On the other hand, his choice of objectives was frequently, especially in the first offensive, governed by the same conditions as apply in desert warfare ; that is, they were chosen rather for their water supply than for their general strategical or tactical importance. If they were not taken, it might be necessary to withdraw to the position from which the attack had started. He was opposed by troops skilful in defence and in rear-guard tactics, especially in the hill country wherein so great a proportion of the operations took place, and of such extraordinary endurance that they seemed to be able to fight by day, break off the action, and march all night, almost indefinitely. His superiority in transport was almost nullified by the facts that British soldiers have greater needs and bigger appetites than Turkish, and that he was often compelled to follow the enemy into roadless country. In such country the road-making operations of the Royal Engineers played a very important part in strategical as well as tactical plans. It would not be too much to say that in all the hill fighting the terrain represented 40 per cent. of the difficulties to be overcome.

The influence of the Commander-in-Chief in the moral sphere can never be too much emphasized in considering this campaign. It is the testimony of the most acute and responsible observers that he restored the old personal relationship between leader and troops which was one of the finest traditions of the British Army in the past and one of the keys to its successes. He was constantly up and down his line, so that there can have been few commanders in modern warfare who were so well known to their troops. All ranks gave him their confidence, and to a force of many nationalities his character and temperament were of inestimable value. His Australian troops, for example, were men of original and independent type, not nurtured in the traditions of British military discipline and inclined to be impatient of them; yet their reliance upon him was complete. In the late war the will of the commander, that determination to conquer, that driving-force which Marshal Foch declared to be the first essential of victory, was too often set to flow through the channel of his generals, to be modified or diverted according to the accidents of individual temperament or attainment. Sir Edmund Allenby, blessed with strength and endurance which made little of very long drives in intense heat and on dusty, bone-shaking tracks, was enabled to communicate it directly also to subordinate officers and the rank and file themselves. In the advance on Nablus he was seen up in front in his car urging on tired men at a moment when his personal influence was the strongest stimulant they could have had, illustrating therein another favourite precept of the Marshal's, that the carrying through of a plan is of even more importance than the plan itself. But perhaps it was the brigade and regimental commanders upon whom his influence was greatest. He saw them and talked with them frequently, and they could not fail to be impressed by his energy and unflinching will. Here, again, he had an advantage over the enemy. It was impossible for his two German opponents, the first a great soldier, the second a good one, and both men of remarkable personality, to influence and inspire in the same fashion troops to whom they were foreigners and infidels. They seem, in fact, seldom to have left their headquarters.

Yet, though Sir Edmund Allenby embarked upon all his greater operations with a fixed determination to carry them through to victorious issue, and refused to let the hunger, thirst, and exposure of his troops check the offensive or the pursuit, in several cases he abandoned an attack promptly when it appeared to him that its objects had ceased to be worth the cost and risk of attaining them. The Battle of Nabi Samweil and the three attacks which followed one another closely in the spring of 1918 (the two raids into Trans-Jordan and the offensive of the XXI Corps at Berukin which took place in the interval between them) are instances of this suppleness of judgment. He recognized that with his superiority in numbers and resources Palestine afforded many opportunities for winning great successes without heavy loss; so that when losses began to grow serious and there were prospects of their increasing, he was prepared, unless the enterprise seemed to him to be vital, to abandon it, and to fight another day in another way.

The only period of the whole campaign which has the interest created by the clash of two great strategists is that from the 6th November 1917—which may be taken as the date on which Marshal von Falkenhayn assumed effective control of the Turkish Armies in the field—to the end of the year. Throughout those disastrous weeks Falkenhayn never lost grip of the situation and never despaired. His two counter-offensives, that launched on the 12th November against the British right flank during the advance up the coast, and still more the assault upon their communications in the hills between the 27th November and the 1st December, were excellently conceived. In each case he effected a notable concentration, considering the slenderness of his means, and struck as hard as he could. The first blow was parried by mobility—the Australian Mounted Division, wide on the right flank, being able to yield ground without endangering the main body—and by pressing the attack further west at Burqa. The long marches made by the Turkish divisions before they attacked had also a big part in the result ; for the men were too weary to exploit their early success. In the case of the second the British had no such recourse. Every yard of ground was valuable here, and the attack had to be gradually worn down by stubborn defence. Falkenhayn's last great operation, the attempt to recapture Jerusalem at the end of December, was less well advised, and seems to have taken too little account of the fatigue of his troops and the reaction upon them of successive defeats. That, indeed, is the general criticism to be made of all his counter-offensives. He asked of his men more than they could give. They were set, while not yet restored in body or spirit from the effects of previous reverses, to make prodigious marches over tracks along which they could not be supplied adequately with food and ammunition. The roads in Rumania, the scene of the Marshal's recent triumphs, had been bad enough, but not so bad as in the Judæan hills. There, too, he had had inferiority of numbers ; but he had commanded German troops, led by officers on whom he could rely for the execution of his orders in spirit as well as in letter, against adversaries less well led and trained. The conduct of operations through Turkish generals—brave, able enough in their fashion, but dilatory, unmethodical, and careless—by means of Turkish troops, against British troops, was another matter ; and it was only by bitter experience that he learnt the difference. Had he come south two months earlier with his reinforcements, the campaign might have followed other lines.

Surprise and the concentration of greatly superior strength in front of his immediate objectives are the keynotes to Sir Edmund Allenby's strategy. Superiority of strength by means of concentration had been obtained often enough in France, and at least partial surprise sometimes, within his experience ; but where the forces on both sides were so dense on the ground, where communications were first-class, and, above all, where the whole front was so fortified that the conditions of an assault resembled those of siege warfare and manœuvre was almost impossible, they could not have the value with which a primitive country and a lightly-held front invested them. The deception of the enemy he attempted by various ruses which almost always succeeded. The faked *dossier* put into the hands of the enemy before Third Gaza, the dummy camps and bustle in the Jordan Valley while the concentration for Megiddo was in progress on the opposite flank, concealed his real intentions. The raids into Trans-Jordan had the secondary object of fixing the enemy's attention on that flank and inducing him to believe that another attack would be launched there.

At Beersheba Sir Edmund Allenby concentrated an infantry corps of three divisions, with one in reserve, against the western defences, and a mounted corps of two divisions east of the town. That is to say, he assured himself of overwhelmingly superior strength at the vital point. Here he staked all upon the capture of the objective within the course of a day; for the Desert Mounted Corps could not, for lack of water, have maintained its position unless it had gained possession of the wells in Beersheba that evening, and the XX Corps depended entirely upon them for its attack on the Sheria defences. At the same time he struck at the defences of Gaza on the Mediterranean shore, in order to hold the enemy's reserves on that flank. And it should be noted that this attack was no pin-prick. It was supported by the bulk of his heavy artillery, was driven home to deep objectives, and was actually one of the most costly of his campaign. A holding attack which does not really attract and pin down the enemy's reserves is fruitless expenditure of energy and of human life. The attack from the east on the Sheria position was delayed by unexpected difficulties in respect of water, but when it was launched it was in superiority of numbers almost as great as that at Beersheba, and appears to have come as an even greater surprise to the enemy command. Three British divisions suddenly swept down from the flank upon a single widely strung-out Turkish division, rolled up its line, and swallowed it up. Meanwhile up in the hills above Beersheba one British division attacked the concentration which the Turks had made to prevent themselves being outflanked and to cover the Hebron road. The progress made by this frontal attack was not great, but its effect was to cover the right of the main assault and prevent the Turks in the hills from reinforcing their breaking front at Tell esh Sheria. With vast differences in circumstances, the principle was that which triumphed at Jena and Auerstadt.

Surprise was again the deciding factor in the capture of the Jerusalem defences. Here a battle had raged for a fortnight, each side attacking in turn. All the attempts of the British to get astride the Jerusalem-Nablus road at Bire or Er Ram had been unavailing, and the subsequent Turkish attacks between Beit 'Ur el Foqa and El Burj had been beaten off after prolonged and bitter fighting. It seemed that deadlock had been reached. But the British commander had now had time to improve his communications. Silently and unobserved he shifted his strength further south, and suddenly assaulted the Turkish defences astride the Jaffa-Jerusalem road. In this case his superiority in numbers was not nearly so great as at Beersheba or Sheria, but surprise did the work. In the grey dawn the British scaled the steep-faced ridges whereon lay the Turkish redoubts and took them while their garrisons were only half awake.

In the final attack on the 19th September 1918 we have again concentration and surprise. But this time the British had what they had lacked at Beersheba, an area of country admirably fitted for their purpose, well watered and affording cover from view. During the flank marches towards Beersheba the enemy had seen a good deal of what was in progress. During the flank marches towards the coast plain he saw nothing whatever. In this case the concentration was the heaviest ever attempted in Palestine, and the surprise was the most complete.

The strategical employment of cavalry in the Third Battle of Gaza and the Battles of Megiddo gives to the campaign an interest not often found in those of other theatres of the war, least of all in France and Belgium, where the numbers of the enemy in proportion to the length of the front and the high quality of his troops allowed that arm few big opportunities after the first month. The capture of Beersheba from the east could not have been effected by infantry, for lack of mobility. The first stage of this battle was perfectly organized. The lack of complete success in the cavalry drive after the Turkish front had been broken at Sheria was due to several causes. In the first place, the concentration was not nearly so heavy as the Commander-in-Chief had hoped, one whole division and one brigade having been left in the hills. In the second place, the long delay in organizing the water supply at Beersheba had exhausted the horses before the moment when they were required to put forth their greatest effort. Then came the unhappy affair at Tell esh Sheria, when the Australian Mounted Division, though there was a gap already opened by the A. & N. Z. Mounted Division on its right, was pushed forward against a section of the front held by infantry and machine guns, and failed to get through that day. Thereafter the prospect of intercepting the enemy divisions between Gaza and Tell esh Sheria faded swiftly. Very different was the result of the strategical use of the Desert Mounted Corps in the Battles of Megiddo. In this case it was called upon to do none of the fighting to break the enemy's line, but was concentrated ready to pass through the gate when once the infantry had swung it open. Its operations were not in the nature of a pursuit until it was ordered to follow the retreating Turkish *Fourth Army* to Damascus, for in the space of the first thirty-six hours it enveloped the *Seventh* and *Eighth Armies* west of Jordan.

The strategical value of the large force of cavalry under Sir Edmund Allenby's command was all the greater because the horses revealed a power of resistance to the extremes of climate and an endurance in huge marches without water that their most sanguine advocates could not have prophesied. Heat, even the sweltering heat of the Jordan Valley in summer, had little effect upon them. But it is the work accomplished entirely without water in the pursuit after the Third Battle of Gaza that is really astounding. Horses of all three mounted divisions went 72 hours—three complete days and nights—without water, and did continuous work during that period. The horses of the Lincolnshire Yeomanry hold the record of 84 hours. Those of the Dorsetshire Yeomanry covered 60 miles in 54 hours without water. Horses of the artillery and of the infantry divisional trains had performances as striking during the same period: those of the XX Brigade R.H.A. marching 50 miles in 56 hours, and those of the 54th Divisional Train 50 miles in 63 hours without water. Even when water was to be had,

ACHIEVEMENT OF HORSES

the majority of these horses were watered once daily only, and in many cases received very small quantities of food during the pursuit.[1] The wastage in the whole Force from 31st October to 31st December 1917 in horses, mules, and donkeys was 10,000, including all battle casualties. Of this figure half, representing 5·75 per cent. of the total strength, was a dead loss.

In the final operations the achievement of the horses lay not in the time they worked without water, which was fairly plentiful throughout, but in the distances they covered. The marches of the 5th Cavalry Division were so remarkable that it is not necessary to give any other figures here. In 38 days the division marched 550 miles. In that period it lost 21 per cent. of its horses from all causes; and it must

---

[1] The following statistics are abstracted from the official history of the "Veterinary Services" (pp. 208–9). The whole of Chapter XI of this volume, devoted to the Veterinary Services in Egypt and Palestine, is well worthy of the study of cavalrymen and perhaps of soldiers interested in mechanical transport:—

Formation or Unit.	Longest period without water.	Work performed during this period.	Average amount of Grain and Fodder daily.
A. & N.Z Mounted Division.	72 hours	Continuous	Grain 9lb. Fodder 4lb. Tibben requisitioned 4 lb.
Aust. Mtd. Division Yeo.Mtd.Div.	,, ,,	,, ,,	Grain 8 lb. Fodder 2 lb.
Bucks Yeo.	,, ,,	,, ,,	Grain and fodder to 26th Nov., 10 lb. Forage obtained locally once.
Dorset Yeo.	54 ,,	60 miles	Grain 9 lb. Tibben occasionally 7lb. Grain and tibben obtained locally once.
Lincoln Yeo.	84 ,,	Continuous	Grain 5 lb. (Maximum 9 lb. grain and 3 lb. hay, 1st–5th Nov.) Small amount of tibben from villages.
XX Brigade R.H.A.	56 ,,	50 miles	Grain 9 lb. Considerable grain requisitioned on 3 occasions.
54th Div. Train	63 ,,	50 ,,	Grain 10 lb. Fodder 7 lb. A little grazing.

be recalled that it fought four considerable actions, at Nazareth, Haifa, Kiswe, and Haritan. An equally strong tribute to horseflesh and horsemastership is to be found in the fact that at the end of the campaign the New Zealand Brigade had 1,056 horses—about 50 per cent. of its establishment—which it had originally brought to Egypt. Generally speaking, the thoroughbred and its cousin the waler proved by far the most successful cavalry horses, and it was found that the better a horse was bred, the longer it lasted. The bigger-boned horse of the half-bred hunter type might carry weight better, but lost condition rapidly and regained it very slowly.[1]

Finally, it must be realized how greatly the surprise concentration for Megiddo was assisted by the British mastery of the air. Mastery such as was attained by the Royal Air Force in the latter part of 1918 depends on numbers less than upon quality. There were doubtless many more British machines than German, but it was the superior speed and climbing power of the fighting machines which contributed so much to keep the British preparations secret, just as, during the greater part of Sir A. Murray's command, a single German squadron had dominated the air by reason of the same advantages.

THE TACTICS OF THE CAMPAIGN.

The student of infantry tactics will find marked differences between those of this theatre and the Western Front. They were due to the facts that in Palestine the quantity of artillery employed in proportion to the length of the front and of ammunition expended in proportion to the number of guns were far smaller, that there was more room for manœuvre, and, at least in the hill country, much better cover for assembly and approach. With few exceptions

---

[1] A word must, however, be said for the hackney, on which few cavalrymen look with favour. Br.-General E. R. C. Butler, Director of Veterinary Services, on examining the horses of the 5th Cavalry Division at Aleppo, found a number of hackneys, apparently twenty years old or more, which he discovered on enquiry had been issued to Yeomanry regiments when there was a great shortage of horses in Great Britain and had served abroad for the greater part of the war. Though in poor condition, these gallant old horses kept their gay carriage, and the fact that they had reached Aleppo convinced him, against his will, of their hardiness and fitness for war.

British attacks were not made behind the dense creeping barrages familiar in France; but they had not, on the other hand, to face protective barrages of anything like the same weight. In consequence infantry was often able to remain in column, following the little donkey-tracks which wind along almost every wadi even in the roughest country, much longer than would otherwise have been possible. For the same reason bold measures in attack paid well, and exposure which would have been fatal in the conditions prevalent in France was often worth risking. The campaign in Palestine was essentially one of movement. The tactics most commonly employed consisted in an approach march and an attack at dawn, generally on a broad front, followed by progression from tactical point to tactical point, on which alone the supporting artillery could bring to bear concentrated fire. Warfare of this nature gave great scope to subordinate commanders of all ranks, but perhaps especially to brigade and battalion commanders. The particular hill set as the objective in orders might be found to be of minor importance because dominated by other ground, or, alternatively, non-existent. Then it was for the initiative and eye for country of the man on the spot to secure the best tactical position. The brigadier's part in a battle in France was often perforce limited to the issuing of his orders—even these being largely imposed on him by superior authority. Here he could constantly influence its fate. Two well-known and successful brigade commanders always fixed their command posts three or four hundreds yards apart, with a special telephone wire in addition to the brigade lines laid between them, so that they could constantly converse as the battle progressed. If one went forward the other remained in command of both brigades. Their battalions they looked upon as interchangeable, and either in emergency used without hesitation the troops of the other.

There was one great advantage possessed by the infantry of the E.E.F. The trench-to-trench assaults of the Western Front were generally so costly that progressive training was all but impossible. Casualties, proportionally heaviest among platoon commanders, non-commissioned officers, and the best of the men, were so high that there could be little continuity of leadership; the battalions engaged in an attack were unable to profit by the lessons of the last. In Palestine the infantry suffered heavy casualties on certain occasions, the 54th Division being particularly unfortunate in this respect in the Second and Third Battles of Gaza; but as a rule losses were not so great as to affect seriously the fighting quality of the unit. Good junior officers and non-commissioned officers nearly always remained, becoming craftier fighters and better leaders of men as they gained experience; and the spirit of the rank and file was not blunted by the prospect, on forming up for an attack, of one-third or two-thirds of their numbers being killed or wounded by nightfall. Nor was there the continuous drain caused by raids for identifications, because they were seldom necessary when agents could pass at will through the lines and a steady trickle of deserters kept the chart of the enemy's dispositions up to date. Another potent source of strain and wastage in France, the systematic searching of roads and camping areas by long-range fire, was almost absent here. The training of the infantry—except for the late-joined Indian units, whose case has been discussed—was always at a high standard. Those who were serving on the Western Front in the summer of 1918 will recall the excellent impression made by the two divisions which arrived from Palestine, and also by the individual battalions which were distributed among a number of divisions and by the splendid battalions of the Machine-Gun Corps formed from Yeomanry regiments. The result of this training was a notable skill in the use of ground which reduced losses from the fire of machine guns, the chief weapon which the troops of the E.E.F. had to face.

One of the most striking features of the campaign was the success attained by the bold use of cavalry for shock tactics. Determination to succeed, instant readiness to charge when opportunity offered, fluid and extended formations, triumphed again and again: in the pursuit after Third Gaza, in the Jordan Valley, and in the drive after Megiddo. It should be noted, however, that mounted action seldom succeeded without careful reconnaissance and fire support. Personal reconnaissance by commanders, from the brigadier downward when possible, proved invaluable in actions such as that of Maghar. Where it was neglected, because of the belief that time did not admit of it, there were sometimes failures, as at Irbid. At Maghar again, which may stand as the classic example of a cavalry charge in Palestine, efficient fire support played a great part in the victory. A cavalry brigade, with a horse-artillery battery generally attached, with its machine-gun squadron and its Hotchkiss-rifle troops, could develop considerable fire power in support of mounted action. The great value of this was in checking the enemy's fire while the cavalry was approaching, probably at the trot, and was still so far off that its moral effect had not yet begun to work upon the opposing troops. When close quarters were reached, when the squadrons drove in spurs and thundered forward with the sun glinting upon swords or lance-heads, the moral effect was overwhelming, especially on troops already beaten, fatigued, or in some degree demoralized. Beersheba and Maghar were also instances of a decision being swiftly got by shock action after dismounted attacks—in one case by dismounted cavalry, in the other by infantry—had failed to obtain it. Haifa was a case in which a bold mounted attack on unfavourable ground produced results that it is practically certain could not have been reached by a dismounted force of similar strength.

It would be rash in the extreme to take the lessons afforded by the tactics of mounted troops in Palestine as absolute; they are chiefly valuable in the conditions of this campaign, though they may have a wider general application. The absence of concentrations of artillery, to which we have referred when dealing with infantry tactics, must be considered here also; so must the fact that the enemy was deficient in aircraft and that the British had superiority in the air almost from the beginning of Sir Edmund Allenby's command. The Turkish machine guns were very numerous and often well handled, but their detachments had not quite the steadiness and imperturbability displayed by the German machine gunners during the first three years of the war. Yet, whatever we may say of the weakness of the Turk, let us not forget that there are few nations which excel his in martial qualities. In the last year of the Great War he was doubtless not what he had been, for the flower of his strength had been destroyed in the Balkan Wars and on the Gallipoli Peninsula; but, at all events as he was represented in formations such as the *19th* and *24th Divisions*, he was still a fine soldier. The lessons of the campaign have this much value at least, that they were learnt at the expense of worthy foemen.[1]

Armoured cars had opportunities in Palestine denied to them in France, in support of mounted troops. They were very valuable on occasion, but it is disappointing, in view of the discussions and tendencies of the present day, to find that they never played a decisive part in any contest. Generally speaking the country was too broken for the armoured car of the time. Interesting studies are afforded by the problem of how far a "mechanized" force could have replaced the cavalry in the campaign, but, while this history, it is hoped, furnishes some material whereon to base them, they do not properly belong to it.[2]

Finally, let us not forget that no great strategical conceptions, no tactical skill, no administrative organization, no wealth of resources, could have prevailed without the valour and endurance which the troops displayed. Howsoever perfect the machine may be in design, unless its material is sound it cannot long stand the strain to which it must needs be subjected in a war of this character. If the proportion of losses was smaller in Palestine than in France, if the conditions were never so horrible as those of

---

[1] It is always a matter of difficulty to compare adequately the military qualities of different nations or armies. One may say that the German soldier was superior to the Turkish, and explain in what this superiority consisted. But to the question, "How much superior was he?" the answer is not so easy. In "The Palestine Campaigns" Colonel A. P. Wavell has sought to define the quality of the Turk by imaginary sporting handicaps, which have at least the merit that they are intelligible to all British readers. At golf the Turk is set to receive five or six strokes from a nation placed at scratch. In a flat-racing handicap he receives nine pounds from the top-weight. It might be added that there are few nations which British students of war would set at scratch or to carry top-weight with the British Empire, or even place between it and Turkey in the handicaps. The writer has discussed the question with British, French, and German soldiers and has found them in agreement that the Turkish soldier, in the rare cases where he has had anything like equality in arms, training, leadership, and equipment, is virtually equal to any. He can almost match any other in every military quality but intelligence, and goes far to atone for lack of that by frugality, patience, and endurance.

[2] The problems to be faced in such studies are the crossing of belts of soft sand, the passage of defiles, in which a single broken-down vehicle might hold up a column, the difficulty of guarding prisoners, and, above all, the supply of petrol and grease. Cavalry, it was proved, can still live on the country; a mechanized force cannot. In some of the hill fighting no mechanical vehicles that have yet been designed would have been of value for fighting, though they might have been useful for supply.

THE SPELL OF PALESTINE

certain periods during the Battles of the Somme in 1916 and of Ypres in 1917, yet in the long run the discomforts were greater. Many passed through three or four years of these discomforts without revisiting their homes. Their spirit and devotion were maintained throughout.

The testimony of officers of all grades of seniority leaves no doubt that the spiritual and historical traditions of the country in which they fought had an influence upon the troops. Rightly, the Commander-in-Chief discouraged the popular use of the word " Crusade " as applied to a campaign wherein Mohammedan troops played a great part and wherein Britain had as allies the descendants of the Crusaders' foes. Apart from considerations of taste and expediency, he did not choose to lay himself open to the retort made at the Peace Conference by King Feisal to M. Pichon:—" And, pray, which of us won the Crusading Wars ? " Yet British soldiers could not be indifferent to the sacred memories of the soil which they trod, or to those of an English King, leader of their forefathers, who set his name near the head of the crowded roll of great warriors that have likewise trodden it. It is, moreover, the unique distinction of Palestine that it is holy ground to men not of one religion only, but of three. Nabi Samweil, for example, around and actually within the buildings of which some of the hottest fighting raged for many days, is the traditional tomb of a prophet venerated by those of both the Christian and Jewish faiths, but it is maintained by Moslem guardians and is a place of Moslem pilgrimage. In the great mosque at Hebron pious Moslems venerate what they believe to be the Cave of Machpelah, wherein were buried the Patriarchs and their families. Into this little land have been compressed an extraordinary share of the world's history and its most momentous spiritual event. It is not astonishing that the troops, as in no other theatre of war, were impressed by its associations and were brought beneath its spell.

APPENDICES.

APPENDIX 1.

TABULAR RECORDS

EGYPT AND

From June 1917 to

THE INVASION OF

Operations.	Battles.		Actions, etc.
	Name.	Tactical incidents included.	
The Second Offensive. (27th Oct.–16th Nov. 1917).	**Third Battle of Gaza.**		
		Capture of Beersheba.	.. .. ..
		[Attack on Gaza Defences.]	.. .. ..
		Capture of the Sheria Position.	.. .. ..
			Affair of Huj. ..

[1] The nomenclature and dates are, generally speaking, those given in the official report where these appear inappropriate. Actions omitted from the Official List are enclosed in to the rough geographical limits laid down by the Committee. Mounted troops, whether armed
[2] For Forces engaged on both sides, see Orders of Battle in Appendix 2 (British), and
[3] Includes only Batteries which could fire on the Western Defences of Beersheba, and the

OF OPERATIONS.

PALESTINE.

the Armistice with Turkey.[1]

PALESTINE—continued.

Limits.		Forces engaged.	
Chronological.	Geographical.	British.	Enemy.
27th Oct.–7th Nov.	North of the Wadi Ghazze.	[2] Sabres—12,000. Rifles—60,000. Guns—418.	Sabres—1,400. Rifles—33,000. Guns—260.
31st Oct.	..	Desert Mounted Corps (Chauvel): A. & N.Z. Mtd. Div., Aus. Mtd. Div., 7th Mtd. Bde. XX Corps (Chetwode): 60th, 74th Divs.; 53rd Div. & Imp. Camel Bde. (not engaged in attack). XCVI. H.A. Group, Berks. Bty. R.H.A., 10th Mtn. Bty. Sabres—8,500. Rifles—27,000 (17,000 engaged). Guns—180.[3] Casualties—1,348. Captures—1,948, 15 guns.	III Corps (Ismet): 3rd Cav., 27th Divs.,2nd, 48th Regts. Sabres—1,100. Rifles—4,300. Guns—28.
1st–3rd Nov. ..		XXI Corps (Bulfin): 54th Div., 156th Bde.; XCVII, 100th, 102nd H.A. Groups and 52nd Divnl. Arty. Rifles—11,000. Guns—148. Casualties—2,696. Captures—446.	XXII Corps (Refet): 53rd Div., 7th Div. (drawn in from Eighth Army Reserve) 3rd Div. (part of). Rifles—8,000. Guns—116.
6th Nov.	..	XX Corps (Chetwode): 60th, 74th Divs., 31st Bde., 10th Divnl. Arty., 10th Mtn. Bty. Rifles—17,000. Guns—168. Casualties—1,750. Captures—600, 12 guns.	XX Corps (Ali Fuad Pasha): 16th Div., 26th Div. (part of); 27th Div. (handful of). Rifles—about 4,000. Guns—about 40.
8th Nov.	..	Warwick and Worcester Yeo. (3 squadrons). Sabres—190. Casualties—93. Captures—70, 11 guns.	Turkish Rear Guard. Rifles—about 600. Guns—12. Casualties—about 200

of the " Battles Nomenclature Committee " (H.M. Stationery Office) with certain alterations square brackets. In each case the actual battlefield has been taken as the area, without regard with the sword or not, are included under "Sabres."
Appendix 4 (Turkish).
Horse Artillery Batteries of the Desert Mounted Corps.

APPENDIX 1

THE INVASION OF

Operations.	Battles. Name.	Tactical incidents included.	Actions, etc.
The Second Offensive. (27th Oct.–16th Nov. 1917)—(contd.).	Third Battle of Gaza—(contd.)		Action of El Maghar —*with subsequent* Occupation of Junction Station.
Jerusalem Operations. (17th Nov.–30th Dec. 1917).	Battle of Nabi Samweil.	.. .. ..	.. .. ..
	(Turkish Counter-Attacks in Defence of Jerusalem.)	.. .. ..	.. .. ..
			Capture of Jerusalem.

[1] These figures are approximate, but the Yeomanry Division, after sending back its rifles for attack.
[2] The number of guns which could be got up varied, but was never more than 18, and only
[3] The British figures include all reinforcements. At the beginning of the attacks the-

APPENDIX 1

PALESTINE—*continued*.

	Limits.		Forces engaged.	
Chronological.	Geographical.	British.		Enemy.
13th–14th Nov.	North of the line Beersheba–Gaza and west of Beersheba–Jerusalem Road.	*Desert Mounted Corps* (Chauvel): A. and N.Z. Mtd., Aus. Mtd., Yeo. Mtd. Divs., 7th Mtd. Bde., Imperial Camel Bde. 12th Light Armoured Motor Bty. *XXI Corps* (Bulfin): 52nd, 75th Divs., 189 Hvy. Bty., 380th Siege Bty. Sabres—11,000. Rifles—14,000. Guns—136. Casualties—1,339. Captures—1,469.		*Eighth Army* (Kress). *XXII Corps* (Refet): 3rd, 7th Divs. *XX Corps* (part of) (Ali Fuad *Pasha*): 26th, 53rd, 54th Divs. 16th Div. (Army Reserve). Rifles—about 9,000. Guns—about 60.
17th–24th Nov.	North and South of the line Hebron–Junction Station.	*XXI Corps* (Bulfin): 52nd, 75th Divs.; B/IX Mtn. Bty. Yeo. Mtd. Div. (under orders of Desert Mtd. Corps till 23rd). Sabres—2,500.[1] Rifles—12,000.[1] Guns—18.[2] Casualties—2,503. Captures—about 150.		*Seventh Army* (Fevzi) *III Corps* (Ismet): 3rd Cav., 24th Divs. *XX Corps* (Ali Fuad *Pasha*): 53rd, 26th Divs. (only a small part of engaged). Sabres—900. Rifles—about 5,000. Guns—about 50. Captures—about 150.
27th Nov.–3rd Dec.	North of the Jaffa–Jerusalem road.	*XXI Corps* (Bulfin), till 12 noon, 28th Nov.; then *XX Corps* (Chetwode): Yeo. Mtd., 52nd, 60th, 74th Divs., 7th Mtd. Bde. *Desert Mtd. Corps* (Chauvel): A. and N.Z. Mtd., Aus. Mtd., 54th Divs., Imperial Camel Bde. Sabres—8,000.[3] Rifles—18,000.[3] Guns—172. Casualties—2,154. Captures—561.		*Eighth Army* (Kress): *XXII Corps* (Refet): 3rd, 7th, 16th, 20th (part of) 54th Divs.; 19th Div. (under Army). *Seventh Army* (Fevzi). *III Corps* (Ismet): 3rd Cav., 24th Divs. *XX Corps* (Ali Fuad): 26th (part of) 53rd Divs. Sabres—800. Rifles—15,000. Guns—about 120. Captures—about 125.
7th–9th Dec.		*XX Corps* (Chetwode): 60th, 74th Divs., "Mott's Detachment" (53rd Div. [less 158th Bde.] XX Corps Cav., 91st H. Bty., 11th Light Armoured Motor Bty.), XCVI H.A. Group, B/IX and 10th Mtn. Btys., 10th A.L.H. Regt. Sabres—500. Rifles—10,000. Guns—142. Casualties—about 700. Captures—454.		*XX Corps* (Ali Fuad): 26th, 27th, 53rd Divs. 150th Regt. Rifles—5,500. Guns—about 50.

horses, had not more than 1,500 rifles, and neither Infantry Division had more than 4,000 reached that number on the last day of the attack—the 24th. Turks were considerably superior in numbers.

APPENDIX 1

THE INVASION OF

Operations.	Battles.		Actions, etc.
	Name.	Tactical incidents included.	
Jerusalem Operations. (17th Nov.-30th Dec. 1917)—(contd.).	Defence of Jerusalem.	.. .. ..	.. .. ..
	—with subsidiary Battle of Jaffa.	.. .. ..	.. .. ..
Operations in and beyond the Jordan Valley (19th Feb.-4th May 1918).[2]	.. .. ..	.. .. ..	Capture of Jericho.
			First Trans-Jordan Raid.
			Turkish Attack on the Jordan Bridgeheads.

[1] The Passage of the Nahr el 'Auja by the 52nd Division is the main incident of this battle, seem that logically the boundary should be extended further east and the operations of the have here, however, followed the Committee's report and included only troops west of the Committee, however, fixes the chronological limits as 21st-22nd December, which is obviously

[2] Here it has been thought proper to depart from the official report, which under this First Action of Es Salt, First Attack on 'Amman, Turkish Attack on the Jordan Bridgeheads, the British Commander-in-Chief to divide the operations, after the Capture of Jericho, into Bridgeheads. This is, perhaps, a matter of opinion, but the boundary given in the official were on both banks of the river, that on the west bank being actually the more dangerous.

[3] Exactly what units arrived as reinforcements is not known. The rifle strengths given

APPENDIX 1

PALESTINE—*continued*.

Limits.		Forces engaged.	
Chronological.	Geographical.	British.	Enemy.
26th–30th Dec.	North and East of the line Hebron–Junctn. Station.	*XX Corps* (Chetwode): 10th, 53rd, 60th, 74th Divs.; XX Corps Cav. Sabres—300. Rifles—25,000. Guns—180. Casualties—about 1,000. Captures—558.	*Seventh Army* (Fevzi): *III Corps* (Ismet). 3rd Cav., 1st, 24th Divs. *XX Corps* (Ali Fuad): 19th, 26th, 53rd Divs., 7th Cav. Regt., 61st Regt. Sabres—1,300. Rifles—16,000. Guns—about 100.
[1] 20th–22nd Dec.	Between the Tul Karm–Junction Station – Jaffa Railway and the Sea.	*XXI Corps* (Bulfin): 52nd Div. 54th Div. (part of); 100th, 102nd H.A. Groups; 1st L.H. Bde., Auckland M.R. Sabres—1,100. Rifles—7,000. Guns—88. Casualties—180. Captures—about 350.	*XXII Corps* (Refet): Caucasus Cav. Bde., 3rd, 7th, 16th Divs. Sabres—1,200. Rifles—5,000. Guns—60.
19th–21st Feb.	Between the Bethlehem – Nablus Road and the Jordan, north of the line Jerusalem–Dead Sea.	*XX Corps* (Chetwode): A. and N.Z. Mtd. Div. (less 2nd L.H. Bde. Group), 60th Div. Sabres—1,800. Rifles—5,000. Guns—54. Casualties—510. Captures—144.	*XX Corps* (Ali Fuad): 53rd Div. and some other troops. Rifles—3,000.
21st March–2nd April.	East of the Jordan.	*Shea's Force* (Shea): A. and N.Z. Mtd., 60th Divs. 10th Hvy. Bty., IX Mtn. Arty. Bde.; Light Armoured Car Bde. Sabres—2,600. Rifles—7,000. Guns—82. Casualties—1,348. Captures—986, 4 guns.	*Fourth Army* (Jemal): [3] 150th Regt. (part of), 145th Regt. German 703rd. Bn.,etc. Sabres—about 500. Rifles—5,000. Guns—about 26.
11th April	The Jordan Valley	A. and N.Z. Mtd. Div., Imperial Camel Bde., 10th Hvy. Bty. 301st Bde., R.F.A. Sabres—2,500. Rifles—2,000. Guns—33. Casualties—100. Captures—141.	48th Div., and other troops, totalling 8 squadrons and 13 Battalions. Sabres—1,000. Rifles—3,000. Guns—about 40. Casualties—472.

and that title might well have been given to it. If it is to be called the Battle of Jaffa, it would 54th and 75th Divisions east of the railway on the 11th and 15th December included. We railway and their operations between the night of the 20th and the 22nd December. The an error, as the crossing began at 8 p.m. on the night of the 20th, and this has been corrected. general heading gives the following actions: Capture of Jericho, Passage of the Jordan, Second Action of Es Salt. It seems simpler and more in accordance with the intentions of the First and Second Trans-Jordan Raids, separated by the Turkish Attack on the Jordan report to the last-named action—" East of the Jordan "—is an error, as the Turkish attacks are the maximum and refer to the last days of the raid.

656 APPENDIX 1

THE INVASION OF

Operations.	Battles.		Actions, etc.
	Name.	Tactical incidents included.	
Operations in and beyond the Jordan Valley (19th Feb.-4th May 1918)—*(contd.).*			Second Trans-Jordan Raid.
Local Operations, 1918	.. .. ..	.. .. ..	Actions of Tell 'Asur.
			Affair of Abu Tulul.
The Final Offensive. (18th Sept.–31st Oct. 1918).	**The Battles of Megiddo.** (i) **Battle of Sharon.** (ii) **Battle of Nablus.**	.. .. .. [Capture of Haifa.]	.. ..

[1] For forces engaged on both sides, see the Orders of Battle in Appendix 3 (British) and
[2] Includes troops from Ma'an northward, but not the Hejaz Expeditionary Force at

APPENDIX 1

PALESTINE—*continued.*

Limits.		Forces engaged.	
Chronological.	Geographical.	British.	Enemy.
30th April–4th May.	East of the Jordan.	*Desert Mtd. Corps* (Chauvel): A. and N.Z. Mtd., Australian Mtd., 60th Divs., 6th Mtd. Bde. (2 Regts.), Imp. Service Cav. Bde. (2 Regts.), 20th Indian Bde., 91st Hvy. Bty., IX Mtn. Arty. Bde., Hong Kong Mtn. Bty., 12 Light Armoured Car Bty. Sabres—6,000. Rifles—7,000. Guns—66. Casualties—1,649. Captures—981.	*Fourth Army* (Jemal): *VIII Corps* (Ali Fuad Bey): 48th and Composite Divs., 3rd Cav. Div., Caucasus Cav. Bde., 24th Div. (less 1 Regt. and Artillery), 3 Coys. German 146th Regt., 3/32nd, 1/58th,1/150th Bns., Circassian Cav. Regt. Sabres—2,000. Rifles—7,000. Guns—about 70. Casualties—about 2,000. Captures—about 100, 9 guns.
8th–12th March	West of the Jordan, and north of the line Jericho–Ram Allah–Jaffa.	*XX Corps* (Chetwode): 10th, 53rd, 74th Divs., 1st L.H. Bde., 181st Bde., Auckland Mtd. Rifles, XCVI and XCVII H.A. Groups, 2 Bdes. 60th Divnl. Arty., 10th Mtn. Bty., 2 Btys. 7th Divnl. Arty. *XXI Corps* (Bulfin): 75th Div., 54th Div. (part of), XCV, 100th, 102nd H.A. Groups, XXI Corps Cavalry. Sabres—1,500. Rifles—20,000. Guns—325. Casualties—1,415. Captures—281.	*Eighth Army* (Jevad): 3rd Cav., 7th Divs. *Seventh Army* (Fevzi): *III Corps* (Ismet): 1st, 24th Divs. *XX Corps* (Ali Fuad): 26th, 53rd Divs. Sabres—800. Rifles—8,000. Guns—about 150.
14th July	The neighbourhood of Abu Tulul and East of the Jordan, near El Hinu.	*Desert Mtd. Corps* (Chauvel): A. and N.Z. Mtd. Div., 2nd Mtd. (later 5th Cav.) Div. (2 Bdes. only). Alwar and Patiala Inf. Bns. Sabres—4,200(2, 500 engaged). Rifles—1,500 (not engaged). Casualties—189. Captures—540.	German 702nd and 703rd Bns., 1 Bn. 146th Regt., 1 Coy. 11th Jäger Regt., Turkish Caucasus Cav. Bde., 2nd (not engaged), 32nd, 58th and 163rd Regts., etc. Sabres—1,200 (800 engaged). Rifles—7,000 (5,000 engaged). Casualties—about 1,000.
19th–25th Sept.	Between the Hejaz Railway and the Sea.	[1] Sabres—11,000. Rifles—56,000. Guns—552.[3]	Sabres—3,000. Rifles—32,000.[2] Guns—370.
23rd Sept.	.. ..	15th Cav. Bde. (less Hyderabad Lancers), "B" Bty. H.A.C., 1 Sqdn. Sherwood Rangers. Sabres—500. Guns—4. Casualties—37, 143 horses. Captures—689, 16 guns.	Turkish Rear Guard (Probably Depot Troops.) Rifles—about 1,000. Guns—16.

Appendix 5 (Turkish).
Medina or troops in Northern Syria.   [3] Includes immobile captured Turkish guns.

APPENDIX 1

THE INVASION OF

Operations.	Battles.		Actions, etc.
	Name.	Tactical incidents included.	
The Final Offensive (18th Sept.–31st Oct. 1918).—(contd.).		[Capture of Samakh.]	.. .. ..
—*Including the Pursuit through Syria* (*26th Sept.–31st Oct.*).	.. .. ..	.. .. ..	Capture of 'Amman. Capture of Damascus.[1] Affair of Haritan, *with subsequent* Occupation of Aleppo

[1] "Actions beyond Jordan," included in the Official Report, has been omitted, as there included.

PALESTINE—*continued.*

Limits.		Forces engaged.	
Chronological.	Geographical.	British.	Enemy.
25th Sept.	.. .. ..	4th L.H. Bde. (less 4th A.L.H. and 5 Troops 12th A.L.H.). Sabres—400. Casualties—78. Captures—364, 1 gun.	German and Turkish Rear Guard. Rifles—about 470.
25th Sept.		A. and N.Z. Mtd. Div. Sabres—2,750. Captures—2,563, 10 guns.	Rear Guard of Turkish *Fourth Army* (Jemal).
1st Oct.	North of the Haifa-Der'a Railway.	*Desert Mtd. Corps* (Chauvel): 4th Cav. Div., 5th Cav. Div. (less 2 Regts.), Aus. Mtd. Div. (less 2 Regts.), 11th and 12th Light Armoured Motor Btys., 7th Light Car Patrol. Sabres—6,000. Guns—28. Captures—about 13,000.	Remnants of *Fourth, Seventh* and *Eighth* Armies.
26th Oct.	.. .. ..	15th Cav. Bde. (less Hyderabad Lancers), 12th Light Armoured Motor Bty. Sabres—500. *Totals for whole of Final offensive:—* Casualties—5,666. Captures—75,000, 360 guns.	Remnants of *Seventh Army* (Mustapha Kemal). Rifles—about 4,000.

were a number of small actions fought by different troops, which cannot conveniently be

APPENDIX 2.

ORDER OF BATTLE

OF THE

EGYPTIAN EXPEDITIONARY FORCE, OCTOBER 1917.[1]

GENERAL HEADQUARTERS.

Commander-in-Chief	General Sir Edmund H. H. Allenby, K.C.B.
Chief of the General Staff	Major-General L. J. Bols, C.B., D.S.O.
Br.-General, General Staff	Br.-General G. P. Dawnay, D.S.O., M.V.O.
Deputy Adjutant-General	Major-General J. Adye, C.B.
Deputy Quartermaster-General	Major-General Sir Walter Campbell, K.C.M.G., C.B., D.S.O.
Attached—	
Major-General, Royal Artillery	Major-General S. C. U. Smith, C.B.
Engineer-in-Chief	Major-General H. B. H. Wright, C.B., C.M.G.

DESERT MOUNTED CORPS.

G.O.C.	Lieut.-General Sir H. G. Chauvel, K.C.M.G., C.B.
Br.-General, General Staff	Br.-General R. G. H. Howard-Vyse, D.S.O.
Deputy Adjutant and Quartermaster-General	Br.-General E. F. Trew, D.S.O.
G.O.C. Royal Artillery	Br.-General A. D'A. King, C.B., D.S.O.

---

[1] Pressure on space has necessitated the abridgement of this and the following Order of Battle—the first on the eve of Third Gaza, the second on that of Megiddo—as compared with those in the previous volume. Headquarters and troops on the Lines of Communication are omitted, as well as those guarding the Canal and stationed in the Western Desert, and all auxiliary units, etc. With regard to artillery, it is to be understood, unless there is a footnote to the contrary, that horse-artillery batteries consist of four 13-pdr. guns, field-gun batteries of six 18-pdr. guns, and field-howitzer batteries of four 4·5-in. howitzers. The howitzer battery is always the third-named in its brigade, and where there are only two batteries they are 18-pdr. It is also to be understood that each mounted brigade has a machine-gun squadron, each infantry brigade a machine-gun company and a light trench-mortar battery.

APPENDIX 2

Australian and New Zealand Mounted Division.

G.O.C. .. .. Major-General E. W. C. Chaytor, C.B., C.M.G.

1st Australian Light Horse Brigade .. .. .. Br.-General C. F. Cox, C.B.
    1st Regt. A.L.H.   2nd Regt. A.L.H.   3rd Regt. A.L.H.

2nd Australian Light Horse Brigade .. .. .. Br.-General G. de L. Ryrie, C.M.G.
    5th Regt. A.L.H.   6th Regt. A.L.H.   7th Regt. A.L.H.

New Zealand Mounted Rifles Brigade .. .. .. Br.-General W. Meldrum, C.B., D.S.O.
    Auckland M.R. Regt.   Canterbury M.R. Regt.   Wellington M.R. Regt.

Artillery .. .. XVIII Brigade R.H.A. (Inverness, Ayr, and Somerset Btys.).

Engineers .. .. A. and N.Z. Field Sqdn.

Australian Mounted Division.

G.O.C. .. .. Major-General H. W. Hodgson, C.B., C.V.O.

3rd Australian Light Horse Brigade .. .. .. Br.-General L. C. Wilson, C.M.G.
    8th Regt. A.L.H.   9th Regt. A.L.H.   10th Regt. A.L.H.

4th Australian Light Horse Brigade .. .. .. Br.-General W. Grant, D.S.O.
    4th Regt. A.L.H.   11th Regt. A.L.H.   12th Regt. A.L.H.

5th Mounted Brigade .. .. Br.-General P. D. Fitzgerald, D.S.O.
    1/1st Warwick Yeo.   1/1st Gloucester Yeo.   1/1st Worcester Yeo.

Artillery .. .. XIX Brigade R.H.A. (Notts. Bty. R.H.A., "A" and "B" Btys. H.A.C.).

Engineers .. .. Australian Mounted Division Field Sqdn.

Yeomanry Mounted Division.

G.O.C. .. .. Major-General G. de S. Barrow, C.B.

6th Mounted Brigade .. .. Br.-General C. A. C. Godwin.
    1/1st Bucks Yeo.   1/1st Berks Yeo.   1/1st Dorset Yeo.

8th Mounted Brigade .. .. Br.-General C. S. Rome.
    1/1st City of London Yeo.
    1/1st County of London (Middlesex) Yeo.
    1/3rd County of London Yeo.

22nd Mounted Brigade .. .. Br.-General F. A. B. Fryer.
    1/1st Lincs. Yeo.   1/1st Staffs. Yeo.   1/1st E. Riding Yeo.

Artillery .. .. XX Brigade R.H.A.[1] (Berks, Hants, and Leicester Btys.)

Engineers .. .. No. 6 Field Sqdn. R.E.

---

[1] Three 18-pdr. btys.

662 APPENDIX 2

Corps Troops.

Machine-Gun Corps	Nos. 2, 3, 11, and 12 Light Armoured Motor Btys.
	Nos. 1 and 7 Light Car Patrols.

Attached.

7th Mounted Brigade	Br.-General J. T. Wigan, D.S.O.
1/1st Sherwood Rangers.	1/1st S. Notts. Hussars.
Attached	Essex Bty. R.H.A.
Imperial Camel Corps Brigade[1]..	Br.-General C. L. Smith, V.C., M.C.
2nd (Imperial) Bn.	3rd (A. and N.Z.) Bn. 4th (A. and N.Z.) Bn.
Attached	Hong Kong and Singapore Mountain Bty.

XX Corps.

G.O.C.	Lieut.-General Sir P. W. Chetwode, Bt., K.C.M.G., C.B., D.S.O.
Br.-General, General Staff	Br.-General W. H. Bartholomew, C.M.G.
Deputy Adjutant and Quartermaster-General	Br.-General E. Evans, D.S.O.
G.O.C. Royal Artillery	Br.-General A. H. Short, C.B.
Chief Engineer	Br.-General R. L. Waller.

53rd (Welsh) Division.

G.O.C.	Major-General S. F. Mott.
158th Brigade	Br.-General H. A. Vernon, D.S.O.
1/5th R. Welch Fusiliers.	1/6th R. Welch Fusiliers.
1/7th R. Welch Fusiliers.	1/1st Herefordshire Regt.
159th Brigade	Br.-General N. E. Money, D.S.O.
1/4th Cheshire Regt.	1/7th Cheshire Regt.
1/4th Welch Regt.	1/5th Welch Regt.
160th Brigade	Br.-General V. L. N. Pearson.
1/4th R. Sussex Regt.	2/4th R. West Surrey Regt.
2/4th R. West Kent Regt.	2/10th Middlesex Regt.
Artillery	265th Brigade R.F.A. (" A," " B," and " C " Btys.).
	266th Brigade R.F.A. (" A," " B," and " C " Btys.).
	267th Brigade R.F.A. (" A " and " B " Btys.).
Engineers	436th, 437th, and 439th Field Coys. R.E.

---

[1] The 1st (A. and N.Z.) Bn. was in the Southern Canal Section. The brigade was never at a strength of more than three battalions.

APPENDIX 2

60th (London) Division.

G.O.C.	Major-General J. S. M. Shea, C.B., D.S.O.
179th Brigade	Br.-General FitzJ. M. Edwards, C.M.G., D.S.O.
2/13th London Regt.	2/14th London Regt.
2/15th London Regt.	2/16th London Regt.
180th Brigade	Br.-General C. F. Watson, C.M.G., D.S.O.
2/17th London Regt.	2/18th London Regt.
2/19th London Regt.	2/20th London Regt.
181st Brigade	Br.-General E. C. Da Costa.
2/21st London Regt.	2/22nd London Regt.
2/23rd London Regt.	2/24th London Regt.
Artillery	301st Brigade R.F.A. ("A," "B," and "C" Btys.).
	302nd Brigade R.F.A. ("A," 413th, and "C" Btys.).
	303rd Brigade R.F.A. ("A," "B," and "C" Btys.).
Engineers	519th, 521st, and 522nd Field Coys. R.E.
Pioneers	1/12th Loyal N. Lancashire Regt.

74th (Yeomanry) Division.

G.O.C.	Major-General E. S. Girdwood.
229th Brigade	Br.-General R. Hoare.
16/Devonshire Regt.	12/Somerset L.I.
14/R. Highlanders.	12/R. Scots Fusiliers.
230th Brigade	Br.-General A. J. M'Neill.
10/E. Kent Regt.	16/R. Sussex Regt.
15/Suffolk Regt.	12/Norfolk Regt.
231st Brigade	Br.-General C. E. Heathcote, D.S.O.
10/Shropshire L.I.	24/R. Welch Fusiliers.
25/R. Welch Fusiliers.	24/Welch Regt.
Artillery	XLIV Brigade R.F.A. (340th and 382nd Btys.).
	117th Brigade R.F.A. ("A," "B," and "C" Btys.).
	268th Brigade R.F.A. ("A," 366th, and "C" Btys.).
Engineers	5th (R. Monmouth) and 5th (R. Anglesey) Field Coys. R.E.

Corps Troops.

Mounted Troops	1/2nd County of London Yeo.
Artillery	XCVI Heavy Artillery Group (15th, 91st, and 181st Heavy Btys.; 378th, 383rd, and 440th Siege Btys.).
Attached	*10th (Irish) Division.*
G.O.C.	Major-General J. R. Longley, C.B.

APPENDIX 2

29th Brigade	Br.-General R. S. Vandeleur, C.M.G.
6/R. Irish Rifles.	5/Connaught Rangers.
1/Leinster Regt.	6/Leinster Regt.
30th Brigade	Br.-General F. A. Greer, D.S.O.
1/R. Irish Regt.	6/R. Munster Fusiliers.
6/R. Dublin Fusiliers.	7/R. Dublin Fusiliers.
31st Brigade	Br.-General E. M. Morris.
5/R. Inniskilling Fusiliers.	6/R. Inniskilling Fusiliers.
2/R Irish Fusiliers.	5/R. Irish Fusiliers.
Artillery	LXVII Brigade R.F.A. (" A," " B," and " C " Btys.).
	LXVIII Brigade R.F.A. (" A," " B," and " C " Btys.).
	263rd Brigade R.F.A. (75th and " C " Btys.).
Engineers	65th, 66th, and 85th Field Coys. R.E.
Pioneers	5/R. Irish Regt.

XXI CORPS.

G.O.C.	Lieut.-General E. S. Bulfin, C.B., C.V.O.
Br.-General, General Staff. ..	Br.-General E. T. Humphreys, D.S.O.
Deputy Adjutant and Quartermaster General	Br.-General St. G. B. Armstrong.
G.O.C. Royal Artillery ..	Br.-General H. A. D. Simpson Baikie, C.B.
Chief Engineer	Br.-General R. P. T. Hawksley.

52nd (Lowland) Division.

G.O.C.	Major-General J. Hill, D.S.O.
155th Brigade	Br.-General J. B. Pollok-M'Call, C.M.G.
1/4th R. Scots Fusiliers.	1/5th R. Scots Fusiliers.
1/4th K.O.S.B.	1/5th K.O.S.B.
156th Brigade	Br.-General A. H. Leggett, D.S.O.
1/4th R. Scots.	1/7th R. Scots.
1/7th Scottish Rifles.	1/8th Scottish Rifles.
157th Brigade	Br.-General C. D. H. Moore, D.S.O.
1/5th H.L.I.	1/6th H.L.I.
1/7th H.L.I.	1/5th Argyll and Suth'd Highrs.
Artillery	261st Brigade R.F.A. (" A," " B," and " C " Btys.).
	262nd Brigade R.F.A. (" A " and " B " Btys.).
	264th Brigade R.F.A. (" A " and " C " Btys.).
Engineers	410th, 412th, and 413th Field Coys. R.E.

54th (East Anglian) Division.

G.O.C.	Major-General S. W. Hare, C.B.
161st Brigade	Br.-General W. Marriott-Dodington.
1/4th Essex Regt.	1/5th Essex Regt.
1/6th Essex Regt.	1/7th Essex Regt.

APPENDIX 2

162nd Brigade	Br.-General A. Mudge.
1/5th Bedfordshire Regt.	1/4th Northamptonshire Regt.
1/10th London Regt.	1/11th London Regt.
163rd Brigade	Br.-General T. Ward, C.M.G.
1/4th Norfolk Regt.	1/5th Norfolk Regt.
1/5th Suffolk Regt.	1/8th Hampshire Regt.
Artillery	270th Brigade R.F.A. ("A," "B," and "C" Btys.).
	271st Brigade R.F.A. ("A" and "B" Btys.).
	272nd Brigade R.F.A. ("B" and "C" Btys.).
Engineers	484th and 486th Field Coys. R.E.

75th Division.

G.O.C.	Major-General P. C. Palin, C.B.
232nd Brigade	Br.-General H. J. Huddleston, D.S.O., M.C.
1/5th Devonshire Regt.	2/5th Hampshire Regt.
2/4th Somerset L.I.	2/3rd Gurkhas.
233rd Brigade	Br.-General the Hon. E. M. Colston, D.S.O.
1/5th Somerset L.I.	1/4th Wiltshire Regt.
2/4th Hampshire Regt.	3/3rd Gurkhas.
234th Brigade	Br.-General F. G. Anley, C.B., C.M.G.
1/4th Duke of Cornwall's L.I.	2/4th Dorset Regt.
123rd Outram's Rifles	58th Vaughan's Rifles (F.F.).
Artillery	XXXVII Brigade R.F.A. (389th, 390th, and 405th Btys.).
	172nd Brigade R.F.A. (391st, 392nd, and 406th Btys.).
	1st S. African F.A. Brigade ("A" and "B" Btys.).
Engineers	495th and 496th Field Coys. R.E.

Corps Troops.

Mounted Troops	Composite Regt. (1 Sqdn. R. Glasgow Yeo., 1 Sqdn. Duke of Lancs. Yeo., 1 Sqdn. 1/1st Herts. Yeo.).
Artillery [1]	XCVII Heavy Artillery Group (189th and 195th Heavy Btys.; 201st, 205th, 300th, and 380th Siege Btys.).
	C Heavy Artillery Group (10th Heavy Bty.; 43rd, 134th, 379th, 422nd, and 423rd Siege Btys.)
	102nd Heavy Artillery Group (202nd Heavy Bty.; 209th, 292nd, 420th, 421st, and 424th Siege Btys.).
Machine-Gun Corps	"E" Company, Tank Corps. 211th Machine-Gun Coy.

---

[1] The XCV H. A. Group from Alexandria joined later. (See p. 324 f.n.)

APPENDICES 2 AND 3

GENERAL HEADQUARTERS TROOPS.
Royal Flying Corps, Middle East.

G.O.C.	Br.-General W. S. Brancker.[1]
Palestine Brigade, R.F.C.	Lieut.-Colonel A. E. Borton, D.S.O.
5th (Corps Artillery) Wing (Nos. 14 and 113 Sqdns. R.F.C.)	
40th (Army) Wing (No. 67 Sqdn. Australian F.C., No. 11 Sqdn. R.F.C.)	
No. 21 Balloon Coy.	
Artillery	VIII Mountain Brigade R.G.A. (10th and 11th Btys. [3·7-in. hows.]).
	IX Mountain Brigade R.G.A. (" A " and " B " [2·75-in.], 12th [3·7-in. hows.] Btys.).
Attached Desert Mounted Corps	7th Mounted Brigade and Imperial Camel Corps Brigade.
Attached XX Corps	10th Division.

APPENDIX 3.

ORDER OF BATTLE

OF THE

EGYPTIAN EXPEDITIONARY FORCE, SEPTEMBER 1918

GENERAL HEADQUARTERS.

Commander-in-Chief	General Sir Edmund H. H. Allenby, G.C.M.G., K.C.B.
Chief of the General Staff	Major-General Sir L. J. Bols, K.C.M.G., C.B., D.S.O.
Br.-General, General Staff	Br.-General W. H. Bartholomew, C.M.G., D.S.O.
Deputy Adjutant-General	Major-General W. G. B. Western, C.B.
Deputy Quartermaster-General	Major-General Sir Walter Campbell, K.C.M.G., C.B., D.S.O.
Attached—	
Major-General, Royal Artillery	Major-General S. C. U. Smith, C.B.
Engineer-in-Chief	Major-General H. B. H. Wright, C.B., C.M.G.

---

[1] Br.-General Brancker succeeded Br.-General W. G. H. Salmond on the 5th November 1917. Br.-General Salmond shortly afterwards returned, succeeding Br.-General Brancker in the command of R.F.C. Middle East on the 3rd January 1918. Lieut.-Colonel Borton was shown as second-in-command of the Palestine Brigade until the 17th December 1917, the G.O.C. Middle East being until that date nominally in command of the Palestine Brigade also.

APPENDIX 3

Desert Mounted Corps.

G.O.C.	Lieut.-General Sir H. G. Chauvel, K.C.B., K.C.M.G.
Br.-General, General Staff	Br.-General C. A. C. Godwin, D.S.O.
Deputy Adjutant and Quarter-master-General	Br.-General E. F. Trew, C.M.G., D.S.O.
G.O.C. Royal Artillery	Br.-General A. D'A. King, C.B., C.M.G., D.S.O.

4th Cavalry Division.

G.O.C.	Major-General Sir G. de S. Barrow, K.C.M.G., C.B.
10th Cavalry Brigade	Br.-General R. G. H. Howard-Vyse, C.M.G., D.S.O.

1/1st Dorset Yeo.　　2nd Lancers.　　38th Central India Horse.

11th Cavalry Brigade	Br.-General C. L. Gregory, C.B.

1/1st County of London (Middlesex) Yeo.
29th Lancers.　　36th Jacob's Horse.

12th Cavalry Brigade	Br.-General J. T. Wigan, D.S.O.

1/1st Staffs. Yeo.　　6th Cavalry.　　19th Lancers.

Artillery	XX Brigade R.H.A. (Berks, Hants, and Leicester Btys.).
Engineers	4th Field Sqdn. R.E.

5th Cavalry Division.

G.O.C.	Major-General H. J. Macandrew, C.B., D.S.O.
13th Cavalry Brigade	Br.-General P. J. V. Kelly, C.M.G., D.S.O.

1/1st Gloucester Yeo.　　9th Hodson's Horse.　　18th Lancers.

14th Cavalry Brigade	Br.-General G. V. Clarke, D.S.O.

1/1st Sherwood Rangers.　　20th Deccan Horse.　　34th Poona Horse.

15th (Imperial Service) Cavalry Brigade .. Br.-General C. R. Harbord, D.S.O.
Jodhpore I.S. Lancers.　　Mysore I.S. Lancers.
1st Hyderabad I.S. Lancers.

Artillery	Essex Battery R.H.A.
Engineers	5th Field Sqdn. R.E.

Australian and New Zealand Mounted Division.
(Formed part of "Chaytor's Force," which appears below.)

Australian Mounted Division.

G.O.C.	Major-General H. W. Hodgson, C.B., C.V.O.
3rd Australian Light Horse Brigade	Br.-General L. C. Wilson, C.M.G.

8th Regt. A.L.H.　　9th Regt. A.L.H.　　10th Regt. A.L.H.

4th Australian Light Horse Brigade	Br.-General W. Grant, D.S.O.

4th Regt. A.L.H.　　11th Regt. A.L.H.　　12th Regt. A.L.H.

668 APPENDIX 3

5th Australian Light Horse Brigade .. .. Br.-General G. M. M. Onslow, D.S.O.
14th Regt. A.L.H.   15th Regt. A.L.H.

Attached—(French) Régiment Mixte de Marche de Cavalerie.

Artillery .. .. XIX Brigade R.H.A. (Notts. Bty. R.H.A.,[1] "A" and "B" Btys. H.A.C.)

Engineers .. .. Australian Mounted Division Field Sqdn.

Corps Troops.

Machine Gun Corps .. .. Nos. 11 and 12 Light Armoured Motor Btys.
Nos. 1 and 7 Light Car Patrols.

XX Corps.

G.O.C. .. .. Lieut.-General Sir P. W. Chetwode, Bt., K.C.B., K.C.M.G., D.S.O.
Br.-General, General Staff .. Br.-General A. P. Wavell, M.C.
Deputy Adjutant and Quarter-master-General .. .. Br.-General C. W. Pearless, C.M.G., D.S.O.
G.O.C. Royal Artillery .. Br.-General A. H. Short, C.B., C.M.G.
Chief Engineer.. .. .. Br.-General R. L. Waller, C.M.G.

10th Division.

G.O.C. .. .. Major-General J. R. Longley, C.B., C.M.G.

29th Brigade .. .. .. Br.-General C. L. Smith, V.C., M.C.
1/Leinster Regt.   1/101st Grenadiers.
1/54th Sikhs (F.F.).   2/151st Indian Infantry.

30th Brigade .. .. .. Br.-General F. A. Greer, C.M.G., D.S.O.
1/R. Irish Regt.   1/Kashmir I.S. Infantry.
38th Dogras.   46th Punjabis.

31st Brigade .. .. .. Br.-General E. M. Morris, C.M.G.
2/R. Irish Fusiliers.   2/101st Grenadiers.
74th Punjabis.   2/42nd Deoli Regt.

Artillery .. .. .. LXVII Brigade R.F.A. ("A," "B," and "C" Btys.).
LXVIII Brigade R.F.A. ("A," "B," and "C" Btys.).
263rd Brigade R.F.A. (75th,[2] 424th, and "C" Btys.).

Engineers .. .. 66th and 85th Field Coys. R.E.
18th Coy. Sappers and Miners.

Pioneers .. .. 2/155th Pioneers.

---

[1] Attached 5th Cavalry Division throughout the operations.
[2] Attached Chaytor's Force for operations.

APPENDIX 3

53rd Division.

G.O.C.	Major-General S. F. Mott, C.B.
158th Brigade	Br.-General H. A. Vernon, D.S.O.
5/6th R. Welch Fusiliers.	4/11th Gurkha Rifles.
3/153rd Indian Infantry.	3/154th Indian Infantry.
159th Brigade	Br.-General N. E. Money, D.S.O.
4/5th Welch Regt.	3/152nd Indian Infantry.
1/153rd Indian Infantry.	2/153rd Indian Infantry.
160th Brigade	Br.-General V. L. N. Pearson.
1/7th R. Welch Fusiliers.	1/17th Infantry.
1/21st Punjabis.	1st Cape Corps.
Artillery	265th Brigade R.F.A. (" A," " B," and " C " Btys.).
	266th Brigade R.F.A. (" A," " B," and " C " Btys.).
	267th Brigade R.F.A. (" A," " B," and 439th Btys.).
Engineers	436th and 437th Field Coys. R.E.
	72nd Coy. Sappers and Miners.
Pioneers	1/155th Pioneers.

Corps Troops.

Mounted Troops	1/1st Worcester Yeo.
Artillery [1]	XCVII Brigade R.G.A.[2] (421st Siege Bty., 1 Gun 387th Bty.).
	103rd Brigade R.G.A. (10th Heavy Bty., 205th and 392nd Siege Btys., 387th Siege Bty. less 1 Gun.).
	39th Indian Mountain Bty.[3]
	Hong Kong and Singapore Mountain Bty.[4]

XXI Corps.

G.O.C.	Lieut.-General Sir E. S. Bulfin, K.C.B., C.V.O.
Br.-General, General Staff	Br.-General H. F. Salt, D.S.O.
Deputy Adjutant and Quartermaster- General	Br.-General St. G. B. Armstrong.
G.O.C. Royal Artillery	Br.-General H. A. D. Simpson Baikie, C.B., C.M.G.
Chief Engineer..	Br.-General R. P. T. Hawksley, D.S.O.

---

[1] The artillery here shown is not that normally attached to the XX Corps, but merely that proportion under its command for the operations of the 19th September. The bulk had been transferred to the XXI Corps, and will be found under that heading.

[2] Sufficient personnel was available to man 2 captured 150-mm. howitzers, 2 captured 105-mm. howitzers, and 2 captured 75-mm. guns, under the command of the XCVII Brigade.

[3] Directly under the orders of the 53rd Division.

[4] Directly under the orders of the 10th Division.

3rd (Lahore) Division.

G.O.C.	Major-General A. R. Hoskins, C.M.G., D.S.O.
7th Brigade	Br.-General S. R. Davidson, C.M.G.
1/Connaught Rangers.	2/7th Gurkha Rifles.
27th Punjabis.	91st Punjabis.
8th Brigade	Br.-General S. M. Edwardes, C.B., C.M.G., D.S.O.
1/Manchester Regt.	47th Sikhs.
59th Scinde Rifles (F.F.).	2/124th Baluchistan Infantry.
9th Brigade	Br.-General C. C. Luard, C.M.G.
2/Dorsetshire Regt.	1/1st Gurkha Rifles.
93rd Infantry.	105th Mahratta L.I.
Artillery	IV Brigade R.F.A. (7th, 14th, and B/69th Btys.).
	VIII Brigade R.F.A. (372nd, 373rd, and 428th Btys.).
	LIII Brigade R.F.A. (66th, 374th, and 430th Btys.).
Engineers	65th Field Coy. R.E.
	20th and 21st Coys. Sappers and Miners.
Pioneers	1/34th Sikh Pioneers.

7th (Meerut) [1] Division.

G.O.C.	Major-General Sir V. B. Fane, K.C.I.E., C.B.
19th Brigade	Br.-General G. A. Weir, D.S.O.
1/Seaforth Highlanders.	28th Punjabis.
92nd Punjabis.	125th Napier's Rifles.
21st Brigade	Br.-General A. G. Kemball.
2/R. Highlanders.	1st Guides Infantry.
20th Punjabis.	1/8th Gurkha Rifles.
28th Brigade (F.F.)	Br.-General C. H. Davies, C.M.G., D.S.O.
2/Leicestershire Regt.	51st Sikhs (F.F.).
53rd Sikhs (F.F.).	56th Punjabi Rifles (F.F.).
Artillery	261st Brigade R.F.A. (" A," " B," and " C " Btys.).
	262nd Brigade R.F.A. (" A," " B," and 438th Btys.).
	264th Brigade R.F.A. (422nd, 423rd, and " C " Btys.).
Engineers	522nd Field Coy. R.E.
	3rd and 4th Coys. Sappers and Miners.
Pioneers	121st Pioneers.

54th (East Anglian) Division.

G.O.C.	Major-General S. W. Hare, C.B.
161st Brigade	Br.-General H. B. H. Orpen-Palmer, D.S.O.
1/4th Essex Regt.	1/5 Essex Regt.
1/6th Essex Regt.	1/7th Essex Regt.

---

[1] Or " (Indian)."

APPENDIX 3

162nd Brigade	Br.-General A. Mudge, C.M.G.
1/5th Bedfordshire Regt.	1/4th Northamptonshire Regt.
1/10th London Regt.	1/11th London Regt.
163rd Brigade ..	Br.-General A. J. M'Neill, D.S.O.
1/4th Norfolk Regt.	1/5th Norfolk Regt.
1/5th Suffolk Regt.	1/8th Hampshire Regt.
Artillery	270th Brigade R.F.A. ("A," "B," and "C" Btys.).
	271st Brigade R.F.A. ("A," "B," and 440th Btys.).
	272nd Brigade R.F.A. ("A," "B," and "C" Btys.).
Engineers	484th, 486th, 495th Field Coys. R.E.

60th Division.

G.O.C.	Major-General J. S. M. Shea, C.B., C.M.G., D.S.O.
179th Brigade ..	Br.-General E. T. Humphreys, D.S.O.
2/13th London Regt.	3/151st Punjabi Rifles.
2/19th Punjabis.	2/127th Baluch L.I.
180th Brigade ..	Br.-General C. F. Watson, C.M.G., D.S.O.
2/19th London Regt.	2nd Guides Infantry.
2/30th Punjabis.	1/50th Kumaon Rifles.
181st Brigade ..	Br.-General E. C. Da Costa, C.M.G., D.S.O.
2/22nd London Regt.	130th Baluchis.
2/97th Deccan Infantry	2/152nd Indian Infantry.
Artillery	301st Brigade R.F.A. ("A," "B," and "C" Btys.).
	302nd Brigade R.F.A. ("A," "B," and 413th Btys.).
	303rd Brigade R.F.A. ("A," "B," and "C" Btys.).
Engineers	519th and 521st Field Coys. R.E.
	No. 1 Coy. Sappers and Miners.
Pioneers	2/107th Pioneers.

75th Division.

G.O.C.	Major-General P. C. Palin, C.B., C.M.G.
232nd Brigade	Br.-General H. J. Huddleston, C.M.G., D.S.O., M.C.
1/4th Wiltshire Regt.	72nd Punjabis.
2/3rd Gurkha Rifles.	3rd Kashmir I.S. Infantry.
233rd Brigade ..	Br.-General the Hon. E. M. Colston, C.M.G., D.S.O., M.V.O.
1/5th Somerset L.I.	29th Punjabis.
3/3rd Gurkha Rifles.	2/154th Indian Infantry.
234th Brigade	Br.-General C. A. H. Maclean, D.S.O.
1/4th Duke of Cornwall's L.I.	123rd Outram's Rifles.
58th Vaughan's Rifles (F.F.).	1/152nd Indian Infantry.

APPENDIX 3

Artillery	XXXVII Brigade R.F.A. (389th 390th, and 405th Btys.).
	172nd Brigade R.F.A. (391st, 392nd, and 406th Btys.).
	1st S. African F.A. Brigade (" A," " B," and " C " Btys.).
Engineers	496th Field Coy. R.E., 10th and 16th Coys. Sappers and Miners.
Pioneers	2/32nd Sikh Pioneers.

Détachement Français de Palestine et Syrie.[1]

Commander	Colonel P. de Piépape, C.B.
Régiment de Marche de Tirailleurs	7me Bn. 1er Tirailleurs Algériens.
	9me Bn. 2me Tirailleurs Algériens.
Régiment de Marche de la Légion d'Orient..	1er and 2me Bns. Arméniens.
	Also 1 Territorial Bn., 1 Coy. Syrians, 1 Sqdn. dismounted Spahis.
Artillery	1 80-mm., 1 75-mm., and 1 65-mm. (mountain) Btys.

Corps Troops.

Mounted Troops	Composite Regt. (1 Sqdn. Duke of Lancs. Yeo., 2 Sqdns. 1/1st Herts. Yeo.).
Artillery	XCV Brigade R.G.A. (181st Heavy Bty., 304th, 314th, 383rd, and 422nd Siege Btys.)[2]
	XCVI Brigade R.G.A. (189th and 202nd Heavy Btys., 378th and 394th Siege Btys.)
	100th Brigade R.G.A. (15th Heavy Bty., 134th and 334th Siege Btys., 1 Section [1 6-in. gun] 43rd Siege Bty., 1 Section 300th Siege Bty.).[3]
	102nd Brigade R.G.A. (91st Heavy Bty., 209th, 380th, 440th Siege Btys., 1 Section [1 6-in. gun] 43rd Siege Bty., 1 Section 300th Siege Bty.)
	VIII Mountain Brigade R.G.A.[4] (11th [3·7-in. hows.], 13th [3·7-in. hows.], and 17th [2·75-in.] Btys.).
	IX Mountain Brigade R.G.A.[5] (10th [3·7-in. hows.], 12th [3·7-in. hows.], and 16th [2·75-in.] Btys.).

---

[1] Under the orders of G.O.C. 54th Division.
[2] And 1 section captured 150-mm. howitzers.
[3] Also 1 improvized 4·7-in. battery.
[4] Attached 54th Division on the 19th September, and 7th Division on the 20th.
[5] Attached 54th Division on the 19th September, and 3rd Division on the 20th.

APPENDICES 3 AND 4

CHAYTOR'S FORCE.

G.O.C. .. .. Major-General Sir E. W. C. Chaytor, K.C.M.G., C.B.
(With Staff of A. and N.Z. Mounted Division.)

Australian and New Zealand Mounted Division.
(As in Appendix 2.)

20th Indian Brigade .. .. Br.-General E. R. B. Murray.
Alwar I.S. Infantry. Gwalior I.S. Infantry.
Patiala I.S. Infantry. 110th Mahratta L.I.
38/R. Fusiliers.
39/R. Fusiliers.
1/British West Indies Regt.
2/British West Indies Regt.
Artillery .. .. 75th Bty. R.F.A.,[1] 29th and 32nd (2·75-in.) Indian Mountain Btys., 195th Heavy Bty. R.G.A.[2]

GENERAL HEADQUARTERS TROOPS.
ROYAL AIR FORCE, MIDDLE EAST.[3]

G.O.C. .. .. Major-General W. G. H. Salmond, D.S.O.
Palestine Brigade R.A.F. .. Br.-General A. E. Borton, D.S.O.
5th (Corps) Wing (Nos. 14, 113, and 142nd Sqdns.).
40th (Army) Wing (Nos. 111, 144, and 145 Sqdns., No. 1 Sqdn. Australian F.C.).
No. 21 Balloon Coy.

APPENDIX 4.

ORDER OF BATTLE OF *YILDERIM*, OCTOBER 1917.

GENERAL HEADQUARTERS.

Commander-in-Chief .. .. Marshal E. von Falkenhayn.
Chief of the Staff.. .. .. Oberst von Dommes.

SEVENTH ARMY.

G.O.C. .. .. General Fevzi Pasha.
III Corps: Colonel Ismet Bey (3rd Cavalry and 27th Divisions, 2nd and 48th Regiments);
24th Division (less 2nd Regiment).

---

[1] From 10th Divisional Artillery.
[2] Also 2 Sections captured 75-mm. guns and 1 Section captured 150-mm. howitzers.
[3] In theory, there is no more reason for including this headquarters than that of the Admiral on the Egyptian Station, for like his, it was, since the formation of the Royal Air Force, an independent command. In practice, where operations were concerned, Major-General Salmond acted under Sir Edmund Allenby's orders.

APPENDICES 4 AND 5

EIGHTH ARMY.

G.O.C. .. .. General Freiherr Kress von Kressenstein.
XX Corps: Colonel Ali Fuad Bey (16th Division [less 48th Regiment], 26th and 54th Divisions);
XIII Corps: Colonel Refet Bey (3rd and 53rd Divisions);
7th Division.

GENERAL HEADQUARTERS TROOPS.

19th Division, 10th Depot Regiment;
German Flying Corps (301st, 302nd, 303rd, and 304th Flight Detachments).

APPENDIX 5.

ORDER OF BATTLE OF *YILDERIM*, SEPTEMBER 1918.

GENERAL HEADQUARTERS.

Commander-in-Chief .. .. Marshal Liman von Sanders.
Chief of the Staff .. .. General Kiazim Pasha.

FOURTH ARMY.

G.O.C. .. .. General Mohammed Jemal Pasha.
II Corps: (Hauran Detachment, 'Amman Division, Ma'an Detachment);
VIII Corps: Colonel Ali Fuad Bey (Caucasus Cavalry Brigade, 48th Division, Composite Division, Mule-Mounted Infantry Regiment, etc.).[1]

Army Troops.

3rd Cavalry Division, German 146th Regiment, 63rd Regiment, etc.

SEVENTH ARMY.

G.O.C. .. .. General Mustapha Kemal Pasha.
III Corps: Colonel Ismet Bey (1st and 11th Divisions);
XX Corps: Major-General Ali Fuad Pasha (24th, 26th, and 53rd Divisions).

EIGHTH ARMY.

G.O.C. .. .. General Jevad Pasha.
XXII Corps: Colonel Refet Bey (7th and 20th Divisions);
Asia Corps: Oberst von Oppen (16th and 19th Divisions, German *Pasha II* Brigade).

---

[1] Single battalions in the heterogeneous collection of troops east of Jordan are not included.

APPENDICES 5 AND 6

46th Division. Army Troops.

GENERAL HEADQUARTERS TROOPS.

109th Regiment (attached Seventh Army), 110th Regiment, 13th and 17th Depot Regiments.
Yilderim Flying Command (1st Pursuit Detachment, 302nd, 303rd, 304th Reconnaissance Detachments).

APPENDIX 6.
GERMAN FORMATIONS WITH *YILDERIM*.[1]

ASIA CORPS (" Pasha II ").

Commander .. .. .. Oberst von Frankenberg und Proschlitz (later Oberst von Oppen).

701st, 702nd, and 703rd Bns. (each with 6 machine guns and 18 light Bergmann machine guns).

To each battalion was attached a machine-gun company of 6 guns, a troop of cavalry, an " infantry-artillery platoon " with 2 mountain guns or howitzers, and a trench-mortar section with 4 mortars.

701st Artillery Detachment (2 4-gun 77-mm., one 4-gun 105-mm. how. btys.).

Machine-Gun Detachment " Hentig."

" PASHA II " REINFORCEMENTS.

Commander .. .. .. Oberst von Oppen
(later Oberstlt. Freiherr von Hammerstein-Gesmold).

Masurian Infantry Regiment 146 (3 bns. each with 6 machine guns).[2]
11th Reserve Jäger Bn. (with 6 machine guns).[2]
Mountain Artillery Detachment (3 4-gun 105-mm. how. btys.).
Mountain Machine-Gun Detachment (4 machine-gun companies).

---

[1] Pioneers, anti-aircraft artillery, medical units, etc., are not included. Aircraft units are given in Appendices 4 and 5. The heavy artillery, machine-gun companies, and trench-mortar units of " Pasha I " (see Vol. I, p. 202) were absorbed by the Asia Corps. It will be seen that, while in infantry the German contribution was only seven battalions, it may be said, in view of the great number of light and heavy machine guns, to have had at least the value of a division in the conditions of the campaign. There were also 24 German, six Turkish, and three Austrian lorry columns under German control.

[2] The number of light machine gun with these battalions is not known.

APPENDIX 7.

FORCE ORDER No. 54.

BY

GENERAL SIR EDMUND ALLENBY, K.C.B.,
Commander-in-Chief, Egyptian Expeditionary Force.

General Headquarters,
22nd October 1917.

Reference Maps : Palestine 1/20,000 ; Palestine 1/63,360.

Maps 2, 4, 6.

1. The latest intelligence regarding the enemy will be issued to all concerned from time to time as the information is received.

2. It is the intention of the Commander-in-Chief to take the offensive against the enemy at Gaza and at Beersheba, and, when Beersheba is in our hands, to make an enveloping attack on the enemy's left flank in the direction of Sheria and Hureira.

3. (*a*) On Zero day the XX Corps (with the 10th Division and the Imperial Camel Brigade attached) and the Desert Mounted Corps (less one mounted division and the Imperial Camel Brigade) will attack the enemy at Beersheba with the object of gaining possession of that place by nightfall.

(*b*) As soon as Beersheba is in our hands and the necessary arrangements have been made for the restoration of the Beersheba water supply, the XX Corps and the Desert Mounted Corps complete will move rapidly forward to attack the left of the enemy's main position, with the object of driving him out of Sheria and Hureira, and enveloping the left flank of his army. The XX Corps will move against the enemy's defences south of Sheria, first of all against the " Qawuqa " line, and then against Sheria and the Hureira defences. The Desert Mounted Corps, calling up the division left in General Reserve during the Beersheba operation, will move north of the XX Corps to gain possession of Nejile and of any water supplies between that place and the right of the XX Corps, and will be prepared to operate vigorously against and round the enemy's left flank if he should throw it back to oppose the advance of the XX Corps.

(*c*) On a date to be subsequently determined, and which will probably be after the occupation of Beersheba and 24 to 48 hours before the attack of the XX Corps on the Qawuqa line, the XXI Corps will attack the south-western defences of Gaza with the object of capturing the enemy's front line system from Umbrella Hill to Sheikh Hasan, both inclusive.

(*d*) The Royal Navy will co-operate with the XXI Corps in the attack on Gaza and in any subsequent operations that may be undertaken by XXI Corps.

4. (*a*) On Z − 4 day G.O.C. XXI Corps will open a systematic bombardment of the Gaza defences, increasing in volume from Z − 1 day to Z + 2 day, and to be continued until Z + 4 day at the least.

(*b*) The Royal Navy will co-operate as follows :—On Z − 1 and Zero days two 6-in. monitors will be available for bombardment from the sea : special objective, Sheikh Hasan. On Zero day a third 6-in. monitor will be available, so that two of these ships may be constantly in action while one replenishes ammunition. On Z + 1 day 6-in. monitors will discontinue their bombardment, which they will re-open on Z + 2 day.

APPENDIX 7

From Z — 1 day the French battleship *Requin* and H.M.S. *Raglan* will bombard Deir Sneid station and junction for Huj, the roads and railway bridges, and camps on the Wadi el Hesi in the neighbourhood, under arrangements which are being made by the Rear-Admiral, Senior Naval Officer, Egypt and Red Sea. *Requin* and *Raglan* will be assisted by a seaplane carrier. From Zero day one 9·2-in. monitor will be available from dawn : special objective, Sheikh Redwan.

(c) From Z — 1 day inclusive demands for Naval co-operation will be conveyed direct by G.O.C. XXI Corps to the Senior Naval Officer, Marine View, who will arrange for the transmission of demands so made. The Rear-Admiral, Senior Naval Officer, Egypt and Red Sea, will be prepared to meet all demands for co-operation so far as the means at his disposal allow.

5. (a) The XX Corps will move into position during the night Z — 1/Zero, so as to attack the enemy at Beersheba on Zero day south of the Wadi es Sabe with two divisions, while covering its flank and the construction of the railway east of Shellal with one division on the high ground overlooking the Wadis es Sufi and Hanafish.

The objective of the XX Corps will be the enemy's works west and south-west of Beersheba as far as the Khelasa–Beersheba road inclusive.

(b) The Desert Mounted Corps will move on the night Z — 1/Zero from the area of concentration about Khelasa and Asluj so as to co-operate with the XX Corps by attacking Beersheba with two divisions and one mounted brigade.

The objective of the Desert Mounted Corps will be the enemy's defences from the south-east to the north-east of Beersheba and the town of Beersheba itself.

6. G.O.C. Desert Mounted Corps will endeavour to turn the enemy's left with a view to breaking down his resistance at Beersheba as quickly as possible. With this in view, the main weight of his force will be directed against Beersheba from the east and north-east. As soon as the enemy's resistance shows signs of weakening, G.O.C. Desert Mounted Corps will be prepared to act with the utmost vigour against his retreating troops, so as to prevent their escape, or at least to drive them well beyond the high ground immediately overlooking the town from the north. He will also be prepared to push troops rapidly into Beersheba in order to protect from damage any wells and plant connected with the water supply not damaged by the enemy before Beersheba is entered. Special instructions will be issued to G.O.C. Desert Mounted Corps, and a copy of these instructions will be forwarded for information to G.O.C. XX Corps.

7. The Yeomanry Mounted Division will pass from the command of the G.O.C. XX Corps at 5 a.m. on Zero day, and will come directly under General Headquarters as part of the General Reserve in the hands of the Commander-in-Chief.

8. When Beersheba has been taken, G.O.C. XX Corps will push forward covering troops to the high ground north of the town to protect it from any counter movement on the part of the enemy. He will also immediately put in hand the restoration of the water supply in Beersheba.

G.O.C. Desert Mounted Corps will be responsible for the protection of the town from the north-east and east. The line of demarcation between the Desert Mounted Corps and the XX Corps will be one drawn from the Mosque at Beersheba and produced through Kh. el Omry, the latter place being in the XX Corps area.

9. As soon as possible after the taking of Beersheba, G.O.C. Desert Mounted Corps will report to General Headquarters on the water supplies

in the wells and wadis east of Beersheba, and especially along the Wadi es Sabe and the Beersheba–Tell el Mila road. If insufficient water is found to exist in this area, G.O.C. Desert Mounted Corps will send back such of his troops as may be necessary to watering places from which he started or which may have been found in the country east of the Khelasa–Beersheba road during the operations.

A preliminary survey having been made, G.O.C. XX Corps will report by wire to General Headquarters on the condition of the wells and water supply generally in Beersheba and on any water supplies found west and north-west of that place. He will telegraph an estimate, as soon as it can be made, of the time required to place the Beersheba water supply in working order.

10. When the situation as regards the water at Beersheba has become clear, so that the movement of the XX Corps and Desert Mounted Corps against the left flank of the enemy's main position can be arranged, G.O.C. XXI Corps will be ordered to attack the enemy's defences south-west of Gaza, in time for this operation to be carried out prior to the attack of the XX Corps on the Qawuqa line of works.

The objective of the XXI Corps will be the defences of Gaza from Umbrella Hill inclusive to the sea about Sheikh Hasan.

11. *Artillery*.

(a) Instructions with regard to the following have been issued separately to all Corps :—

    (i) Amount of Corps Artillery allotted.
    (ii) Amount of ammunition to be on Corps charge prior to operations.
    (iii) The amount of ammunition per gun that will be delivered daily at respective railheads, and the day of commencement.
    (iv) The amount of transport allotted for forward supply from railheads.

(b) The general average for one day's firing has been calculated on the following basis :—

Field and Mountain Guns / Mountain Howitzers	150 rounds per gun.
4·5-in. Howitzers	120 ,, ,,
60-pdr. / 6-in. Howitzers	90 ,, ,,
8-in. Howitzers	60 ,, ,,
6-in. VII	60 ,, ,,

This average expenditure will only be possible in the XXI Corps up to Z + 16 and for the Desert Mounted Corps and XX Corps to Z + 13. After these dates (if the average has been expended), the daily average will have to drop to the basis of 100 rounds per 18-pdr. per day and other natures in proportion.

12. *Aircraft*.

(a) Army Wing.

Strategical reconnaissance, including the reconnaissance of areas beyond the tactical zone and in which the enemy's main reserves are located, also distant photography and aerial offensive, will be carried out by an Army Squadron under instructions issued direct from General Headquarters. Protection from hostile aircraft will be the main duty of the Army Fighting Squadron.

A bombing squadron will be held in readiness for any aerial offensive which the situation may render desirable.

(b) Corps Squadrons.

The Corps Squadrons will undertake artillery co-operation, contact patrols, and tactical reconnaissance for the Corps to which they are attached.

In the case of the Desert Mounted Corps, one flight from the Corps Squadron attached to the XX Corps will be responsible for the above work.

Photography of trench areas will normally be carried out daily by the Army Wing.

13. *Communications.*

(a) Messages between the Army and the Royal Navy will normally be transmitted by telephone through the Senior Naval Officer at Marine View, where there will be a Naval W/T Station as well as at Deir el Balah. Direct wireless communication with the Senior Naval Officer afloat will only be used by General Headquarters and in case of emergency.

(b) The Director of Army Signals will arrange for the construction of the following semi-permanent telegraph lines, in addition to lines provided by Corps for their own use :—

Qamle to Khelasa and Asluj	(4 wires)
Shellal to Imara and Kharm	(6 ,,)
Qamle to El Baqqar	(8 ,,)
El Baqqar to Beersheba	(4 ,,)

Signal Offices at Qamle, and at Imara and Kharm when railhead reaches those places, will be arranged for by the Director of Army Signals.

14. No maps will be carried into action other than the following :—

1/20,000 (Sheets required by formations or units concerned).
Palestine, 1/63,360 squared map.
Africa, 1/125,000, Rafah and Beersheba sheets.

All ranks are forbidden to carry into action any letters, papers, orders or sketches which, in the event of their capture, would give any useful information to the enemy.

15. One General Staff Officer from General Headquarters for liaison purposes will be attached to each Corps Headquarters during operations.

General Officers Commanding Corps will arrange between themselves for interchange of the necessary liaison officers.

16. *Medical.*

(a) Three Casualty Clearing Stations at Imara will serve the XX Corps and the Desert Mounted Corps. Two Casualty Clearing Stations at Deir el Balah will serve the XXI Corps. A Casualty Clearing Station for light cases from all Corps will be placed at Rafah, and an Egyptian Hospital for prisoners of war will be at Imara.

In order that the Casualty Clearing Stations at Imara may be erected as rapidly as possible, the sites will be carefully laid out beforehand, the tents will be placed in readiness on the ground, and 50 E.L.C. labourers will be assigned to each Casualty Clearing Station to assist in its erection, beginning at sunset on Z − 1 day, before which time no tents will be erected.

(b) The transport of casualties to Casualty Clearing Stations will be effected by the mobile portion of Field Ambulances and by the Motor Ambulance Convoy, two sections of which will be assigned to the XX Corps and Desert Mounted Corps and one to XXI Corps.

(c) The D.D's.M.S. of Corps will be responsible for the evacuation of casualties to the Casualty Clearing Stations assigned to them by the Director of Medical Services or his representative.

The Inspector Palestine L. of C. will be responsible for the evacuation from the Casualty Clearing Stations westwards as far as Qantara. The

Director of Medical Services will be responsible for the evacuation from Qantara to the Base Hospitals.

(*d*) The hospital trains east of the Suez Canal will be controlled by the A.D.M.S. Palestine L. of C., to whom instructions have been issued. The hospital trains will be supplemented by returning empty truck trains for slight cases.

(*e*) Nos. 7, 4, and 6 Advanced Depots of Medical Stores will be at Deir el Balah, Rafah, and Imara respectively.

17. *Prisoners of War.*

A reception compound for prisoners of war has been arranged at Shellal in addition to the existing compound at Deir el Balah. Prisoners will be sent back from the reception compounds to the main compound which has been established at Rafah.

Arrangements will be made by the Inspector Palestine L. of C. for receiving prisoners of war at railhead on both lines, and for escorting them to the rear. Should the Inspector Palestine L. of C. not have sufficient guards and escorts for these duties, he will demand the additional personnel from the Officer Commanding Palestine L. of C. Defences.

The general procedure in regard to prisoners of war is laid down in General Routine Order 3005 of 30th September 1917.

18. In addition to the existing arrangements for synchronization throughout the force by means of the Signal Service, the Wireless Station at General Headquarters will send out to Army Corps and the Navy daily at 12.30 p.m. the official time for use during operations.

19. The date of Zero will be notified in due course.

20. General Headquarters will remain in its present position.

L. J. BOLS.

Major-General, Chief of the General Staff, Egyptian Expeditionary Force.

APPENDIX 8.

Secret.

XX CORPS INSTRUCTION.

G.O.14/9.

Reference | 1 : 125,000 and 1 : 20,000 Maps.

Maps 4, 5.

Tracing " A " referred to is issued with XX Corps Order No. 10.

1. (*a*) The G.O.C. XX Corps, in co-operation with the Desert Mounted Corps, intends to attack and destroy the enemy's detachment at Beersheba, to envelop the enemy's left flank, and to drive him out of Sheria and Hureira.

(*b*) On a date to be notified later (Z day) two divisions of the XX Corps will attack the Beersheba works between the Fara–Beersheba and the Khelasa–Beersheba roads, while the third division with attached troops covers the left flank of the Corps from a position on the general line between Kh. es Sufi and El Girheir and thence to Point 510 (3 miles W. of El. Girheir).

(*c*) The XX Corps Reserve (1 Division less 1 Brigade) will be at Shellal.

(*d*) The Desert Mounted Corps (less 1 Division) will co-operate on the right of the XX Corps and attack the enemy's defences from the south-east to the north-east of Beersheba and the town itself.

(*e*) One Division of the Desert Mounted Corps will be at Shellal in G.H.Q. Reserve.

APPENDIX 8

2. *Dispositions and Objectives—Desert Mounted Corps.*

The Anzac Mounted Division and the Australian Mounted Division of the Desert Mounted Corps will march from Asluj and Khelasa respectively on the night Z − 1/Z *via* W. el Imshash–Thaffa–Goz ez Shegeib.

The Anzac Mounted Division, which will lead, will deploy by 9 a.m. on Z day between the Beersheba–Hebron road and the Beersheba–Khasim Zanna road on the front Bir es Sqati–Khasim Zanna.

Objectives—Tell es Sabe, Beersheba, Hill 970 north of Beersheba.

One Brigade of the Anzac Mounted Division will move to the neighbourhood of Bir es Sqati to watch the Beersheba–Hebron road and protect the right flank.

The Australian Mounted Division will follow the Anzac Mounted Division in its approach march.

The 7th Mounted Brigade will move from Esani *via* the Broken Earth Road and Goz Sheihili to the neighbourhood of Goz en Na'am on night Z − 1/Z.

The tasks allotted to the Australian Mounted Division and 7th Mounted Brigade will be communicated to the G.O.C. 60th Division separately.

3. *Dispositions and Objectives—XX Corps.*

(i) The objective of the attack by the XX Corps on Z day is the capture of the line of works between the Khelasa–Beersheba road and the Wadi es Sabe, the capture of the enemy guns between Beersheba and the trenches west of the town, and in co-operation with the cavalry to drive the enemy from the remainder of his defences at Beersheba.

Right Division.—The 60th Division with the Corps Cavalry Regiment attached.

Left Division.—The 74th Division.

(ii) " Smith's Group " (Brigadier-General C. L. Smith, V.C., I.C.C. Brigade), consisting of two battalions 53rd Division and the I.C.C. Brigade, is placed under the command of G.O.C. 74th Division to hold the ground from the Wadi es Sabe inclusive at H.14 central to the right of the 53rd Division about Hill 765 (T.24.c.).

(iii) The 53rd Division (less 1 Artillery Brigade) with 1 Infantry Brigade and 1 Artillery Brigade of the 10th Division and 1 Heavy Battery attached will occupy the line Hill 765 (T.24.c.)–Point 790 (Y.7.)–Point 770 (T.4.)–Point 730 (R.33.)–Point 630 (Q.22.)–Hill 465 (Q.13.)–Hill 430 (L.30.)[1] to secure the left flank of the XX Corps against a hostile counterstroke from Abu Hureira, keeping as large a mobile reserve as possible for offensive action in co-operation with the Corps Reserve.

The 53rd Division will be prepared to attack the Beersheba garrison if it retreats by the Beersheba–Gaza road, or to block its escape by night. In this case reinforcements from the Corps Reserve would be placed at the disposal of the G.O.C. 53rd Division.

(iv) 10th Division (less 1 Artillery Brigade, 1 4·5-in. Battery, 1 Infantry Brigade and Pioneer Battalion) will be Corps Reserve on the east bank of the Wadi esh Shellal ready to co-operate with the 53rd Division against any attack from the direction of Hureira.

The G.O.C. 10th Division will also be responsible for protection of the line of communications east of the Wadi Ghazze.

Certain troops will be allotted by G.H.Q. for the local protection of Shellal, Imara and Kharm, under O.C. Palestine L. of C. Defences, and the G.O.C. 10th Division will be kept informed as to their numbers.

G.O.C. 10th Division will be at 53rd Division headquarters during Z day.

---

[1] The dispositions of these troops are clearly shown on Map 5, though the points named are not marked.

(v) The Yeomanry Mounted Division will be G.H.Q. Reserve on Z day at Shellal, west of the Wadi Ghazze.

(vi) The lines on which divisions will deploy and boundaries between divisions are as shown on Tracing " A."

4. *Plan of Attack.*—(a) Orders for the march to the position of deployment, which will be completed by 4 a.m. on Z day, will be issued separately.

(b) The attack on the enemy position will be made in two stages.

1st Stage.—Attack on advanced works in H.29.c. and H.35.

2nd Stage.—Attack on the main line running from Z.29 inclusive through H.36.d. and c., H.35.b., H.29.d., b., a., H.23, H.17 to the Wadi es Sabe.

(c) *Attack on Advanced Works.*—The attack on the advanced works is being made by the 181st Infantry Brigade, 60th Division, at an hour to be fixed by the G.O.C. 60th Division, and will be preceded by a bombardment of the enemy's line from the Khelasa Road as far north as work Y.28 (exclusive) which is to begin as early as the light will permit.

The artillery preparation by the 60th Division for the attack on the enemy's advanced works will be assisted by the 74th Division, which will include works Z.15 and Z.16 in their scheme for artillery bombardment and by one Siege Battery, XCVI Heavy Group.

During the attack on the enemy's advanced works the remainder of the 60th Division and the 74th Division will conform to the advance of the attacking brigade, and the 74th Division will push forward infantry to connect with the left of the 60th Division.

(d) *Attack on the Main Line.*—The objective of the attack is the main line of the enemy trenches between the Khelasa–Beersheba road and the Wadi es Sabe, and the enemy guns between Beersheba and the trench line.

The position will be consolidated after capture and outposts will be placed approximately on the " Blue " Line (Tracing " A ") to cover the consolidation of the position and reorganization of the attacking troops. No troops will be pushed forward beyond the " Blue " Line [1] without orders from divisional headquarters except for the capture of enemy guns, which may be undertaken at the discretion of subordinate commanders.

The 60th Division and 74th Division are both attacking with two brigades, and the third brigade in divisional reserve. The left brigade of the 60th Division will direct, and although the advance of the 74th Division must be simultaneous with that of the 60th Division, the line from which the 74th Division will advance to the attack will be slightly refused on the left so that the right flank of the attack engages the enemy first.

The time for the commencement of the attack will depend on the progress of wire-cutting by artillery, and the attack will be ordered to begin by the G.O.C. 60th Division after he is satisfied that the wire on his front is sufficiently cut, and after he has received a report from the G.O.C. 74th Division to the same effect.

The G.O.C. 74th Division will keep the G.O.C. 60th Division informed of the progress of wire-cutting on his front, and if there is likely to be a prolonged delay in the completion of the operation after the 60th Division is ready, the hour for the commencement of the attack will be referred by the G.O.C. 60th Division to Corps headquarters.

(e) The task of " Smith's Group " under the orders of the G.O.C. 74th Division will be to deal with any counter-stroke against the left of

---

[1] The " Blue " Line is shown in red as " Objective of XX Corps " on Map 5.

the 74th Division and to prevent the transfer of troops to reinforce the enemy on the front of attack of the 60th and 74th Divisions by holding the enemy to his trenches north of the Wadi es Sabe.

The right of " Smith's Group " will work forward along the Wadi es Sabe and its northern bank to within effective range of the enemy works north of the wadi, timing its progress by the left of the 74th Division.

(f) In the event of orders being issued from XX Corps headquarters for an attack on the enemy trenches north of the Wadi es Sabe after the capture of the trenches south of the wadi, the G.O.C. 74th Division will be placed in charge of the operation and will be allotted an infantry brigade of the 53rd Division to assist him. This brigade will pass through the line held by " Smith's Group," after which the group will be broken up, the two battalions of the 53rd Division in the group reverting to the command of the G.O.C. 53rd Division and the I.C.C. Brigade coming into Corps reserve. The Corps Field Artillery Brigade (see para. 5 [i]) and at least one field artillery brigade of the 53rd Division will be placed at the disposal of the G.O.C. 74th Division to support the attack. All the available batteries of the XCVI Heavy Artillery Group will be employed under the orders of the G.O.C.R.A., XX Corps, to assist the operation.

5. *Artillery.*—(i) The allotment of artillery is as follows :—
XCVI Heavy Artillery Group.—(Less 1 Heavy Battery) for counter battery work.
  2 Heavy Artillery Batteries, 60-pdr.
  2 Siege Batteries, 6-in. Howitzer.
  1 Field Battery (4·5-in. Howitzer) from 10th Division.
Corps Field Artillery Brigade.
  266th Field Artillery Brigade detached from 53rd Division.
60th Division.
  60th Divisional Artillery.
  3·7-in. Howitzer Battery.
  1 18-pdr. Battery Yeomanry Mounted Division.
74th Division.
  74th Divisional Artillery.
53rd Division.
  53rd Divisional Artillery (less 266th F.A. Brigade).
  1 Heavy Artillery Battery (60-pdr.).
  1 Field Artillery Brigade, 10th Division.
10th Division.
  10th Divisional Artillery (less 1 Field Artillery Brigade, and 1 4·5-in. Howitzer Battery).

(ii) The task of the XCVI Heavy Artillery Group, which in the first instance will be in position west of and in the vicinity of Abu Yahia and North of the Fara–Beersheba road at Taweil el Habari (approximate positions shown on Tracing " A ") will be to neutralize the enemy's artillery. Fire to be opened as soon as the light will permit of observation. One 6-in howitzer battery will bombard a portion of the enemy's works prior to the attack of the 60th Division on the advanced line near Point 1070.[1] Objective to be selected and communicated to the O.C. XCVI Heavy Artillery Group by G.O.C. 60th Division. This battery will revert to counter-battery work under the orders of the O.C. XCVI Heavy Artillery Group as soon as the infantry assault on the advanced works takes place.

(iii) The Corps Field Artillery Brigade (266th Brigade R.F.A.) which moves into position north of the Wadi es Sabe in Squares B.6 and

---

[1] Point 1069 on Map 5.

B.12 under the orders of the G.O.C. 74th Division, will be placed temporarily at his disposal. The Corps Commander cannot at present foresee the manner in which he may employ this brigade during the later stages of the action, and Corps headquarters will be informed before its batteries are committed to more forward positions from which they cannot be extricated.

During both stages of the attack G.O.C. 74th Division will employ a portion of this brigade in combination with the right artillery brigade of the 53rd Division to bombard the enemy's line north of the Wadi es Sabe (see para. 4 [a]). The bombardment will be sufficiently intense to make the enemy believe that the frontage of the main attack extends north of the Wadi es Sabe. Particular attention must be paid to keeping down flanking fire against the left of the 74th Division as it moves forward during the second stage of the attack from enemy works Y.58 to salient at Y.49 both inclusive.

The G.O.C.R.A. XX Corps, after consultation with the G.O's.C. 74th Division and 53rd Division, will allot a dividing line between the zones of the Corps Field Artillery Brigade and the right artillery brigade of the 53rd Division for bombardment of the enemy's line north of the Wadi es Sabe.

(iv) After the capture of the enemy's main line, some guns of the 60th and 74th Divisions will be allotted the task of dealing with the enemy's works north and south of the front of attack in case the enemy holds his ground on the flanks, while others move forward as soon as possible to the conquered position to pursue the enemy with fire and to deal with hostile counter-attacks.

6. *Dispositions Evening Z Day.*—It is essential to continue the advance at the earliest possible moment north and north-west of Beersheba against the enemy's positions south of the Wadi es Sheria and south and south-east of Abu Hureira, and with this object in view water development at Beersheba will be proceeded with immediately after the capture of the town.

Although it is impossible to lay down the movements of the XX Corps on Z day after the capture of the enemy trenches, the Corps Commander will aim at the following distribution by the evening of Z day.

> *I.C.C. Brigade.*—North of and covering Beersheba on a line astride the Beersheba–'Ain Kohle track, sufficiently far forward to deny the enemy positions from which the town can be shelled.
>
> *60th Division.*—On the conquered position, with some troops in Beersheba to begin water development as soon as possible.
>
> *74th Division.*—In the triangle formed by the Fara–Beersheba and Gaza–Beersheba roads, east of Kh. es Sufi, with one Artillery Brigade and one Infantry Brigade in readiness to move to the support of the I.C.C., routes for which will be reconnoitred as early as possible.
>
> *53rd Division* (with 1 Infantry Brigade and 1 Artillery Brigade 10th Division attached).—On the line Kh. es Sufi–Bir Imleih– El Girheir with outposts covering the left of the 74th Division and holding the approaches from the Wadi es Sufi and Wadi Imleih.
>
> *10th Division* (less 1 Infantry Brigade and 1 Artillery Brigade).— About Shellal.
>
> *XX Corps Cavalry Regiment.*—Withdrawn to water in the Mirtaba Valley.

It is hoped that at least 1 Cavalry Division will be in the water area about Bir Salim Abu Irqaiyiq and Tell es Sabe, holding the approaches to Beersheba from the east and watching the Hebron road.

APPENDICES 8 AND 9

7. The outline of plans for the second stage in XX Corps G.O. 14/4 of 28th September 1918, and G.O. 14/7 of 11th October 1917 cannot be developed further at present and will depend on the course of events between now and the evening of Z day.

8. Acknowledge.

W. H. BARTHOLOMEW,
Br.-General, General Staff, XX Corps.

Headquarters XX Corps.
22nd October 1917.
Issued at 12 noon.

APPENDIX 9.
Secret.

XX CORPS ORDER No. 12.

BY

LIEUT.-GENERAL SIR P. W. CHETWODE, Bart., K.C.M.G., C.B., D.S.O., Commanding XX Corps.

Headquarters XX Corps,
26th October 1917.

Reference Maps : Palestine 1/20,000 ; 1/125,000.

1. (a) On Z day (date to be communicated later) the G.O.C. **Maps 4, 5.** XX Corps intends to attack the enemy's works west and south-west of Beersheba in co-operation with the Desert Mounted Corps, whose primary objectives are the enemy's defences from the south-east to the north-east of Beersheba and the town of Beersheba.

(b) After the capture of Beersheba, the task of the Desert Mounted Corps is to drive the enemy off any positions within artillery range of the town, enveloping and attacking his left flank if he retreats in a northerly or north-westerly direction.

2. The attack by the 60th and 74th Divisions of the XX Corps and Desert Mounted Corps on the defences of Beersheba will be carried out in accordance with paragraphs 1 to 5 (inclusive) of the XX Corps Scheme of Operations already issued under XX Corps No. G.O.14/9 dated 22nd October 1917.

3. After the capture of the enemy's works by the 60th and 74th Divisions, the I.C.C. Brigade will be prepared to march to relieve the Desert Mounted Corps on the high ground north of Beersheba : dividing line between the two Corps a line from the Mosque at Beersheba through Kh. el Omry (latter place inclusive to the XX Corps).

4 (i) The 53rd Division may be called upon to attack the enemy's western flank to hinder or prevent his retreat by routes leading north or north-west from Beersheba.

The crossings over the Wadi es Sufi will be reconnoitred early on the morning of Z day with a view to the rapid movement of troops by routes through and south of Kh. Abu Irqaiyiq.

(ii) The Corps Reserve (10th Division less 1 Brigade) will be prepared to move from 6.30 a.m. on Z day.

5. The Yeomanry Mounted Division, which is in G.H.Q. Reserve about Shellal and Hisea from 5 a.m. on Z day, furnishes posts to watch the area between the Wadi Ghazze and the Wadi esh Sheria north of an east-and-west line through El Imara. Headquarters of Division at D.15.d.

6. No maps other than the following will be used:—
   Palestine : 1/20,000, 1/63,360.
   Rafah and Palestine : 1/125,000.

All ranks are forbidden to carry into action letters, papers, orders, or sketches which would give useful information to the enemy.

7. Separate instructions have already been issued as to :—

Ammunition Supply.	Prisoners of War.
Employment of Aircraft.	Liaison.
Communications.	Distribution of Pioneer Labour and Water Development.

8. Watches will be synchronized from Advanced Corps headquarters at 5.15 p.m. on Z — 1 day.

9. Reports to Advanced Corps headquarters at El Baqqar (A.5.d.) from 5 p.m. Z — 1 day.

10. Acknowledge.

W. H. BARTHOLOMEW,
Brigadier-General, General Staff, XX Corps.

Issued at 10 p.m.

APPENDIX 10.

Secret.

DESERT MOUNTED CORPS OPERATION ORDER No. 2.

26th October 1917.

Reference Map : 1/125,000.

Information.

Maps 4, 5. 1. The Army will attack on Z day, with the primary object of
Sketch 3.   capturing Beersheba.[1]

. . . .

Yeomanry Mounted Division passes from the command of G.O.C. XX Corps into G.H.Q. reserve at 5 a.m. on Z day. Special instructions regarding its rôle will be issued direct by General Headquarters.

Intention.

2. The tasks of the Desert Mounted Corps are to
   (a) Attack Beersheba from the east so as to envelop the enemy's left rear ; and
   (b) Seize as much water supply as possible in order to form a base for future operations northwards.

Orders to Troops.

3. In consequence, the Corps will move on the evening of Z — 1 day in accordance with the attached march table,[2] and with the following tasks :—

---

[1] Here follows the rôle of the XX Corps, and the statement that the defences of Gaza will be bombarded.

[2] It has not been thought necessary to attach the march table, as the moves are given in detail in the text, and are shown on Sketch 3.

APPENDIX 10

(a) *A. and N.Z. Mounted Division*

1st Objective :—High ground north of and overlooking the line Bir el Hamam–Bir Salim Abu Irqaiyiq–Point 1020, East of Bir Hassan.

2nd Objective :—Bir es Sqati–Tell es Sabe.

The aim will be to advance in strength against this objective at 9 a.m.

Protective detachments (to be reduced to a minimum) will be left to watch for a hostile advance between the Tell el Mila road (inclusive) and Bir es Sqati (exclusive).

A Brigade (less 1 regiment) will hold the ground about Bir es Sqati and Kh. el Jubbein.

3rd Objective :—Point 1020, north-east of Sabe–Point 970–Mosque.

Main body of the Division will not advance to this objective till orders are received from Corps headquarters.

(b) *1 Regiment and 2 Machine Guns Australian Mounted Division*
will march immediately behind the two leading brigades A. and N.Z. Mounted Division. On reaching the track junction W/N.1,[1] this detachment will, unless it receives orders to the contrary from G.O.C. A. and N.Z. Mounted Division, move westwards in order to take up a position astride track W. about 2 miles from Iswaiwin.

It will be prepared to act as either advanced or left flank guard to Australian Mounted Division, according to circumstances. It will also endeavour to get into signalling communication with 7th Mounted Brigade, and to locate the enemy's left flank about Ras Ghannam. It will revert to the command of G.O.C. Australian Mounted Division as soon as it leaves track N.1.

(c) *Australian Mounted Division* (less 1 Regiment, 2 Machine Guns, and 1 Section L.A.M. Battery)
will concentrate near Iswaiwin by 9.30 a.m. and will send forward reconnaissances in order to be prepared for an advance either westwards on Beersheba or northwards to assist A. and N.Z. Mounted Division.

1 Brigade will come into Corps reserve.

The Divisional Commander and the Commander of the Brigade in Corps reserve will report to Corps headquarters as soon as the head of their respective formations reaches the position of assembly.

(d) *7th Mounted Brigade*
will, by 6.30 a.m., establish observation posts on the line Point 1210, 1 miles due south of Ras Ghannam–Goz en Naam.

The Brigade will be assembled south of this line ready to act in accordance with instructions which are issued separately. Signalling communication will be established with Australian Division south-west of Khashm Zanna, and close touch maintained with XX Corps Cavalry Regiment.

1 Section L.A.M. Battery and 1 Ford Car are placed at the disposal of G.O.C. in accordance with the next sub-paragraph.

---

[1] Just north of Iswaiwin. N. track was that from Asluj to Bir Arara, N.1 track that from Thaffa to Khashm Zanna, W. track that from north of Iswaiwin to Beersheba.

APPENDIX 10

(e) *1 Section L.A.M. Battery Australian Mounted Division and 1 Car No. 7 Light Car Patrol*

will move, under instructions to be issued by A.D.A.S., so as to reach Goz Itwail es Semin at 6 a.m. They will then come under the orders of G.O.C. 7th Mounted Brigade.

Transport.

4. (a) B Echelons (including those of Ammunition Column) remain at the disposal of the Divisional and 7th Mounted Brigade Commanders, but will not be moved before daylight.

(b) Camel Water Convoys for A. & N.Z. and Australian Mounted Divisions will move in rear of all fighting troops, under orders to be issued by Divisions, so as to be at the track junction M/N. at 8 a.m.

(c) Trains will move under instructions to be issued by D. A. & Q.M.G.

(d) No moves, other than those laid down in the march table and sub-para. (b) above, will take place between 5 p.m. Z − 1 day and 5 a.m. Z day.

Traffic.

5. (a) During halts all troops will clear the road or track. The road must be cleared at all times for staff officers, gallopers, and despatch riders.

(b) Transport which becomes blocked must at once clear the route for fighting troops.

Administration of Beersheba.

6. G.O's.C. A. & N.Z. and Australian Mounted Divisions will each tell off the following details for duty in Beersheba :—

1 Field Officer as Administrative Commandant ; 1 Officer as adjutant; 4 M.M.P.

In the event of details of both divisions being in Beersheba, G.O.C. Australian Mounted Division will be responsible for the administration of the town until further orders are received.

Work on water supply in the town itself will be taken over as early as possible by the XX Corps, but measures for water reconnaissance and protection of wells will at once be taken by the first troops entering.

Prisoners.

7. Prisoners can be evacuated either to Corps headquarters, where the A.P.M. will establish a collecting station, or to Infantry Divisional collecting stations, the locations of which will be notified by A.P.M.

Aerial Reconnaissance.

8. R.F.C. Liaison Officer will arrange for reconnaissances in accordance with instructions which are communicated separately.

Maps and Papers.

9. Care will be taken to ensure that no officer or man goes forward in possession of maps or papers (except such as are essential to the conduct of operations) which, if captured, would give information of value to the enemy.

Time.

10. Watches will be synchronized, under arrangements to be made by A.D.A.S., at 1 p.m. on Z − 1 day.

Reports.

11. Reports :—

(a) Up to 1 a.m. Asluj Station.
(b) Thence to 6 a.m. cross-roads N/N. 1.
(c) Thence onward track junction N.1/W.

The above times are liable to alteration.

R. G. HOWARD-VYSE,
Brigadier-General, General Staff, Desert Mounted Corps.

APPENDIX 11.

XXI CORPS ORDER No. 11.

24th October 1917.

Ref. Maps : Palestine 1/63,360 ; Gaza 1/20,000 ; Trench Map 1/10,000.

1. The disposition of the enemy is given in the attached sketch. Map 6.

2. The Corps Commander intends to attack the enemy's right flank from Umbrella Hill (inclusive) to the Sea, on a night (X — 1/X) and at an hour (Z) to be named later. The furthest objectives to be seized and consolidated will include Umbrella Hill, El Arish Redoubt, Magdhaba Trench, Gibraltar, Island Wood, Rafah, Yunis, and Balah Trenches and Sheikh Hasan. Advanced posts are to be sent to occupy trenches in G. 21, 22, and 28. Every endeavour is to be made to push beyond the limits of these objectives provided the tactical situation is thereby improved.

3. The attack will be carried out under the orders of Major-General Hare, commanding 54th Division. The following troops will be placed at his disposal for this purpose :—

> 54th Division.
> 52nd Divisional Artillery.
> 156th Infantry Brigade ⎫
> 412th Field Company R.E. ⎬ 52nd Division.
> 1st Lowland Field Ambulance ⎭
> 211th Machine-Gun Company.
> 1 Battery 9th B.M. Artillery Brigade.

After the capture of Sheikh Hasan, 1 mobile section 9th B.M. Artillery Brigade may be withdrawn under Corps instructions.

4. The attack on Umbrella Hill is to be carried out as a distinct operation and some hours in advance of the main attack.

5. A bombardment of the enemy's defences from Fryer Hill *via* Outpost Hill to the Sea will be carried out from X — 6 day onwards. His wire will be cut during this bombardment from Middlesex Hill to the Sea.

6. The attack will be supported by the Royal Navy, the Corps Heavy Artillery, Tank Detachment, and such guns of the Machine-Gun Companies in the Edinburgh and Carnarvon Sectors as can be spared from defensive purposes.

From X — 3 day (inclusive) all demands for Naval co-operation will be made through the Senior Naval Officer, Marine View.

7. The routes and objectives of the tanks will be :—

> (a) 1 tank Philistine Hill–Magdhaba–Crested Rock–Island Wood.
> (b) 1 tank El Arish Redoubt–Maghaba, then as in (a).
> (c) 1 tank Rafah Redoubt ; Rafah, Yunis, Balah Trenches–Sheikh Hasan.
> Not to move north of Rafah Redoubt before Z + 55,
> nor of John Trench before Z + 110,
> nor of Balah Trench before Z + 125.
> (d) 1 tank Rafah Junior–Rafah Redoubt–Rafah, Yunis, Balah Trenches–Sheikh Hasan.
> Times as for (c).

(e) 1 tank Beach Post–Cricket Redoubt–Gun Hill–Sheikh Hasan–
Trenches in G. 21, 22, and 28.
Not to move north of Beach Post before Z + 55,
nor of Cricket Redoubt before Z + 110,
not to reach Gun Hill before Z + 120.

(f) 1 tank Sea Post–Beach Post–Cricket Redoubt–Gun Hill–
Sheikh Hasan–Trenches in G. 21, 22, and 28.
Times as for (e).

All tanks will return to Sheikh Ajlin on completion of duty.
The H.Q. Tank Detachment will be at Marine View. Two tanks will be in reserve at Sheikh Ajlin.

8. A contact aeroplane will pass over the line as follows :—

5.45 a.m. Umbrella Hill to Rafah Trench (both inclusive),
6.45 a.m. Rafah Trench to Sheikh Hasan (both inclusive).

Flares are to be lit by troops in the furthest objectives of the lines named, when called upon by Klaxon horn.

9. The following troops will be in Corps reserve :—

Regent's Park .. Cdr. Brig.-Gen. C. R. Harbord.
(Q.10) ..   .. I.S.C. Bde. (less 2 squadrons).
            Corps Cavalry Regiment.
Regent's Park .. Cdr. Brig.-Gen. Hamilton Moore.
            157th Infantry Bde.
            413th Field Coy. R.E.
            2nd Lowland Field Ambulance.
Wadi Simeon .. Cdr. Brig.-Gen. H. J. Huddleston.
(T.5) ..   .. 232nd Infantry Bde.
            2 Sections 495th Field Coy. R.E.
            1 Section 123rd Field Ambulance.

The G.O.C. Sheikh Abbas Sector may call upon 2 battalions of the Corps Reserve troops at the Wadi Simeon for the defence of his line, notifying Corps H.Q. of his action.

10. The following subsidiary operations will be carried out on the dates and by the formations stated :—

Night	Formation	Operation
X − 8/X − 7.	75th Division.	Advance our line from direction of Mansura to the Donga (R.11).
X − 2/X − 1.	75th Division.	Raid on Outpost Hill.
X − 1/X	Composite Force.	Advance our line towards Atawine Redoubt.
X/X + 1.	75th Division.	Raid on Outpost Hill.

11. From X − 6 to X − 2 day (both inclusive) the official time will be sent out daily at 2 p.m. on the telephone by the General Staff to all concerned.

From X − 1 day (inclusive) watches will be synchronized at 2 p.m. at Advanced Corps H.Q. Representatives will attend from all Divisions, O.C. Heavy Artillery, and the I.S.C. Bde. The G.O.C. 54th Division will arrange for synchronization with the O.C. Tank Detachment.

12. Advanced Corps H.Q. will be established on Raspberry Hill at 4 p.m. on X − 1 day.

E. T. HUMPHREYS,
Brigadier-General, General Staff, XXI Corps.

Issued at 9 p.m.

APPENDIX 12.
Secret.

XX CORPS ORDER No. 13.

BY

LIEUT.-GENERAL SIR P. W. CHETWODE, BT., K.C.M.G., C.B., D.S.O., Commanding XX Corps.

Headquarters XX Corps.
5th November 1917.

Reference Maps : 1-in. (Palestine) ; 1/20,000.

1. The G.O.C. XX Corps intends to resume the attack on November Maps 4, 8. 6th, with the object of securing the Sheria water supply and capturing the Qawuqa trench system as far as and inclusive of the long communication trench S.78–S.56 inclusive, 1¾ miles south-east of Hureira. The attack must be pressed with the utmost rapidity and determination, as the enemy must be given no respite until his resistance is broken down, and it is essential to secure the water at Sheria before nightfall.

2. The Desert Mounted Corps, to which the 53rd Division will be attached temporarily from 6 a.m. on November 6th, is allotted the following tasks :—
  (a) To protect the right of the XX Corps.
  (b) To take advantage of any retirement of the enemy to press forward and seize the Nejile and Jemmame water supplies.

The 53rd Division is about 'Ain Kohle, and will extend its left so as to occupy the general line Kuweilfe–Rujm el Dhib. The Yeomanry Mounted Division of the Desert Mounted Corps is to be concentrated south-west of 'Ain Kohle by 7 a.m. on November 6th, ready to close the gap between the 53rd Division and 74th Division, which attacks on the right of the XX Corps, and to take advantage of any enemy retirement to push forward to the line Kh. Abu Rasheid–Ez Zubala [1]—and thence to the right of the 74th Division.

The artillery of the Yeomanry Mounted Division will march at the head of its division to the position of concentration and will be placed in the first instance at the disposition of the G.O.C. 53rd Division, under special instructions to be given by the G.O.C. Desert Mounted Corps.

3. Divisions will move as follows to positions of assembly, to be reached before dawn on November 6th [2] :—
  (i) *74th Division.*—Leading brigade to positions west of the Wadi Union, as near as possible to the flank of the enemy works running eastwards from the railway ; the remaining brigades of the division being echeloned on its right flank in readiness to meet any counter-attack by enemy troops from a north-westerly direction.
  (ii) *60th Division.*—Leading brigade in position on the enemy's outpost position in W.3 and W.4.
  (iii) During the night November 5/6th the 10th Division will concentrate between the left of the 60th Division and the Gaza–Beersheba road at Point 570, one infantry brigade to be in position by 4 a.m. on November

---

[1] These places are north of the Wadi Khuweilfe, and 5 and 3 miles respectively east of the railway.

[2] Positions and objectives are clearly marked on Map 8, so that there is no need of the map references given in the following paragraphs.

6th, to attack on the left of the 60th Division ; remaining infantry of the division in covered positions near culvert in R.12.d.

4. (i) 74th, 60th and 10th Divisions of the XX Corps will attack on November 6th in the order named from right to left, tasks and objectives as below, 74th Division being the leading and directing division :—

74th Division, First Objective.—The line of enemy's works east of the railway at Point P.21.b.55. After reaching the railway the tasks of the 74th Division will be :—

(a) To protect the right of the 60th Division and drive the enemy out of Sheria ;

(b) To seize the high ground north of Sheria to protect the water supply ;

(c) To assist as far as possible the attack of the 60th Division on the enemy work west of the railway by such artillery as can be spared.

60th Division, First Objective.—Works of the Qawuqa system west of the railway and north of a line through P.27 central and O.24 central as far as the communication trench S.78–S.56 inclusive. After attaining the first objective the task of the 60th Division will be to assist if necessary the 74th Division to secure the high ground north of Sheria and covering the water supply at that place.

10th Division.—The 10th Division will employ one infantry brigade, supported by all the artillery of the division, to attack the works of the Qawuqa system south of the boundary allotted to the 60th Division. The remaining two brigades of the 10th Division will be concentrated behind the brigade allotted to the attack, will be in Corps reserve, and will not be employed without the sanction of Corps headquarters.

(ii) The attack of the 74th Division will be made as early as possible on November 6th, the infantry of the 60th and 10th Divisions moving forward during the initial stages sufficiently to cover suitable positions from which their artillery can begin the preliminary bombardment of the Qawuqa system.

G.O's.C. 10th and 60th Divisions will report to Corps headquarters when they consider the artillery preparation to be complete.

(iii) Exact boundaries between divisions to be arranged between G.O's.C. concerned.

5. The Heavy Artillery Group, less 1 60-pdr. battery attached to 53rd Division, will move into positions north of the Gaza–Beersheba road to support the attack under the orders of the G.O.C.R.A. XX Corps, who will allot objectives to the Group Commander.

6. The closest signal communication and liaison will be maintained between divisions, responsibility for connection being from left to right.

7. Orders for movements of trains and camel convoys will be issued by the D.A. & Q.M.G. XX Corps.

8. Reports to XX Corps Advanced headquarters at Beersheba.

9. Acknowledge.

W. H. BARTHOLOMEW,
Brigadier-General, General Staff, XX Corps.

Issued at 8.30 a.m.

APPENDIX 13.
TELEGRAPHIC ORDERS BY DESERT MOUNTED CORPS.

Anzac, Ausdiv., Yeodiv., 5th Bde., 60th Div., 3rd L.H. Bde., R.F.C. Liaison Officer, G.H.Q., XX Corps, XXI Corps, 74th Div., G.O.C.R.A., D.A. & Q.M.G.

G.A.208.   6th November (11.45 p.m.).

Operation Order No. 4. XX Corps were everywhere successful to-day and are now on the line Kh. Umm el Bakr–Kh. Barrata–G. central [1]–G.25 central–O.17. Desert Mounted Corps, less troops under Major-General Barrow (vide G.A.204) and with 60th Division attached will advance to-morrow to secure the water at Jemmame and Huj with a view to cutting off or pursuing the Gaza garrison. Advance will proceed with the utmost vigour. Anzac Mounted Division will pass through our infantry west of Kh. Umm el Bakr at 5 a.m., advanced guard to Corps: 1st objective Kh. Umm Ameidat–Kh. Shuteiwy el Oseibi. Ammunition dump at Ameidat Station to be destroyed. Reconnaissances on Nejile and Jemmame. Yeomanry Field Squadron is attached this division. Ausdiv. will march at 2 a.m., first destination south bank of Wadi Sheria west of railway. 5th Brigade will march at same time to same destination by east of railway. 3rd L.H. Brigade will march at 7 a.m. to Irqaiyiq and thence to Sheria, to which place orders will be sent; march at 5 miles per hour. 60th Div. as soon as it is watered and fed will be directed *via* Kh. Zuheilika on Huj with object of supporting left flank of right group. The echelons of ammunition columns are placed at disposal of G.O.C.R.A. The remainder of echelon trains camel convoys will move under orders of D.A. & Q.M.G. The aerial reconnaissance of area Kh. Zubala–Nejile–Jemmame–Hureira has been ordered for 7 a.m.

Maps 2, 4, 8.

APPENDIX 14.

Secret.
XXI CORPS ORDER No. 12.

12th November 1917.

Reference: 1-in. Map.

1. The enemy holds the line Beit Jibrin (D.2)–Tell et Turmus (K.24)–El Qastine (K.11)–Yazur (H.28)–Burqa (B.23). It is estimated that he has 13,000 men on this extended line of 12 miles. These men have all been battered and have taken part in the recent retreat. He has no reserves.

Map 9. Sketch 10.

2. The 75th Division is on the front Es Suafir el Gharbiye–Beit Duras. The 52nd Division extends the front to the north-west as far as Sdud (inc.) and is attacking Burqa to-day. The Desert Corps protects both flanks of the XXI Corps.

---

[1] Should probably be G.26 central. That point and G.25 central are both just north of the Wadi esh Sheria. As has been explained, there were in fact no troops of the XX Corps north of the wadi at the time this order was issued.

3. The Corps Commander intends to attack the enemy to-morrow, the final objective being the Jaffa–Jerusalem railway.

4. The 75th Division will attack on the line Tell et Turmus–El Qastine–Yazur (all inc.). It is to be noted that the high ground at Tell et Turmus commands El Qastine.

As soon as the above line has been captured the 75th Division will seize El Mesmiye (J.32).

5. The 52nd Division will attack the line Yazur (exc.)–Beshshit (Y.16) (inc.), and will then advance and take Qatra (Z.13).

6. The attacks mentioned in paras. 4 and 5 will commence at 8 a.m. A bombardment of the enemy's defences is to begin at 7 a.m.

7. The Desert Mounted Corps is co-operating as follows :—

(*a*) 1 division on right flank which is directed on Et Tine (L.5)–Qezaze (P.23) and Junction Station (P.7). The right boundary of the 75th Division, after the capture of Tell et Turmus, will be the El Qastine–Junction Station road.

(*b*) 2 divisions on left flank directed on Beshshit and Yibna (V.22). The left boundary of the 52nd Division will be the Burqa–Beshshit–Qatra road (inc.).

8. One infantry brigade 54th Division will be in Corps reserve. It will reach Julis (F.18) at 9 a.m. 13th inst.

9. As positions are seized, the artillery is to be prepared to move rapidly forward to positions further in advance.

10. All localities inside the zone of operations of divisions which are occupied by Desert Mounted Corps will be taken over by divisions at the earliest possible moment so as to release the cavalry. The 52nd Division will seize the high ground north of Yibna and consolidate a strong position astride the Yibna–Jaffa road.

11. A pause will be made on the line El Mesmiye–Qatra sufficient to enable guns to be brought forward, ammunition replenished, and fresh troops to be pushed forward to the final objective Junction Station–El Mansura. The point of junction of divisions will be about Square J.8. The G.O.C. 52nd Division will be responsible that touch is maintained with the 75th Division.

12. On moving forward, after the pause mentioned in para. 11, the final objective will be :—

75th Division :—Junction Station–Umm Kelka [1] (inc.).
52nd Division :—Umm Kelka (exc.) to Wadi el Male (inc.). This line is to be strongly consolidated.

13. All ranks are to be given a hot meal before the attack commences.

14. Contact aeroplanes will pass over at 7 and 9 a.m., 12 noon, and 4 p.m. Troops will wave their hats when called upon by Klaxon horn.

15. Prisoners are to be sent to Es Suafir el Gharbiye or Sdud, from which places they will be collected by squadrons of the I.S.C. Brigade and escorted to Beit Hanun, where they will be handed over to the 54th Division.

16. Ammunition dumps have been established at Julis and Hamame (Z.12).

17. Battle headquarters of 75th Division will be on hill ½ mile south-west of Es Suafir el Gharbiye.

---

[1] Not on maps. About one mile south of El Mansura.

Battle headquarters of 52nd Division will be at Sdud.

18. Corps Battle headquarters will open on hill ½ mile south-west of Es Suafir el Gharbiye at 8 a.m. A visual signalling station will be established there.

19. Acknowledge.

E. T. HUMPHREYS,
Brigadier-General, General Staff, XXI Corps.

Issued at 1.30 p.m.

APPENDIX 15.

Secret.

DESERT MOUNTED CORPS OPERATION ORDER No. 7.

12th November 1917.

Reference Maps : 1/250,000 ; *Jerusalem.*

Information.

1. (*a*) It is estimated that the enemy has 13,000 men on the line Beit Jibrin–El Qastine–Burqa.

Map 9.
Sketch 10.

(*b*) XXI Corps is on the front Tell et Turmus–Sudd, with 75th Division on the right and 52nd Division on the left.

Intention.

2. Desert Mounted Corps and XXI Corps will attack to-morrow with the object of securing the railway junction N.N.E. of Qezaze.[1]

3. XXI Corps will attack at 8 a.m., with a preliminary bombardment at 7 a.m.

First Objective :—Line El Mesmiye–Qatra.

Second Objective :—Station N.N.E. of Qezaze and El Mansura.

A halt will be made on the first objective sufficient to allow of guns and fresh troops being brought up.

4. Desert Mounted Corps will co-operate by vigorous action in advance of the flanks of the infantry.

Final Objective :—A line from a point on the railway due east of El Mansura to Ne'ane.

Orders to Troops.

3. (*a*) *Australian Mounted Division* will be responsible for the protection of the right flank of the infantry. As soon as the enemy shows signs of weakening it will push forward with the objective of Qezaze and Junction Station.

Dividing line between Australian Mounted Division and 75th Division is El Qastine–'Amwas road, inclusive to 75th Division.

(*b*) *Yeomanry Mounted Division*, with I.C.C. Brigade attached, will, with its main advanced guard, pass Tell el Kharrube[2] at 8 a.m.

First Objective :—Beshshit, exclusive, to Yibna, inclusive.

Second Objective :—'Aqir, inclusive, to bridgehead east of Yibna, inclusive.

A detachment will be left in Yibna until relieved by the Infantry.

---

[1] Junction Station is actually north by west of Qezaze.
[2] A mile and a half south-west of Yibna.

Dividing line between 52nd Division and mounted troops is road Burqa–Beshshit–Qatra–El Mansura, all inclusive to 52nd Division.

(c) *A. & N.Z. Mounted Division* will be in a position of readiness south-west of Sdud by 8 a.m. It will follow Yeomanry Mounted Division closely, prepared either to support it or to move forward to the final objective, which will be as given in para. 4. The Division will be under Corps headquarters, but in case of there being a risk of delay in communication with Corps headquarters, G.O.C. Yeomanry Mounted Division will issue instructions to A. & N.Z. Mounted Division direct.

(d) *7th Mounted Brigade* will be in Corps reserve and will be in a concealed position west of Beit Affe by 8 a.m.

(e) *I.C.C. Brigade* will be at Sdud by 6 a.m. G.O.C. will report to G.O.C. Yeomanry Mounted Division at Pt. 140, Sdud, as soon as the head of his Brigade arrives.

6. XXI Corps will take over at earliest possible moment the defence of any localities inside its zone which are occupied by Desert Mounted Corps beforehand. It will also, as soon as possible after its capture, place a garrison in Yibna and on the high ground north of it.

7. G.O's.C. both Yeomanry and A. & N.Z. Mounted Divisions will be prepared, as soon as the infantry have consolidated the position of El Mansura, and on receipt of orders from Corps headquarters, to move on Er Ramle and Lydda in order to capture prisoners and do as much damage as possible to the enemy.

8. Arrangements must be made for the demolition of the bridge over the Wadi Merubba north of Junction Station immediately the station is reached ; also for demolition of railway line to greatest possible distance northwards.

9. Reports to Point 331 until further notice. Mounted messengers may also be sent to the hill south-west of Es Suafir el Gharbiye, at which place the Corps Commander will be. The Report Centre will afterwards move *via* El Qastine–'Amwas road.

10. Acknowledge.

R. G. HOWARD-VYSE,
Brigadier-General, General Staff, Desert Mounted Corps.

APPENDIX 16.

Secret.

XXI CORPS ORDER No. 14.

18th November 1917.

Reference Map : 1 in. to 1 mile.

Maps 2, 10. 1. (a) The Yeomanry Division moved to-day on Shilta (J.14) and Beit 'Ur et Tahta (O.33). It moves to-morrow on Bire (U.22).

(b) The enemy is in small scattered parties, with some artillery and machine guns, in the hills between Latron [1] (M.9) and the Jerusalem–Bire road. He holds a line covering 'Amwas and Latron from K.35–M.9. He also has trenches in M.21, M.20 and M.25 and a gun about M.21.d.

Strong enemy detachments were to-day in Jimzu (B.12.).

He is evacuating Jerusalem, his troops and transport moving north along the Bire road.

---

[1] 1 mile south-west of 'Amwas.

APPENDIX 16

2. The Corps Commander intends to advance to-morrow with the 52nd and 75th Divisions on the line Qaryet el 'Inab (S.29)–Beit Liqya (Q.13) and, on the 20th November, he proposes to get astride the Jerusalem –Bire road, in the neighbourhood of Bire, and cut off the troops retreating from Jerusalem.

No operations are to be undertaken within a six-mile radius of Jerusalem.

3. The following moves will be completed by 4 p.m. to-morrow :—

(a) *75th Division* will attack enemy's line at Latron and 'Amwas and seize those places by noon. Headquarters and two Brigade Groups will then move forward to Qaryet el 'Inab, the other Brigade Group remaining at 'Amwas.

(b) *52nd Division* :—2 Brigade Groups will move from Lydda to Beit Liqya.

Headquarters and Brigade Group will move to Berfilya (H.28).

4. The 54th Division will act as a pivot to the operations of the rest of the XXI Corps and will hold and consolidate the places named below.

It will move as follows :—Headquarters and two Brigade Groups, also Heavy Battery, area Ramle–Lydda : Headquarters at Lydda. A garrison of not less than one battalion is to be detached to Beit Dejan (L.24).

One Brigade Group to Abu Shushe (D.27) sending one company to Junction Station as escort to prisoners.

5. The Heavy Battery now with the 75th Division will join the 54th Division at Sidun as soon as the line Latron–'Amwas has been captured. The G.O.C. 75th Division will inform the G.O.C. 54th Division of its despatch.

The Mountain Artillery now with 52nd Division will join the 75th Division at 'Amwas to-morrow.

The 75th Division will send a party to be at El Qubab (K.19) at noon to escort it.

G.O.C. 75th Division will notify Corps headquarters of the time it joins.

6. One Mounted Brigade, Australian Division, is protecting the right flank of the Corps.

The G.O.C. this brigade is to report to G.O.C. 75th Division to-night. He will keep in close touch with this Division throughout operations.

The reports of this brigade will be sent to Corps headquarters through the 75th Division.

7. An aeroplane will fly over the 'Amwas position about 6 a.m. and will drop its report at XXI Corps and 75th Division headquarters at 0.3.a.

Another aeroplane will fly over the area round Jimzu and drop its report at XXI Corps and 52nd Division headquarters at Lydda.

8. Prisoners of War will be sent to Junction Station.

9. Collecting Station will be at Junction Station.

10. Corps Battle headquarters will be established at El Qubab at 4 p.m. to-morrow. A visual signalling station will be established at Abu Shushe.

11. Acknowledge.

E. T. HUMPHREYS,
Brigadier-General, General Staff, XXI Corps.

Issued at 5.30 p.m.

APPENDIX 17.
Secret.

XX CORPS ORDER No. 17.

Advanced Headquarters XX Corps.
5th December 1917.

Reference : 1 in. Map.

Map 11.
Sketch 19.

1. The XX Corps, pivoting on the Nabi Samweil and Beit Izza defences, will attack the enemy south and west of Jerusalem, and the Corps Commander intends :—
   (a) To secure the general line Point 2670 Kh. Ras et Tawil (Z.7)–Nabi Samweil ;
   (b) To block the approaches to Jerusalem from Jericho.

2. The 53rd Division (less one brigade group) with the Corps Cavalry Regiment attached will advance on December 6th from the Dilbe area to the Bethlehem–Beit Jala area, which must be reached on December 7th.

3. (i) The attack of the XX Corps will be carried out on December 8th by the 53rd Division (less one brigade group), 60th Division, and 74th Division (less one brigade group), in the order named from right to left.
   (ii) The 53rd Division will protect the right flank of the Corps, operating under special instructions attached to this order.
   (iii) The dividing line between the 60th and 74th Divisions will be the 'Inab–Jerusalem road as far as Lifta (village and road inclusive to the 60th Division) and thence the Wadi Beit Hannina as far as Y.15.d.66.[1]

4. The attack will be divided into four stages, and the tasks and objectives of the 60th and 74th Divisions in each stage are as follows :—
   1st Stage.—The 60th Division will capture the enemy works between the railway in B.36 [1] and the 'Inab–Jerusalem road in Y.25.[1]
   74th Division will capture the enemy works covering Beit Iksa between the 'Inab–Jerusalem road in Y.25 and the Wadi el 'Abbeide (T.12.d).
   The commencement of the advance of the 74th Division will be timed by that of the 60th Division ; G.O.C. 60th Division to report to Corps headquarters by 8 a.m. on December 6th the hour at which his assault will take place.
   2nd Stage.—The 60th Division will advance to the line of the Jerusalem–Lifta road on the approximate front H.11.c.45–Lifta (inclusive).
   3rd Stage.—The 60th Division will advance to the general line of the track which leaves the Jerusalem–Nablus road at H.5.d.96 and runs through Y.28 to the Wadi Beit Hannina in Y.21.
   The 74th Division will advance to the spur which runs south-east from Nabi Samweil and on which is marked the word " Tombs " in square Y.8.c. and Kh. Ras el Bad in Square Y.14.b.
   4th Stage.—The 60th Division will advance to a line astride the Jerusalem–Nablus road about Shafat and push forward thence to secure the high ground about Kh. Ras et Tawil.
   The 74th Division will link up with the 60th Division, occupying Beit Hannina if the ground is suitable for this purpose.
   The G.O's.C. 53rd Division and 60th Division will arrange to send out patrols to establish communication, and will arrange for co-operation between the 53rd Division group east of Jerusalem (*vide* Instructions to

---

[1] As objectives and boundaries are shown on Map 11, it is unnecessary to endeavour to describe these points.

G.O.C. 53rd Division) and the right flank of the 60th Division north of Jerusalem.

5. The XCVI Heavy Artillery Group (less one 6-in. battery at Beit Liqya) will be placed from 9 a.m. on December 7th under the command of the G.O.C. 60th Division, who will be responsible for its employment in consultation with the G.O.C. Royal Artillery XX Corps, who will be at 60th Division headquarters.

6. Orders for movement of trains and convoys will be issued by D.A. & Q.M.G. XX Corps.

7. Reports to Advanced XX Corps at Latron.

8. Acknowledge.

L. R. SCHUSTER, MAJOR,
for
Brigadier-General, General Staff, XX Corps.

Issued at 4.30 p.m.

Secret.

INSTRUCTIONS TO G.O.C. 53RD DIVISION
REFERENCE XX CORPS ORDER NO. 17.

Ref.: 1 in. Map.

1. It is important that you should reach the line Sur Bahir–Sherafat **Map 11.** by dawn on December 8th, so that you may be in a position to co-operate **Sketch 19.** with the 60th Division.

Should the resistance of the enemy be so great that you are unable to reach this line in time to co-operate with the 60th Division, the General Officer Commanding 60th Division will be instructed to detach troops to advance east from about 'Ain Karim towards the Hebron–Jerusalem road to prevent the escape of the enemy on your front either by the Jerusalem–Nablus road or by the Jerusalem–Jericho road.

2. (i) In the more likely case that you are able to break the enemy's resistance south of the line Sur Bahir–Sherafat, you will advance on December 8th from the line Sur Bahir–Sherafat in two groups.

(ii) The right group will move at dawn towards Jerusalem and pass thence south of the town to seize a position to command the Jerusalem–Jericho road and to protect the XX Corps against attacks from the east and north-east of Jerusalem.

(iii) The left group will advance between the Hebron–Jerusalem road and the general line Sherafat–Malha–J of Jerusalem to co-operate with and protect the right flank of the 60th Division.

This group should endeavour to cross the railway as soon after dawn as possible.

The further progress of the group will be regulated by that of the 60th Division until the group reaches the area west of Jerusalem, whence it will make no further advance unless necessary to assist the right of the 60th Division in the further advance to its final objective.

3. As soon as you are able to pass troops round the southern and south-eastern outskirts of Jerusalem, you will push forward a portion of the Corps Cavalry Regiment to discover whether there are any formed bodies of the enemy on that road within a distance of six miles of Jerusalem. It is probable that on the day after the attack the regiment will be ordered to reconnoitre as far as the town of Jericho.

4. The city of Jerusalem will not be entered, and all movements by troops and vehicles will be restricted to roads passing outside the city.

5. You must make every possible use of visual signalling and other means to communicate your progress to 60th Division, and full information of the means which will be at your disposal is being forwarded under separate letter.

L. R. SCHUSTER, MAJOR,
for
Brigadier-General, General Staff, XX Corps.

Advanced Headquarters XX Corps.
5th December 1917.

APPENDIX 18.

Secret.

60TH DIVISION ORDER No. 60.[1]

5th December 1917.

Reference Map : 1/63,360.

Map 11.
Sketch 19.

1. The XX Corps is attacking the Jerusalem Defences from the west and south-west with the 60th and 74th Divisions. The 53rd Division is advancing on Jerusalem *via* the Hebron road.

The attack of the 60th and 74th Divisions will pivot on Nabi Samweil, 74th Division conforming to the advance of the 60th Division on its successive objectives, with the object of seizing the general line Point 2670–Nabi Samweil.

One brigade 53rd Division on Z day will advance on the general line Sherafat–Malha–J of Jerusalem, its rôle being to protect the right flank of the 60th Division.

Another brigade 53rd Division will advance direct on Jerusalem with the object of protecting the right flank of the Corps, eventually seizing a line covering the Jericho road and the north-east of Jerusalem.

2. *Concentration.*

On the night Z − 1/Z :

179th Brigade Group (179th Inf. Bde., 10th Mountain Battery, B/IX Mountain Battery, Section 521st Field Company R.E., Company Pioneers, Detachment 2/4th Field Ambulance) on a special scale of mule transport, will cross the Wadi es Sarar north of Setuf and seize the high ground in B.29, which will be reached under cover of darkness.

180th Brigade Group (180th Inf. Bde., 519th Field Company R.E., 2 platoons Pioneers, 2/5th Field Ambulance) will move to a position of assembly in B.2.d by the 'Inab–Jerusalem road, and thence to a position of deployment from which the Deir Yesin spur and the high ground east of Qalonye can be assaulted at dawn.

181st Brigade Group (181st Inf. Bde., 522nd Field Company R.E., less rear party, 2/6th Field Ambulance) will be concentrated in A.6.a and b by dawn on Z day, less M.G. Coy., which will be in position on the ridge south-east of Qastal to support the advance of the attacking brigades if required.

---

[1] This order is given as a good specimen of divisional orders in these conditions. It is of no more importance than that of the 74th Division, but to save space one only is printed.

3. *Objectives:*
(a) First Objective.—H.9 central–H.7b–H.1a.
(b) Second Objective.—Main road from H.11c.45 to Lifta.
(c) Third Objective.—Road junction H.5d.97, along ridge running through Y.28 central and 3rd N of Wadi Beit Hannina.
(d) Fourth Objective.—Point 2670 Ras et Tawil–Wadi Beit Hannina in Y.10c.

4. *Boundaries:*
(a) Boundary between 60th and 74th Divisions: 'Inab–Jerusalem road (inclusive to 60th Division) to H.2a, thence the Wadi Beit Hannina.
(b) Between 179th and 180th Infantry Brigades: Wadi running through B.18a and b, H.13a and b–road junction in H.9b–Shafat (inclusive to 180th Brigade) to the Nablus–Jerusalem road (inclusive to the 179th Brigade).

5. *Method of Attack.*
At dawn (Zero hour and Z day will be communicated later):
The two attacking brigades will capture the first objective. At the same hour 74th Division will assault the Beit Iksa trenches.
Pauses will be made at each objective to enable the infantry to reorganize. Except for these pauses the advance to the final objective will be as rapid as possible.
The 179th Infantry Brigade will be the directing brigade throughout the operation.
During the advance to the third objective, the left brigade of the 53rd Division, if it has room to act, will assist the right of the 60th Division. If it has not, it will go into reserve west of Jerusalem and will only be employed on the direct request of the B.G.C. 179th Infantry Brigade for support, should the latter require help in gaining his final objective.
In the event of the 53rd Division being held up in its advance on Sherafat and Malha, one battalion of the reserve brigade will be placed under the orders of B.G.C. 179th Brigade to protect the right flank.

6. *Artillery.*
The artillery plan will be issued separately. The artillery (except mountain) will be under divisional control at the commencement of the operation. Later, as soon as it is possible for batteries to get forward after the second objective has been taken, a group will come under the orders of the B.G.C. each attacking brigade.

7. *Mounted Troops.*
One squadron 10th Australian Light Horse, now at Er Ras, will march to El Khudr, so as to reach there one hour before dawn on Z day. This squadron will gain touch with the 53rd Division advancing along the Hebron road, and keep touch between the two divisions during the operation. 10th A.L.H. (less one squadron) will come under the orders of the XX Corps.

8. Priority on the Jerusalem road will be given to artillery and ammunition in that order.
Brigaded transport of 179th and 180th Infantry Brigades will remain in bivouacs until after the capture of the second objective and until Fergusson's and Bayley's Groups have moved forward. They can then move forward at the discretion of Brigadiers.
There will be no double banking on the main road, except by guns and ammunition wagons moving at a trot, and motor cars.

9. Arrangements will be made by the A.A. & Q.M.G. to ensure that the inhabitants of 'Inab, Soba and Setuf are confined to their villages during the night Z − 1/Z.

10. Watches will be synchronized on Z − 1 day at 12 noon and 5 p.m.

11. Divisional Report Centre will close in its present position at 4 a.m. on Z day and open at B.1.b.56 at the same hour.

12. Acknowledge.

A. C. TEMPERLEY,
Lieutenant-Colonel, General Staff.

Issued at 1 p.m.

APPENDIX 19.

Secret.

52ND DIVISIONAL SECTION ORDER No. 3.

17th December 1917.

Reference Maps : Palestine 1/63,360 and attached Hecto.

Map 12.
Sketch 20.

1. Information regarding the enemy's dispositions will be issued separately as and when received.

2. The 52nd Division will cross the 'Auja and establish itself on the right bank on the line Kh. Hadra–Sh. Muwannis–Tell er Ruqti in order to form a bridgehead from which further operations can be developed.

3. On night X − 1/X day, at a Zero hour to be notified later, the 52nd Division will cross the river as follows :—

(*a*) A Bn. 156th Inf. Bde. will cross the 'Auja in rafts and form a covering party to the N.E. for the construction of a light bridge capable of taking infantry in single file at Z.19c.–Crossing C.1.[1]

(*b*) A Bn. 157th Inf. Bde. will cross the 'Auja in rafts and form a covering party to the N.W. for the construction of a light bridge capable of taking infantry in single file at Z.19b.–Crossing C.2.[1]

(*c*) B and C Bns. 156th Inf. Bde. will cross the river by the bridge and form up under cover of the covering parties, D Bn. remaining in reserve.

(*d*) B and C Bns. 157th Inf. Bde. will cross by ford in Y.18,[2] according to time-table attached, D Bn. remaining in reserve.

4. (*a*) Whether the crossing is a surprise or not, all ground gained must be held, so that the programme shall be carried out without deviation.

(*b*) G.O.C. 155th Inf. Bde. should be prepared to demonstrate vigorously towards F.13[3] if our crossing is discovered, prior to Zero + 150, but he will not so demonstrate without a definite order from Div. H.Q.

(*c*) The guiding principle must be that not a single man more than is necessary is sent N. of the river until our objectives are attained.

5. Moves subsequent to those outlined in para. 3 will take place according to attached time-table, which must be adhered to.

6. The final objectives will be :—
155th Inf. Bde.   Kh. Hadra.
156th Inf. Bde.   High ground north of Muwannis and Slag Heap Farm.
157th Inf. Bde.   Tell er Ruqti.
As the ground is unreconnoitred, it is left to G.O's.C. Inf. Bdes.

---

[1] These crossings are shown on Map 12.
[2] At the river's mouth.
[3] East of Hadra Bridge and south of the 'Auja.

APPENDIX 19

discretion whether they will advance or modify their line on arrival at their objective or subsequently at daylight, bearing in mind the provisions of para. 2. Similarly, it is impossible to lay down dividing lines for the zones of attack. G.O's.C. Inf. Bdes. will concert measures at daylight to define their respective points of junction.

7. After the passage of 157th Inf. Bde. over the ford Y.18, B.G.R.A. will be prepared to push forward two batteries by the ford in Y.18 for the closer support of the infantry, when ordered to do so by Div. H.Q.

8. C.R.E. will arrange to throw one barrel bridge to take infantry in fours, as soon as possible after Muwannis is taken, near confluence of Nahr el Baride with Nahr el 'Auja. One bridge to take infantry in fours will be thrown as early as possible in Y.24b.[1]

9. On Zero − 1 day [2] an iron ration will be issued in lieu of the ordinary ration.

10. Not less than 200 rounds S.A.A. per man will be carried.

11. Watches will be synchronized at 10 a.m. and 4 p.m. on X − 1 day under arrangements to be made by O.C. Divl. Signal Coy.

12. Reports to Div. H.Q. at H.18 [3] every half-hour after Zero hour.

Acknowledge.

G. N. HOLDICH,
Lieut.-Colonel, G.S., 52nd Division.

Issued at 6 a.m., 18th.

---

[1] Near the mouth, south-east of the ford.
[2] *Sic.* X is used to define the day elsewhere in the orders.
[3] Tel Aviv, the Jewish township north-east of Jaffa.

APPENDIX 19

TIME TABLE.

Hour.	155th Inf. Bde.	156 Inf. Bde.	157th Inf. Bde.	Right Group R.A.	Left Group R.A.
Zero.	—	3 Bns. crossing river, rafts and bridges C.1, C.2.	1 Bn. crosses river, rafts.	Slow bombardment according to "drill" of the previous nights.	Slow bombardment according to "drill" of the previous nights.
Z+150	Construction light bridges Z.28a; demonstrations in F.13.	A. Bn. moves to take Slag Heap Farm. B. and C. Bns. move to take Orange Groves.	A. Bn. moves to seize trenches in Y.18.d. and assault trenches Z. 13.	Orange Groves, Muwannis, Slag Heap Farm, trenches Z.13.a and d.	Orange Groves, Muwannis, Slag Heap Farm, trenches Z.13.a and d.
Z+170	do.	2 Bns. move through or round Orange Groves.	—	Lifts from Orange Groves to trenches S.W. Muwannis.	—
Z+180	do.	—	Seizes trench Y.18.d.	—	—
Z+190	do.	A. Bn. assaults Slag Heap Farm.	Assaults trenches Z.13.a.	—	Lifts from Slag Heap Farm and Z.13.a. to trenches Z.7.a.
Z+200	do.	—	Assaults trenches Z.13.b.	—	Lifts from Z.13.b. to trenches Z.7.a.
Z+230	do.	B. Bn. assaults trenches S.W. Muwannis. C. Bn. assaults trenches S.E. Muwannis.	—	Lifts from trenches S.W. Muwannis to those S.E. Muwannis.	—
Z+260	2 Bns. cross river and deploy.	—	Head of 157th Bde. crosses Ford Y.18.b.	Lifts from S.E. Muwannis to protective barrage and Hadra area selected points.	—
Z+350	—	—	Deploys under cover Z.13.a and b.	—	—
Z+360	2 Bns. move to assault Hadra.	—	—	Lifts from selected points to Hadra.	—
Z+380	—	—	Assaults Z.7.a.	—	Lifts to trenches Z.1.b. and Z.2.a.
Z+390	—	—	Assaults Z.8.a.	—	do.
Z+410	—	—	Assaults Z.1.b. and Z.2.a.	—	do.
Z+420	2 Bns. assault Hadra.	—	—	Lifts to protective.	Lifts to protective.

Note.—Although Map 12 is not squared, the square numbers are written where necessary against the objectives, so that they can be identified on the map.

APPENDIX 20.
Secret.

To
GENERAL OFFICER COMMANDING
60TH DIVISION.

G.Z. 27/9. 16.3.18.

Major-General J. S. M. Shea,
C.B., D.S.O.
Commanding
60th Division.
A. & N.Z. Mtd. Division.
1st Imperial Camel Brigade.
1 Heavy Battery.
IX B.M.A. Brigade.
13th Pontoon Park R.E.
Desert Corps Bridging Train.

1. You are placed in command of the **Map 16.** troops named in the margin [1] for the **Sketch 24.** purpose of occupying Es Salt and destroying the railway at and south of 'Amman to a sufficient extent to cause a complete cessation of railway traffic.

2. The troops under your command will concentrate in accordance with the instructions already issued (this office G.Z.27/7 dated 15th March 1918).

3. Operations will begin on the night 19th/20th March, the passage of the Jordan being forced as soon after dark on the evening of the 19th as possible. Bridgeheads will be formed east of the river to cover the construction of
    (a) Temporary bridges (one to carry lorries);
    (b) A permanent bridge.
The distribution of your troops and the routes used for your advance beyond the Jordan are left to your discretion, but Es Salt must be occupied by the 60th Division and the destruction of the railway will be carried out by the mounted troops.

4. The objectives to be selected on the railway will be such that their destruction will make it impossible for the enemy to use the line for a prolonged period. The actual choice of these objectives must be left to the officer allotted the task of railway destruction, but, so far as it is possible to obtain information at present, the following appear to be the points it is most essential to destroy, in their order of importance.
    i. The 'Amman Viaduct.
    ii. A masonry bridge which is believed to exist between the viaduct and the tunnel south of the station.
    iii. 'Amman Station, with its water tanks, turn-table, and repair shed.
    iv. Rails and bridges between 'Amman Station and Libban Station, which are to be destroyed by explosives.
    v. 'Amman tunnel. This objective should be attacked by a special party to be detailed from the Imperial Camel Brigade under the command of Major Henry.
    vi. The nearest railway bridge north of 'Amman, which is about 7 miles distant. (Masonry bridge of six 20-foot arches over stream 40 feet wide.)

5. During the operation one infantry and one artillery brigade of the 53rd Division, under the command of Brigadier-General Pearson, will be responsible, operating under Corps instructions, for watching the

---

[1] A circular memorandum, subsequently issued, laid down that these troops were to be known as " Shea's Force."

approaches of the Wadi el 'Auja from the north and for protection of your lines of communication west of the river. The communications already existing from your present divisional headquarters to the 181st Brigade must be left intact for the use of the brigade of the 53rd Division mentioned above, which will be under the direct command of the Corps Commander.

6. During your operations, if the situation makes it necessary, it is proposed to carry out certain demonstrations on the front now held by the 74th and 10th Divisions, which it is hoped may assist in preventing the enemy from attempting to reinforce his troops east of the Jordan.

Instructions have also been issued for the destruction if possible of the bridge over the Jordan at Jisr ed Damiye by bombing machines of the Royal Flying Corps, but you must reckon with the possibility of the transfer of troops from the country west of the Jordan to Es Salt by this and other routes and of an attack on your left flank.

So far as they can be ascertained, you will be kept informed of the movements of the enemy and particularly of any accession to his strength in the 'Amman and Es Salt areas.

7. As soon as the railway about 'Amman has been destroyed, your force, less a detachment at Es Salt and necessary troops to protect the line of communication, will probably be withdrawn to the present area occupied by your division.

The strength of the detachment left at Es Salt will be governed by the situation, but it will probably consist of one mounted brigade, one battalion, and one battery, and its mission will be to garrison Es Salt and keep the railway from being repaired. Additional troops to protect the line of communication to this detachment must also remain east of the Jordan, and the Corps Commander thinks that it will probably be necessary to leave behind another mounted brigade, supplemented by one or two infantry detachments for that purpose. The bridges over the Jordan will be guarded in the first instance by infantry detachments.

It is possible, however, that you may be called upon to undertake further operations against the enemy now in the Tafila area, should he return to the 'Amman area before you leave. Should this be the case, it might become necessary to reduce your force, as the system of supply and the amount of supplies accumulated have been calculated on the assumption that your whole force can remain east of the Jordan for seven days.

It is impossible at present to say what number of troops could be maintained east of the Jordan after the seventh day, but the situation will be carefully watched at Corps headquarters and will be kept in mind before any orders for operations covering a more extended period are issued.

8. Guides will be provided for your columns, as required, by Captain Mackray, Intelligence Officer, Jerusalem, who has already made provision for them and has been instructed to comply with your requirements. He will be at your disposal during operations and will be responsible for the arrangements to notify the Arabs of your arrival at Es Salt and 'Amman, native messengers being used for this purpose. Information has already been communicated to him by G.H.Q. as to the positions in which he is likely to find the Arab detachments. You can expect no direct co-operation from the Arabs, who will, however, it is hoped, eventually advance to Madeba on their receiving an assurance that you have established yourself at Es Salt and 'Amman.

9. Further information as to the scope of aeroplane reconnaissance in connection with your operations will be sent you shortly. In order

that the troops under your command may be kept informed of the situation as revealed by aeroplane reconnaissance you should select landing grounds east of the Jordan, both in the area occupied by the mounted troops and by the infantry. To assist you in the selection of these landing grounds two officers of the Royal Flying Corps, who will be provided with the necessary apparatus for marking the grounds, will be attached to you.

10. Separate instructions as to the organization of the communication service will be issued to you.

W. H. BARTHOLOMEW,
Brigadier-General, General Staff, XX Corps.

APPENDIX 21.

Strictly Secret.

OPERATIONS OF XXI CORPS.

S.G.113.
1.4.18.

1. *Objects*:
The operations of the XXI Corps have two objects in view :—   Maps 2, 17.
(a) To inflict a defeat on the enemy and to capture as many of his troops and guns as possible.
(b) To advance the front held by the XXI Corps to the approximate line Kh. el Fakhakhir [1]–Bidya–'Azzun–Jiyus–Kh. Ibreike [2]–Mouth of the Nahr el Faliq.

2. *Outline of Plan*:
The plan is, first, to push forward the left of the Corps about 2,000 yards to enable artillery to be advanced for the bombardment of the enemy defences at Jaljulye, Byar 'Adas, and the Tabsor defences.

The main attack will come shortly afterwards from the right and right centre, in order to make a gap in the enemy's line about Jaljulye and Qalqilye, through which the cavalry division will advance in order to block the enemy's line of retreat in the neighbourhood of Et Tire.

At the same time the Tabsor system will be cleared by sweeping along it from east to west.

3. *Details of the Plan*:
Z − 7 *day*.—It is hoped that a brigade group will be placed by G.H.Q. under the orders of G.O.C. XXI Corps. This will be called "Corps Brigade Group." As the 75th Division advances northwards this group will be responsible for the protection of the right flank of the Corps, and for preventing the enemy from working in behind the right flank of the 75th Division.

The operations will be divided into three stages :—
1st Stage.—Preliminary Operations.
2nd Stage.—Capture of enemy's 1st-line system.
3rd Stage.—Consolidation of the position.

---

[1] A mile and a half north of Berukin.
[2] One mile N.N.E. of Qalqilye.

APPENDIX 21

1st Stage (Preliminary Operations).

About Z − 6 day.—75th Division will advance its right flank to include Kh. Susie,[1] Sh. Subi, and 'Arara, at the same time driving out the enemy who threaten its right flank from Berukin and El Kufr.

Z − 5 day.—After dark the 7th (Indian) Division will take over the extreme left of the 54th Division up to and including Transfluvia.[2]

Z − 4/Z − 3 night.—The 7th Division will advance its line about 2,000 yards and will dig a line of works. Before daylight as many men as possible will be withdrawn to the original line, leaving only sufficient to hold the works, and these will take every precaution not to show themselves during Z − 3 day. On the same night forward gun positions will be prepared and ammunition brought forward.

Z − 3 day.—The 7th Division will move its reserve brigade to the neighbourhood of Jlil.

Z − 3/Z − 2 night.—The 7th Division will complete its advanced line and will hold it. The Artillery will be moved into its forward positions and their ammunition supply completed.

Z − 2 day.—The 7th Divisional Artillery and the left flank Heavy Artillery will register from their new positions. If the flashes will not disclose their position too much, they will shell back areas during Z − 2/Z − 1 night.

On this day the 75th and 54th Divisions will advance to the line Bidya–Kufr Qasim.

Z − 2/Z − 1 night.—The Artillery of the 75th and 54th Divisions and the Heavy Artillery on that flank will be advanced to suitable positions to take part in the operations of Z day.

On this night also the cavalry division will move to Mulebbis, and take every care to conceal itself until required.

Z − 1 day.—The Artillery of the left flank will commence the bombardment of Jaljulye, Qalqilye, and the Tabsor system, paying especial attention to back areas during Z − 1/Z night.

2nd Stage (Capture of Enemy's 1st-Line System).

Z day.—The left flank Artillery continues the bombardment. On the right flank the 75th and 54th Divisions advance as follows:—

75th Division advances to the line 'Azzun–Kh. el Khareije [3] and in conjunction with it the 54th Division advances to the neighbourhood of Kh. el Khareish,[4] extending its right flank to Hable as soon as the 75th Division has taken that place. The 54th Division will then be facing roughly north-west.

A selected force of the 54th Division will take Jaljulye, and at the same time the 75th Division will take Qalqilye and Kh. Ibreike. (It is important that these places should be taken before midnight, and the earlier it is done the better.)

This will make a gap east of the line Jaljulye–Qalqilye, through which the cavalry division can pass.

Z/Z + 1 night.—As soon as it is dark the cavalry division will move across from Mulebbis to the neighbourhood of Majdal Yaba, and as soon as Jaljulye, Qalqilye, and Kh. Ibreike are reported to be taken, it will move northwards to Qalqilye.

---

[1] On the south bank of the Wadi el Lehham, south-west of Sh. Subi.
[2] The spit of land between the Nahr el 'Auja and the Wadi Ishkar.
[3] Half a mile south-east of Qalqilye.
[4] A mile and a half S.S.E. of Hable.

APPENDIX 21

Z + 1 day.—At dawn a bombardment of Byar 'Adas and the Tabsor system will be opened. At the same time the 54th Division will advance from the vicinity of Jaljulye with its right directed on Kufr Saba and its left on Byar 'Adas. This advance will be pushed in a north-westerly direction to the west of Tabsor at about 0 84.A.14.

At dawn also the cavalry division will push forward with all speed to Et Tire to close the line of retreat of the enemy northwards between the Qalqilye-Tul Karm road and Kh. ez Zerqiye.[1]

At dawn on this day the Royal Navy will appear off the Nahr el Faliq in order to prevent the enemy from withdrawing northwards by the ford and bridge near its mouth. The remaining crossing over the marsh at 0 84 S.16 will be closed by fire from the Royal Navy and from the left flank Heavy Artillery, by means of aeroplane observation. During operations this point will be called Zerqiye Crossing.

In the event of the enemy being in full retreat northwards before the cavalry division reaches Et Tire, the cavalry, having first taken steps to block the gap at Et Tire, will carry out an energetic pursuit, but will not go beyond a rough east-and-west line through Tul Karm.

As soon as the 54th Division reaches Tabsor the 7th Division will push forward its left and secure the two crossings over the Nahr el Faliq, forming a bridgehead there.

The 54th Division will bivouac for the night of Z + 1/Z + 2 on the line Kufr Saba-Tabsor facing north, with a line of outposts in front, linking up with the 75th Division immediately west of the railway at Kh. Ibreike, and with the 7th Division at about 0 84 A.3 central.

3rd Stage (Consolidation of the Position).

It is intended to keep the 54th Division in the Tabsor defences as short a time as possible. It will be relieved by the 7th Division, and will move across to the right flank and relieve the Corps Brigade Group.

The approximate line to be taken up and consolidated will be :—

54th Division: Kh. el Fakhakhir–Bidya–Kh. Kefar Thilth.

75th Division: Kh. Kefar Thilth (excl.)–'Azzun–Jiyus–Kh. Ibreike (incl.).

7th Division: Kh. Ibreike (excl.)–Miske–Kh. Maleika–Bridgehead north of Nahr el Faliq.

H. F. SALT,
Brigadier-General, General Staff, XXI Corps.

Headquarters XXI Corps.
1st April 1918.

---

[1] This line is a paraphrase of the original, to enable the intention of the order to be more easily followed on the map.

APPENDIX 22.

Secret.

DESERT MOUNTED CORPS OPERATION ORDER No. 16.

27th April 1918.

Reference Map : 1 in. = 1 mile.

Information.

Map 18.
Sketch 24.

1. Information about the enemy will be issued separately.

Intention.

2. The Corps Commander intends to envelop the right of the enemy's main forces about Shunet Nimrin, capture Es Salt, and advance to the line Qasr, 142.T.9–Pt. 2900,[1] 142.O.35.

Orders to Troops.

3. In consequence, the following moves will take place on April 30th.

Major-General J. S. M. Shea, C.B., C.M.G., D.S.O.
A. & N.Z. Mounted Division (less 1st L.H. and XVIII R.H.A. Brigades).
60th Division (less 1 Bde. Group).
XX R.H.A. Bde. (less 1 Bty.).
91st Heavy Battery R.G.A.
IX Mountain Artillery Bde. (less 1 Battery).
No. 11 L.A.M. Battery.
1 squadron Hyderabad Lncrs.
Patiala Infantry Battalion.

Major-General H. W. Hodgson, C.B., C.V.O.
Australian Mounted Division.
1st A.L.H. Brigade.
Hong Kong and Singapore Bty.
1 Battery IX Mountain Artillery Brigade.
No. 12 L.A.M. Battery.

(a) *Major-General J. S. M. Shea, C.B., C.M.G., D.S.O.*, will attack about one hour before dawn. He will (i) Employ 1 Mounted Regiment, 1 Squadron Hyderabad Lancers, and 1 Battalion Patiala Infantry to seize the enemy's advanced works near Qabr Said and Qabr Mujahid (tracks nos. 2 and 3).
(ii) Occupy the line Ma'qqer ed Derbasi–Tell el Mistah–El Haud.
(iii) Direct A. & N.Z. Mounted Division to advance to the line Qasr, 142.T.9–Es Salt.
A. & N.Z. Mounted Division, when clear of the infantry, will come under direct orders of Corps headquarters.

(b) *Major-General H. W. Hodgson, C.B., C.V.O.*, will advance rapidly northwards east of the Jordan not later than 4 a.m. He will place one mounted brigade, supported by at least two R.H.A. Batteries, facing north-east astride the Umm esh Shert–Jisr ed Damiye and Es Salt–Jisr ed Damiye tracks.
With the remainder of his force he will move on Es Salt from west and north-west.

When Es Salt is occupied dispositions will be made to protect it on the north ; one brigade will advance to Pt. 2900, 142.O.35, and a detachment will move towards Shunet Nimrin with the object of capturing the enemy retiring in front of Major-General Shea.

Corps headquarters will be prepared to assume direct command of the brigade facing Jisr ed Damiye, when Major-General Hodgson considers it more convenient.

---

[1] Close to 'Ain Hummar, west of Suweile.

APPENDIX 22

(c) The dividing line between A. & N.Z. and Australian Mounted Divisions east of Es Salt will be a line from Es Salt to Pt. 2900, 142.O.35, inclusive to Australian Mounted Division.

The Wadi Arseniyet [1] track (No. 6) is allotted to Major-General Shea, east of the spring in 127.O.6, exclusive.

Br.-General C. L. Smith, V.C., M.C. I.C.C. Brigade. 1/1st Staffordshire Yeomanry (less 1 squadron). XVIII R.H.A. Brigade. 383rd Siege Battery R.G.A.	(d) Br.-General C. L. Smith, V.C., M.C., will, by 4 a.m., have thrown forward his right to about 113.X.23.a,[2] and have established a post of at least one section in a position to command the right bank of the Jordan near the bend in 113.X.17.d.[3]

(e) *20th Indian Infantry Brigade* (less Patiala Infantry and detachments) will be employed, from 5 a.m. onwards, in improving the approaches to the Ghoraniye bridgehead. Two sections, total not less than 25 men, will be permanently stationed at the bridges from 6 p.m. on April 29th onwards, to render assistance in case of a block : they may, however, be withdrawn in the event of the brigade being required to occupy the bridgehead.

(f) *6th Mounted Brigade including 1 R.H.A. Battery*, and *Imperial Service Cavalry Brigade* (less 1 Squadron and detachments) will, by 9 a.m., be assembled in Corps reserve, about two miles west of El Ghoraniye, and north and south respectively of the road. They will reconnoitre routes towards Umm esh Shert east of the Jordan and towards El Musallabe, 113.W.34.

Approach March.

4. The approach march in connection with the above will be conducted as follows :—

(a) XX Brigade R.H.A. (less 1 Battery) will come under the orders of Major-General Shea on arrival at Tal 'at ed Damm on the morning of April 29th. On the night April 29th/30th as much of the march as possible will be conducted in darkness.

(b) The Ghoraniye crossings are allotted to Major-General Hodgson from 10 p.m. to 2.30 a.m., during which period Major-General Shea will have no troops on the approaches. Major-General Hodgson will emerge from the bridgehead by No. 6 road only.

Communication with Artillery.

5. A. & N.Z. Mounted Division will use red and yellow flags, the remainder of the Corps red flares, to indicate the position of the most advanced troops to the artillery.

Ammunition Supply.

6. (a) An ammunition dump has been formed west of Ghoraniye Bridge 115.L.12.b. A second will be formed at Shunet Nimrin as early as possible.

(b) G.O.C. R.A. will assume control of ammunition columns as under :—

(i) Of Major-General Shea's Force and A. & N.Z. Mounted Division, on occupation of the line Tell el Mistah–El Haud.

(ii) Of Major-General Hodgson's Force, on reaching Es Salt.

---

[1] Read Wadi Abu Turra.
[2] North of the Mellaha and 2 miles north-west of Umm esh Shert.
[3] Where the Jordan turns eastward a mile and three-quarters N.N.W. of Umm esh Shert.

APPENDIX 22

Aeroplane Co-operation.

7. The following have been arranged.

(a) Aeroplane contact patrols of the area of operations from 5.30 to 7 a.m., 11 a.m. to 12.30 p.m., and 3.30 to 5 p.m.

(b) Tactical reconnaissance of the area of operations, not going more than 10,000 yards beyond our front line, from 9 to 10.30 a.m., 1 to 2.30 p.m., and 3 to 4.30 p.m.

(c) Strategical reconnaissance of the Nablus–Jisr ed Damiye–Es Salt and 'Amman–Es Salt roads at about 12 noon and 4 p.m.

(d) Artillery observation (one machine) throughout the day.

Messages from (a) and (b) will be dropped on A. & N.Z. and Australian Divisional as well as on Corps headquarters. Those from (c) on Corps headquarters only.

Medical.

8. Receiving Stations will be established on the east bank of the Jordan near the bridge.

Prisoners.

9. *Prisoners' Collecting Station* will be established at the entrance to the Ghoraniye Bridgehead on No. 5 road.[1] G.O.C. Imperial Service Cavalry Brigade will detail two troops to report to Corps A.P.M. there at 4 a.m.

Traffic Control.

10. Corps A.P.M. will issue instructions as to traffic control, paying particular attention to the Ghoraniye crossings.

Relay Posts.

11. O.C. Escort Squadron will detail one troop to establish a chain of relay posts from Advanced Corps headquarters behind Australian Mounted Division, to connect with the brigade of that division facing Jisr ed Damiye. To be in position by 5 a.m. and to remain there until withdrawn by Corps headquarters.

Documents.

12. All ranks will be searched for documents before going into action.

Gallopers.

13. A. & N.Z. and Australian Mounted Divisions will each detail an officer galloper to be at Advanced Corps headquarters at 4 a.m. : 6th Mounted and Imperial Service Cavalry Brigades will each detail an officer galloper to be at Advanced Corps headquarters at 9 a.m.

Reports.

14. Advanced Corps headquarters will be established at 3 a.m. at 113.L.12.a.2.1. Telegraphic address—Advanced Descorps.

15. Acknowledge.

R. G. HOWARD-VYSE,
Brigadier-General, General Staff, Desert Mounted Corps.

Issued at 3.45 p.m.

---

[1] The main Jericho–Es Salt road.

APPENDIX 23.
Secret and Personal.

FORCE ORDER No. 68.

BY

GENERAL SIR EDMUND ALLENBY, G.C.M.G., K.C.B.,
Commander-in-Chief, Egyptian Expeditionary Force.

General Headquarters,
9th September 1918.

Reference Maps : 1/40,000 ; 1/63,360.

1. The Commander-in-Chief intends to take the offensive. The Army, pivoting on its positions in the Jordan Valley, will attack on the front between the high ground east of El Mughaiyir (113.Q.5) and the sea with the object of inflicting a decisive defeat on the enemy and driving him from the line Nablus–Samaria–Tul Karm–Cæsarea. **Maps 2, 2A, 19. Sketch 24.**

2. The XXI Corps, with 5th Australian Light Horse Brigade, 60th Division, and Détachement Français de Palestine–Syrie attached, will attack the enemy's right, and when his trench systems between Et Tire and the Nahr el Faliq have been captured, will advance eastwards to drive the enemy from the line Deir Sharaf–Samaria–Tul Karm.

As soon as the crossings over the Nahr el Faliq and the marshes to the east have been cleared of the enemy by the advance of the XXI Corps, the Desert Mounted Corps (4th and 5th Cavalry Divisions and Australian Mounted Division [less 1 brigade]), passing round the left of the XXI Corps, will advance to El 'Affule and Beisan to cut the enemy's railway communications and to block his retreat in a northerly and north-easterly direction.

The XX Corps (less 60th Division) will attack astride the Nablus road to gain possession of a line south of Nablus from which it will be in a position to co-operate with XXI Corps and to advance to the high ground north and north-east of Nablus.

3. (*a*) The XXI Corps, employing five divisions, will attack, on a day to be notified later and known as Z day, on the front Umbrella Hill (C.4/U.6)–sea.

Objective : The line Three Bushes Hill (C.4/N.25)–high ground C.3/K.14 [1]–foothills east of Qalqilye–north-eastern edge of Et Tire (D.3/Y.13)–north bank of the Nahr el Faliq.

The infantry will advance to the assault under an artillery barrage, which will be put down at the hour at which the infantry leave their positions of deployment. This hour will be known as the " XXI Corps Zero Hour." There will be no preliminary bombardment.

(*b*) Immediately the objective allotted in (*a*) above has been gained, the Corps, pivoting on its right, will wheel to the east, clear the Qalqilye–Tul Karm road, advance to seize the high ground east of the railway between Deir Sharaf and 'Atara, and be prepared to pursue the enemy in the direction of Jenin.

One division of the Corps, with the 5th Australian Light Horse Brigade attached, will advance *via* Tul Karm on 'Atara (098.B.27), blocking the railway line between Samaria and Jenin as early as possible.

When the 5th Australian Light Horse Brigade is no longer required by the General Officer Commanding XXI Corps it will revert to the command of the General Officer Commanding Desert Mounted Corps.

---

[1] The spur south-east of Hable.

APPENDIX 23

(c) The right division of the XXI Corps will not advance further east than an approximate north and south line through Bidya unless required to assist the XX Corps, which will be operating on its right.

4. The Desert Mounted Corps (less 5th Australian Light Horse Brigade attached XXI Corps) will move to positions of readiness behind the XXI Corps during the night Z — 1/Z, and will begin its advance to the El 'Affule area immediately the infantry has secured the crossings over the Nahr el Faliq and the Kh. ez Zerqiye marsh.

First Objective : The line Qaqun–Jelame–Tell edh Dhrur (083.K.20)–Hadera.

The advance by the Desert Mounted Corps will be continued as soon as possible and with the utmost speed to El 'Affule by the Jelame–Kh. es Sumra–El Lajjun and the Hadera–Ez Zerganiya–J'ara–Abu Shushe roads. Every effort will be made to prevent the escape of Turkish rolling-stock by cutting the railway lines from Jenin and Haifa to El 'Affule at the earliest possible moment.

The General Officer Commanding Desert Mounted Corps, retaining sufficient troops in the El 'Affule–Jenin–El Lajjun area to close the Turkish lines of retreat to the north and north-west, will push on to close the roads which converge on Beisan from the Jordan Valley and Nablus.

Special instructions will be issued to the General Officer Commanding Desert Mounted Corps and sent for information to General Officers Commanding XX and XXI Corps.

5. Two Torpedo-boat Destroyers of the Royal Navy will co-operate in the attack, operating with the XXI Corps in its advance to the Nahr el Faliq and later with the Desert Mounted Corps.

The mission of the Destroyers will be to deny to the enemy the use of the coast road south of Haifa.

Special instructions for the employment of the Destroyers will be issued through the Rear-Admiral, Senior Naval Officer, Egypt and Red Sea, and copies forwarded to General Officers Commanding XXI and Desert Mounted Corps.

6. (a) On the evening of Z — 1 day, the XX Corps will advance its right to the general line (ref. 1/40,000 map, Sheet C.5) :—Valley View,–El Mughaiyir (Q.5)–Hindhead (0.33)–Sh. Muhammad (0.26)–Nairn Ridge (0.31).

(b) The date on which the XX Corps will begin its advance from the front El Mughaiyir–Ra-fat will depend on the rate of progress of the XXI Corps, but divisions must be concentrated and ready to attack by 6 p.m. on Z day.

The attack by the Corps will be made by two groups operating from the right and left flanks of its line and converging on to the approximate line 'Aqrabe–Beita–Jemma'in–Kefar Haris.

The Right Group will advance from near El Mughaiyir along the high ground which runs in a northerly direction to 'Aqrabe. The Left Group will advance along the Furqa–Selfit–Iskaka ridge and the ridge which runs from Kh. Susie [1] (099.A.2) in the direction of Kefar Haris between the Wadi el Mutwy and the Wadi 'Auwad.

From the line 'Aqrabe–Beita–Jemma'in–Kefar Haris the Corps will be prepared to move forward rapidly to secure the high ground north and north-east of Nablus and to pursue the enemy towards Beisan.

7. "Chaytor's Force," on which the Army will pivot during the operations, will be responsible for the defence of the front :—North end

---

[1] South of Sh. Subi.

of Dead Sea–Ghoraniye Bridgehead–'Auja Bridgehead–Mussalabe–En Nejme (exclusive) (113.S. 24).

If the enemy reduces his strength in the Jordan Valley the Force may be required to advance as far as Jisr ed Damiye or to send a detachment east of the Jordan to join hands with an Arab force from the south, but no movement in either direction except as referred to below will be made without sanction from General Headquarters.

Although Major-General Sir E. W. C. Chaytor will not commit his force to an advance, he will take such measures as he finds possible, from Z day inclusive, to make the enemy believe that attacks both east and west of the Jordan are imminent and so prevent the enemy from concentrating troops to attack the right flank of the XX Corps.

8. The XXI Corps will be responsible for control of traffic in the Coastal Plain north of the line Rantye–crossing over the Nahr el Baride [1] (071.J.3)–Sheikh Abd en Nabi (070.Y.29) (all inclusive). All traffic south of this line including Sarona will be controlled by Palestine Lines of Communication.

The Tabsor–Hadera road and the route along the sea beach will be allotted to the Desert Mounted Corps when required. An additional bridge over the Nahr el Faliq will be constructed by the XXI Corps for the use of the Desert Mounted Corps. The troops of the XXI Corps will have precedence over the existing bridge at D.3/N.6.c.9.8. Desert Mounted Corps trains will be given precedence over XXI Corps trains and Desert Mounted Corps Reserve Parks over XXI Corps Reserve Parks on all roads on Z day.

9. No maps, other than the following, will be used during operations:—

1/20,000 (XXI Corps only).   Palestine 1/63,360.
1/40,000.   Haifa 1/250,000.

10. Instructions as to the allotment of artillery, the organization and tasks of the Royal Air Force, Communication Services, Medical Services and Supply Services have been issued separately.

11. Watches will be synchronized by General Headquarters time, which, from the date of this order, will be sent out daily by wireless signal at 8.15 a.m. and 6 p.m.

L. J. BOLS,

Major-General, Chief of the General Staff, Egyptian Expeditionary Force.

APPENDIX 24.

Strictly Secret.

XXI CORPS ORDER No. 42.

17th September 1918.

Reference Map : 1/40,000, Sheets C.2, 3, 4, D.3, 4.

1. A summary of the latest information regarding the enemy's Maps 2, dispositions is being issued separately to all concerned. 19, 20.

2. The Corps Commander intends on a day to be notified later and known as Z day to assault the enemy's Tabsor and Et Tire defences between the foot-hills and the Sea, and after these defences are captured

---

[1] Sarona Bridge on Maps 19 and 20.

to advance eastwards into the hills on a front extending from the Wadi Deir Ballut to the Tul Karm–Mas'udye road. These operations will be carried out in accordance with XXI Corps Instructions Nos. 1 to 7 and Administrative Instructions No. S.A.8, already issued to all concerned.

3. The Corps Commander again emphasizes the importance of time. It is of vital importance that the enemy's defences shall be broken through with the utmost determination and rapidity; and once broken through that the 3rd (Lahore) and 7th (Meerut) Divisions face east and sweep forward on their march through the foot-hills, gaining the undermentioned line as rapidly as possible :—

Wadi Qana (excl.)–'Azzun–Jiyus–Felamiye–Taiyibe or further east if possible.

The whole of the success of these operations depends on the rapidity of movement of the infantry, in order to allow no time for the enemy to meet our onslaught. All commanders must carefully guard against embarking on side issues, and must keep steadily in view the gaining of their objectives well east in the foot-hills, and ensure that their troops are ready to continue the pursuit without pause or delay as long as the enemy are in front of them.

The operations call for self-sacrifice, determination and endurance of a high order, but if the total destruction of the enemy's forces in front of us can be achieved by 48 hours' concentrated exertion, the result will more than repay any hardships endured.

The Corps Commander therefore expects commanders to take risks and act with the utmost boldness with their leading troops, relying on their reserves to meet unexpected eventualities.

4. The objectives of the XXI Corps on Z day will be :—

1st Objective : Three Bushes Hill–Surrey Hill—Qasim [1] Wood–Jevis Tepe–Byar 'Adas–Trenches G.35–G.28–G.30–F.37–F.39–F.4–C.39–C.38– Trench junction in A.8.1.0.1.–C.7–C.6.[2]

2nd Objective : Three Bushes Hill–Scurry Hill–Crown Hill–High Ground N. of Wadi Qana–foot-hills E. of Qalqilye–Et Tire line of defences– Bridgehead north of Nahr el Faliq.

3rd Objective : Ra-fat–Kh. Kefar Thilth–'Azzun–Jiyus–Felamiye– Taiyibe–Tul Karm ; but this does not prohibit formations pushing beyond this line if they have the opportunity.

Reports will be sent directly these objectives are reached.

5. As soon as the XXI Corps has captured the Et Tire line and secured the crossings over the Nahr el Faliq, the Desert Mounted Corps has orders to begin its advance northwards along the coast, extending if necessary as far east as Zerqiye Crossing.

It is most important that, as soon as the infantry have broken through the enemy's defences and have pushed eastward their covering troops, the Desert Mounted Corps should start on its northward journey as soon as possible, and the 7th (Meerut) and 60th Divisions will help in every way and will give it a clear start at the earliest possible moment. The details of Desert Mounted Corps and XX Corps plans of operations have been communicated confidentially to Divisional Commanders.

6. The positions of Divisional Battle H.Q. at XXI Corps Zero Hour will be :—

54th Division : P.20.d. (N.W. of Muzeira).
3rd Division : C.22.d.2.4.
75th Division : C.9.c.
7th Division : X.11.d.8.0.
60th Division : Arsuf.

---

[1] The woodland south-east of Kufr Qasim.
[2] Generally the front system of trenches from Kufr Saba to the sea.

APPENDIX 24

7. The following will be the allotment of water areas for Z evening:—

54th Division : Ras el 'Ain and all sources in the hills between Wadi Deir Ballut and Wadi Qana (both inclusive).

3rd (Lahore) Division.—Jaljulye and all sources in the hills between Wadi Qana and Wadi Sir (both inclusive).

7th (Meerut) Division.—Qulunsawe, Taiyibe and all sources in the hills between Wadi Sir (inclusive) and the line Feron–Kufr el Lebad (inclusive).

Et Tire will also be allotted to the 7th Division.

60th Division.—Tul Karm area.

75th Division.—Miske area and the Kh. ez Zerqiye marshes.

8. Every commander down to platoon commanders will be given the compass bearing of his line of advance against the Tabsor defences.

9. Red, blue and yellow flags have been issued to Divisions. These will be used as follows:—

(a) *Yellow Flags.*—To be carried by platoons to show their own and neighbouring divisions and the artillery the position of the most forward line of infantry. These flags will never be stuck in the ground but will be waved by the leading platoons. It is of the utmost importance that no troops other than those in the front line should display their yellow flags.

(b) *Red and Blue Flags.*—These will be employed for marking trench crossings.

10. Instructions regarding the action of the Corps Heavy Artillery and Mountain Artillery are being issued by G.O.C.R.A. XXI Corps.

The Corps Commander attaches the greatest importance to every gun—heavy, field and mountain—opening fire exactly at XXI Corps Zero Hour.

11. No written orders, marked maps, or other documents which would be of value to the enemy are to be carried by company and platoon commanders or other ranks during the advance.

12. No railways will be cut except at Iktaba and 'Ajje, and at these places only the permanent way will be damaged, bridges and tunnels being left intact. It is of great importance that the railway at 'Ajje should be cut during $Z/Z + 1$ night.

When any engines or rolling stock are captured an immediate report will be sent in, giving all details, so that engine-drivers and repair gangs may be sent up.

Telegraph lines are not to be destroyed unless specially ordered by Divisional Commanders, as they will be required for our own use.

13. Casualty Clearing Stations will be opened at Wilhelma for the 54th, 3rd (Lahore) and 75th Divisions, and at Jaffa for the 7th (Meerut) and 60th Divisions. A C.C.S. will be opened as soon as possible at Jaljulye once the troops have reached their objectives in the foot-hills.

14. Watches will be synchronized by telephone on $Z - 1$ day at 12 noon and 6 p.m. Synchronization is not to be carried out by telephone lower than Brigade H.Q.

15. (a) Reports will be sent in by Divisions on Z day at the following times:—

   (i) Hourly up to 12 noon.
   (ii) On the capture of each of the various objectives.
   (iii) At 4 p.m.
   (iv) On the moves of Divisional H.Q.
   (v) On the occurrence of any other important events.

(*b*) Subsequent to Z day, situation reports will reach XXI Corps H.Q. at 7 a.m., 11 a.m., and 4 p.m. daily. In addition, changes in the situation will be reported as they occur.

(*c*) A report will be sent daily to announce the arrival of water and rations at the Divisional refilling points, and also a report on the general physical condition of the troops.

(*d*) All situation reports will be addressed to the Advanced Corps H.Q., and repeated to flank Divisions, to supporting Heavy Artillery Brigade and to Aeronautics 113.

(*e*) When advanced XXI Corps H.Q. opens, messages concerning operations will be addressed to " Adv. XXI Corps "; but Intelligence messages will be addressed " XXI Corps."

(*f*) All references will be to the 1/40,000 map.

16. Headquarters XXI Corps will be at C.3/Z.28 central. Advanced XXI Corps will probably open on the afternoon of Z day in the neighbourhood of C.3/B.25.b.

17. Z day and XXI Corps Zero Hour will be notified separately to all concerned.

18. Acknowledge by wire.

H. F. SALT,
Brigadier-General, General Staff, XXI Corps.

Issued at 7 a.m.

APPENDIX 25.

Secret.

XX CORPS OPERATION ORDER No. 42.

13th September 1918.

Reference Maps : 1/40,000 ; 1/63,360.

Maps 2, 19, 20.

1. On Z day, the date of which will be notified later, the Army will take the offensive. The object is to inflict a decisive defeat on the enemy, and to advance to the general line of the high ground Meshariq Nablus[1]–Yasid (098.L.9)–Sh. Beiazid (098.K.9)–'Atara–Jebel Bir 'Asur (098.B.25)–Bala (098.A.22)–Yemma (083.N.26).

2. (*a*) The main attack will be made by the XXI Corps with five divisions against the enemy's right between the foot-hills east of the railway and the sea. This attack will commence on Z day at an hour which will be known as " XXI Corps Zero hour."

(*b*) As soon as the crossings over the Nahr el Faliq are cleared of the enemy by the advance of the XXI Corps, the Desert Mounted Corps, passing round the left of the XXI Corps, will be directed on El 'Affule and Beisan with the object of cutting the enemy's railway communications and blocking his retreat in a northerly and north-easterly direction.

(*c*) As soon as the XXI Corps has gained the general line Three Bushes Hill (04/N.25)–High ground 03/K.14–Foot-hills east of Qalqilye–north-eastern edge of Et Tire (D.3/Y.13)–north bank of the Nahr el Faliq, it will move north-eastwards and advance to seize the high ground east of the railway between Deir Sheraf and 'Atara.

One division and a cavalry brigade will advance *via* Tul Karm on

---

[1] The high ridge south of the Wadi el Far'a. Yasid and Sh. Beiazid are respectively 5 miles N.N.E. and 6 miles N.N.W. of Nablus.

APPENDIX 25

'Atara; while two other divisions will advance up the El Funduq road on Deir Sheraf, and by Felamiye–Beit Lid on Mas'udye respectively.

The right division of the XXI Corps (54th Division) will not advance further east than an approximate north and south line through Bidya, unless required to assist the XX Corps.

(d) "Chaytor's Force" will hold the present front in the Jordan Valley, and may be required later to advance as far as Jisr ed Damiye.

3. The XX Corps will attack astride the Nablus Road to gain possession of a line south of Nablus, from which it will be in a position to co-operate with XXI Corps and to advance to the high ground north and north-east of Nablus.

The date and hour of the advance of the XX Corps will depend upon the progress of the main attack and the action of the enemy. The 10th Division will be prepared to advance by 6 p.m. on Z day, if circumstances demand it. The date and hour of the main advance of the 53rd Division will be as soon as possible after the 10th Division commences its advance.

4. The advance of the XX Corps will take the form of a converging attack from the two outer flanks directed on the general line 'Aqrabe–Jemma'in–Kefar Haris. The centre of the enemy's line, from Norfolk Hill to the Wadi er Rum, will not be attacked at all.

From the 'Aqrabe–Jemma'in–Kefar Haris line the advance will be continued, so as to reach as early as possible the line 'Aqrabe–'Awerta–Sh. Selman el Farsi and any other positions which it is found desirable to seize prior to an advance against the high ground about Nablus.

5. The 10th and 53rd Divisions will therefore be concentrated as under, the centre of the present Corps front being taken over by a mixed force under the command of Lieut.-Colonel S. Watson, 1/155th Pioneers, to be known as "Watson's Force."

53rd Division.—To be concentrated east of the Nablus Road in the approximate area Nejme [1]–Kh. Abu Falah–Mezra esh Sherqiye–Dar Jerir before dawn on Z − 1 day.

10th Division.—To be concentrated in the approximate area Nabi Salih–Kufr 'Ain–Berukin–El Kufr (less detachments left temporarily between 'Arura and Kufr 'Ain and between El Kufr and Ra-fat) before dawn on Z day.

6. On the night of Z − 1/Z the 53rd Division will bring up its right flank and seize the general line Square Hill (P.31.c.)–Hindhead–Nairn Ridge, preparatory to the general advance.

7. When the order for the general advance is given, "Watson's Force" will remain in position, while the 10th and 53rd Divisions advance to the following objectives :—

53rd Division.

1st Objective.—The line Dome–Pt. 2905 (0.17.b.)–Ras et Tawil, the left being extended to secure the works in O.13 and J.18, if found necessary.

2nd Objective.—Majdal Beni Fadl–Qusra–Sh. Halim.

3rd Objective.—The high ground south of 'Aqrabe–Qabalan.

4th Objective.—The high ground north of 'Aqrabe–'Awerta.

The 53rd Division will be prepared to piquet the roads leading from the valley into its right flank, between El Mughaiyir and Majdal Beni Fadl ; and, if necessary, to push detachments with artillery eastwards

---

[1] Nejme and Dar Jerir are just south of the southern boundary of Maps 19 and 20.

down these roads, to assist the forward movement of a portion of Chaytor's Force, should this latter receive orders to advance.

10th Division.
  1st Objective.—The general line of the Furqa defences in B.6.c.–Kh. esh Shellal–high ground in T.13.[1]
  2nd Objective.—The high ground Sh. Abu Zarad–Merda–Kefar Haris–Haris.
  3rd Objective.—High ground south of Quza–Et Tarud–Maza Abd el Haqq–'Alim el Hada.
  4th Objective.—The Sh. Selman el Farsi ridge, throwing out a defensive flank to the north-west as may be found necessary.

The 10th Division will establish touch with the division of the XXI Corps advancing up the El Funduq road on its left as early as possible.

8. It is of great importance that the actions of both divisions should secure the road junction in Z.14 [2] early in the advance, and thus shorten their lines of supply.

9. 53rd and 10th Divisions will establish Battle headquarters at or near Jalud and Selfit respectively as soon as the situation permits.

10. Paragraphs 1, 2, and 3 of these orders are not to appear in any written orders; and only such portions of them will be communicated verbally to Brigade Commanders as is essential for the performance of their tasks. Brigade and Regimental orders will define only their own objectives and those of units in immediate touch with them; and will give no indication of the general Corps plan.

No written orders of any description are to be taken into action; officers will mark immediate objectives only on their maps, inconspicuously.

11. The Artillery Plan, Administrative instructions, and instructions on Signals, Co-operation with R.A.F., and for "Watson's Force" are being issued separately.

12. Advanced Corps Battle headquarters will be established at Ram Allah on "Z" day.

13. Acknowledge.

A. P. WAVELL,
Br.-General, General Staff, XX Corps.

Issued at 12.30 p.m.

APPENDIX 26.

Secret.

DESERT MOUNTED CORPS OPERATION ORDER No. 21.

12th September 1918.

Reference Maps: 1/40,000; 1/63,360.

Maps 2, 20, 21.

1. *Information.*—(a) On Z day at Zero hour the Army is taking the offensive, pivoting on its positions in the Jordan Valley (Chaytor's Force), and attacking on the front between the high ground east of El Mughaiyir (113.Q.5) and the sea, with the object of inflicting a decisive defeat on the enemy and driving him from the line Nablus–Samaria–Tul Karm–Cæsarea.

---

[1] About Point 1755 between the Wadis el Mutwy and 'Auwad.
[2] On the Damascus road, immediately south of the Wadi el Jenab.

(b) The XXI Corps, with 5th A.L.H. Brigade, 60th Division, and French detachment, are to drive the enemy from the line Deir Sharaf–Samaria–Tul Karm.

(c) The XX Corps is attacking astride the Nablus Road to gain the high ground north and north-east of Nablus.

2. *Intention.*—The task of the Desert Mounted Corps (less A. & N.Z. Mounted Division) is to advance to El 'Affule–Beisan, cut the enemy's railway communications at their most vital point, and get in a position to strike the enemy's columns if they endeavour to escape in a northerly or north-easterly direction.

3. *Orders to Troops.*—In consequence the Corps will move on Z day with the above object in view as follows :—

(a) (i) *The 5th Cavalry Division* (plus 12th L.A.M. Battery and No. 7 Light Car Patrol, less 2 gun cars) to be in a Position of Readiness in rear of the 60th Division by 5 a.m.

(ii) *The 4th Cavalry Division* (plus 11th L.A.M. Battery and No. 1 Light Car Patrol) to be in rear of 7th (Indian) Division by 6 a.m.

(iii) *Australian Mounted Division* to be in the Sarona area vacated by 4th Cavalry Division by 7 a.m.

(b) When the XXI Corps has opened the way for crossing the Nahr el Faliq and Kh. ez Zerqiye marsh :—

(i) *5th Cavalry Division* (plus 12th L.A.M. Battery and No. 7 Light Car Patrol, less 2 gun cars) will advance on :—

1st Objective, the line Tell edh Dhrur (exclusive)–Hadera–the Sea, securing in the first place the crossings over the Nahr Iskanderune.

Thence moving with utmost speed to a position north of El 'Affule by the Hadera–Ez Zerganiya–Kh. es Shrah–Abu Shushe road.

Touch must be maintained with the 4th Cavalry Division on its right.

Should any portion of the enemy's force retreat in the direction of Haifa, only sufficient troops to keep touch with them and protect the line of communication should be detached.

The passage of the remainder of the Corps through the Musmus Defile must be protected from the north by a detachment left in the neighbourhood of J'ara for this purpose. This detachment will not be recalled without reference to Corps.

In advancing on the El 'Affule road the Haifa railway should be cut and dispositions should ensure a detachment visiting Nazareth, with a view to capturing influential prisoners and important documents.

The division will be prepared to operate towards Jenin and Beisan according to circumstances.

The conditions for the advance will be as laid down in the instructions issued under S.G.920/11 of 12th September.

(ii) *4th Cavalry Division* (plus 11th L.A.M. Battery and No. 1 Light Car Patrol) will advance on :—

1st Objective, the line Qaqun–Jelame–Tell edh Dhrur (inclusive), keeping touch with the 5th Cavalry Division on its left.

The advance will be continued with the utmost speed *via* the Jelame–Kh. es Sumra–El Lajjun road to El 'Affule. On no account will the division be diverted from its objective by the presence of hostile troops in the Tul Karm–Qulunsawe–Et Tire area ; these will be dealt with by the XXI Corps.

The railways from El 'Affule to Jenin, Beisan, and Haifa, will be cut as soon as possible.

On arrival at El 'Affule a detachment will be sent to seize the roads and railway bridges over the Jordan at Jisr el Majami', moving *via* Nein,

Endor, Sirin. The railway bridge at Jisr el Majami' will be prepared for demolition but will not be destroyed so long as it can be held.

From El 'Affule the advance will continue as early as possible on Beisan with a view to closing the roads converging on that place from the Jordan Valley and Nablus.

The conditions for the initial advance will be as laid down in the instructions issued under S.G. 920/11 of the 12th September.

(iii) *Australian Mounted Division* (less 5th A.L.H. Brigade) will move across the 'Auja into the position of readiness vacated by the 4th Cavalry Division directly that division is clear.

Thence it will move to a position on or about the Nahr Iskanderune on receipt of orders from Corps headquarters; thence follow the remainder of the Corps.

It will be prepared to send a detachment of one brigade or less from El Lajjun to block the roads and railway passing through Jenin and to gain touch with the 5th A.L.H. Brigade, which is to rejoin the division in this area.

(iv) *R.H.A.*—Directly the initial barrage under which the infantry advance and which commences at an hour known as " XXI Corps Zero Hour " is complete, the R.H.A. batteries will rejoin their divisions under divisional arrangements, after reference to G.O.C.R.A. XXI Corps.

4. *Dividing Line.*—The Dividing Line between 4th and 5th Cavalry Divisions will be Tabsor–El Mughaiyir–Tell edh Dhrur–Qannir–Kefrein–Buseile.

5. *Demolitions.*—Demolitions on railways should be limited to such as can be easily repaired.

6. *Naval Co-operation.*—Torpedo-boat Destroyers are co-operating in the attack and later in the advance of this Corps along the coast. Care must be taken to display the Red and Yellow Troop Flags as prominently as possible for the information of the Navy.

7. *Allotment of Roads.*—The Tabsor–Hadera road and route along the Beach is allotted to this Corps when required. If 4th and 5th Cavalry Divisions both cross the Nahr el Faliq by the Beach and Coast road, the following roads are allotted after the Nahr el Faliq is crossed :—

(a) *4th Cavalry Division.*—Tabsor–El Mughaiyir–Zelefe road crossing the Iskanderune at Kh. esh Sh. Mukammad in G.19.b. central, branching off the main road at P.1.c. central or G.25.c.2.2.

(b) *5th Cavalry Division.*—Arsuf–Mukhalid–Hadera road crossing the Iskanderune by bridges in F.30.b. central.

(c) *Australian Mounted Division.*—Tabsor–El Mughaiyir–Zelefe road, crossing the Iskanderune by bridges in F.30.b. central.

An additional bridge over the Nahr el Faliq is being constructed by the XXI Corps for the use of the Desert Mounted Corps.

The troops of the XXI Corps have precedence over the existing bridge at (D.3) N.6.c.9.3. Desert Mounted Corps train and park have precedence over XXI Corps trains and parks on all roads on " Z " Day.

8. *Traffic.*—If the 4th Cavalry Division follows the 5th Cavalry Division along the Coast road, it will follow immediately behind the fighting troops, the transport of 5th Cavalry Division giving way and keeping clear of the roads.

9. *Maps.*—No maps other than the following will be used during operations :—

Palestine. 1/40,000.
1/63,360.
Haifa. 1/250,000.

10. *Instructions.*—Instructions regarding R.A.F., Communications, Medical, Administrative and Supply Services, Traffic Control and Prisoners, Ammunition Supply, Engineer Arrangements are being issued separately.

11. *Time.*—Watches will be synchronized daily, commencing from receipt of this order, by the time received by Wireless from G.H.Q. every day at 8.15 a.m. and 6 p.m.

12. The date of Z day and Zero hour will be communicated verbally to those concerned.

13. *Reports.*—Reports to Advanced Corps headquarters at Pt. 121 in Z.27.b.4.7. on Z day until it moves forward. Advanced Report Centres will be communicated.

14. Acknowledge.

C. A. C. GODWIN,
Br.-General, General Staff, Desert Mounted Corps.

Issued at 11.30 p.m.

APPENDIX 27.

TELEGRAPHIC ORDER BY DESERT MOUNTED CORPS.

G.A.72. 26th September 1918 (7 p.m.).

Ausdiv., Fourcav., Fivecav., XX Corps, XXI Corps, G.H.Q. (O), D.A. & Q.M.G., G.O.C.R.A., C.R.E., D.D.M.S.

Seventh and Eighth Turkish Armies have been destroyed. Fourth Army is retreating on Damascus *via* Der'a. Desert Mounted Corps will move on Damascus. 4th Cavalry Division is moving on Der'a under separate instructions, and will move thence to Damascus. Australian Mounted Division followed by 5th Cavalry Division will move *via* Jisr Benat Yakub and El Quneitra. The march will be so regulated that the Australian Mounted Division arrives at El Quneitra in the early morning of 28th inst. and will form on the plain to allow 5th Cavalry Division to debouch. Australian Mounted Division should start from El Quneitra at 5 p.m. on 28th inst. and endeavour to reach Damascus in the early morning of 29th inst. 5th Cavalry Division will closely follow Australian Mounted Division in order to support and provide as imposing a force as possible on approaching Damascus. Divisions should move on as broad a front as ground permits. On arrival at Damascus a defensive position will be taken up on high ground commanding the town, and dispositions made by leading division to secure all hostile approaches. Town will be left under its present civil administration, and no national flags will be flown. Only fighting wheels will accompany troops; all other wheels will be concentrated under divisional control. After Tiberias fighting troops of 5th Cavalry Division will have precedence over Australian Division Mounted transport. Desert Mounted Corps Report Centre will open at Tiberias to-morrow at 10 a.m. and then will follow in rear of 5th Cavalry Division. Acknowledge. Addressed Ausdiv., Fourcav., Fivecav., repeated XXI Corps, XX Corps. G.H.Q. (O), Chaytor's Force, D.A. & Q.M.G., G.O.C.R.A., C.R.E., D.D.M.S., A.D.A.S.

Maps 1, 2A, 3.

GENERAL INDEX.[1]

Abd el Kader, 591.
Abdulla el Feir, 404
Abdulla, the Emir, 397, 398, 409, 410, 609, 624
Abu Shushe, Action at, 178
Abu Tulul, Affair of, 429; simultaneous cavalry action, 434
Adye, Maj.-Gen. J., 23, 412
Agamemnon (British battleship), 620, 627
Agostino, Lieut.-Col. F. d', 260
Air Force, Royal (*see also* Flying Corps, Royal), organization of on eve of Megiddo, 460; value of in concealing preparations, 462; effective work of in attack, 487; bombing of Wadi el Far'a by, 502; co-operation of with Arabs, 565; its mastery of the air, 642
Albright, Major M. C., 121
Aleppo, capture of. *See* Megiddo, Battles of
Alexandretta, projects for landing at, 27, 297, 610, 618
Ali Bey, Col., 557, 558
Ali Fuad Bey, Col., 366
Ali Fuad Pasha, Col. (later Maj.-Gen.), 31, 35, 106, 141, 155, 190, 217, 291, 366, 613
Ali Ihsan Pasha, Gen., 622, 623
Ali Riza Pasha el Rikabi, Gen., 586, 593, 607
Ali, the Emir, 397, 398, 409
Allenby, Gen. Sir Edmund H. H., arrives in Cairo, 1; 2, 7, 8; states his requirements, 12; transfers G.H.Q. to Palestine, 13; receives general instructions, 15; his plan of attack on Gaza-Beersheba line, 17; 21; his orders for this attack, 28; discusses policy with C.I.G.S., 26, 32, 54, 55; his peremptory message at Beersheba, 57; his readiness to exploit events, 63; 66, 78; postpones Sheria attack, 88; authorizes attack on Khuweilfe, 95; orders cavalry to advance on Huj, 107; 111, 123, 124, 126, 139; disregards threatened counter-attack, 146;

Allenby, Gen. Sir Edmund H. H. (*continued*)—
is prepared to attack Junction Station, 154; gives instructions for capture of station, 156; his correspondence with Government, 157; decides to advance into hills, 184, 188; 197; orders a diversion in the plain, 208; orders XXI Corps to discontinue attacks, 212; orders XX Corps to relieve XXI, 219; enters Jerusalem, 259; approves plans for advance north of Jerusalem and Jaffa, 265; 276, 277, 290, 291; is called on to exploit success, 293; his criticism of Government's suggestions, 294; 299, 302, 305; decides to advance his right to Wadi el 'Auja, 310; decides to destroy Hejaz Railway at 'Amman, 328; breaks off attack on 'Amman, 345; his plans in March, 350; authorizes Gen. Bulfin to discontinue Berukin operation, 356; orders demonstration in Jordan Valley, 361; his objects in second Trans-Jordan raid, 364; 385; authorizes withdrawal from Es Salt, 386; 387; 389; realizes importance of Arab campaign, 395; 397; 400, 401, 406, 408, 410, 411, 412; is called on to send troops to France, 413; begins reorganization, 414; protests against withdrawal of 54th Div., 418; his reason for holding Jordan Valley, 423; 437; his plans for final offensive, 447; expands original scheme, 449; his orders for final offensive, 455; 461; refuses to intervene in discussion between Gens. Bulfin and Chauvel, 465; his confidence in success, 468; 532; reveals intention of capturing Damascus, 560; his orders, 561; his demands of the Arabs, 563; his interview with Feisal, 592; 594, 596; orders occupation of Riyaq,

---

[1] Names in orders of battle and operation orders, which appear in appendices, are not indexed.

725

GENERAL INDEX

Allenby, Gen. Sir Edmund H. H. (*continued*)—
601; orders occupation of Homs and Tripoli, 605; 606; issues instructions for administration of territory, 607; decides to advance to Aleppo, 609; refuses to stop Gen. Macandrew's advance, 611; 614; 618; his difficulties after Armistice, 622; visits Constantinople, 623; 629, 631; his summary of the campaigns, 632; his advantages and difficulties, 634; his moral influence, 635; his strategy, 636; 645; discourages use of word "Crusade," 647
Amet, Vice-Admiral, 620
'Amman, attacks on in March, 335; capture of in September, 552
Anderson, Lieut.-Col. J., 269, 272
Andrew, Lieut. R. H., 260
Andrews, Pte. R. W. J., 252
Anley, Br.-Gen. F. G., 162, 163
Aphis (British river gunboat), at Third Gaza, 65
Apsley, Capt. Lord, 577
Arab Campaign, progress of after capture of 'Aqaba, 328, 364, 395; value of to British, 396, 408; Arab victory at Tafila, 402; organization of Arab forces, 405; Ma'an operations, 406; attacks on railway near Der'a, 466, 563; capture of Der'a, 567; attacks on Turks on Pilgrims' Road, 585; attack on Aleppo, 613; occupation of Muslimiya Station, 617; occupation of Medina, 624
Arab Northern Army, composition, 397; 405, 406
Arab Southern Army, 409
Arbalète (French destroyer), 65
Arif, Mohammed, 140
Armistice with Turkey, 618; terms of, 625
Armitage, Capt. R., 253
Armstrong, Lieut.-Col. A., 161, 202, 479
Armstrong, Br.-Gen. St. G. B., 510
Army of Occupation, composition of, 623
Artillery, counter-battery work of at Beersheba, 45, 51; at Gaza, 64, 73; marches of in Judæan Hills, 207, 287; is reinforced on the 'Auja, 266; value of in advance of XXI Corps in March, 323,

Artillery (*continued*)—
325; concentration of for final offensive, 456; effect of in final offensive, 472; "mechanization" of on Nablus Road, 497
Auda Abu Tayi, 407, 564, 566, 585
'Auja, Nahr el, demonstration over, 214; passage of, 265

Baghdad, German scheme for recapture of, 4, 13
Bagot-Chester, Capt. W. G., 67
Bailey, Lieut.-Col. P. J., 372
Bainbridge, Br.-Gen. P. A., 443
Balfour Declaration, 410, 420
Barada Gorge, blocking of. *See* Megiddo, Battles of
Barker, Capt. G. P., 317
Barqusya, Turkish counter-attack at, 146
Barrow, Maj.-Gen. Sir G. de S., 125, 126, 166, 167, 178, 192, 196, 199, 200, 207, 220, 221, 224, 226, 227, 235, 412, 415, 420, 465, 514, 515, 518, 519, 539, 581–4, 586
Barrow's Detachment (*see* " Corps," Arms and Formations Index)
Barry, Major F. R., 252
Bartholomew, Br.-Gen. W. H., 88, 260, 412, 561
Bayley, Lieut.-Col. H., 252, 256
Beck, Major W., 252
Beersheba, capture of. *See* Gaza, Third Battle of
Beirut, occupation of. *See* Megiddo, Battles of
Bell, Lieut.-Col. G. J., 431
Bell-Irving, Capt. W. O., 230
Berukin, Action of, 350
Bingham, Lieut. C. R., 570
Böhme, Oberst, 392–4
Bolingbroke, Major A. J., 337
Bols, Maj.-Gen. Sir L. J., appointed C.G.S., 16; 88, 260, 356
Borton, Lieut.-Col. A. D., V.C., 108
Borton, Br.-Gen. W. M., 260
Boughey, 2/Lieut. S. H. P., V.C., 234, 235
Bourchier, Lieut.-Col. M. W. J., 377, 542, 568, 569, 590
Bourne, Lieut.-Col. G. H., 432
Bowker, Br.-Gen. W. J., 316, 317
Bowman-Manifold, Br.-Gen. M. G. E., 459
Boyd, Capt. J. M., 556
Boyle, Capt. W. H. D., R.N., 395
Brémond, Col. E., 623

GENERAL INDEX

Breslau (German cruiser), 296
Brest-Litovsk, Treaty of, its effect in Palestine, 444
Brierty, Lieut. A. R., 115
Broadbent, Br.-Gen. E. N., 561
Bronsart von Schellendorff, Gen., 6
Brown, Lieut.-Col. J., 222
Browne, Lieut.-Col. J. G., 167, 557
Bulfin, Lieut.-Gen. Sir E. S., appointed to command of XXI Corps, 16, 64; his orders for Gaza attack, 66; 74, 124; his orders for pursuit, 129; 132, 144, 146; receives instructions for capture of Junction Station, 156; issues his orders, 158; 175; orders advance into hills, 189; orders 75th Div. to reach Bire at all costs, 193; 194, 196, 197, 201, 207, 208, 211, 219; takes over command in plain from Gen. Chauvel, 265; subordinates his plan for 'Auja crossing to Gen. Hill's, 267; 270, 275, 353, 356, 448; his views on concentration of cavalry for Megiddo, 464; his orders for Megiddo, 469; his orders for 20th Sept. 1918, 504; his tribute to his staff, 510; his decision regarding Ladder of Tyre, 602; 605
Burney, Br.-Gen. P. de S., 313
Burqa and Brown Hill, action at, 152
Buta Khan, Naik, 482
Butler, Br.-Gen. E. R. C., 642
Buxton, Major I., 317
Buxton, Major R. V., 408, 563

Caccia, Comdt., 260
Cain, Capt. J. R., 104
Caldecott, Major A. H., 498
Calvert, Lieut.-Col. C. A., 225, 230
Camel Transport Corps, 142, 185, 190, 263, 342, 454, 457, 562, 584
Cameron, Lieut.-Col. D., 377
Cameron, Lieut.-Col. D. C., 556, 557
Campbell, Maj.-Gen. Sir Walter, 23, 143, 188, 268, 301, 440
Captures, at Beersheba, 51, 59; at Gaza, 74; at Sheria, 100; in pursuit, 113; in capture of Junction Station, 163, 169, 172; in capture of Jerusalem, 246; in operations north of Jerusalem, 290; in Actions of Tell 'Asur, 322, 326; in first Trans-Jordan raid, 347; in second Trans-Jordan raid, 389; in Affair of Abu Tulul, 433,

Captures (*continued*)—
436; in Battles of Megiddo, 473, 476, 500, 502; (total of XX Corps), 503; (total of XXI Corps), 510; at Nazareth, 527; at Jenin, 531; at Beisan, 533; at Haifa, 537; at Jordan fords, 539, 540, 541; at Samakh, 544; by Chaytor's Force on Jordan, 552; and at 'Amman, 554; and at Ziza, 558; (total of Chaytor's Force), 558; on road to Damascus, 570, 571, 573, 575, 576; at Damascus, 589, 590, 591; (total of Desert Mtd. Corps up to Damascus), 593; (total in final offensive), 618; by Arabs at Medina, 624
Carlyon, Sergt. E., 432
Cassels, Lieut.-Col, G. R., 162, 198, 212, 354
Casualties—
British, at Beersheba, 52, 60; at Gaza, 74; at Sheria, 100, 109; at Khuweilfe, 105; at Hureira, 110; at the Wadi el Hesi, 134, 136; at Burqa and Brown Hill, 154; in capture of Junction Station, 164, 172; in defence of Nabi Samweil, 204; in attacks on El Jib, 206, 211; at Beit 'Ur el Foqa, 234, 236; in capture of Jerusalem, 246, 249; up to capture of Jerusalem, 290; in Actions of Tell 'Asur, 322, 326; in First Trans-Jordan raid, 347; at Berukin, 357; in Turkish attacks on Jordan Bridgeheads, 361; in Second Trans-Jordan raid, 389; in attack on "Sisters," 425; in Affair of Abu Tulul, 433, 436; in Battles of Megiddo, 476, 500, 502; (total of XX Corps), 503; (total of XXI Corps), 509; (total of Chaytor's Force), 559; (total of Desert Mtd. Corps up to Damascus), 594; at Haritan, 615; (total in final offensive), 618; (total from Jan. 1915 to Armistice), 618
Turkish, from 31st Oct. to 31st Dec. 1917, 262; at Berukin, 357; in attacks on Jordan Bridgeheads, 361; in second Trans-Jordan raid, 394. *And see* Captures

GENERAL INDEX

Cavalry, strategical use of, 639; marches of without water, 640; tactics of, 644

Channer, Lieut.-Col. G. K., 203

Charles, Lieut.-Col. E. M. S., 290, 303

Chauvel, Lieut.-Gen. Sir H. G., appointed to command of Desert Mtd. Corps, 16; 26, 30, 41; his orders for Beersheba attack to be pressed, 57; 86, 87; advises postponement of Sheria attack, 88; 95, 107; 109; his orders for pursuit of the enemy, 112, 114, 117; 119, 124; points out weariness of horses, 126; 143, 146, 147; receives instructions for capture of Junction Station, 156; issues his orders, 158; 174, 175; orders occupation of Ramle and Lydda, 178; orders demonstration over Nahr el 'Auja, 214; 224, 225, 265, 302; his plans for Second Trans-Jordan raid, 365, 369; his conversation with Gen. Grant, 372; 375, 377, 380, 382; orders withdrawal from Es Salt, 385, 386; 448; his views on concentration of cavalry, 464; his orders for Megiddo, 513; 524, 528, 529; orders interception of Turks at Jenin, 530; orders advance on Haifa, 534; orders interception of Turks at Jordan fords, 538; 542; receives instructions to capture Damascus, 560; drops detachment at Quneitra to guard communications, 569; 574, 576; his entry into Damascus, 593; 601, 605, 606, 611

Chaytor, Maj.-Gen. E. W. C., 55, 56, 86, 112, 113, 117, 143, 167, 214, 223, 308, 337, 340–3, 345, 346, 358, 361, 362, 377–9, 383, 386, 389, 450, 463, 466, 549–52, 555, 557, 558

Chaytor's Force (see " Corps," Arms and Formations Index)

Chetwode, Lieut.-Gen. Sir P. W., Bt., his appreciation of situation in June 1917, 7; appointed to command of XX Corps, 16; 26, 32; his orders for Beersheba attack, 44; 48; directs assault to be launched, 49; 79, 81, 84; advises postponement of Sheria attack, 88; 90; his orders for

Chetwode, Lieut.-Gen. Sir P. W. (*continued*)—
Sheria attack, 94; 95, 96, 99, 109, 124, 125, 126, 140; takes over command in Judæan Hills, 228; orders attacks on Foqa to be discontinued, 236; decides to shift his right closer to Jerusalem, 237; his instructions to Gen. Mott, 239; his orders for capture of Jerusalem, 240; 243, 247; his messages to Gen. Mott, 250; 251, 254, 256, 258, 260; his plan for advance north of Jerusalem, 275; learns of projected Turkish attack, 278; his subsequent action, 282; success of his plan, 286, 288; orders the advance to cease, 290; 302; his plan for occupation of Jericho, 303; 321, 331, 334; 362, 365, 449, 466; his orders for Megiddo, 471; 491, 497; orders advance on Nablus, 499

Christie, Lce.-Corpl. J. A., V.C., 274

Church, Pte. H. E., 252

Clarke, Br.-Gen. G. V., 574–6

Clayton, Br.-Gen. G. F., 260, 300, 301

Climate. See Palestine

Clowes, Major M., 216

Collins, Corpl. John, V.C., 50

Colston, Br.-Gen. the Hon. E. M., 160, 163, 194, 197, 198, 201, 205, 206, 355, 426

Comet (British destroyer), at Third Gaza, 65

Connaught, H.R.H. the Duke of, 334

Cook, Lieut.-Col. J. B., 134, 170, 209

Cooke, Major E. M. D. H., 253

Coutelas (French destroyer), at Third Gaza, 65

Cox, Br.-Gen. C. F., 56, 145, 308, 342, 358, 359, 388, 432, 551

Crawford, Major A., 234, 235

Cripps, Lieut.-Col. the Hon. F. H., 168, 172, 179

Da Costa, Br.-Gen. E. C., 46, 48, 313, 340, 341, 486

Dalmeny, Lieut.-Col. Lord, 260

Damascus, advance to and capture of. See Megiddo, Battles of

Davenport, Major W. A., 398, 409

Davidson, Br.-Gen. S. R., 476

Davies, Br.-Gen. C. H., 426, 483

GENERAL INDEX 729

Davies, Br.-Gen. G. F., 440
Davison, Capt. D. S., 518, 519
Dawnay, Lieut.-Col. A. G. C., 406, 407, 412
Dawnay, Br.-Gen. G. P., 8, 260
Dear, Lieut.-Col. H. J., 247
Deedes, Lieut.-Col. W. H., 260
Dempsey, Capt. J. A. D., 308
Deshon, Lieut.-Col. F. G. T., 317
Dickson, Lieut. A. F., 436
Dixon, Lieut. E. W., 104
Doig, 2/Lieut. P. W. K., 530
Dommes, Oberst v., 155
Donkey transport, 263
Druid (British destroyer), 471, 485
Duffy, Pte. James, V.C., 284
Dundas, Major W. L., 356

Edwardes, Br.-Gen. S. M., 478, 505
Edwards, Br.-Gen. Fitz J. M., 46, 98, 246
Edwards, 2/Lieut. J. W., 121
Egypt, unrest in, 300, 624
Egyptian Camel Corps, 406, 407, 564
Egyptian Expeditionary Force, strength of in October 1917, 35; administrative changes in, 299; despatches troops to France, 350; 364, 412; reorganization of on Indian basis, 411; state of in late summer 1918, 438; leave in, 443; strength of in September 1918, 452; sickness in at end of campaign, 597; reorganization of after Armistice, 623; its part in the Great War, 633; spirit and devotion of, 646
Egyptian Labour Corps, 93, 185, 337, 454, 497
Enver Pasha, 4, 5, 183, 445, 619
Espérey, Gen. Franchet d', 619
Essad Bey, Col., 349, 392, 394
Eustace, Lieut.-Col. H., 491
Evans, Br.-Gen. E., 22

Fakhri Pasha, Gen., 624
Falkenhausen, Lieut.-Col. v., 393, 394
Falkenhayn, Gen. v., appointed to command of *Yilderim*, 4; abandons Baghdad scheme, 6; 7, 36; gives way to Kress about reserves, 43; 62; orders evacuation of Gaza, 76; 89; orders counter-attacks north of Beersheba, 106; 139; orders with-

Falkenhayn, Gen. v. *(continued)*—
drawal from Tell esh Sheria, 141; 150; prestige of, 155; 156; decides to turn to the offensive, 155; 183, 190; orders general withdrawal after loss of Junction Station, 217; sees an opportunity to counter-attack in the hills, 218; 220, 228, 236; his attempt to retake Jerusalem, 278; its failure, 290; his report to Germany, 291; his recall, 310; 326; his operations against the Arabs, 328; 404; estimate of, 636
Fane, Maj.-Gen. Sir V. B., 350, 481, 514
Fauconneau (French destroyer), at Third Gaza, 65
Feisal, the Emir, 328, 329, 364, 397, 401, 406, 409, 566, 591, 592, 605, 606, 609–11, 625, 647
Fevzi Pasha, Gen., 42, 140, 182, 236
Findlay, Lieut.-Col. J. M., 204
Fitzgerald, Capt. G. M., 600
Fitzgerald, Br.-Gen. P. D., 115, 120
Flying Corps, Royal (*see also* Air Force, Royal), activity of at Third Gaza, 40; in pursuit, 138; after capture of Jerusalem, 258, 290; in capture of Jericho, 309
Foch, Marshal, 635
Foqa, Beit 'Ur el, evacuation of by Yeomanry Mounted Div., 227; attack on by 25/R. Welch Fus., 231; by 16/Devonshire, 235
Force in Egypt, 300
Forester (British destroyer), 471, 485
Fortescue-Wells, Lieut.-Col. L., 268
Forth, Lieut.-Col. N. B. de Lancey, 103, 104
Foster, Lieut.-Col. W. J., 515, 519
Foulkes-Taylor, Lieut. C. D., 374
Fournet, Admiral Dartige du, 419
France, claims of in Syria, 591, 608
Frankenberg u. Proschlitz, Oberst v., 352
French Army—
 Détachement Français de Palestine et de Syrie (D.F.P.S.), composition of, 419; 452, 456, 464, 469, 470, 473, 476, 505, 607
 Regiments, Cavalry—
  Régiment Mixte de Marche de Cavalerie (R.M.M.C.), 487, 509, 571–3, 607

730 GENERAL INDEX

French Army (*continued*)—
  Regiments, Infantry—
    Régiment de Marche de la Légion d'Orient, 473, 622
    Régiment de Marche de Tirailleurs, 473, 474
Frey, Major, 495, 520
Fryer, Br.-Gen. F. A. B., 170, 171, 201

Garland, Major H., 399
Gaza, Third Battle of, the plan of attack, 25; approach march to Beersheba, 37; Turkish attacks on outposts, 37; attack of XX Corps, 48; of Desert Mounted Corps, 55; charge of 4th L. H. Bde., 58; attack on Gaza defences, 69; operations north of Beersheba, 79, 101; attack on Sheria position, 95; attack on Khuweilfe, 101; advance of cavalry, 111; charge of Huj, 120; advance of XXI Corps, 130; capture of Wadi el Hesi defences, 131; capture of Sausage Ridge, 133.
Gell, Major, P. F., 435, 437, 615
George, Lce.-Corpl. T. B., 531
German aid to Turkey, 3, 444
Gibbs, Pte. R. A., 584
Gillman, Maj.-Gen. W., 297
Girdwood, Maj.-Gen. E. S., 44, 49–51, 81, 96, 248, 286, 289, 312, 315, 317, 320
Glynton, Major G. M., 163
Godwin, Br.-Gen. C. A. C., 168, 169, 172, 178, 179, 224, 226, 227, 378, 388, 412
Goeben (German battle cruiser), 296
Gough-Calthorpe, Vice-Admiral the Hon. Sir S. A., 620, 621, 625
Gould, Major G., 518, 578, 580
Grafton (British cruiser), 65, 275
Grant, Br.-Gen. W., 57, 115, 226, 369, 372, 373, 375, 378, 384, 388, 389, 542, 544, 545, 569
Grassman, Hauptm., 349
Gray-Cheape, Lieut.-Col. H. A., 120
Green, Lieut-Col. (later Br.-Gen.) W. G. K., 521, 578, 581, 582
Greer, Br.-Gen. F. A., 288, 500, 501
Gregory, Br.-Gen. C. L., 514, 539–41, 585
Gregory, Commander G., R.N., 143

Hache (French destroyer), at Third Gaza, 65
Halil Pasha, 6

Hamid Bey, Lieut.-Col., 404
Hammerstein-Gesmold, Oberstlt. Freiherr v., 594, 595
Harbord, Br.-Gen. C. R., 130, 378, 434, 535, 536, 614
Hardy, Thomas, quoted, 518
Hare, Maj.-Gen. S. W., 67, 69, 274, 473, 474, 476
Haritan, Affair of. *See* Megiddo, Battles of
Harter, Lieut. J. C. H., 225
Hawksley, Br.-Gen. R. P. T., 510
Heathcote, Br.-Gen. C. E., 49
Hecker, Rittmeister, 527
Hejaz, campaign in the. *See* Arab Campaign
Henderson, Lieut. L. J., 433
Hesi, Wadi el, capture of. *See* Gaza, Third Battle of
Hext, Br.-Gen. L. J., 96
Heywood-Lonsdale, Lieut.-Col. H., 232
Hikmet Bey, 620, 625
Hill, Lieut.-Col. E. F. J., 602
Hill, Maj.-Gen. J., 132, 133, 135, 144, 166, 201, 208, 209, 211, 268
Hills, Lieut. C. H., 269
Hoare, Br.-Gen. R., 47, 248
Hodgson, Maj.-Gen. H. W., 57, 115, 118, 146, 174, 234, 353, 369, 373, 379, 380, 382, 383, 385–7, 390–2, 394, 416, 529, 531, 544, 568, 569, 571, 574, 590, 593
Holden, Lieut.-Col. H. N., 536, 615
Hornsby, Capt. H. P., 615
Horses, achievements of. *See* Cavalry
Hoskins, Maj.-Gen. A. R., 476, 505
Howard-Vyse, Br.-Gen. R. G. H., 373, 387, 412, 514, 515
Huddleston, Br.-Gen. H. J., 153, 160, 194, 355, 426, 479, 480
Huj, Affair of. *See* Gaza, Third Battle of
Humphreys, Br.-Gen. E. T., 337, 371, 412, 508
Hurcomb, Sergt. F. G., 252
Hurst, Major H. C., 216
Hussein Husni, Lieut.-Col., 62, 77, 150, 154, 155, 182, 183, 236, 349, 357, 404
Hussein Ibn Ali, King of the Hejaz, 402, 410, 564, 608
Hutchinson, Lieut.-Col. F. P., 324
Hutchison, Major J. R., 579, 582

Infantry tactics, 642
Influenza. *See* Sickness

GENERAL INDEX

Ismet Bey, Col., 34, 54, 60, 61, 62
Izzet Pasha, Marshal, 5, 619, 620
Jackson, Capt. M. H., 539
Jackson, Rear-Admiral T., 65, 268, 275, 297, 471
Ja'far Pasha el Askeri, 397, 401, 405
Jaffa, occupation of, 184; Battle of, 265
Jarvis, Lieut.-Col. F. W. 316
Jemal Pasha, Gen. Ahmed, *Biyuk*, opposes Baghdad scheme, 4; his departure to Europe, 310, 327
Jemal Pasha, Maj.-Gen. Mohammed, *Kuchuk*, 327, 343, 348, 393, 394, 511, 552, 589, 595, 605
Jericho, capture of, 302
Jerusalem, capture of, 237; incidents in surrender of, 252; C.-in-C.'s entry into, 259; British defence of, 275
Jevad Pasha, Gen., 312, 327, 468, 511, 546, 595
Jewish Colonies, 176
Jewish Legion, 420
Jones, 2/Lieut. G. E., 333
Jordan, passage of the, 328
Jordan Bridgeheads, Turkish attacks on, 358
Jordan Valley, conditions of, 305, 422
Joyce, Major P. C., 398, 405, 406
Judæan Hills, advance into, 189
Junction Station, Capture of, 158. See also Maghar Ridge

Karanbahadur Khan, Rifleman, V.C., 355
Kearsey, Lieut.-Col. A., 209
Kelly, Br.-Gen. P. J. V., 120, 369, 374, 379, 382, 388, 391, 522, 524, 576, 606
Kemball, Br.-Gen. A. G., 425, 482
Kendall, Capt. C., 203
Kensington, Lieut.-Col. Lord, 232
Kiazim Pasha, Gen., 311, 527
King, Br.-Gen. A. D'A., 534
King, Lieut. W. K., 434
Kinnear, Lieut.-Col. W., 283
Kisch, Capt. E. R., 245
Kitson, Capt. R. B., 161
Knowles, Lieut.-Col. G., 518
Kress von Kressenstein, Gen. Freiherr, 4, 7, 34, 36, 43, 54; his action at Beersheba, 61; Turkish criticism of, 62; 63; his comments on Gaza attack, 76; 106, 139, 141, 163, 222, 311; his recall, 312

Ladybird (British river gunboat), at Third Gaza, 65
Lafone, Major A. N., V.C., 38, 39
Lambert, Major W. J., 615
Lapwing (British destroyer), 275
Latham, Major A., 485
Lawrence, Lieut.-Col. H. M., 321
Lawrence, Capt. (later Lieut.-Col.) T. E., 260, 398, 400, 402, 404–6, 563, 565, 582, 583, 585, 591
Lawson, Lieut.-Col. E. F., 540, 541
Lebon, Comdt., 572
Leggett, Br.-Gen. A. H., 67, 152, 210, 211, 271
Leslie, Lieut.-Col. (later Br.-Gen.) W. S., 483, 508, 606, 607
Liman von Sanders, Gen., 7; succeeds Falkenhayn, 310; his characteristics, 311; his new methods of holding front, 326; 343, 346; his action in first Trans-Jordan raid, 392; 408, 427, 429; his account of Affair of Abu Tulul, 437; recognises decline of Turkish morale, 438; protests against withdrawal of German troops, 445; 450, 452, 468; his orders on 19th Sept. 1918, 511, 520; escapes capture at Nazareth, 526; 542; at Samakh and Der'a, 545; 570, 573, 588; orders stubborn retirement to Damascus, 594; 605, 613; his departure, 621
Lizard (British destroyer), 275
Lloyd George, Right Hon. D., 261, 294, 297
Longley, Maj.-Gen. J. R., 110, 276, 282, 283, 286, 290, 321, 427, 492, 500, 501
Luard, Br.-Gen. C. C., 477
Lucas, Major G. W. C., 436
Lyall, Major R. A., 480
Lynden-Bell, Maj.-Gen. A. L., 17

M.15, *M.29*, *M.31*, *M.32* (British monitors), 65; *M.15* sunk by submarine, 66; *M.29*, 275; *M.31*, 275; *M.32*, 275
Ma'an, operations against, 406
Macandrew, Maj.-Gen. H. J. M., 415, 417, 434, 522–4, 527, 528, 574, 575, 591, 593, 601, 606, 610, 611, 613, 616, 617, 624
Macansh, Lieut. J. D., 433
Macauley, Br.-Gen. Sir. G., 9, 20, 439
McDougall, Capt. A., 38

732 GENERAL INDEX

McIntyre, Capt. R. H. M., 613
Mackenzie, Lieut.-Col. C. M., 245, 280, 307
McKenzie, Lieut. P. W., 238, 239
McLaurin, Lieut.-Col. A. M., 599
Maclean, Br.-Gen. C. A. H., 198, 204, 354, 480
McClelland, Lieut. T., 138
McMurrough-Kavanagh, Major A. T., 417
M'Neill, Br.-Gen. A. J., 49, 51, 96, 248, 473, 474
Maghar Ridge, capture of, 166
Malaria. *See* Sickness
Mardon, Lieut.-Col. A. C., 236
Marriott-Dodington, Br.-Gen. W., 68
Mason, Lieut.-Col. G. K. M., 378, 581
Massy, Br.-Gen. E. C., 191, 207
Maulud Pasha, 401, 407
Maxwell, Lieut.-Gen. Sir J., 299, 300, 629
Medical organization, 23, 264, 322, 425, 460
Medina, surrender of. *See* Arab Campaign.
Megiddo, Battles of; preparations for, 447; attack of XXI Corps in, 472; capture of Tul Karm, 487; attack of XX Corps in, 488; final infantry operations in, 496; advance of cavalry, 513; capture of El 'Affule, 520; attack on Nazareth, 525; interception of Turks at Jenin, 530; capture of Haifa, 534; actions at Jordan fords, 538; capture of Samakh, 542; operations east of Jordan, 547; advance to Damascus, 560; action at Sa'sa', 569; action at Kaukab, 572; blocking of Barada Gorge, 572; actions near Kiswe, 574; action at Irbid, 577; action at Remta, 581; occupation of Der'a, 583; capture of Damascus, 586; actions outside Damascus on Homs road, 589; occupation of Beirut, 602; occupation of Homs and Tripoli, 604; capture of Aleppo, 609; action at Haritan, 613
Meldrum, Br.-Gen. W., 55, 56, 91, 343, 549–51
Mercer, Lieut. W. B., 123
Mesopotamia, campaign in, 3, 8, 298, 618

Meta'ab, Sheikh, 403
Military Resources Board, 440
Moberley, Lieut.-Col. A. H., 324
Money, Maj.-Gen. Sir A. W., 300, 607
Money, Br.-Gen. N. E., 85, 258, 301, 490
Monro, Gen. Sir Charles, 414
Moore, Br.-Gen. C. D. H., 132, 133, 135, 136, 145, 175, 195, 210, 234
Moore, Lieut.-Col. W. H., 324
Morris, Br.-Gen. E. M., 98, 99, 427, 494
Morrison, Col. F. L., 132
Mott, Maj.-Gen. S. F., 81, 85, 87, 89, 90, 94, 95, 104, 105, 125, 237, 239–42, 250, 251, 264, 283, 287, 315, 489, 491, 492, 497, 499
Mott's Detachment (*see* "Divisions," Arms and Formations Index)
Mudge, Br.-Gen. A., 68, 475
Mulliner, Capt. W. A., 238, 239
Murray, Gen. Sir A. J., 20, 299, 300, 415, 440, 629, 642
Murray, Br.-Gen. E. R. B., 362
Musallabe, Turkish attack on. *See* Jordan Bridgeheads.
Mustapha Kemal Pasha, Gen., 5, 6, 445, 495, 546, 595, 605, 613, 616–18, 621, 622, 625

Nabi Samweil, Battle of, 197
Nablus, Battle of. *See* Megiddo, Battles of
Naper, Capt. W. L., 260
Nasir, Sherif, 402, 611
Naval assistance, at Gaza, 65, 73; at Nahr el 'Auja, 275; in Action of Berukin, 353; in Arab operations, 395; in Battles of Megiddo, 471, 485; in general, 634. *And see* Transport by sea.
Nazareth, attack on. *See* Megiddo, Battles of
Nes Ziyona, action at, 177
Newcombe, Lieut.-Col. S. F., 54, 64, 82, 83, 398
Nihad Pasha, Gen., 622
Nur Ahmad, Risaldar, 576
Nuri Bey, Col., 583, 606, 613
Nuri esh Shalaan, 564, 566

Olden, Lieut.-Col. A. C. N., 530, 588, 589, 591
Onslow, Lieut.-Col. (later Br.-Gen.) G. M. M., 368, 371, 378, 415, 487, 504, 572

GENERAL INDEX 733

Oppen, Oberst v., 495, 506, 511, 512, 532, 539, 545, 546, 594, 595, 599, 605
Ordnance services, 443
Orpen-Palmer, Lieut.-Col. (later Br.-Gen.) H. B. H., 110, 474
Osborne, Lieut.-Col. R. H., 417, 521

Palestine, administration of, 300, 591; climatic conditions of, 18, 144, 158, 241, 278, 292, 422; physical conditions of, 186, 304, 451; spiritual influence of, 647. *And see* Jordan Valley, Syria, and Trans-Jordan
Palin, Maj.-Gen. P. C., 153, 159, 162, 163, 190, 197, 206, 479, 480
Pan-Islamism, 2
Pan-Turanianism, 2
Pan-Turkism, 2, 4, 444
Papen, Major v., 392
Parsons, Lieut.-Col. J. W., 233, 543
Paterson, Lieut.-Col. A. W. S., 320
Paton, Major R. W., 134
Patterson, Lieut.-Col. J. H., 553, 555
Patterson, Lieut. R. R. W., 531
Peake, Capt. F. G., 407, 565
Pearless, Br.-Gen. C. W., 309, 331
Pearson, Br.-Gen. V. L. N., 85, 89, 251, 320, 489
Perkins, Lieut. C. H., 168
Philby, Mr. H. St. J., I.C.S., 410
Pichon, M., 647
Picot, M. Georges, 260
Piépape, Col. P. de., 260, 473, 604, 607
Pipe-line in Sinai, 13, 25
Pisani, Capt., 405, 564
Policy of the campaigns, 628
Pollok-M'Call, Br.-Gen. J. B., 132, 133, 135, 164–6, 169, 172, 209, 225, 226, 273
Powell-Edwards, Capt. G. H., 97
Powell-Edwards, Lieut.-Col. H. I., 317, 319
Prentis, Lieut.-Col. W. S., 480
Price, Major F. G., 253
Prigge, Major, 527
Primrose, Major the Hon. Neil, 180
Propaganda, British, 445

Raglan (British monitor), at Third Gaza, 65
Raids during stationary warfare, 25, 67, 214, 228, 230, 265, 426

Railways (British), 9; doubling of in Sinai, 13, 15, 20, 185, 293, 439; in Palestine, 20, 40, 185, 188, 237, 292, 295, 439, 563, 600
Railways (Turkish), 26, 294, 330, 407, 445, 451, 454
Raouf Bey, 620, 625
Rashid, Sa'ud Ibn Abd el Aziz Ibn, 398, 400
Rasim Bey, 403
Rees, Major, J. G., 232, 233
Rees, Capt. T. W., 482
Refet Bey, Col., 35, 76, 141, 468, 480
Requin (French coast-guard ship), at Third Gaza, 65
Reynolds, Capt. A., 99
Roads. *See* Transport
Robertson, Br.-Gen. A. B., 412, 419
Robertson, Capt. H. C. H., 167
Robertson, Major K., 518
Robertson, Gen. Sir W. R., is unable to meet all C.-in-C.'s demands, 14; discusses policy with C.-in-C., 26; 157; his memorandum of 26th Dec., 295
Robinson, Major J. F. M., 170, 171, 173
Romanes, Lieut.-Col. J. G. P., 69, 204
Rome, Br.-Gen. C. S., 168, 199, 227
Rothschild, Major Evelyn de, 180
Rowan-Hamilton, Lieut.-Col. G. B., 480
Royston, Br.-Gen. J. R., 57
Ruses, British, 30, 41, 62, 66, 461, 638
Rushdi Bey, Maj.-Gen., 539
Russell, Lieut.-Col. R. E. M., 23
Russia, effect of her collapse, 3, 295
Ryrie, Br.-Gen. G. de L., 55, 56, 127, 128, 336, 382, 391, 548, 555, 558

Saadullah Bey, Col., 620, 625
Sackville, Lieut.-Col. Lord, 316
Said, Mohammed, 589, 591
Saint-Quentin, Comdt. R. de, 260
Salmond, Br.-Gen. W. G. H., 565
Salt, Br.-Gen. H. F., 412, 510
Samakh, capture of. *See* Megiddo, Battles of
Sangster, Lieut.-Col. P. B., 541
Sa'ud, Abd el Aziz Ibn, 410, 624, 625
Scott, Lieut.-Col. W. H., 590
Scully, Lieut.-Col. V. M. B., 285
Sedgewick, Sergt. J., 252
Shaitan Singh, Risaldar, 437

734 GENERAL INDEX

Sharon, Battles of. *See* Megiddo, Battles of
Shea, Maj.-Gen. J. S. M., 44, 45, 48, 49, 81, 108, 116, 119, 220, 243, 247, 253, 254, 287, 304, 309, 331, 332, 334, 335, 338, 341, 342, 345, 358, 367, 368, 373, 381, 384, 419, 427, 484, 486, 487, 522
Shea's Force (*see* " Corps," Arms and Formations Index)
Sherifial Camel Corps, 564
Short, Br.-Gen. A. H., 95
Shukri Pasha, 591, 593
Sickness in Sept.–Oct. 1918, 597
Simon-Eberhard, Hauptm., 363
Simpson-Baikie, Br.-Gen. H. A. D., 73, 352, 456
Singhji, Gen. Sir Pertab, 424
Smith, Br.-Gen. C. L., V.C., 44, 358, 389, 427, 493, 502
Smith's Group (*see* " Brigades," Arms and Formations Index)
Smith, Capt. Ross, 565
Smuts, Lieut.-Gen. J. C., his mission to Palestine, 297, 411, 413, 632
Sommerville, Major C., 346
Staunch (British destroyer), at Third Gaza, 65 ; sunk by submarine, 66
Stedall, Major L. P., 38
Steuber, Obergeneralarzt, 83, 598
Stewart-Richardson, Lieut.-Col. N. G., 234
Storrs, Col. R., 300
Streatfeild, Lieut.-Col. H. S., 313, 314
Supplies Control Board, 440
Supply service, development of, 439
Supreme War Council, its decision regarding Palestine, 296
Sutcliffe, Capt. O. D., 490
Sykes, Sir Mark, Bt., 261
Sykes-Picot Agreement, 410, 592, 607
Syria, administration of, 591, 607, 623 ; physical conditions of, 604

Tafila, Action at, 402
Talaat Pasha, 4, 619
Tanks, at Gaza, 68, 71, 72
Tell 'Asur, Action of, 310 ; simultaneous action of XXI Corps, 323
Thornhill, Corpl. F. S., 245
Thorpe, Lieut.-Col. H., 81
Tiller, Major, 480
Todd, Lieut.-Col. T. J., 599
Tooth, Major S. A., 381, 384

Townshend, Maj. Gen. C. V. F., 620
Train, Corpl. C. W., V.C., 245
Trans-Caucasia, 3
Trans-Jordan, physical conditions of, 329 ; operations in, in March, 328 ; in April and May, 364 ; in September, 552
Transport, general problem of, 19, 634 ; in attack on Gaza–Beersheba line, 21, 40 ; in subsequent pursuit, 126, 138, 142, 157 ; in Judæan Hills, 191, 193, 194, 197, 201, 213, 237, 239, 243, 256, 263, 276, 290, 292, 303, 313, 322 ; in capture of Jericho, 309 ; in Trans-Jordan operations, 331, 336, 346, 367, 383, 387 ; in final offensive, 457, 492, 504 ; in cavalry break-through, 538 ; in advance to Damascus, 562, 584, 600
Transport by rail. *See* Railways
Transport by sea, 8, 20, 143, 185, 268, 292, 440, 442, 600, 634
Trew, Br.-Gen. E. F., 84, 367, 562
Turkish Army, on Gaza–Beersheba line, 8 ; estimated strength of in July 1917, 12 ; in October 1917, 33 ; 42 ; evacuates Gaza, 75, 76 ; panic in on 9th Nov., 141, 154 ; counter-attacks at Barqusya, 146 ; split in two by capture of Junction Station, 181, 184 ; stands to defend Jerusalem, 201 ; counter-attacks in defence of Jerusalem, 220 ; evacuates Jerusalem, 252; its losses up to capture of Jerusalem, 226 ; attempts to retake Jerusalem, 279 ; attacks Jordan Bridgeheads, 358 ; its successful counter-attack on 1st May, 374 ; strength of on Hejaz Railway, 408 ; wretched state of in August 1918, 445 ; strength of in September 1918, 452 ; its general retreat, 511 ; its retreat intercepted at Jenin, 530 ; and at Beisan, 533 ; and at Jordan fords, 538 ; and at Damascus, 590 ; sickness in, 598 ; attempted reorganization of at Aleppo, 613, 617 ; losses of in final offensive, 618 ; and in Great War, 619 ; demobilization of, 623 ; qualities of, 645
Turkish Army—
Second Army, 5, 452, 454, 546, 595, 622

GENERAL INDEX

Turkish Army (*continued*)—
 Fourth Army, 4–6, 327, 348, 392, 404, 452, 454, 540, 545, 547, 548, 552, 560, 561, 566, 567, 580, 582, 584, 585, 595, 605, 617, 640
 Sixth Army, 5, 311, 622, 623
 Seventh Army, 5, 42, 83, 139, 140, 154, 175, 182, 184, 201, 217, 220, 236, 291, 326, 348, 445, 452, 454, 495, 512, 532, 540, 548, 550, 552, 595, 605, 640
 Eighth Army, 36, 47, 61, 69, 76, 127, 139, 140, 154, 173, 175, 181, 182, 184, 217, 220, 236, 312, 326, 349, 351, 452, 454, 468, 495, 510, 511, 532, 546, 595, 640
 Asia Corps (German troops). *See* Pasha II. Headquarters as corps command, 352
 Hejaz Expeditionary Force, 402, 408, 454
 Pasha II (Asia Corps), formation of, 5; 7, 43, 236, 348, 357, 362, 363, 392, 426, 444, 478, 495, 506, 510, 511, 539, 542, 594, 601, 605
 Yilderim (Army Group F), 5–7, 24, 35, 36, 41, 43, 62, 155, 182; its failure, 310; 311, 437, 444, 450, 467, 496, 511, 545, 601
Tyrrell, Lieut.-Col. G. G. M., 130

Valintine, Capt. R., 121, 123
Vandeleur, Br.-Gen. R. S., 283, 285, 427
Vaughan, Capt. E. W. D., 578, 580
Vernon, Br.-Gen. H. A., 101, 104, 105, 318, 496
Versailles. *See* Supreme War Council
Vigors, Major M. D., 576, 577, 586
Voltigeur (French destroyer), at Third Gaza, 65

Walker, Major G. H., 385
Waller, Br.-Gen. R. L., 93, 276, 303, 497
War Cabinet, its instructions to Sir Edmund Allenby, 15, 26, 157, 193
Ward, Br.-Gen. T., 68

Water Supply, in attack on Beersheba, 11, 17, 19, 22, 29, 33, 37, 39, 56, 59; in attack on Sheria position, 64, 79, 81, 85, 90, 92; in pursuit, 118, 127, 143; value of Junction Station for, 164; in Judæan Hills, 188, 276, 313; in final offensive, 472, 507, 510; and horses, 544. *And see* Pipe-line
Watson, Major A. C., 123
Watson, Br.-Gen. C. F., 46, 100, 247, 253, 254, 333, 334, 485
Watson, Lieut.-Col. G. B., 466, 471, 497
Watson, Br.-Gen. H. D., 300
Watson's Force (*see* " Brigades," Arms and Formations Index)
Wavell, Br.-Gen. A. P., 260, 296, 412
Weir, Major F. J., 433
Weir, Br.-Gen. G. A., 481, 483, 507, 606
Wemyss, Vice-Admiral Sir R. E., 395
Western, Maj.-Gen. W. G. B., 412
Wheler, Major G. B. H., 575
Whitfield, Pte. H., V.C., 319
Wigan, Br.-Gen. J. T., 80, 181, 224, 225, 514, 519
Wiggin, Major W. H., 120
Wildblood, Lieut.-Col. E. H., 427
Wilhelma, defence of, 221
Williams, Lieut.-Col. H. J., 120, 383
Williamson-Oswald, Lieut. - Col. (later Br.-Gen.), 64, 324
Willmer, Major, 545
Wilson, Lieut.-Col. the Hon. G. G., 208, 224
Wilson, Gen. Sir H. H., (C.I.G.S.), 414, 417, 447, 609
Wilson, Br.-Gen. L. C., 57, 369, 373, 374, 391, 530, 570, 574, 588, 595
Wilson, President, 618
Wingate, Gen. Sir R., 300, 397, 608, 624
Winterton, Major Earl, 565
Wood-Hill, Lieut.-Col. C., 551
Wright, Maj.-Gen. H. B. H., 22

Younger, Lieut.-Col. J., 233

Zeid, the Emir, 398, 402, 403, 405
Zionism, 625

INDEX TO ARMS, FORMATIONS, AND UNITS.

Artillery—
  Batteries, Field—
    428th—505 ; 527th—317
  Batteries, Garrison, Heavy—
    10th—307, 331, 358, 361, 497, 502 ; 15th—95, 324 ; 91st—102, 238, 241, 257, 313, 315, 367, 484 ; 181st—95, 324 ; 189th—159, 214, 324 ; 195th—313, 317 ; 202nd—324
  Batteries, Garrison, Mountain—
    10th—47, 96, 244, 283, 315, 389 ; 11th—431 ; 16th—381
  Batteries, Garrison, Siege—
    43rd—324 ; 134th—324, 353 ; 205th—497 ; 209th—324 ; 304th—324 ; 334th—313 ; 378th—95 ; 380th—160, 214, 324, 484 ; 383rd—95, 307, 313, 361, 378 ; 387th—492 ; 440th—95
  Batteries, Horse—
    Ayrshire—80, 358 ; Berkshire—47, 168, 172, 180, 219, 378, 388, 578 ; Essex—80, 118, 416, 522, 533, 574, 575 ; Hampshire—38, 539, 541, 585 ; H.A.C. " A "—376, 572 ; H.A.C. " B "—57, 120, 149, 230, 376, 388, 431, 522, 535, 536, 606 ; Inverness-shire—56, 86, 181, 214, 230, 358, 550 ; Leicestershire—179, 189, 219, 375, 388 ; Nottinghamshire—59, 118, 376, 431, 531, 568, 572 ; Somersetshire—56, 177, 216, 342, 348, 358
  Battery, Mountain—
    Hong Kong and Singapore—189, 199, 200, 234, 248, 338, 368, 373, 380, 431, 500, 501
  Battery, Indian Mountain—
    29th—550

Artillery (continued)—
  Brigades, Field—
    IV—478 ; XXXVII—207, 208, 266 ; XLIV—47, 96, 283, 317 ; LXVII—283, 317, 498, 500 ; LXVIII—109, 283, 317, 498, 500, 501, 502 ; 117th—47, 96, 283, 317 ; 172nd—324 ; 261st—164, 166, 207 ; 262nd—144, 191, 207 ; 263rd—283, 285, 317, 494 ; 264th—131, 132, 133, 153, 166, 194, 207, 229, 483 ; 265th—85, 242 ; 266th—47, 85, 499 ; 268th—47, 96, 97, 227, 283 ; 270th—214, 216, 325 ; 272nd—222, 223, 325 ; 301st—47, 247, 358, 367, 421, 486 ; 302nd—47, 247, 288, 313, 367, 431 ; 303rd—47, 252, 253, 335
  Brigade, South African Field—
    1st—138, 153, 160, 190, 266, 267, 325, 356, 480
  Brigades, Garrison—
    LXI—64 ; XCV—324 ; XCVI—45, 98, 241, 244, 283, 287, 313 ; XCVII—313 ; 100th—266, 269, 324 ; 102nd—269, 324 ; 484, 563 ; 103rd—496, 502
  Brigades, Garrison, Mountain—
    VIII—353, 507, 508 ; IX—165, 166, 190, 205, 244, 283, 331, 340, 367, 428, 475, 505, 506
  Brigades, Horse—
    XVIII—347, 368 ; XX—368, 416, 640, 641

Camel Corps Brigade, Imperial—16, 36, 79, 81, 90, 101, 103, 107, 124, 125, 140, 148, 166, 167, 173, 176, 178, 180, 213, 223, 230, 331, 332, 336, 337, 338, 341, 343, 358,

---

[1] Formations and units in orders of battle and operation orders, which appear in appendices, are not indexed.
As in the first volume, the new titles of Indian regiments are given in shortened form after the old, enclosed in square brackets, so as to enable the reader of the future easily to identify the regiment.

Camel Corps Brigade, Imperial (*continued*)—
360, 361, 365, 366, 368, 373, 375, 389, 408, 414; reorganized as 5th Australian L.H. Brigade, 415; 430

———, Regiments—
1st (A. & N.Z.) Bn., 344, 360, 415
2nd (Imperial) Bn., 87, 91, 176, 338, 344, 360, 415
3rd (A. & N.Z.) Bn., 102, 103, 105, 176, 178–80, 415
4th (A. & N.Z.) Bn., 91, 176, 178, 223, 230, 339, 341, 343, 345, 415

Cavalry—
Brigades (Australian)—
1st Light Horse—53, 56, 57, 86, 87, 101, 111, 112, 117, 118, 128, 143, 145, 148, 149, 154, 173, 176, 181, 214, 269, 304, 307, 313, 332, 336, 337, 340, 347, 349, 358, 359, 368, 369, 372, 380, 383, 384, 385, 387, 388, 431, 434, 466, 549–55
2nd Light Horse—36, 37, 52, 53, 55, 56, 79–8, 81, 86, 87, 89, 91, 101, 111–3, 116–8, 127, 146, 148, 174, 175, 214, 230, 336–9, 341–3, 345, 347, 358, 367, 368, 373, 380, 382, 383, 385, 387, 389, 431, 433, 466, 549, 552, 554, 555, 558, 593
3rd Light Horse—56, 57, 79, 107, 111, 112, 116–20, 122, 124, 144, 147, 151, 152, 175, 224, 229, 230, 234, 235, 369, 373, 374, 379, 380, 382, 383, 385, 386–8, 390, 391, 529–32, 534, 543, 544, 568–71, 573, 586, 588, 591, 593
4th Light Horse—54, 57, 59, 111, 114–6, 118, 119, 127, 144, 149, 150–2, 160, 174, 175, 223, 224, 226, 227, 234, 369, 371, 374, 376–9, 383, 384, 386, 388, 389–91, 393, 431, 438, 529, 531, 532, 534, 542–5, 568–71
5th Light Horse—formed, 414; 416, 417, 420, 455, 464, 469, 484, 487, 504, 509, 513, 529, 534, 568, 572, 573, 586, 593

Cavalry (*continued*)—
Brigades (*continued*)—
New Zealand Mounted Rifles, 37, 53, 55–7, 79, 89, 90, 101, 111, 124–6, 148, 173, 175–8, 181, 184, 214, 215, 304, 307, 332, 336–9, 341, 343–6, 358, 361, 367, 368, 375, 377, 431, 549–51, 553, 554, 558, 642
5th Mounted, 37, 57, 58, 86, 87, 89, 91, 101, 106, 111, 112, 114, 116, 118–20, 149, 174, 175, 198, 213, 223, 229, 234, 365, 369, 373, 374, 379, 380, 382–5, 387–91, 411, 415, 416. *And see* 13th Cavalry Brigade
6th Mounted, 112, 148, 166, 179, 180, 196, 199–201, 220, 224, 226, 227, 230, 231, 365, 368, 373, 377, 378, 386, 388, 411, 416. *And see* 10th Cavalry Brigade
7th Mounted, 16, 53, 54, 58, 79–81, 86, 91, 101, 111, 114, 117, 118, 127, 129, 148, 174, 175, 181, 189, 213, 221, 223, 226, 227, 229, 234, 414, 416, 430, 431, 434, 436. *And see* 14th Cavalry Brigade
8th Mounted, 37, 39, 148, 167, 168, 173, 179, 189, 192, 196, 200, 205, 219, 220, 227, 230, 231, 365, 416. *And see* 11th Cavalry Brigade
22nd Mounted, 167, 170, 173, 176, 179, 180, 189, 192, 196, 199, 200, 224–7, 231, 365. *And see* 12th Cavalry Brigade
10th (formerly 6th Mounted), 412, 416, 514, 515, 518, 519, 521, 532, 577–84
11th (formerly 8th Mounted), 416, 514, 515, 519, 542, 546, 580–3, 585, 586
12th (formerly 22nd Mounted), 416, 514, 515, 519, 521, 580–3
13th (formerly 5th Mounted), 416, 521–5, 527, 532, 533, 535, 576, 577, 591, 606, 617
14th (formerly 7th Mounted), 416, 430, 524, 525, 528, 532, 536, 576, 586, 591, 601, 615, 617

INDEX TO ARMS, FORMATIONS, AND UNITS 739

Cavalry (continued)—
  Brigades (continued)
    15th (Imperial Service), 73, 119, 130, 137, 141, 144, 365, 368, 378, 411, 414, 416, 430, 431, 436, 524, 528, 529, 535, 612, 613
  Divisions—
    Australian Mounted, in Desert Mounted Corps, 16; Third Gaza, concentration, 36, approach march, 53; capture of Beersheba, 55; 79; relieves Yeomanry Div., 91; 107; at Sheria 7th Nov., 111; 119, 127, 144; in counter-attack at Barqusya, 146; 158, 163, 173, 175, 181, 183, 189, 190, 213, 219, 223, 286, 303, 353; Second Raid into Trans-Jordan, 365, 368, 371, 373, 375, 378, 382, 384, 389, 416, 431; task in final offensive, 449; concentration, 463, 467; advance on 20th Sept., 529; advance on Jenin, 530; capture of Samakh, 542; 562; advance on Damascus, 567; blocking of Barada Gorge, 573; 576; capture of Damascus, 586; 588; actions north of Damascus, 589; 606, 617; transferred to Egypt, 623; 641

    Australian and New Zealand Mounted, in Desert Mounted corps, 16; Third Gaza, concentration, 36, approach march, 52; capture of Beersheba, 55; operations north of Beersheba, 1st/2nd Nov., 79; 3rd/5th Nov., 86; 111; advance from Sheria, 117; pursuit, 9th Nov., 124; 140, 414; halts to rest, 143; 148, 167, 173; operations 14th–16th Nov., 175; 189; demonstration over 'Auja, 213; capture of Jericho, 302, 304, 307; raid on 'Amman, 331, 335, 337, 343; withdrawal from 'Amman, 345; Turkish attack on Jordan bridgeheads, 358; demonstration of 18th April, 361; Second Raid into Trans-

Cavalry (continued)—
  Divisions (continued)—
    Australian and New Zealand Mounted (continued)—
      Jordan, 365, 368; 416, 424; Turkish attack on Abu Tulul, 19th July, 429; task in final offensive, 450, 456; 463; operations 18th Sept., 549; advance on 21st Sept., 550; advance on 'Amman, 552; capture of 'Amman, 554; interception of Ma'an garrison, 555; 593; transferred to Egypt, 623; 641
    Yeomanry Mounted, in Desert Mounted Corps, 16; task at Third Gaza, 29; in outpost line, 36; 46, 91; 94, 97, 107, 111, 112, 124, 144, 146, 148, 149, 159; in action at El Maghar, 13th/14th Nov., 166; 173, 175; at Abu Shushe, 178; advance into Judæan Hills, 189, 191, 193, 196; attack on Beitunye, 199; 205, 207, 219; heavily counter-attacked, 220; 224; loss of Foqa, 226; relief of, 230; 290, 364; reorganized with Indian cavalry regiments as 4th Cavalry Division, 411, 414, 423; 641
    1st Mounted. See 4th Cavalry Division.
    2nd Mounted. See 5th Cavalry Division
    4th, formation, 415; in Desert Mounted Corps, 416; 423; task in final offensive, 449, 513; concentration, 463, 465, 467; advance on 19th Sept., 514, 518; capture of El 'Affule, 520; and of Beisan, 521; 533; actions at Jordan fords, 538; 562, 567, 569, 574; advance to Damascus, 577; action at Irbid, 577; at Der'a, 582; 586; sickness in, 597; outstanding horsemanship of, 600; 601, 605, 610; in Army of Occupation, 623
    5th, formation, 415; in Desert Mounted Corps, 416; 423; 429, 431; action in Jordan valley, 14th July, 434; task

740 INDEX TO ARMS, FORMATIONS, AND UNITS

Cavalry (continued)—
  Divisions (continued)—
    5th (continued)—
      in final offensive, 449, 513; concentration 463, 465; advance on 19th Sept., 522; attack on Nazareth, 525; capture of Haifa, 532, 534; 561; actions at Kiswe, 575; 586; occupation of Riyaq, 601; advance to Homs, 605; advance to Aleppo, 610; action at Haritan, 614; in Army of Occupation, 623
  Regiments (Australian)—
    1st Light Horse, 86, 112, 117, 118, 181, 322, 342, 359, 372, 375, 376, 383, 431-3, 554, 555
    2nd Light Horse, 56, 86, 181, 335, 340, 342, 359, 431, 432, 434
    3rd Light Horse, 56, 86, 112, 117, 118, 336, 337, 342, 359, 431, 551
    4th Light Horse, 58, 119, 151, 152, 376, 377, 532, 542, 568-71, 590
    5th Light Horse, 80, 113, 117, 128, 337, 339, 358, 385, 433, 554, 558
    6th Light Horse, 80, 113, 214, 341, 381, 549
    7th Light Horse, 25, 55, 80, 91, 117, 127, 128, 230, 341, 360, 368, 371, 378, 382, 415, 549, 554, 558
    8th Light Horse, 53, 80, 81, 150, 234, 374, 380, 385, 388, 530, 532, 534, 545, 570
    9th Light Horse, 149, 150, 189, 373, 531, 568-70, 573, 586, 590
    10th Light Horse, 199, 229, 243, 246, 250, 259, 373, 380, 382, 386, 530, 531, 556, 568, 570, 582
    11th Light Horse, 58, 115, 149, 161, 226, 233, 372, 374, 376-8, 384, 529, 543, 544, 569
    12th Light Horse, 58, 115, 119, 127, 137, 377, 542, 544, 545, 569
    14th Light Horse, 415, 504, 509, 568, 569, 572, 573
    15th Light Horse, 415, 569

Cavalry (continued)—
  Regiments (New Zealand)—
    Auckland Mounted Rifles, 55-7, 148, 177, 215, 216, 269, 275, 309, 313, 314, 334-6, 343, 378, 550, 551
    Canterbury Mounted Rifles, 55, 57, 79, 90, 177, 215, 216, 344, 378, 384, 388, 551, 553, 554
    Wellington Mounted Rifles, 53, 79, 177, 178, 184, 215, 306-8, 336, 338, 339, 344-6, 433, 550, 551
  Regiments (Yeomanry)—
    Berks, 168, 169, 178-80, 196, 199, 200, 221, 226
    Buckinghamshire (R. B. Hussars), 166-9, 179, 180, 199, 200, 221, 226, 227, 420, 641
    Composite Regt. (XXI Corps), 130, 131, 133, 137, 300, 327, 479, 508, 602, 603, 607
    Dorset, 168-70, 179, 180, 196, 199, 200, 226, 365, 378, 386, 388, 515, 581 640, 641
    Duke of Lancaster's Own (see Composite Regt.)
    Glasgow, (Q.O.R. Dragoons) (see Composite Regt.)
    Gloucestershire (R.G. Hussars), 37, 89, 116, 120, 149-51, 199, 234, 379, 524-7, 577
    Herts (see Composite Regt.)
    Lincolnshire, 200, 224, 225, 640, 641
    1/1st City of London (Rough Riders), 38, 199, 205, 220, 227
    1/1st County of London (Middlesex), 38, 39, 173, 221, 227, 365, 378, 539-41
    1/2nd County of London (Westminster Dragoons), 47, 54, 126, 238, 254, 257, 282
    1/3rd County of London (Sharpshooters), 38, 167, 189, 199, 200
    Nottinghamshire—
      1/1st Sherwood Rangers, 80, 81, 118, 224, 225, 365, 382, 388, 430, 434-6, 536, 537, 569, 574, 601
      1/1st South Notts Hussars, 54, 80, 81, 83, 86, 106, 181, 183, 225

Index to Arms, Formations, and Units 741

Cavalry (continued)—
 Regiments (Yeomanry) (continued)—
  Staffordshire (The Q.O.R. Regt.), 170, 171, 180, 196, 224, 365, 368
  Warwickshire (Hussars), 87, 89, 120–3, 149, 150, 365
  Worcestershire (The Q.O.W. Hussars), 89, 120–3, 150, 151, 382, 383, 466, 497, 501, 541
  Yorkshire—
   1/1st East Riding, 170, 171, 176, 199, 200, 201, 224, 227
 Regiments (Indian)—
  2nd Lancers, 515, 518–20, 577–80, 582
  6th Cavalry [18th Cavalry], 519
  9th Hodson's Horse [4th Lancers], 523–8, 576
  18th Lancers [19th Lancers], 523–6, 533
  19th Lancers, 521, 522, 600
  20th Deccan Horse [Royal Deccan H. (9th)], 417, 430, 520, 524, 575
  29th Lancers (R. Deccan H. (9th)], 539, 541, 585
  34th Poona Horse [17th Cavalry], 417, 430, 436, 520, 575
  36th Jacob's Horse [The Scinde H. (14th Cav.)], 514, 515, 520, 539–41
  38th Central India Horse [21st Horse], 533, 542, 543, 579–81
  1st Hyderabad I.S. Lancers, 130, 190, 197, 202, 365, 368, 378, 416, 430, 532, 535, 569, 613, 614
  Jodhpore I.S. Lancers, 414, 416, 424, 430, 434–7, 536, 538, 614, 615
  Mysore I.S. Lancers, 130, 365, 378, 416, 430, 434–6, 524, 535–7, 614, 615

Corps—
 Desert Mounted, formation, 16; 17, 19; G.H.Q. orders to, 28; concentration, 36; 45, 47, 51; orders to divisions and approach march, 52; attack on Beersheba, 55; captures Beersheba, 59; operations north of Beersheba, 1st/2nd

Corps (continued)—
 Desert Mounted (continued)—
  Nov., 78; 3rd–5th Nov., 84; 91; attack on Tell Khuweilfe, 101, 105; orders to break through at Sheria, 107; operations 7th Nov., 111; affair at Huj, 117; advance to Mediterranean shore, 124; 129, 130; operations against Junction Station, 158, 167; 188, 189; 207, 208; demonstration across 'Auja, 213, 221; operations 29th Nov.–3rd Dec., 230; 262; 302; Second Raid into Trans-Jordan, 365; reorganization, 416, 420; Turkish attack at Abu Tulul, 429; task in final offensive, 448, 455, 457; concentration, 461, 467; orders of, 513; advance on 19th Sept., 513, 522, 529; operations 21st Sept., 532; 22nd Sept., 534; capture of Haifa, 535; operations 23rd Sept., 538; 24th Sept., 542; 561; advance on Damascus, 561, 567, 574, 577; capture of Damascus, 586; entry into Damascus, 593; sickness in corps, 597; advance to Riyaq, 601; advance to Homs, 605; advance to Aleppo, 610, 616; in Army of Occupation, 623
 XX, formation, 16; 17; G.H.Q. orders to for Third Gaza, 28, concentration, 36; approach march and orders, 44; artillery allotment, 45; attack on Beersheba defences, 48; operations 1st/2nd Nov., 78, 3rd–5th Nov., 84; 91; capture of Sheria position, 92; capture of Hureira Redoubt, 108; 111; 124, 125, 142, 157, 188; relieves XX Corps, 218, 228; attack on Jerusalem defences, 237, 243; operations 8th Dec., 243; capture of Jerusalem, 252; advance on 9th Dec., 256; 262; preparations for advance northwards, 275; Turkish counter-attacks, 279; British attack launched, 282; capture of Jericho, 303; action at Tell 'Asur, 310; passage of the Jordan, 328; attacks on 'Amman, 335; withdrawal

742 INDEX TO ARMS, FORMATIONS, AND UNITS

Corps (continued)—
  XX (continued)—
    from 'Amman, 343; 368; task in final offensive, 449, 455, 465, 471; attack 18th Sept., 488; operations 20th Sept., 496; advance on Nablus, 499; 503, 560; transferred to Egypt, 623
  XXI, formation, 16; 17; Third Gaza, G.H.Q. orders to, 28; plan of attack, 63; artillery concentration and bombardment, 64; naval assistance, 65; orders for attack on Gaza defences, 69; 74; Turkish withdrawal, 75; comparison British and enemy strengths, 76; 124, 126, 127, 128; capture of Wadi el Hesi defences, 129; 142, 143; operations at Sdud, 10th Nov., 144; capture of Burqa, 146; operations against Junction Station, 157, 185, 188; advance into Judæan Hills, 189; capture of Nabi Samweil, 197; attacks on El Jib, 205; Turkish counter-attacks, 218; operations 27th Nov., 219; relieved, 228; 262; passage of Nahr el 'Auja, 265; 303; advance on 12th March, 323; 439; task in final offensive, 448, 455; concentration, 464; plan of attack, 469; orders of, 471; attack of 19th Sept., 472; operations 20th Sept., 504; 21st Sept., 509; 560, 561, 563; occupation of Beirut, 602; occupation of Tripoli, 605, 607
  Barrow's Detachment, north of Beersheba, 107, 124
  Chaytor's Force, rôle in final offensive, 450, 456, 458; takes over Jordan valley, 463, 466; attack 20th Sept., 547; capture of 'Amman, 552; interception of Ma'an garrison, 555
  Shea's Force, operations in and beyond Jordan valley, 331, 350

Divisions—
  3rd (Lahore), arrival, 413, 417, 418; task in final offensive, 449, 458; concentration, 464;

Divisions (continued)—
  3rd (Lahore) (continued)—
    attack 19th Sept., 470, 476; operations 20th Sept., 504, 505; 561; in Army of Occupation, 623
  7th (Meerut), arrival, 293, 298; relieves 52nd Div., 350, 352, 412; 411, 417, 418; operations 8th June, 425; raid on Piffer Ridge, 426; task in final offensive, 449, 458; concentration, 464; 470, 472; attack on 19th Sept., 481; 504; operations 20th Sept., 507; 21st Sept., 509; 514; 561, 563, 597, 601; advance on Beirut, 602; advance to Tripoli, 605; in Army of Occupation, 623
  10th, ordered to Egypt, 15; in XX Corps, 16; 39; Third Gaza, orders to, 45; 51; operations against Sheria position, 95, 98, 99; capture of Hureira, 109; 126, 219, 229; relieves 52nd Div., 282, 284; operations 28th Dec., 286, 288, 290; action at Tell 'Asur, 313, 317, 320; 323, 354, 357, 368; reorganized with Indian battalions, 411; raid on 12th Aug. (Kh. Gharabe), 427; task in final offensive, 449, 465; attack 19th Sept., 491; operations 20th Sept., 498; march on Nablus, 500; 502; transferred to Egypt, 623; 629
  13th (in Mesopotamia), 298, 411
  52nd (Lowland), in XXI Corps, 16; 67, 75, 128; capture of Wadi el Hesi defences, 129, 138; 142; action near Sdud, 144; capture of Burqa, 146; 158, 161, 162; operations against Junction Station, 164, 169, 172; 175, 188; advance into Judæan Hills, 189, 191, 194; battle of Nabi Samweil, 197, 199, 201, 204; 207; attack on El Jib, 208; 214, 219; moves to aid of Yeomanry, 223; 225, 227; 29th Nov.–3rd Dec., 229, 231, 233; relieved by 10th Div., 236; passage of Nahr el 'Auja, 265, 268, 270, 274; departs for Western front, 350, 412

INDEX TO ARMS, FORMATIONS, AND UNITS 743

Divisions (*continued*)—
53rd, in XX Corps, 16; Third Gaza, concentration, 36; orders to, 44; 51; operations north of Beersheba, 1st/2nd Nov., 79; 3rd-5th Nov., 84; 94; attacks on Tell Khuweilfe, 101; 107, 111, 124, 188, 237; advance up Hebron Road, 238; advance on Jerusalem, 243, 246, 250; operations 9th Dec., 256; 276; operations 16th and 21st Dec., 277; Turkish attack on, 281; advance on 28th Dec., 286; in Jericho operations, 304, 306; operations at Tell 'Asur, 312, 313, 314, 318, 321; operations of 159th Bde. at Berukin, 353, 356, 358; reorganized with Indian battalions, 412, 418; task in final offensive, 449, 465; preliminary advance on 18th Sept., 471; attack 19th Sept., 488, 491; operations 20th Sept., 496, 499; 21st Sept., 499; 500; transferred to Egypt, 623
54th (East Anglian), in XXI Corps, 16; attack on Gaza defences, 67, 69, 74; enters Gaza, 75; 188, 214, 219; attacked at Wilhelma, 221, 227, 228; battle of Jaffa, 265, 267, 269, 274; operations 12th March, 323; 353; 418; task in final offensive, 449, 458; concentration, 464; attack 19th Sept., 470, 472, 473; 504, 563; transferred to Egypt, 623
60th, in XX Corps, 16; Third Gaza, concentration, 36; orders for attack, 44; approach march, 46; attack at Beersheba, 48; operations against Sheria position, 95, 98; attack north of Wadi esh Sheria, 108, 113, 114, 116; operations 8th Nov., 117; 124, 126, 140, 208, 213; at Nabi Samweil, 218; 229; preparations for attack on Jerusalem defences, 237; attack on Jerusalem defences, 243, 244, 251; 252; operations 9th Dec., 256, 258; 276, 277, 278; Turkish attack on, 279; advance on 28th Dec.,

Divisions (*continued*)—
60th (*continued*)—
286, 288; operations against Jericho, 304, 306, 309; operations at Tell 'Asur, 313, 314, 318, 322; passage of the Jordan, 331, 335; advance on Es Salt, 337; 339; attack on 'Amman, 341; withdrawal from 'Amman, 343; second raid into Trans-Jordan, 365, 367, 369, 374, 379, 380, 384, 389; reorganized with Indian battalions, 411; raids on 12th August, 428; task in final offensive, 449, 458; concentration, 464; 467, 470, 472; attack on 19th Sept., 484; operations 20th Sept., 504, 508; transferred to Egypt, 623; 629
74th (Yeomanry), in XX Corps, 16; Third Gaza, concentration, 39; orders for attack, 44; approach march, 47; attack on Beersheba defences, 48; 81, 87; operations against Sheria position, 94, 95, 98; 101; 108; 126, 213, 219; advance into Judæan Hills, 229; attacks on Foqa, 230, 235; preparations for attack on Jerusalem defences, 237, 240; attack on Jerusalem defences, 243, 248; operations 9th Dec., 256, 257, 258; 276, 277; operations 27th Dec., 283, 286; advance on 28th Dec., 288, 303; operations at Tell 'Asur, 312, 313, 315, 318, 321; 351; relieved, 358, 364; departs for Western front, 413
75th, 14, 15; in XXI Corps, 16; Third Gaza, 67, 74, 137, 138, 142, 144, 146, 158; attack on Junction Station, 159; 164, 175; 188; advance into Judæan Hills, 189, 190, 193; battle of Nabi Samweil, 197, 201; attack on El Jib, 205; 208; 214, 218, 219, 265, 266; operations 12th March, 323; action of Berukin, 352; 357; reorganized, 412, 417, 418; task in final offensive, 449, 458; concentration, 464; attack 19th September, 470, 472, 479; at Qantara as general reserve, 623; 629

744 INDEX TO ARMS, FORMATIONS, AND UNITS

Divisions (*continued*)—
  Mott's Detachment, in capture of Jerusalem, 238, 243, 246, 250, 264

Engineers—
  Army Troops Coy., 14th—510
  Bridging Train, Desert Mounted Corps, 331, 367, 569
  Field Companies—
    410th—164, 272, 273; 412th—67, 70, 196, 207, 271, 273; 413th—13, 132, 144, 268, 272; 436th—257; 437th—90; 495th—138, 324; 519th—333, 388; 521st—244, 333; 522nd—47, 313
  Field Squadrons—
    4th—522; 5th—612; A. & N.Z.—111, 215, 335; Aust. Mtd. Div.—174, 181
  Pontoon Park, 13th—331, 459, 484
  Sappers and Miners—
    3rd Coy.—602; 4th—602; 10th—324; 72nd—491
  Signal Troop, 5th—611
  Survey Section, G.H.Q., 26

Flying Corps (R.F.C., later R.A.F.)—
  Balloon Coy., 21st—461
  Squadrons, No. 14—460; No. 111—461; No. 113—460, 523; No. 142—460; No. 144—461; No. 145—461
  Wings, 5th—138, 460; 40th—40, 138, 460

Infantry—
  Brigades—
    7th—476, 478, 505, 506, 561
    8th—476, 478, 505, 506
    9th—476, 505, 506
    19th—481, 483, 507, 508, 606, 607
    20th—362, 365, 368, 377, 379, 424, 452, 463, 466, 549, 552, 553
    21st—425, 482, 483, 507, 508, 561
    28th—426, 481, 483, 507–9, 561, 623
    29th—283, 285, 288, 317, 318, 320, 427, 428, 492, 493, 498, 500, 502
    30th—46, 51, 258, 283, 285, 288, 317, 318, 320, 493, 500–2
    31st—98, 99, 109, 110, 283, 284, 317, 318, 320, 492–4, 498, 500, 501

Infantry (*continued*)—
  Brigades (*continued*)—
    155th—132, 137, 141, 148, 159, 164, 165, 169, 172, 194, 207, 208, 221, 223, 225, 227–9, 230, 269, 270, 272
    156th—67–9, 138, 147, 152, 165, 173, 191, 194, 196, 204, 205, 208–10, 219, 227, 229, 234, 269, 270
    157th—75, 131, 133, 134, 141, 144, 146, 147, 165, 173, 191, 192, 194, 210, 211, 219, 220, 230, 234, 269, 270, 275
    158th—36, 37, 44, 85, 89, 90, 101, 102, 105, 281, 282, 287, 289, 314, 315, 318, 490, 491, 496, 497, 499, 500
    159th—85, 87, 105, 257, 281, 289, 318, 320, 353, 356, 489, 490, 496, 497, 499
    160th—81, 85, 87, 89, 90, 251, 277, 281, 307, 321, 489, 491, 496, 499
    161st—68, 71, 75, 214, 216, 228, 275, 473–5
    162nd—68, 72, 75, 221, 274, 324, 325, 475
    163rd—68, 71, 228, 267, 473
    179th—36, 46, 47, 49, 50, 98, 99, 116, 119, 140, 208, 218–20, 244, 246, 256, 257, 279, 286, 306, 307, 332, 335, 337, 338, 341, 346, 367, 369, 375, 380, 381, 384, 389, 390, 428, 484, 508, 509
    180th—46, 98, 99, 108, 109, 219, 220, 244, 247, 252, 259, 278, 281, 287–9, 307, 332, 338, 341, 347, 361, 362, 367, 369, 380, 384, 389, 484, 485
    181st—46–9, 99, 100, 108, 244, 247, 256, 257, 280, 281, 286, 288, 306, 307, 313, 322, 332, 334, 335, 337–9, 343, 346, 365, 385, 389, 428, 484, 486, 487, 509
    229th—47, 87, 96–8, 233, 235, 248, 257, 283, 284, 289
    230th—47, 48, 50, 96, 97, 100, 248, 249, 257, 287, 289, 316, 317, 319, 321, 473
    231st—47, 48, 50, 51, 96, 97, 228, 230, 233, 234, 248, 249, 256, 257, 277, 278, 283, 286, 307, 312, 315, 318, 319, 321

INDEX TO ARMS, FORMATIONS, AND UNITS   745

Infantry (continued)—
  Brigades (continued)—
    232nd—138, 147, 159, 160, 162, 190, 193, 197, 202, 205, 266, 267, 324, 353–5, 357, 426, 479–81
    233rd—67, 75, 147, 153, 159, 160, 162, 175, 194, 197, 198, 202, 265, 354, 355, 357, 479, 481
    234th—147, 160, 161, 174, 175, 181, 197, 198, 202, 208, 324, 325, 354, 355, 357, 479–81
    Composite Force, formation, 16; at Third Gaza, 74, 111, 137, 362
    Smith's Group, at Third Gaza, 44, 50, 51
    Watson's Force, 466, 471, 497
  Regiments—
    Infantry of the Line and Territorial—
      Argyll and Sutherland Highlanders, 1/5th Bn., 135, 136, 145, 146, 211, 234, 272
      Bedfordshire, 1/5th Bn., 221, 230, 274, 475
      Black Watch (Royal Highlanders), 2nd Bn., 425, 482, 483
      ——, 14th Bn., 98, 233, 284, 287
      Buffs (East Kent), 10th Bn., 49, 249, 316, 319–21
      Cheshire, 4th Bn., 242, 258
      ——, 7th Bn., 240, 242, 251
      Connaught Rangers, 1st Bn., 476, 506
      ——, 5th Bn., 285, 286, 318, 321, 476, 506
      Devonshire, 1/5th Bn., 161, 191, 197, 202, 206, 324, 354
      ——, 16th Bn., 235
      ——, 2/4th Bn., 355
      Dorsetshire, 2nd Bn., 477, 507
      ——, 2/4th Bn., 197, 198, 201, 203, 325, 354, 356
      Dublin Fusiliers, Royal, 7th Bn., 285
      Duke of Cornwall's L.I., 1/4th Bn., 198, 202, 203, 212, 325
      Essex, 1/4th Bn., 74, 214–7, 474
      ——, 1/5th Bn., 71, 228, 474
      ——, 1/6th Bn., 71, 72, 214–6, 474, 475

Infantry (continued)—
  Regiments (continued)—
    Infantry of the Line and Territorial (continued)—
      Essex, 1/7th Bn., 474, 475
      Hampshire, 1/8th Bn., 71, 473
      ——, 2/4th Bn., 198, 202, 203, 265–7, 355
      ——, 2/5th Bn., 154
      Herefordshire, 1st Bn., 102, 103, 105, 287
      Highland L. I., 1/5th Bn., 132, 135, 136, 195, 234
      ——, 1/6th Bn., 132, 135, 136, 145, 195, 199, 269, 272
      ——, 1/7th Bn., 132, 133, 136, 195, 271, 272
      Inniskilling Fusiliers, Royal, 5th Bn., 284, 320
      ——, 6th Bn., 110, 284, 288
      Irish Fusiliers, Royal, 2nd Bn., 99, 110, 318, 494, 498
      ——, 5th Bn., 99, 109, 110, 284, 318, 320
      Irish Rifles, Royal, 6th Bn., 285, 320
      King's Own Scottish Borderers, 1/4th Bn., 133, 134, 165, 166, 172, 209, 225, 226, 273
      ——, 1/5th Bn., 133, 165, 166, 172, 209, 226, 227, 273, 274
      Leicestershire, 2nd Bn., 484, 561, 602
      Leinster, 1st Bn., 285, 318, 427, 428, 493
      ——, 6th Bn., 285, 286
      London Regiment, 1/10th Bn., 72, 221, 475, 476
      ——, 1/11th Bn., 274, 475
      ——, 2/13th Bn., 46, 50, 98, 119, 244–6, 279, 280, 307, 370, 381, 384
      ——, 2/14th Bn., 49, 116, 119, 244–6, 335, 370
      ——, 2/15th Bn., 50, 116, 119, 244, 245, 280, 307, 338, 370, 371, 381
      ——, 2/16th Bn., 98, 119, 244, 245, 279–81, 307, 370, 371, 384
      ——, 2/17th Bn., 100, 109, 246, 247, 254, 257, 333, 341, 343, 345, 370, 381

INDEX TO ARMS, FORMATIONS, AND UNITS

Infantry (*continued*)—
Regiments (*continued*)—
Infantry of the Line and Territorial (*continued*)—
London Regiment, 2/18th Bn., 98, 246, 247, 278, 307, 333, 341, 344, 345, 370, 374, 381, 384
——, 2/19th Bn., 98, 220, 246, 247, 252, 288, 307, 333, 335, 369, 370, 485, 486
——, 2/20th Bn., 99, 100, 109, 229, 247, 252, 257, 281, 288, 306, 333, 342, 370
——, 2/21st Bn., 257, 314, 334, 340, 341, 343, 344
——, 2/22nd Bn., 48, 49, 108, 314, 336, 341, 343, 344, 486
——, 2/23rd Bn., 108, 244, 246, 306, 313, 314, 341, 343
——, 2/24th Bn., 48, 256, 257, 280, 314, 334, 335, 345
Loyal North Lancashire, 12th Bn., 244
Manchester, 1st Bn., 478, 505
Middlesex, 2/10th Bn., 104, 251, 277, 281, 282, 307
Munster Fusiliers, Royal, 6th Bn., 288
Norfolk, 1/4th Bn., 71, 266, 473, 474
——, 1/5th Bn., 71, 228, 473, 474
——, 12th Bn., 249, 316, 319, 321
Northamptonshire, 1/4th Bn., 73, 221–3, 475, 476
Queen's (R. West Surrey), 2/4th Bn., 251, 277, 281
Royal Fusiliers, 38th Bn., 420, 424, 463, 549, 552
——, 39th Bn., 420, 463, 549, 555
——, 40th Bn., 420
Royal Irish, 1st Bn., 288, 318, 320, 493, 501, 502
——, 5th Bn., 286, 318
Royal Scots, 1/4th Bn., 68, 70, 153, 154, 210, 227, 228, 271
——, 1/7th Bn., 71, 153, 210, 271, 272
Scots Fusiliers, Royal, 1/4th Bn., 133, 134, 166, 170, 172, 223, 225, 234, 235, 273

Infantry (*continued*)—
Regiments (*continued*)—
Infantry of the Line and Territorial (*continued*)—
Scots Fusiliers, Royal, 1/5th Bn., 133, 134, 165, 166, 170, 172, 209, 226, 273
——, 12th Bn., 248, 284
Scottish Rifles, 1/7th Bn., 68, 69, 70, 204, 210, 229, 270, 271
——, 1/8th Bn., 68–71, 153, 204, 210, 271
Seaforth Highlanders, 1st Bn., 482, 507
Shropshire L. I., King's Own, 10th Bn., 230–4, 315, 318
Somerset L.I., 1/5th Bn., 160, 161, 194, 201, 202, 204–6, 355, 356, 479, 480
——, 12th Bn., 248
——, 2/4th Bn., 193, 199, 354
Suffolk, 1/5th Bn., 71, 473, 474
——, 15th Bn., 249, 316, 317, 319
Sussex, Royal, 4th Bn., 85, 101–4
——, 16th Bn., 51, 96, 97, 316, 317, 319
Welch, 1/4th Bn., 251, 258
——, 1/5th Bn., 257, 258
——, 4th/5th Bn., 491, 499
——, 24th Bn., 97, 233, 234, 318
Welch Fusiliers, Royal, 1/5th Bn., 50, 85, 87, 90, 102, 103, 315, 318
——, 1/6th Bn., 50, 102, 105, 315, 318, 321
——, 5th/6th Bn., 490, 499
——, 1/7th Bn., 102–4, 287, 490
——, 24th Bn., 50, 233
——, 25th Bn., 50, 231, 232
Wiltshire, 1/4th Bn., 160, 161, 194, 201, 202, 204, 205, 479
Regiments (Indian)—
1st Guides Inf. [5/12th Frontier Force], 425, 481, 482, 507, 508
2nd Guides Inf. [10th/12th Frontier Force], 419, 485, 486
1/17th Infantry, 490, 497

INDEX TO ARMS, FORMATIONS, AND UNITS 747

Infantry (continued)—
Regiments (Indian) (continued)—
20th Punjabis [2/14th Punjab], 481–3, 507
1/21st Punjabis [10/14th Punjab], 489, 490
27th Punjabis [3/15th Punjab], 476, 506
28th Punjabis [4/15th Punjab], 482, 508
2/30th Punjabis [1/16th Punjab], 419, 486
38th Dogras [2/17th Dogra], 501, 502
2/42nd Deoli, 498
47th Sikhs [5/11th Sikh], 478, 505
1/50th Kumaon Rifles [1/K. Rifles, 19th Hyderabad], 485
51st Sikhs [1/12th Frontier Force], 509
53rd Sikhs [3/12th Frontier Force], 484, 509, 602
1/54th Sikhs [4/12th Frontier Force], 428, 429, 493, 498
56th Punjabi Rif. [2/13th Frontier Force Rif.], 483, 484
58th Vaughan's Rif. [5/13th Frontier Force Rif.], 161, 190, 197, 199, 266, 267, 352, 355, 480
59th Scinde Rif. [6/13th Frontier Force Rif.], 478, 479, 505, 506
72nd Punjabis [3/2nd Punjab], 479, 480
74th Punjabis [4/2nd Punjab], 494
91st Punjabis [3/8th Punjab], 476, 477, 505, 506
92nd Punjabis [4/8th Punjab], 484, 483
93rd Burma Inf. [5/8th Punjab], 477, 478, 506
2/97th Deccan Inf. [3/19th Hyderabad], 485, 486
1/101st Grenadiers [1/4th Bombay Grenadiers], 428, 493, 498
2/101st Grenadiers, 498
105th Mahratta L.I. [2/5th Mahratta L.I.], 477, 478
110th Mahratta L.I. [3/5th Mahratta L.I.], 362
121st Pioneers [10/2nd Bombay Pioneers], 602
123rd Outram's Rif. [4/6th Rajputana Rif.], 162, 163, 199, 202, 203, 356, 357

Infantry (continued)—
Regiments (Indian) (continued)—
2/124th Baluchistan Inf. [10/10th Baluch], 478
125th Napier's Rif. [5/6th Rajputana Rif.], 482, 507
130th Baluchis [5/10th Baluch], 486
2/151st Indian Inf., 493, 498
3/151st Punjabi Rif., 508
1/152nd Indian Inf., 480, 481
2/152nd Indian Inf., 487
3/152nd Indian Inf., 490, 491
1/153rd Indian Inf., 490
2/153rd Indian Inf., 491, 497
3/153rd Indian Inf., 490, 500
3/154th Indian Inf., 500
1/155th Pioneers, 466
2/155th Pioneers, 466
1/1st Gurkha Rif., 477
2/3rd Gurkha Rif., 153, 154, 191, 194, 197, 202, 205, 206, 266, 325, 354, 355, 479
3/3rd Gurkha Rif., 67, 161, 197, 198, 202, 204, 205, 265, 355, 426
2/7th Gurkha Rif., 476
1/8th Gurkha Rif., 482
1st Kashmir I.S. Inf., 493, 502
3rd Kashmir I.S. Inf., 480
Alwar I.S. Inf., 436
Patiala I.S. Inf., 368, 371, 381, 385, 389, 436, 549
Regiments (Overseas Dominions)—
South African—
1st Cape Corps, 418, 490
British West Indies—
1st Bn., 16, 207, 424, 463, 549, 550–2
2nd—424, 463, 549–51, 559
3rd—424
4th—424
5th—424

Medical—
Field Ambulances—
2nd Australian L.H., 558
2/6th London, 313
3rd Lowland, 164
Machine-gun Squadrons—
15th—614; 17th—378, 519; 2nd Australian L.H.—100, 104, 105, 118, 125; New Zealand, 216; 2nd New Zealand, 415, 573, 593

748   Index to Arms, Formations, and Units

Machine-Gun Companies—
  18th—522 ; 134th—481 ; 156th—271 ; 159th—258 ; 229th—161 ; 230th—161, 202 ; 231st 161, 203

Motor Batteries and Patrols—
  Light Armoured Car Brigade, 331
  Light Armoured M.B.—
    No. 2—225, 479, 484, 509, 602, 607, 610
    No. 3—215, 281
    No. 11—80, 111, 238, 375, 379, 513, 515, 530, 535, 569, 610

Motor Batteries and Patrols (*continued*)—
  Light Armoured M.B. (*contd.*)—
    No. 12—111, 163, 175, 190, 193, 368, 376, 522, 534, 545, 601, 610, 614
  Light Car Patrols—
    No. 1—80, 111, 513, 535, 610
    No. 2—610
    No. 7—238, 522, 534, 601, 610, 613

Tank Detachment, Palestine, 68, 72

Printed under the authority of His Majesty's Stationery Office
by William Clowes & Sons, Ltd., London and Beccles.

(103) Wt. 28491—2323. 3000. 10/30. W. C. & S., Ltd. Gp. 301.

9 781845 749507